ARCHAEOLOGIES OF THE PUEBLO REVOLT

Frontispiece. *Hector at the Ships*, lithograph by Diego Romero. Photograph by Wendy McEahern.

ARCHAEOLOGIES
of the
PUEBLO REVOLT

*Identity, Meaning, and Renewal
in the Pueblo World*

Edited by
ROBERT W. PREUCEL

THE UNIVERSITY OF NEW MEXICO PRESS ◆ ALBUQUERQUE

© 2002 by the University of New Mexico Press
All rights reserved
First edition
First paperbound printing, 2007
Paperbound ISBN 978-0-8263-4246-1

11 10 09 08 07   1 2 3 4 5

Library of Congress Cataloging-in-Publication Data:

Archaeologies of the Pueblo Revolt : identity, meaning, and renewal
in the Pueblo World / edited by Robert W. Preucel.—1st ed.
          p.   cm.
Includes bibliographical references and index.
        ISBN 0-8263-2247-6 (cloth : alk. paper)
    1. Pueblo Revolt, 1680. 2. Pueblo Indians—Antiquities.
3. Pueblo Indians—Historiography. I. Preucel, Robert W.
E99.P9 A7 2002
978.9'02—dc21

                                2001006062

DESIGN: *Mina Yamashita*

Contents

List of Figures / vi

List of Tables / vii

Acknowledgments / ix

Author Affiliations / x

Preface

The Holy War / xi

Herman Agoyo

PART ONE   Introduction

Chapter 1

Writing the Pueblo Revolt / 3

Robert W. Preucel

PART TWO   Place, Settlement, and Architecture

Chapter 2

Dowa Yalanne: The Architecture of Zuni Resistance
and Social Change during the Pueblo Revolt / 33

T. J. Ferguson

Chapter 3

Mission and Mesa: Some Thoughts on the
Archaeology of Pueblo Revolt Era Sites in the
Jemez Region, New Mexico / 45

Michael L. Elliot

Chapter 4

Transformations of Place: Occupational History and
Differential Persistence in Seventeenth-Century
New Mexico / 61

Mark T. Lycett

PART THREE   Material Culture Meanings

Chapter 5

Crossed Cultures, Crossed Meanings: The Manipulation of
Ritual Imagery in Early Historic Pueblo Resistance / 77

Jeannette L. Mobley-Tanaka

Chapter 6

Acts of Resistance: Zuni Ceramics, Social Identity,
and the Pueblo Revolt / 85

Barbara J. Mills

Chapter 7

Ceramic Semiotics: Women, Pottery, and Social Meanings
at Kotyiti Pueblo / 99

Patricia W. Capone and Robert W. Preucel

Chapter 8

History in Stone: Evaluating Spanish Conversion Efforts
through Hopi Rock Art / 114

Kurt E. Dongoske and Cindy K. Dongoske

Chapter 9

Signs of Power and Resistance: The (Re)Creation
of Christian Imagery and Identities in the
Pueblo Revolt Era / 132

Matthew J. Liebmann

PART FOUR   Social and Political Dynamics

Chapter 10

Re-imagining Awat'ovi / 147

Peter Whiteley

Chapter 11

Social Memory and the Pueblo Revolt:
A Postcolonial Perspective / 167

Michael V. Wilcox

Chapter 12

Pueblo-Spanish Warfare in Seventeenth-Century New
Mexico: The Battles of Black Mesa, Kotyiti, and
Astialakwa / 181

Rick Hendricks

Chapter 13

Pueblo and Apachean Alliance Formation in the
Seventeenth Century / 198

Curtis F. Schaafsma

Chapter 14

The Persistence of the Corn Mothers / 212

Joseph H. Suina

Index / 217

List of Figures

Frontispiece:

Hector at the Ships, lithograph by Diego Romero

1.1 Locations of major Mission Pueblos during the seventeenth century – 10

1.2 Adolph Bandelier at Pecos – 11

1.3 Locations of major post-Revolt Refuge villages – 12

1.4 Frank Hamilton Cushing's Plan of Dowa Yalanne – 13

1.5 Locations of Pueblito Sites post-1730 – 14

1.6 Construction episodes at Pueblito sites – 16

1.7 Plan of Unit 1 at Las Majadas site – 17

2.1 Mesa of Dowa Yalanne from rooftops of Zuni Pueblo – 32

2.2 Archaeological remains on Dowa Yalanne – 34

2.3 The 38 major buildings on Dowa Yalanne – 34

2.4 Cholla cacti on roomblocks of Dowa Yalanne – 35

2.5 Space syntax analysis of Dowa Yolanne – 36

2.6 Roomblocks in three size classes of buildings on Dowa Yolanne, with RCI values – 37

2.7 Hemenway Expedition Map, ca. 1888 – 39

2.8 Box plots of RRA values for historic Zuni settlements – 41

2.9 *Victory on Top of Dowa Yalanne—1680* – 42

3.1 Map of Jemez region – 45

3.2 Map of Giusewa – 48

3.3 Sketch map of Patokwa – 50

3.4 Detail of 1779 Miera y Pacheco map – 50

3.5 Parsons's sketch map of Jemez Pueblo – 51

3.6 Architectural features of Astialakwa – 52

3.7 Warrior petroglyph at Astialakwa – 52

3.8 Sketch map of Boletsakwa – 53

3.9 Bedrock grinding feature at Boletsakwa – 54

4.1 Location of Galisteo Basin and Paaco – 64

4.2 Mission sites in Galisteo Basin and surrounding area – 65

4.3 San Cristobal, location of historic roomblocks – 66

4.4 San Cristobal, high-density contexts within historic roomblocks – 67

4.5 Paaco – 69

4.6 Paaco, Plaza Surface 2 – 69

4.7 Paaco, Plaza Surface 3 – 70

5.1 Prehistoric glazeware bowl with double-bar crosses – 80

5.2 Prehistoric kiva mural from Pottery Mound – 80

5.3 Two glazeware bowls with similar design layouts – 81

5.4 Ritual figures from two Tabira black-on-white vessels – 83

6.1 Map of Zuni area – 87

6.2 Kechipawan Polychrome jar from Hawikku – 89

6.3 Matsaki Polychrome bowl from Hawikku – 89

6.4 Early Matsaki Polychrome bowl interiors – 90

6.5 Late Matsaki Polychrome bowl interiors – 90

6.6 Late Matsaki Polychrome bowl interiors – 91

6.7 Late Matsaki Polychrome bowl from Hawikku – 91

6.8 Hawikuh Polychrome jar from Hawikku – 92

6.9 Hawikuh Polychrome jar designs with Roman cross – 92

6.10 Ashiwi Polychrome jar from Zuni Pueblo – 92

6.11 Ashiwi Polychrome jars – 93

6.12 Ashiwi Polychrome designs – 94

6.13 Zuni Polychrome bowl exterior – 95

6.14 Zuni Polychrome feather designs – 95

7.1 Location map of Kotyiti Pueblo – 100

7.2 Map of Kotyiti plaza pueblo and rancheria – 101

7.3 Kotyiti Glaze Polychrome jar – 102

7.4 Percentage of primary material inclusions – 106

7.5 Distribution of sherds – 107

7.6 Double-headed key motif – 108

7.7 Hooked triangle motifs – 109

7.8 "Sacred mountain" motifs – 109

7.9 Shield motif on Tewa Polychrome jar – 110

8.1 Hope Mesas indicating location of villages – 115

8.2 Example of common rock art elements associated with water sources – 122

8.3 Typical rock art representations, Pueblo III–IV period – 123

8.4 Western shield from Kawaika'a – 124

8.5 Shield with cross form Panel A – 126

8.6 Rock art forms with crosses – 126

8.7 Depiction of a Spanish rider on a horse – 127

8.8 Stick figures carrying a long stick or pole – 128

9.1 Map of Revolt-era sites – 135

9.2 Traditional Pueblo images, Frijoles Canyon – 136

9.3 West wall, Panel B, Frijoles Canyon – 137

9.4 Spanish colonial art – 139

9.5 Katsina images – 140

10.1 Item 306, Spanish Archives of New Mexico – 157

10.2 Passage in Item 306 – 159

12.1 Battle Sites, 1694 – 180

12.2 San Ildefonso Mesa – 185

12.3 Mesa of La Cieneguilla de Cochití – 189

12.4 Guadalupe Mesa – 191

13.1 Map of New Mexico made in Paris in 1657 by Nicolas Sanson – 200

13.2 Detail of Miera y Pacheco map of 1778 – 209

List of Tables

3.1   Tree-ring Dates from Boletsakwa – 54

3.2   Jemez Mission Identifications through the Years – 55

3.3   Distance Data Cited in Vargas Journals – 57

3.4   Mission and Pueblo Locations and Dates in Jemez Area – 58

4.1   Late Prehistoric and Historic Pueblo Settlements in
       Galisteo Basin and surrounding areas – 64

6.1   Periods, Collections, and Ceramic Types in Zuni Ceramic
       Analysis – 88

6.2   Design Occurrences by Period 92

7.1   Historic Period Painted Ware Assemblages – 103

7.2   Design Elements on Local Glazewares – 107

Acknowledgments

This volume has its origins in two interrelated projects. The first of these is the ongoing collaborative research I have been privileged to conduct with the Pueblo of Cochiti. Since 1995, we have been gathering archaeological, historical, and oral historical information on the ancestral Cochiti village known as Kotyiti (Old Cochiti). This village was built and occupied during the interregnum between the Pueblo Revolt of 1680 and the military campaigns of Diego de Vargas in 1694.

I am grateful to the each of the members of the Kotyiti Research Project team: Leslie Atik, Patricia Capone, Virginia Ebert, Elga Jefferis, John Patrick Montoya, J. R. Montoya, Thurman Pecos, Wilson Romero, Jr., Bob Sharer, Nick Stapp, Gilbert Quintana, James Quintana, Loa Traxler, April Trujillo, Martina Valdo, Michael Walsh, Courtney White, Michael Wilcox, and Lucy Williams. Thanks are also due to Mike Bremer, Rita Skinner, and Mike Elliott of USFS Santa Fe National Forest, to Douglas Bailey and his staff of USACE Cochiti Dam, to Fred Dixon, Jim and Becky Mullane of Dixons Ranch, and to Chip Wills of the University of New Mexico, to Ron and Jeff Atik of Oolight Media, and to Jerry Sabloff, Douglas Walker, Annette Merle-Smith, Ruth Scott, and the American Philosophical Society for financial support. I would especially like to acknowledge the support of the members of the Cochiti Pueblo Tribal Council.

The second project is a session I organized for the 64th annual meeting of the Society for American Archaeology in Chicago. The idea of the session was to bring together a group of archaeologists, cultural anthropologists, and historians to explore the indigenous strategies of resistance and accommodation to Spanish authority that emerged during the seventeenth and early eighteenth centuries and that have, in part, created the identities and social configurations of Pueblo peoples today. I would like to thank Eric Blinman, Patricia Capone, Cindy and Kurt Dongoske, Michael Elliott, T. J. Ferguson, Rick Hendricks, Mark Lycett, Barbara Mills, Jeanette Mobley-Tanaka, Curtis Schaafsma, Katherine Spielmann, Joseph H. Suina, John Ware, Peter Whiteley, and Michael Wilcox for their willingness to participate in the session. A special thanks is also due to David Hurst Thomas who served as the discussant.

This volume would not have been possible without the assistance of a number of individuals and institutions. I have benefited from ongoing conversations with Herman Agoyo, Roger Anyon, Jonathan Batkin, Stefanie Beninato, Mike Bremer, Patricia Capone, Kurt Dongoske, T. J. Ferguson, Genevive Head, Tim Kohler, Charles and Pat Lange, Frank Matero, Barbara Mills, Diego Romero, Curtis and Polly Schaafsma, Douglas Schwartz, James Snead, Dede Snow, Joseph H. Suina, David Hurst Thomas, John Torres, Mike Walsh, Mike Wilcox, and Chip Wills. I am grateful to Jerry Sabloff, director of the University of Pennsylvania Museum of Archaeology and Ethnology, for research support and to Matt Liebmann, my research assistant. I also wish to acknowledge the University of New Mexico Press, particularly Luther Wilson, director of the Press, Durwood Ball, former acquisitions editor, Evelyn Schlatter, current acquisitions editor, Amy Elder, manuscripts editor, and Allan McIntyre, copy editor. Finally, I reserve my greatest appreciation for the advice and encouragement of my wife Leslie Atik.

Author Affiliations

HERMAN AGOYO is a former governor of Okay Ow-ingah (San Juan Pueblo) and the founder of the Po'pay statue project.

PATRICIA W. CAPONE is an associate curator and repatriation coordinator at the Peabody Museum of Harvard University in Cambridge, Massachusetts.

CINDY K. DONGOSKE is an archaeologist working for Carter and Burgess, Inc. in Phoenix, Arizona and a former archaeologist for the Hopi Tribe.

KURT E. DONGOSKE is a senior archaeologist working for URS Corporation in Phoenix, Arizona, and a former archaeologist for the Hopi Tribe.

MICHAEL L. ELLIOTT is an archaeologist working for Jemez Mountains Research Center and the former forest archaeologist for the Santa Fe National Forest in Santa Fe, New Mexico.

T. J. FERGUSON is president of Heritage Resource Management Consultants in Tucson, Arizona, and former director of the Zuni Archaeology Project.

RICK HENDRICKS is a historian working for the Department of Archives and Special Collections at New Mexico State University Library, Las Cruces, and a former member of the Vargas Project.

MATTHEW J. LIEBMANN is an associate professor in the Department of Anthropology at the College of William and Mary in Williamsburg, Virginia, and former NAGPRA Coordinator for the Pueblo of Jemez.

MARK T. LYCETT is an assistant professor in the Department of Anthropology, University of Chicago, Chicago, Illinois.

BARBARA J. MILLS is a professor in the Department of Anthropology at the University of Arizona in Tucson.

JEANNETTE L. MOBLEY-TANAKA is lead faculty in anthropology in the Department of Social and Behavioral Sciences at Front Range Community College, Larimer Campus in Fort Collins, Colorado.

ROBERT W. PREUCEL is an associate professor in the Department of Anthropology at the University of Pennsylvania and Gregory Annenberg Weingarten Associate Curator of North America, University of Pennsylvania Museum in Philadelphia.

CURTIS F. SCHAAFSMA is emeritus curator of anthropology at the Museum of Indian Arts and Culture, Museum of New Mexico in Santa Fe and the former State Archaeologist for New Mexico.

JOSEPH H. SUINA is an associate professor in the College of Education at the University of New Mexico in Albuquerque, and a former governor of Cochiti Pueblo.

PETER WHITELEY is curator of anthropology at the American Museum of Natural History in New York City.

MICHAEL V. WILCOX is an assistant professor in the Department of Cultural and Social Anthropology at Stanford University in Palo Alto, California.

Preface

The Holy War

Herman Agoyo

Oway wa haa an bayo—Once upon a time, I was born at *Ohkay Owingeh* (San Juan Pueblo). Early on in my education, while attending the San Juan Pueblo Day School (1941–1948), now known as the Ohkay Owingeh Community School, I developed a love of history. I then attended the Santa Fe Indian School (1948–1954) and took all the required history courses. My interest in history continued into college (1954–1958), where I minored in the subject. I recall researching and writing a "term paper" on the Louisiana Purchase. Yet at no time during my formal education did I ever learn anything of Indian history or about the famous Pueblo Revolt of 1680. Indeed, one recurring thought was that we as Indians did not have a history.

Today, I still have mixed emotions about my education. As a child, I was very fortunate to have a grandpa who, during the winter months, shared with me many fireside stories. I recorded some of these stories and translated them into English in 1960. Grandpa also exposed me to ceremonial activities where I heard more stories and songs of the *towa* (people). I was being taught Indian history, but because Indian history was not written down and presented in school, I grew up thinking that we did not have a history.

Although I did not myself experience the physical abuse of hand slapping, the scolding and other punishable measures for speaking one's native tongue in school as did my parents' generation, I was nonetheless sensitive

to a curriculum that lacked Indian history and failed to recognize the enormous contributions made by the Indian people to the world.

Some of my Indian teachers in Santa Fe passionately advocated academic Indian Studies, but the attitude that "our students were not going to be tested on knowledge of themselves" always prevailed and besides, the school was already providing ample instructions in home economics, art, weaving, drafting, cabinet making, bakery, farming, and silversmithing. The result of this curriculum was that it did not encourage, much less prepare, a student for college. Furthermore, many Indian children suffered from a lack of self-worth and tried to suppress their feelings; those who could not cope, got into trouble, and were dismissed from school.

It took an invitation from the Smithsonian Institution in 1976 to alert me to the impending 300th anniversary in 1980 of the Great Pueblo Revolt of 1680. I was a member of the San Juan Pueblo delegation (there were forty of us) and we justified our participation in the Bicentennial Celebration in Washington, D.C., by dedicating it to Popé, since the Revolt and the 1776 American Revolution were based upon similar beliefs and principles.

Consider the following quote:

> [A]n autocratic foreign government which ruled by decree, taxed them unjustly, gave them no voice in governmental decision making and denied them freedom to worship as they chose. It was a system to which they had been subjected for years during this time uncorrected grievances and hostile, even cruel, treatment at the hands of the representatives of a monarchy housed in luxurious places across the Atlantic Ocean had forced them to a point of no return. They had to drive the Europeans out of their country even though they lacked the empire's arms and military might. So the men gathered clandestinely in their villages to plot an uprising and select their best men as leaders. This was done in great secrecy, mindful of the possibility of information leaking to the

enemy; some of the family members of the revolutionaries were in the foreigners' camp, working for and sympathizing with the ruling order [Sando 1998:3].

This description might seem to refer to the patriots of Concord and Lexington, Massachusetts, but it does not. Instead, it refers to the patriots of the Pueblo people, "who in 1680, nearly a century before the more celebrated revolution of 1776, staged the first successful American revolution against a foreign colonial power, Spain" (Sando 1998:3).

The main leader of the Revolt was a man from Ohkay Owingeh named *Pop'ay* (Ripe Pumpkin). To the Spaniards, he was known as "El Popé." In the history of Pueblo Indians and Spanish relationships, Popé's presence is recorded in the year 1675 when he and 46 other Pueblo men were persecuted and indicted in Santa Fe for the alleged practice of sorcery. As a result of the trial, three men were sentenced to die by hanging. The Pueblo villages sent a delegation to Santa Fe to protest this treatment and threaten war. Fearful for his life, Governor Juan Francisco de Treviño released the prisoners and allowed them to return to their homes.

Among historians, there is much speculation on Popé's role in the Indian Pueblos' socio-political and religious structure. It is likely that he was a religious leader, because this role would have given him access to the inner sanctuary of Taos Pueblo from where he planned the Great Pueblo Revolt of 1680. On December 19, 1681, a Tesuque Pueblo Indian named Juan testified under oath that the chief mover of the Pueblo Revolt was a "native of the Pueblo of San Juan, named El Popé" (Hackett and Shelby 1942:233–234). In the days following, other Indians, also under oath, identified Popé as the leader of the Revolt. In 1980, San Juan Pueblo elders revealed Popé's lineage, moiety and approximate residence in the pueblo. His role after the Revolt is unclear, but the historic event that he led in 1680 is as important to such American ideals of independence and religious freedom as is the better-known American Revolution of 1776.

In 1980, New Mexico Indian Pueblos and the Hopi Nation commemorated the Tricentennial of the Great Pueblo Revolt with dignity and respect (Agoyo 1980). Everyone was mindful of the many lives lost on both sides during the Revolt. Incidentally, bloodshed began very early during Indian-Spanish encounters at Zuni, Cicuye (Pecos), the Tiwa villages of Arenal and Moho, and Acoma. Two particularly bloody episodes that still live in Pueblo memory are associated with the acts of Francisco Vásquez de Coronado and Juan de Zaldívar.

In 1539, the Zunis killed Estevanico, a black man from Azamore, Morocco, who served as a guide to the Fray Marco de Niza expedition because he made demands and crossed the forbidden line of white cornmeal. A year later, Coronado retaliated. With his awesome horses and firearms, he attacked Hawikuh and defeated the Zunis (Kessell 1979). After the battle of Hawikuh, and after concluding a meeting with Cicuye emissaries, Coronado marched north to the Rio Grande Valley, where he "passed through the cluster of pueblos they called the province of Tiguex, and apparently traveled as far north as Taos" (Kessell 1979:8).

Upon returning from Taos, Coronado's expedition camped near Cicuye and, with El Turco and Sopete as guides, continued their search for gold and other riches to the eastern plains. They eventually reached present-day Kansas, the disappointing Quivira region where they found the "Wichitas living along the great bend of the Arkansas River" (Kessell 1979:23). It was during this trip when El Turco met his fate. He was choked to death with a garrote by Melchior Pérez, because he lied about the gold and was conspiring with the Wichitas and, "furthermore, the people of Cicuye had asked him to lead the Spaniards astray on the plains because lacking provisions, their horses would die and when they returned weak the people of Cicuye would kill them" (Kessell 1979:23).

Disappointed, the expedition led by Captain Hernando de Alvarado and Father Juan de Padilla, returned to Cicuye and proceeded on to the Tiguex province, near present-day Bernalillo, where they evicted the Indians from their homes. When the Indians refused to submit to additional Spanish orders war was declared on the pueblos of Arenal and Moho in 1541, which resulted in Tiwa warriors being burned at the stake and women and children being taken captive (Kessell 1979:19).

While Coronado was exploring the Quivira region, another group of soldiers, led by Captain Tristande Arellano returned to Tiguex. Fearing that Cicuye warriors might ambush Coronado, Arellano in the late summer of 1541 returned to Cicuye where he was attacked, and after four days of fighting defeated the pueblo. Coronado left New Mexico in April 1542, leaving behind Father Juan de Padilla and other friars and his dream of finding the fabled Seven Cities.

Fifty-six years would pass before Pueblo Indians would again do battle with the Spaniards. This new battle took place on December 4, 1598 at Sky City (Acoma) where Maese de Campo Juan de Zaldívar, the elder nephew of Governor Juan de Oñate y Salazar, stopped to obtain food and supplies. He was invited to the village on the top of the mesa where he "walked into a trap." During hand-to-hand combat Zaldívar and a few of the soldiers were killed. This situation created a crisis and the friars that had been dispatched on September 9, 1598 from San Juan Pueblo to the various Pueblo provinces were called back to the first capital. There they helped in the crisis, "dutifully citing scripture, church father, philosophers and legalist, concluded" a just war be declared and "that until the Spaniards laid waste the defiant fortress-Pueblo of Acoma, there could be no peace in the land" (Kessell 1979:85).

Taking 70 soldiers—about half the colony's total force—Vicente de Zaldívar set forth to avenge his brother and to humble the rebels of Acoma. Incredibly enough, he did just that. In a bold and well-engineered two-day assault, he carried and sacked the "impregnable stronghold." According to Spanish sources, the Acoma men, sensing defeat, began to kill one another and their families rather than surrender. The invaders took as many captives as they could, "upwards of five hundred men, women, and children."

At populous Santo Domingo, an elated Oñate met

the returning heroes and dealt with the Acoma prisoners. All the Pueblos watched. They did not understand the formalities of the trial that the Spaniards recorded so diligently, but they understood the brutal results. The governor sentenced Acoma males, 25 years and older, to have one foot hacked off. Like the young men and women prisoners, these defeated and mutilated warriors were also required to serve 20 years as slaves of the invaders. Two Hopis caught at Acoma were to lose their right hands and "be set free in order that they may convey to their land the news of this punishment" Kessell 1979:86).

Since 1980, I have continued to lecture on the Revolt and directed from the New Mexico side the re-creation of the carrying of the knotted cord from Taos to Hopi in 1980, 1985, and 1990. In 1680, runners were sent to all the Pueblos, which included the Hopis, taking a knotted cord. Each day a single knot would be untied, and when there were no knots remaining, that would be the day of the Revolt (Agoyo 1980).

In 1998, the State of New Mexico and its Hispanic citizens commemorated the 400th anniversary of the establishment of the first Spanish settlement and capital of New Mexico. Juan de Oñate, the first colonizer, became a focal point of controversy that continues to this day because there is no agreement on how to appropriately memorialize this historic event.

Again, Ohkay Owingeh played a key role in renewing historical ties with Spain. Since the pueblo hosted the first settlement at San Gabriel de Yungé from 1598 to 1610, an ongoing dialogue now exists with Spain for future cultural, educational, and business venture exchanges. Pledges to support mutual concerns and heal old wounds were made at a historic gathering when the Vice President, his wife, and nineteen Spanish delegates met with the New Mexico Indian Pueblo leaders in Ohkay Owingeh on April 29, 1998.

Another very significant and important development was the passage by the New Mexico Legislature, in 1997, of Senate Bill 404, sponsored by Senator Manny Aragon (D) Bernalillo. This action signed into law by Governor Gary Johnson created a nine-person Statuary Hall Commission, with the sole responsibility to raise funds to create a statue of the likeness of Popé and enshrine him at the Statuary Hall in Washington, D.C. This legislation too, had its adversaries whose outlandish claims against Popé's heroic efforts only strengthened the resolve of the commission to fulfill its solemn obligation.

I have witnessed the re-awakening of interest in the historical facts and circumstances regarding the Revolt among the public. This interest is well served by the publication of new books by both Indian and non-Indian historians. These include books by such distinguished scholars as J. Manuel Espinosa (1988), Andrew Knaut (1995), David Weber (1999), and Joe Sando (1998) of Jemez Pueblo. Many scholars now point to the logical conclusion that the Revolt was "a holy war" for the Pueblos.

This book contributes to this new interest in Pueblo history—it is the kind of book I wish had been available when I was growing up. It is distinctive because of its use of archaeology, in conjunction with history and oral history, as a way of approaching the events and meanings of our Holy War. There may be some mistakes in interpretation here and there, but overall the different chapters tell us many new things and reveal new possibilities for future collaboration and research. I now pass the story on to you, *Hawee.*

References Cited

Agoyo, Herman
1980   The Tricentennial Year in Pueblo Consciousness. *El Palacio* 86:27–31.

Espinosa, J. Manuel (editor)
1988   *The Pueblo Indian Revolt of 1696 and the Franciscan Missions in New Mexico: Letters of the Missionaries and Related Documents.* University of Oklahoma Press, Norman.

Hackett, Charles W., and Charmion C. Shelby (editor and translator)
1942   *Revolt of the Pueblo Indians of New Mexico, and Otermín's Attempted Reconquest, 1680–1682.* Coronado Cuarto Centennial Publications, 1540–1949. 2 Vols. University of New Mexico Press, Albuquerque.

Kessell, John L.
1979   *Kiva, Cross, and Crown: The Pecos Indians and New Mexico, 1540–1840.* National Park Service, Washington, D.C.

Knaut, Andrew L.
1995   *The Pueblo Revolt: Conquest and Resistance in Seventeenth-Century New Mexico.* University of Oklahoma Press, Norman.

Sando, Joe
1998   *Pueblo Profiles: Cultural Identities through Centuries of Change.* Clear Light Publishers, Santa Fe.

Weber, David J. (editor)
1999   *What Caused the Pueblo Revolt of 1680?* Bedford/St. Martins, Boston.

PART ONE
Introduction

Chapter 1

Writing the Pueblo Revolt

Robert W. Preucel

On August 10, 1680, the Pueblo Indians of the Spanish province of New Mexico, along with their Navajo and Apache allies, rose up against the Spanish colony to initiate one of the most successful rebellions in the history of the New World.[1] After 82 years of living under foreign rule, Pueblo leaders fashioned a military alliance that transcended longstanding rivalries. In a co-ordinated attack, warriors across the Pueblo world killed their Franciscan missionaries and destroyed their mission churches. For nine days, they besieged the Spanish capital of Santa Fe, finally forcing Antonio de Otermín, the Governor of New Mexico, to retreat in ignominy to El Paso del Norte (now Ciudad Juárez, Mexico). A total of 401 Spanish colonists and 21 Franciscan missionaries lost their lives in the uprising. The number of Pueblo people killed is not recorded.

Immediately following the Revolt, Pueblo people revived their traditional ceremonies, rebuilt their kivas, and reconsecrated their shrines. They also instigated major shifts in settlement; many Pueblo people vacated their mission villages and established new mesatop strongholds for defensive purposes. Without a common enemy, however, the Pueblo confederation broke down and two factions emerged. The Keres, Jemez, Taos, and Pecos began fighting against the Tewa, Tanos, and Picuris. The Spaniards quickly capitalized upon this discord to make a series of reconquest attempts. Otermín, himself, returned in 1681, but his attempt

failed due to the hostilities of the Cochiti people. Other ill-fated attempts included those of Pedro Reneros de Posada in 1688 and Domingo Jironza Petrís de Cruzate in 1689. Some of these attempts at reconquest were quite bloody—for example, Cruzate destroyed Zia Pueblo, killing hundreds of Indians. On August 10, 1692, twelve years to the day of the Revolt, Diego de Vargas, the newly appointed Governor of New Mexico, initiated his own reconquest. He reached Santa Fe without opposition, and on September 14, proclaimed its peaceful surrender in what is popularly called the "Bloodless Reconquest of New Mexico."

The story of the Pueblo Revolt and its aftermath would seem to be well documented. Indeed, it has been the subject of substantial historical analysis (Espinosa 1988; Hackett and Shelby 1942; Jones 1989; Knaut 1995; Sando 1979; Weber 1999) and interpreted for popular audiences (Baldwin 1995; Folsom 1973; Ortiz 1980; Sanchez 1989; Sando 1998; Silverberg 1970; Simmons 1980). Yet, there still remain a number of outstanding questions. For example, is the Revolt best understood as a single anomalous event, or is it better seen as part of a broader strategy of indigenous resistance that characterized the entire period of Spanish colonization? If the latter, what were the antecedent events leading up to the Revolt of 1680? How were Pueblo people able to transcend village rivalries and establish strategic alliances with the Navajo and Apache? How did Pueblo people reconfigure their lives during their period of freedom? What were the material expressions of the new social and political identities that emerged? What are the meanings of the Revolt to Pueblo people today?

Why did the Pueblos Revolt?

The Pueblo Revolt of 1680 is an enduring topic in Borderlands history and Southwestern anthropology.[2] Historians have typically regarded it as an extraordinary and pivotal event in Southwestern history and, accordingly, have sought to understand its causes and consequences. Their overarching framework has been the expansion of the Spanish empire and the creation of frontiers or borderlands as zones of cultural interaction (Bannon 1974; Bolton 1916; Guy and Sheridan 1998; Hall 1989; Weber 1992). However, as David Weber (1999:8) points out, there has been considerable disagreement on the question of causality.

One area of debate centers on the relative importance of religious persecution and economic oppression. Hubert H. Bancroft, for example, articulated both of these theses, but clearly favored the religious persecution view and, moreover, considered it to be congruent with the perspective held by the Spaniards themselves. He writes that the Pueblos, "were required to render implicit obedience (to the Spaniards), and to pay heavy tribute of pueblo products and personal service. Their complaints, however, in this direction are not definitely known. The Spaniards in their later gathering of testimony ignored this element of secular oppression, if, as can hardly be doubted, it existed, and represented the revolt to be founded exclusively, as it was indeed largely, on religious grounds" (Bancroft 1889:174).

The evidence for religious persecution during the seventeenth century is substantial and unambiguous. One of the goals of the Franciscan order was to convert native subjects to Christianity and this required that all traces of native religion be eradicated. Franciscan priests routinely burned kivas and ceremonial paraphernalia in a public display of the superiority of their religion. They also imprisoned traditional ceremonial leaders on charges of

"witchcraft" and, in some cases, executed them. One of the most notable instances occurred in 1675 when Governor Juan Francisco de Treviño began a campaign against idolatry and arrested 47 "sorcerers." One of these men was Popé of San Juan Pueblo, who subsequently became one of the principal leaders of the Revolt.

An advocate of the economic oppression thesis is Ralph Emerson Twitchell. He wrote, "(e)verywhere the Spaniard was regarded as a tyrant. The fetters which had been forged seemed to be tightly riveted. The native was required to render implicit obedience and to pay heavy tribute in the products of their labor and personal service . . . all burned with a desire to rid themselves of the system of tyranny which had been their portion for nearly a hundred years" (Twitchell 1914:354–355, 357). This "system of tyranny" was based upon economic exploitation sanctioned by the *encomienda,* a royal right granted by the Governor of New Mexico to leading colonists that allowed them to collect tribute from the Indian households of a particular pueblo. Tribute was collected twice a year with cotton cloth and hides gathered in May and corn gathered after the harvest in October. The encomienda also carried with it the responsibility to provide for the spiritual welfare of the Indians and protection against the marauding Apache and Navajo. In 1639, the number of encomenderos was officially set at 35 (Scholes 1935:79).

Two factors heightened the effects of the encomienda among the Pueblos. First, the amount of tribute was not stable. In 1643, it was reassessed due to the decline in Pueblo population, itself a response to persistent drought and disease. The result of the reassessment was that encomienda tribute was shifted from households to individuals (Forbes 1960:139). This new burden caused some families to flee to the Apache for refuge. Second, individual encomenderos often abused their rights and neglected their responsibilities. One common strategy was to acquire land adjacent to their tributary pueblo, nominally to ease the collection of tribute, but with the result of illegally obtaining Indian labor and stealing Indian land (Gutiérrez 1991:106).

It seems clear that the phrasing of this debate in oppositional terms, where religion and economy are regarded as alternatives, actually reveals very little about why the Pueblos revolted when they did or how they accomplished their objectives. Indeed, as Alfonso Ortiz (1994) reminds us, there is no sharp divide between sacred and secular, religion and economy for Pueblo people. From this perspective, economic oppression was simultaneously an assault upon Pueblo labor and subsistence as well as an attack upon Pueblo religion and worldview.

Another area of debate turns on whether the Revolt was a unique event or the product of longstanding resistance to Spanish colonial rule. Van Hastings Garner is perhaps the leading advocate of the former view. He regards the Revolt as the outcome of a particular convergence of historical factors including famine, disease, and Apache raiding (Garner 1974). His thesis is that remarkably stable economic relations between Europeans and Indians characterized the first part of the seventeenth century. This stability was not enforced by a dominant power, but rather grew out of mutual dependence. The Pueblos provided the Spaniards with labor, textiles, and food, and they, in turn, received military protection, new crops, and advanced technology. According to Garner, the Pueblo people chose to revolt only because of a breakdown in this implied contract caused by a combination of environmental and political factors.

In sharp contrast, Andrew Knaut (1995) has proposed that the Pueblos offered meaningful resistance to Spanish authority throughout the entire seventeenth century. One form of resistance was the secret observance of traditional ritual practices. For example, he notes that the so-called "conversions" did not necessarily signify the complete renunciation of traditional Pueblo beliefs and practices. Rather they had the effect of driving traditional ceremonial observances underground, out of sight of the Spanish friars and colonists. He cites as evidence for this the case of Pindas, who served as the guardian of the San Juan mission church and who also presided over a traditional child's naming ceremony in a kiva (Knaut 1995:80–81).

Other forms of resistance included mobility and warfare. Knaut (1995:74) writes that many Pueblo people chose life as refugees in their own land over Christian baptism." Typically, they fled to mountainous areas on the peripheries of the Spanish colony. From these vantage points, many plotted armed warfare. The first villages to revolt—Jemez in 1623, Zuni in 1632, and Taos in 1639—were located in precisely those areas that were the most difficult to control from Santa Fe. Knaut (1995:164–166) also discusses a series of broad based, multi-village revolt attempts. The earliest of these took place in the 1650s, during the Governorship of Hernando de Ugarte y la Concha (1649–1653). It involved people from Isleta, Alameda, San Felipe, Cochiti, Jemez, and Apache, but was discovered and its leaders were hanged as traitors. A second revolt, this time involving the Salinas Pueblos and led by Esteban Clemente, was planned during the Governorship of Fernando de Villanueva (1665–1668), but it too was discovered and Clemente executed.

These acts of resistance must have had carried considerable cumulative weight in the social memory of the Pueblo people. It seems particularly significant that Clemente's revolt was directly modeled upon the 1650s revolt attempt. "*Just as they had plotted during the government of General Concha,* they must destroy the whole body of Christians, not leaving a single religious or Spaniard" (Hackett and Shelby 1942:II:300, my emphasis). This statement implies that plans for a unified military action had circulated widely among the Pueblos decades prior to the successful Revolt of 1680.[3]

Finally, there is debate regarding the Revolt leadership. Most authors identify Popé as the primary architect. For example, Marc Simmons (1980:13) has written that Popé was "the key figure in pulling together diverse factions among the Indians and forging a loose coalition capable of opposing the Spaniards." Similarly, J. Manuel Espinosa (1988:32) writes that Popé was "the leader of the Pueblo revolt" and a "notorious enemy of the Spaniards." This position is based largely upon the testimony of four Indian prisoners captured by Otermín during his failed reconquest bid in 1681 (Hackett and Shelby 1942). Popé is thus popularly regarded as both "the genius and symbol of the spectacular revolt" (Josephy 1958:68).

In a controversial thesis, Fray Angélico Chávez (1967) has proposed that the motivating force behind the Pueblo Revolt was not Popé but rather Domingo Naranjo, a man of mixed African and Indian heritage. He cites the testimony of Pedro Naranjo of San Felipe Pueblo who stated that the Indian lieutenant of Poheyemu (a Pueblo mythological culture hero) was "very tall, black, and had very large yellow eyes" and was greatly feared (Hackett and Shelby 1942:5).[4] Chávez tentatively identifies Pedro Naranjo as either this Domingo Naranjo, or his brother. In any event, he proposes that Naranjo "insinuated himself among the ritual leaders of the pueblos" and "cleverly employed the myth of Pohé-yemo to unite the ever-dissident Pueblo Indians for a successful blow" (Chávez 1967:89). He then conducts a genealogical analysis of the Naranjo family of Santa Clara Pueblo and claims to discover historical connections that support his view.

Stefanie Beninato (1990) has recently challenged Chávez's thesis.[5] She suggests that the documentary evidence does support the idea that the Naranjo family of Santa Clara Pueblo played a leadership role in the resistance to the Spaniards. However, she counters Chávez's assertion that Domingo Naranjo was the sole leader with two arguments. First, she contends that it would have been highly unlikely that an adult non-Pueblo individual could have assumed such position of power in Pueblo society at that time. Second, she suggests that the concept of a single leader was not culturally viable within Pueblo society and, therefore, the Revolt was likely the product of multiple leadership. In support of her case, she draws attention to other leaders cited in the Otermín documents but who have been typically overlooked by historians—individuals such as El Saca and El Chato of Taos, and El Taque of San Juan.

Anthropologists, by contrast, have tended to interpret the Revolt in processual terms and highlight its social and ideological dimensions. One perspective sees it as a response to acculturation. Edward Spicer (1962:567), for example, writes that on the one hand, the conquest stimulated a vigorous borrowing of Spanish ideas and practices among native peoples and led to the growth of a common culture. But on the other, it stimulated the Indians to resist the loss of their identity in a variety of ways. The Revolt was a unique attempt to drive out the Spanish from the Pueblo world facilitated by the creation of a supra-village organization. Once this objective was accomplished, the supra-village organization collapsed without a lasting political outcome, such as an institutionalized confederacy or a common policy for addressing Spanish retaliation. As Spicer (1962:163) puts it, the Revolt was "an extreme reaction to an extreme situation."

Another view has focused upon the social mechanisms that facilitated the Revolt. Edward Dozier (1970) drew attention to the importance of medicine societies as a means of establishing a supra-village confederation. He shows that these societies are present at every Pueblo village and, despite linguistic differences serve to structure inter-Pueblo ceremonial interaction. "Attendance and participating in the esoteric rites of the village associations are open only to members, but members of such organizations from other villages are welcome to attend the meetings and rites of the associations" (Dozier 1970:56). He further suggests that these ceremonial associations and their secretive nature played a major role in Popé's success.

Yet another perspective has emphasized the Revolt's strategic character and its ideological legitimation. For Alfonso Ortiz, the Revolt marked an intensive period of "cultural revitalization" associated with massive population movements and dislocations. He writes, "if the Pueblos by this time still did not share a sense of cultural similarity, they certainly shared at least a sense of common historical destiny (Ortiz 1994:300). He further suggests that the Spaniards unwittingly gave the Pueblos a set of political institutions, which they used most effectively to resist both the Spaniards and later colonial powers (Ortiz 1969, 1994).

Similarly, Daniel Reff (1995) has recently characterized the Pueblo Revolt as an expression of a millenarian movement.[6] He suggests that the leaders asserted supernatural guidance and "employed images and symbols with formal (e.g., black complexion, glowing eyes) and behavioral (e.g., intervening) attributes consistent with the Spaniards' Counter-Reformation notions of the devil and his active participation in human affairs" (Reff 1995:65). He observes that this rhetoric, ironically, affirmed the missionaries' sense of self and legitimized their war against the "troops of the demons of hell."

A key contextual factor in his explanation is disease-induced population collapse. He notes that a devastating epidemic immediately preceded the Revolt, a time when the Pueblo population is thought to have declined by 80 percent or more. The loss of elders, as the bearers of sacred knowledge, would have been devastating and those that survived would have seen their authority erode because of their inability to adequately explain or prevent disease. At the same time, it would have become clear that the Franciscan priests were similarly unable to prevent or stem epidemics. This situation coupled with economic exploitation by missionaries and colonists led to broad disaffection and provided fertile ground for the Revolt.

I have recently reviewed the evidence for cultural revitalization and concluded that Pueblo leaders combined aspects of messianism, nativism, and revivalism into a distinctive cultural expression (Preucel 2000). Of the three, the messianic component is perhaps the least well developed. In Pueblo society ritual leaders are not considered to be divine and, therefore, it seems unlikely that Popé should be considered a messiah. Indeed, it is clear that Popé was one of a number of important leaders including El Saca and El Chato of Taos, Francisco Tanjete of San Ildefonso, and Alonzo Catiti of Santo Domingo. Popé does, however, seem to have been the public spokesperson of the movement—the individual most responsible for its rhetorical form and persuasive power.

The nativistic component of the movement, in contrast, is clearly in evidence. The Otermín documents give a sense of the popular anti-Catholic discourse that spread throughout the Pueblo world following the Revolt. They reveal that Popé and his associates demanded that the people "instantly break up and burn the images of the holy Christ, the Virgin Mary and the other saints, the crosses . . . burn the temples, break up the bells, and separate from the wives whom God had given them in marriage and take those whom they desired" (Hackett and Shelby 1942:247). In addition, there was also a strong revivalistic character to the movement. This can be seen in the creation of a new ideology that required people to live in accordance with the "laws of the ancestors" (Hackett and Shelby 1942:248).

Oral History and the Pueblo Revolt

Historians and archaeologists have been slow to appreciate the value of Pueblo oral history in understanding the events surrounding the Pueblo Revolt. For example, Weber (1999:8–9) has written that "Pueblo oral traditions have not provided significant insights into the Pueblo Revolt" and that "we must listen to Pueblo voices through Spanish interlocutors." This assessment is contradicted, however, both by the published literature on Pueblo oral history and by the contemporary practice of Pueblo storytelling.

There have been several focused attempts to collect oral history of the Revolt period. Joe Sando, for example, has made use of Jemez oral history collected in 1970 to write his contribution on the Pueblo Revolt in the *Handbook of North American Indians, Volume 9: Southwest* (Sando 1979) and his various histories of the Pueblo people (Sando 1982, 1992, 1998). Among the things he discusses are the evidence for multiple leadership, the spiritual guidance provided by the Twin War Gods, and the need for ritual purification following military action.

In 1982, Andrew Wiget published a study of four Hopi oral history accounts that refer to the Revolt period (see Dongoske and Dongoske, Chapter 8). These are by Wikvaya (recorded in 1902 by H. R. Voth), Emil Pooley (recorded in 1967 as part of the Duke Oral History Project), Edmund Nequatewa (published in 1936), and Robert Sakiestewa (recorded in 1967 as part of the Duke Project). These accounts provided considerable information on life under Spanish rule. In particular, they highlight such things as the dictatorial nature of the friars, the forced labor in building the missions, the seduction of Hopi women, the raiding of kivas and sacred ceremonies, the punishment for failing to attend mass, and the drought and famine. They also reveal important details about the Revolt itself including the leadership role of Badger clan and the strategic alliance of Awatovi, Shungopovi, and Oraibi. The Pooley account, for example, states that the attack on Oraibi mission took place in the early morning and that the Hopi may have been impersonating katsinas. The Wikvaya account relates that the church was looted for timber and its bells are still held by the Agave society.

In 1988, the Pueblo of Zuni received a grant from the National Endowment for the Arts to document contemporary Zuni storytellers and create a series of radio programs (Wiget 1991:19). The stories recorded included several different accounts of the events of the Pueblo Revolt period.

A popular Zuni account is the story of Father Juan Greyrobe. Father Greyrobe (*Kwan Tátchui Lók'yana*) was a Franciscan priest who apparently was permitted to join the Zuni people in their move to their mesa village on Dowa Yalanne (Cushing 1896:330–331; Davis 1869:79; see Ferguson, Chapter 2). Possible historical confirmation for this story is found in Diego de Vargas's journal account of his visit to the mesa village in 1692. Upon entering a second-story room, Vargas was astonished to find an altar with two large tallow candles burning and various ecclesiastical objects (Kessell et al. 1995:207). Vargas, however, makes no mention of a priest so, if Father Greyrobe was present, he chose to conceal himself from the Spaniards. Wiget (1991:19) suggests that a pro-Catholic faction that formed around this charismatic young priest may have maintained this altar.

Other Zuni accounts mention the role of medicine society chiefs during the Revolt as well as describe two attacks on Dowa Yalanne not documented in the Spanish sources. One specifies that, "the leader of the revolt was the keeper of the great shell, who said that he was not afraid, as he had plenty of medicine to destroy the enemy" (Stevenson 1904:286–289). Another version of this story relates how Zuni priests of the Great Shell Society attempted to "poison" the Spaniards by placing shells in the springs (Wiget 1991:19). Yet another story recounts two Spanish attacks on the mesa, one which is resisted by supernatural means and a second which is prevented by Father Greyrobe who threw a buckskin down off the mesa with a message that convinced the Spaniards of their peaceful intentions (Wiget 1991).

There are several accounts of Vargas's military campaigns after the "bloodless" reconquest. One story, collected by Ruth Benedict (1931), gives a Cochiti perspective on Vargas's attack on Kotyiti Pueblo on April 17, 1694 that challenges the official version recorded by Vargas. The story indicates that Vargas's campaign was successful because he captured a Cochiti man living at Jemez and then tortured him until he finally agreed to lead the Spaniards up the secret trail known as the "Moon trail" (Benedict 1931:185–186). Vargas's own journal account, however, makes no mention of this (Kessell et al. 1998:191–192). Another related story is the story of the "lost Cochiti treasure" (Applegate 1932). When the people of Kotyiti saw the Spaniards approaching, the cacique and his helper gathered together all the village valuables to keep them out of Spanish hands and buried them in a secret location. However, during the battle, they were killed and the location where they hid the valuables was lost.

Several Jemez accounts give versions of Vargas's attack on Astialakwa Pueblo. On July 24, 1694, Vargas stormed San Diego Mesa (Kessell et al. 1998:324–327). After a fierce battle, he succeeded in capturing the village and took 361 women and children as prisoners. Fifty-five Jemez warriors were killed in the battle and another 12 to 15 by Eusebio de Vargas's men. Seven Pueblo men jumped off the cliff edge to escape from the Spaniards. According to Jemez oral history, just at that moment, an image of San Diego appeared on the cliff face and the people who jumped landed safely on their feet (Sando 1982:120). Today, the image of San Diego is venerated as a shrine.

Yet another group of stories are associated with the Revolt of 1696. On June 4, the northern Pueblos rose up in rebellion and killed five missionaries. Fray Alonso de Cisneros, assigned to the mission of San Buenaventura de Cochití, managed to escape certain death by fleeing to the safety of San Felipe Pueblo, which remained loyal to the Spaniards. According to one account, the Cochiti people sought his death because he had had sexual relations with a married woman (Benedict 1931:193). His escape was facilitated because the sacristan dressed him in woman's clothes and led him out of the pueblo. Lange (1990:10) writes that this incident is still familiar to many Cochiti people and one of the favorite stories of "the old days." This same story was also told at San Felipe Pueblo (Bandelier 1892:191–192). One account states that the Cochiti people pursued the priest intending to kill him, but withdrew as soon as he reached the safety of San Felipe. Another version says that the Cochiti laid siege to Old San Felipe on the mesa and cut off its access to water, but were repulsed due to the miraculous intervention of the rescued missionary.

There is a large body of Hopi stories associated with the tragic event that took place at Awatovi in 1700 (see Whiteley, Chapter 10). This incident has been called "one of the most significant events in Hopi history" and was, in part, precipitated by the reintroduction of Catholicism (James 1974:62). Vargas visited Awatovi in 1692 taking possession of it in the name of the crown as part of his reconquest. In 1700, Fray Juan de Garaicoechea visited Awatovi and found that the convent had been repaired and that its people were eager to receive missionaries (Bandelier 1892:371). This public acceptance of Christianity, however, outraged the other Hopi villages and several leaders (including an Awatovi leader) made the fateful decision to attack Awatovi to purge the district of the influence of the Spaniards. Oral history reveals that the Hopi associated Catholicism with the return of *koyaanisqatsi* (rampant corruption and social turmoil). According to one account, the attackers pulverized chili pods and scattered the powder into the kivas, which were then set afire (Lomatuway'ma et al. 1993:401).[7]

This review of Pueblo oral history reveals important

contextual information about the Revolt not present in the Spanish ethnohistorical narratives. For example, it suggests that one of the reasons for the Revolt was the sexual abuse of Pueblo women by Franciscan priests. This motive, however, is never acknowledged by the Spaniards in their explanations of the Revolt, although it is noted in the litigation related to the disputes between church and state (Scholes 1936, 1942). In addition, it reveals the persistent factionalism within different communities that appears to have been heightened by the return of the Spaniards. Many Pueblo people had close family and economic ties with the Spaniards and were reluctant to participate in the violence of the Revolt and, indeed, welcomed back the Spaniards during the Reconquest. Finally, these accounts highlight the mystical character of specific events and the popular belief (shared by the Spaniards) in supernatural intervention.

Archaeology and the Pueblo Revolt

Until quite recently, the Pueblo Revolt has not been the subject of sustained archaeological research. The reasons for this are complex and can be attributed in part to the intellectual interests of scholars working within the traditions of culture historical and processual archaeologies (Wilcox and Masse 1981). Nonetheless, we can identify four interrelated sub-fields that need to be brought together in order to understand the processes, events, and meanings of the Pueblo Revolt. These subfields are Mission archaeology, Refuge site archaeology, Pueblito archaeology, and Spanish site archaeology.

Mission Archaeology

The missions of Arizona and New Mexico are prominent architectural signs of the colonial encounter (Figure 1.1). Some missions, such as Abó and Quarai, lie in ruin while others, like San Esteban de Acoma, are still in use. The archaeology of these (and other) mission sites occupies a special place within Southwestern studies. Mission archaeology helped constitute the field of Spanish Colonial period history (Ayers 1995:62) and played a central role in establishing the scientific basis of Southwestern archaeology.

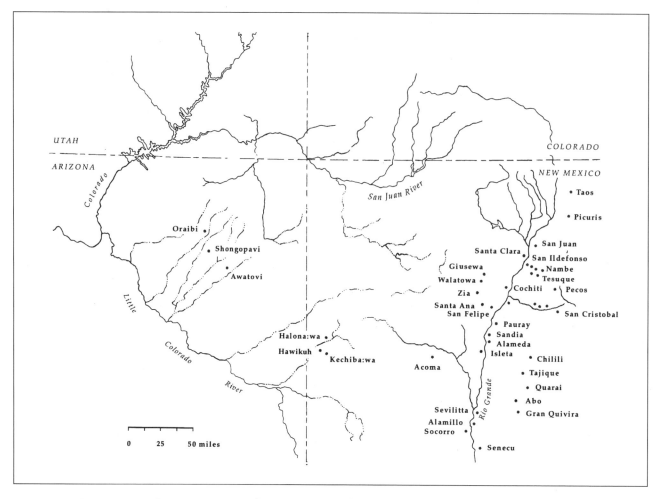

Figure 1.1. Locations of major Mission Pueblos during the seventeenth century.

The beginnings of Mission archaeology can conveniently be set at 1880 with Adolph Bandelier's pioneering work at Pecos Pueblo.[8] Bandelier was hired by the Archaeological Institute of America to write a historical introduction to the Pueblo Indians (Lange and Riley 1996:38). Bandelier sought out the Archbishop of Santa Fe and in conversations with the local priests learned of Pecos as a place worthy of investigation (Lange and Riley 1966:26). He visited the site from August 28 to September 6, and made surface collections and photographed and measured the ruins (Figure 1.2). This work provided the basis for his history (Bandelier 1881).

The first recorded excavation of a mission site is Edgar Lee Hewett's work at Giusewa in 1910. Although there is some debate in the literature, Giusewa is now considered to be the location of San José de los Jemez (Elliott 1993;

Elliott, Chapter 3). Hewett directed a joint School of American Research and the Bureau of American Ethnology summer field school focusing upon the prehistoric village of Tyuonyi in Frijoles Canyon (now Bandelier National Monument). At the end of the season, he moved his operation to the Jemez district and spent a week excavating Giusewa. Hewett prepared a report on his work, but it has never been located (Elliott 1993:18). The only available description is due to Hodge (1918a) who noted that they excavated about 30 burials from the "old cemetery" and "found no indication of Spanish influence."

In 1912, Mission archaeology was placed upon a sound scientific footing with Nels Nelson's investigations of the mission pueblos of the Galisteo Basin for the American Museum of Natural History in New York. These sites included San Cristobal, San Lazaro, San Marcos, San

Pedro, and Galisteo Pueblos as well as several other non-mission villages. Because of the availability of historical and ethnographic data, Nelson (1914:9) felt that it might be possible to arrive at "sound conclusions regarding the culture, character, and interrelations of the early historic Rio Grande villagers of the sixteenth and seventeenth centuries, and that much accomplished, the elucidation of the problems presented by the Pueblos of prehistoric times should be an easier task." His goal was, therefore, to "prosecute a piece of research work in the most scientific manner, namely, by working back from the known to the unknown" to document the nature of the links between Pueblo history and prehistory (Nelson 1914:9). Nelson's (1916) excavations from 1912–1914 at San Cristobal not only established the basic chronological sequence for the Rio Grande region, but they also demonstrated the viability of stratigraphic excavation, which revolutionized American archaeology (Willey and Sabloff 1980:84–89).

In 1915, Alfred V. Kidder selected Pecos Pueblo for intensive research because of its deep chronological time depth. He wrote that "(t)here is, indeed, no known ruin in the Southwest which seems to have been lived in continuously for so long a period" (Kidder 1924:1). Kidder was hopeful that Pecos Pueblo would provide evidence of stratified remains that might reveal the development of Pueblo arts and thus assist in placing prehistoric and historic pueblo villages in an accurate chronological sequence. From 1915 to 1929, he directed ten field seasons at Pecos under the auspices of Phillips Academy, Andover. This resulted in a series of progress reports (Kidder 1916, 1917, 1926a, b), a summary of its history and excavations up to 1922 (Kidder 1924), studies of ceramics (Kidder and Amsden 1931; Kidder and Kidder 1917; Kidder and Shepard 1936), a study of artifacts (Kidder 1932), a study of the human remains (Hooton 1930), and a synthesis (Kidder 1958).

At the same time, Frederick Webb Hodge conducted excavations at Hawikuh Pueblo in the Zuni District (from 1917–1923 with a hiatus in 1922) under the joint sponsorship of the Bureau of American Ethnology and the Museum of the American Indian, Heye Foundation

Figure 1.2. Adolph Bandelier at Pecos (Bandelier 1881:Plate VI).

(Smith et al. 1966). Hodge, like Nelson and Kidder, was attracted to the village, "partly by the important role that the pueblo and its inhabitants played in the Spanish history of the Southwest from 1539 to 1672" (Hodge 1937:xv). One of his research questions addressed the extent of Spanish influence at the village and he concluded that ceramic designs revealed no Spanish influence and that, "objects of stone, wood, and bone had not given way to those of metal to any extent even at the time of the abandonment of Hawikuh" (Hodge 1918b:376).

From 1935–1939 John O. Brew of the Peabody Museum of Harvard University began a major research project at Awatovi in the Hopi District. He writes, "the chief reason for the selection of Awatovi, instead of one of the other large ruined pueblos in the Jeddito, for major excavation was the apparent assurance, obtained in preliminary reconnaissance, that it held the longest record of occupation" (Brew in Montgomery et al. 1949:vii). The Awatovi Expedition produced reports on the excavation of 21 sites (Daifuku 1961), and various specialized studies (Gifford and Smith 1978; Hack 1942a, 1942b; Lawrence 1951; Olsen 1978; Smith 1971; Woodbury 1954), including the Awatovi kiva murals (Smith 1952). Of special interest here is Ross Montgomery's study of mission architecture, which was able to distinguish between pre- and post-Revolt buildings (Montgomery in Montgomery et al. 1949). For example, he proposed that the barracks-stable was built in 1700 on the basis of the modernity of its plan, the use of 90-degree corners, and the character of the walls.

Except for stabilization associated with the creation

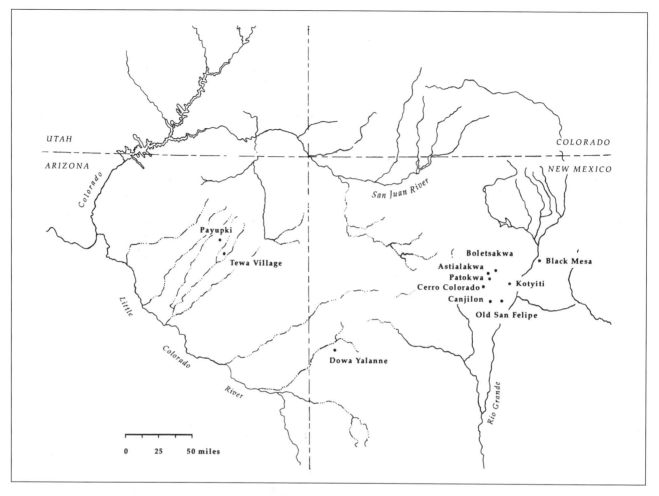

Figure 1.3. Locations of major post-Revolt Refuge villages.

of the New Mexico State Monuments (Hewett and Fischer 1943), very little work took place at mission sites until the 1960s.[9] Herbert Dick's research at Picuris Pueblo stands out as a rare example of collaboration with an Indian tribe. Dick established his project from 1961 to 1965 with the support of the Picuris Tribal Council and the Fort Burgwin Research Center of Southern Methodist University. He selected Picuris because he considered it to be the longest continually inhabited settlement in North America (Dick and Adler 1999). Dick's research design had five goals, one of which involved documenting the evidence of post-contact culture change and acculturation. Unfortunately, very little of this research has been published (but see Adler and Dick 1999).

Beginning in the 1990s, there has been a renewed interest in Mission archaeology, much of it stimulated by the potential of mission sites for addressing social questions of economic organization and cultural identity in the colonial context. Kate Spielmann (1993, 1994), for example, has been focusing upon the evolution of craft specialization at Quarai. Mark Lycett (1997, 1998, 1999, 2000, Chapter 4) has been investigating the relationships between Spanish colonization and the historical transformation of indigenous societies at Paaco (San Pedro). But the largest current project is the San Marcos Project jointly directed by Ann Ramenofsky and David Hurst Thomas. Ramenofsky has been mapping the native Pueblo component of the site while Thomas (1999) has been conducting test excavations of the church-convento complex in order to determine the construction sequence.

Refuge Site Archaeology

The second subfield is Refuge site archaeology. Following the Pueblo Revolt of 1680, there was a dramatic shift in Pueblo settlement; numerous mission villages were vacated and new mesatop communities were established (Figure 1.3) (Ferguson and Preucel, in press). Although the significance of these sites for understanding the transition to the modern period has long been recognized, they have not been systematically studied and Al Schroeder's (1970:68) suggestion that research should focus upon "the part played by various aspects of culture in selecting new or refuge sites or areas during the Pueblo rebellion period" is only now being addressed.

The earliest archaeological documentation of refuge villages was conducted by Bandelier as part of his Southwestern archaeological surveys for the Archaeological Institute of America. From 1880 to 1885, he visited and mapped the villages of Kotyiti (Potrero Viejo) (Lange and Riley 1966:139–140, 151), Old San Felipe (Lange and Riley 1966:273–275; Lange et al. 1975:68–69), and Dowa Yalanne (Toyoalana) (Lange and Riley 1970:47–51).

In 1888, Frank Hamilton Cushing conducted an archaeological survey at Dowa Yalanne for the Hemenway Southwestern Archaeological Expedition. He was particularly interested in evidence of Zuni social structure following the Revolt of 1680. His map of the Dowa Yalanne settlement, made with the assistance of George Bigelow, an engineer, identified seven different clusters that he interpreted to represent the "Seven Cities of Cibola" (Figure 1.4) (Cushing 1890:156). An isolated, square house of four rooms defined each of these clusters. He regarded this house to be "the connecting link" between the House of the Priests of the prehistoric period (here he is referring to the Classic period Hohokam site of Casa Grande) and the kiva of the historic Zuni (Cushing 1890:156–157, n.1).

The first and, to date, only excavation of a refuge community was performed in 1912 at Kotyiti Pueblo by Nels Nelson in the context of the Archer M. Huntington survey of the American Museum of Natural History (Nelson n.d.). Clark Wissler, Curator of Anthropology, directed

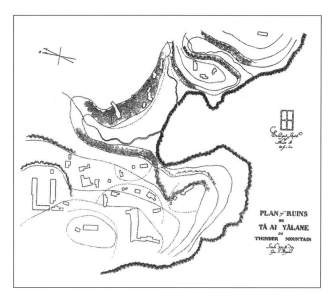

Figure 1.4. Frank Hamilton Cushing's Plan of Dowa Yalanne (Cushing 1890).

Nelson to work at Kotyiti because of its potential in addressing "historical problems" (Letter from Clark Wissler to Nels Nelson, dated May 23, 1912, AMNH archives). Presumably, Wissler had learned of Kotyiti from Adolph Bandelier who held a brief appointment from 1903–1906 at the American Museum (Lange and Riley 1996). In a two-week period, from November 3 to the 15, Nelson excavated 135 ground floor rooms of the plaza pueblo along with a few rooms at an adjacent village. Nelson was discouraged with the results of his excavations, largely because they yielded so few "museum quality" artifacts. He catalogued only 125 specimens.

In 1916, Leslie Spier, also of the American Museum of Natural History, conducted an archaeological survey of sites in the Zuni district (Spier 1917). The purpose of his survey was to elucidate the temporal relations among the different sites in order to provide a background for ethnological research. Taking as his inspiration the methods of Nelson and Alfred Kroeber, he mapped and collected sherds from several post-conquest refuge sites including Towwayallanna (Dowa Yalanne), Wimmayawa (Wimaya:wa), and Kolliwa.[10]

Several refuge villages were visited by H. P. Mera of the Laboratory of Anthropology as part of his survey of glazeware sites in the Northern Rio Grande region. His

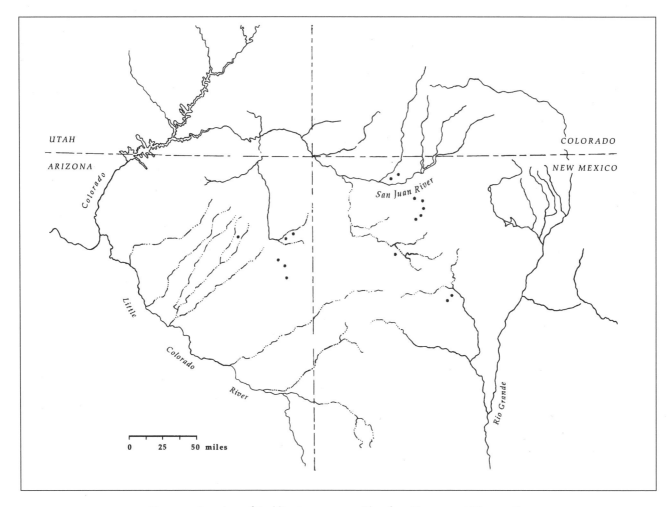

Figure 1.5. Locations of Pueblito sites post-1730 (data from Towner 1996:Figure 7.6).

goal was to "gain a general idea of the movements and shifts in a population, in some ways diverse in composition, but which, on the other hand, possessed in common certain cultural features that may be used as indices" (Mera 1940:1). The refuge sites he visited include Kotyiti, Cerro Colorado, Black Mesa, Old Santa Ana, Old San Felipe, and Astialakwa. He noted that all of these sites could be considered defensive in terms of their locations.

In 1987, T. J. Ferguson began dissertation fieldwork at Zuni Pueblo authorized by the Zuni Tribal Council and conducted under the auspices of the Zuni Archaeology Program. His goal was to investigate the formal characteristics of Zuni architecture and investigate how these were related to changing social structure from the historic to modern periods (Ferguson 1996). Using a space syntax approach, he analyzed 14 different sites with preserved

architecture, including Dowa Yalanne, Wimaya:wa, Kyaki:ma Refuge site 11, and Kyaki:ma Refuge site 12.[11] This research has produced a number of related publications on Zuni settlement (e.g., Ferguson 1992; Ferguson and Mills 1987; Ferguson et al. 1990).

Ferguson's study of Dowa Yalanne is of particular significance since it focuses upon the reshaping of Zuni social structure at a critical juncture in their history (see Ferguson, Chapter 2). He identifies two separate patterns within the settlement—a cluster of two large roomblocks possibly representing village-level social groupings and a cluster of smaller dispersed roomblocks of lineages or clan segments. He notes that the former roomblocks contain almost half of the total number of rooms in the settlement. From this, he infers a substantial amount of social experimentation. He also shows that the spatial structure of Dowa Yalanne was highly distributed and well integrated, a pattern markedly different from that of the earlier villages of Hawikuh, Kechiba:wa and Kyaki:ma, and seemingly at odds with the defensive character of the settlement (Ferguson 1996:119). This led him to conclude that the mesa itself, and not the formal architectural arrangement of the village, provided defensibility.

In 1995, I established the Kotyiti Research Project with the Pueblo of Cochiti to investigate the social processes surrounding the founding and occupation of Kotyiti Pueblo. In the course of three field seasons (1996, 1997 and 1998), we have documented and mapped the plaza pueblo and its adjacent rancheria. Our results demonstrate that these two sites were contemporaneous and formed a single community (Preucel 1996, 2000a). They also reveal the significance of architecture in actively furthering the popular revivalist discourse. The form of the plaza pueblo, in particular, appears to have been built to assert certain elements of the Keresan cosmology (Preucel 2000a,b; Snead and Preucel 1999) and may have even have been conceptualized as White House, the ancestral Keresan village where people and katsinas lived together in harmony (Ferguson and Preucel, in press).

Pueblito Archaeology

The third subfield is Pueblito archaeology. Pueblitos are small masonry structures concentrated mainly in the Gobernador and Largo Canyon areas of northwestern New Mexico in an area known to the Navajo as *Dinétah* (Figure 1.5). These sites have played a key role in the interpretation of Navajo cultural changes during the seventeenth and eighteenth centuries (Hogan 1991, Towner 1996). They were originally seen as evidence for Pueblo refugees fleeing the Spaniards to live with the Navajo after the Revolt of 1696. More recently, they have been reinterpreted as indigenous Navajo sites built to withstand Ute incursions.

The refugee hypothesis was first proposed by A. V. Kidder on the basis of his investigation of three pueblito sites in the Gobernador district in 1912. In his description, he noted their defensive locations and the co-occurrence of pueblo-type rooms with collapsed log structures closely resembling modern Navajo hogans (Kidder 1920). He also observed a corner fireplace with a hood, wood hewn with metal axes, cow and sheep bones, and historic Puebloan ceramics. From these data, he concluded that these sites were built during the Historic period and proposed that their builders were either indigenous peoples probably in contact with the Navajo or some other people who made circular earth covered lodges of wood, or Jemez refugees who joined the Navajo at the time of the Revolt of 1696. Because he could find no ethnohistorical evidence in support of his first thesis, he favored the Pueblo refugee hypothesis.

A number of pueblitos were identified and excavated in the early twentieth century and most scholars adopted Kidder's view (see Towner and Dean 1996 for a summary). For example, Keur concluded that the mixture of Pueblo and Navajo traits at these sites indicated that they were built by "uprooted Puebloans (who) joined the erstwhile hostile Navajos to hide out against a common foe" (Keur 1944:86). Similarly, Dittert (1958) defined the Gobernador phase (A.D. 1700–1775) in the Navajo Reservoir District as a period of intensive "acculturation" between the Navajo and Pueblo refugees. The only cautionary note to this picture was Roy Carlson's (1965:98) observation that the tree-ring dates and ceramic types indicated an occupation in the first quarter of the eighteenth century, some 20 years after the 1696 Revolt.

Kidder's thesis has now been reevaluated on two fronts. First, new dendrochronological dates have been obtained and these indicate that most pueblitos are too late to have been occupied immediately following the 1696 Revolt, as originally pointed out by Carlson (Figure 1.6) (Fetterman 1996; Towner 1992, 1996). Only a single site, the Tapacito Ruin, is known to have been built during this period (Towner and Dean 1992). Second, the historical literature has been reassessed and little evidence has been found to support the idea that large groups of Pueblo people were living with the Navajo (Hogan 1991). For example, Roque de Madrid's Navajo campaign in 1705 ran across only one Jemez woman (Hendricks and Wilson 1996). A new

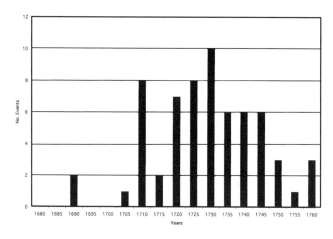

Figure 1.6. Construction episodes at Pueblito sites
(from Towner 1996:Figure 7.4).

consensus has seemingly emerged that regards these sites as indigenous Navajo habitations built for protection against Ute raids.

The redating of the pueblitos is an important contribution. It is worth noting however, the discovery that the majority of the pueblitos were constructed in the mid-eighteenth century does not rule out Pueblo involvement (Carlson 1965:98).[12] It simply means that they could not have been built by Pueblo refugees fleeing the Rio Grande Valley after the 1696 Revolt. Additional historical research is needed on the state of Spanish-Pueblo relations during the first half of the eighteenth century. There is, in fact, evidence for the return of a repressive regime of religious persecution that may have inspired Pueblo people to take refuge with the Navajo. For example, Governor Juan Ignacio Flores Mogollón initiated a vigorous campaign against the use of kivas and destroyed several at Nambe, Tesuque, San Juan, Galisteo, Pecos, Jemez, Laguna, Acoma, and Halona in 1714 (Kessell 1992).[13]

Spanish Site Archaeology

The fourth subfield is Spanish site archaeology. This heading refers to the archaeology of the royal villa of Santa Fe as well as the archaeology of the rural settlement of the Spanish colonists occupied during the seventeenth and early eighteenth centuries. Unlike Mission archaeology, it has received surprisingly little attention from professional

archaeologists with most sites having been recorded in the context of salvage or cultural resource management projects (Ayers 1995). An understanding of these sites is crucial since they, too, were the sites of Pueblo servitude and were therefore targeted for attack during the Revolt.

The archaeology of the city of Santa Fe is poorly known in part because very little research has been conducted and published.[14] Perhaps the best-known project is the salvage excavations at the Palace of the Governors, known to the Spaniards as the *casas reales*. This research is noteworthy because it has produced evidence for both the Spanish occupation prior to the Revolt as well as data on the subsequent Pueblo reoccupation of and remodeling of the Palace after the Revolt. When Vargas took ritual possession of Santa Fe in 1692, he found that the Indians had transformed the casas reales into a walled and fortified pueblo village (Kessell and Hendricks 1992:396).

In 1973, Cordelia Snow directed a salvage excavation in the Palace in the context of a repair and restoration project (Snow 1974). Beneath the floor of two rooms, she discovered a series of nine bell-shaped storage pits in an area that had once been extramural. The pits, likely used for the storage of grain, had been filled in with broken pottery and food bones that dated to the Revolt period. Objects of Indian manufacture included projectile points, chipped stone tools, manos, turquoise beads, worked selenite, a clay pipe, a ceramic figurine, bone needles and awls, and an antler tool (Snow 1974:17). Spanish items modified by Indians include majolica sherds that had been worked into spindle whorls and pendants.

Some areas of the Palace revealed evidence of substantial architectural remodeling. For example, the rooms to the south of the great center wall were sub-divided into smaller pueblo-style rooms. Doors and windows were closed up and access was gained by ladders through roof openings. In her analysis of this excavation, Donna Seifert (n.d.) noted that the Indians did not eliminate all Spanish practices and material culture, but retained certain features, such as Spanish-sized adobes and corner fireplaces. There is even evidence that the Indians built a Spanish-style system of running water. A small trench lined with wood and sand led from the plaza into the residential areas.

Relatively few Spanish rural sites of the Colonial/Revolt period have been studied archaeologically. The best examples are those that were excavated as part of the Cochiti Dam Archaeological Project. Two ranchos, the Cochiti Springs site and the Las Majadas site, date to the Revolt/Spanish Colonization phase (A.D. 1598–1680). The Cochiti Springs site consists of approximately 12 to 18 rooms arranged around a central plaza and a series of corrals (Snow 1979). Corner fireplaces were found in three rooms, one of which had a raised hearth. Although the ceramic assemblage was dominated by Pueblo pottery, more than four different types of Mexican majolica were present. Las Majadas is formed of five rooms arranged in an "L" shape and a corral (Figure 1.7) (Snow 1973a). Several rooms contained corner fireplaces and one may have had a bi-level fireplace. Spanish artifacts recovered included chain mail, forged nails and Mexican majolica. Cordelia Snow (1979:219) has speculated that these sites may have been the residences of either Francisco Luján, *teniente* of Cochiti Pueblo in 1643, José Telles Jiron, encomendero of Cochiti Pueblo and San Felipe by 1661, Varela de Losada, *alcalde mayor* of Cochiti in 1661, or Cristóbal Fontes, alcalde mayor in 1663. Both sites seem to have been abandoned sometime prior to the 1680 Revolt.

The Cochiti Dam Project recorded eighteen sites that dated to the post-Revolt/Spanish Colonial phase (A.D. 1696–1821). Some of these were sizeable settlements while others were small single-family homes, possibly seasonally occupied. Snow (1979) has summarized the evidence for these arguing that, although there is evidence for farming, these sites are clearly associated with the raising of livestock as a primary economic pursuit. This focus also has an effect upon the kinds of residences built. She writes, "because landowners were frequently not in residence, little substantial architecture was necessary so long as shelter was provided for the shepherds and herders as they cared for the livestock" (Snow 1979:225).

One of the most unusual of these sites is the Torreon site, a defensive structure completely enclosed by a perimeter wall with two towers in the southwest and northeast

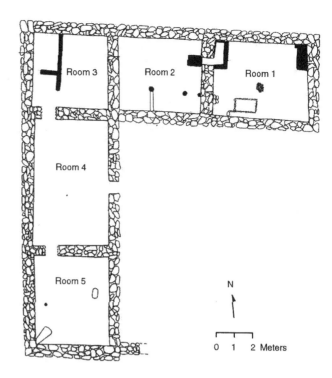

Figure 1.7. Plan of Unit 1 at the Las Majadas site (LA 591) (after Snow 1973a).

corners (Snow 1973b). The ceramics recovered consist of both Pueblo types and five different types of Mexican majolica, Chinese porcelain, glass, and metal. In addition, an unusually large number of butchered cattle, sheep, and goats were found. This faunal assemblage led Snow (1979:221) to speculate that the site may have been a small military garrison established by Governor Francisco Cuervo y Valdés for protection against Apache raids.

New Perspectives on the Pueblo Revolt

In this volume, we seek to offer new perspectives on the Pueblo Revolt that both build upon and transcend the limitations of Borderlands histories and standard acculturationist narratives. Most of the contributions address aspects of Mission and Refuge archaeologies and engage with one of two themes. The first is the dialectical relation between acts of resistance and structures of domination as mediated by material culture. The second is the character of the various discourses that constitute the documentary, oral historical, and archaeological records of the seventeenth and early eighteenth centuries.

What emerges, then, is not a single, definitive archaeology of the Pueblo Revolt, but rather multiple archaeologies of Pueblo resistance to Spanish colonial rule that are contoured by the interests, perspectives, and experiences of individual authors.

Domination and resistance are key topics in the anthropology of colonialism. Most contemporary scholars approach these concepts from a Gramscian point of view and regard hegemony as the cultural practices and social institutions employed by politically repressive regimes to insure consent and compliance. Resistance is theorized as the gradual awareness among social groups through a "war of positions" of their common interest in opposing ruling forces. The problem with this approach turns on the extent to which it can be argued that the hegemonic ideology subsumes all forms of resistance. Or, stated another way, how hegemonic is hegemony?

Scott (1990) has recently argued for an alternative view that holds that even in situations of conflict the public claims of subordinate groups nearly always have a strategic or dialogic dimension that shapes the forms they take. Because of this, it is difficult to know from the public claim alone what is due to caution and what is an indication of acceptance of the dominant ideology. In order to address this point, Scott proposes an analytical distinction between public and hidden transcripts. The former refers to the open interaction between subordinates and those in power. The latter refers to the discourses that takes place beyond the direct observation of those in power and includes speeches, gestures, and practices that confirm, contradict or otherwise comment upon what appears in the public transcript. This approach provides a more nuanced understanding of "passive resistance" (Adams 1989).

For the Pueblo people, resistance to the Spaniards generated a new form of historical consciousness. As a public transcript, the Revolt represented a strategic vehicle for rejecting Spanish hegemony and returning to a life lived according to "the law of the ancestors" (Hackett and Shelby 1942:248). In the aftermath of the Revolt, Pueblo peoples were encouraged to rid themselves of the material signs of Spanish religious authority—the mission churches, bells, crosses, and holy images—to the extent of "washing even their clothing, with the understanding that there would thus be taken from them the character of the holy sacraments" (Hackett and Shelby 1942:247). For the first time in recorded history, Pueblo peoples thought of themselves as a collective with a common genealogy and purpose. In this moment, we see the origins of a trans-Pueblo ethnicity (cf. Comaroff and Comaroff 1992:245).

There is compelling evidence that Pueblo leaders did not restrict themselves to indigenous symbols and meanings to further their cultural revitalization movement, rather they crafted a new discourse on identity that selectively played upon elements of Spanish, Pueblo, and Mexican Indian beliefs and practices. For example, Pedro Naranjo's statement (Hackett and Shelby 1942:246–247) identifies the deities that appeared to Popé as Tilini, Caudi, and Tleume, names that appear to be of Nahuatl origin (Beninato 1990) and the lake of Copala, which seems to combine an indigenous pueblo emergence story with a mythical Aztec kingdom (Tyler 1952). This discourse can also be seen in the use of Spanish material culture and practices by Pueblo leaders in their public appearances. For example, immediately after the Revolt of 1680, Popé and Alonso Catiti parodied the Spanish church and crown in a feast at Santa Ana Pueblo. Popé took a chalice and toasted Catiti saying, "To your Paternal Reverence's health" and Catiti responded saying, "Here's to your Lordship's health, Sir governor" (Twitchell 1914:273).

On the surface, this use of non-Pueblo symbols and meanings would appear to contradict the calls for nativism and revivalism. However, a more nuanced reading reveals the semiotic processes by which Pueblo people used symbols and meanings to fashion new identities (see Liebmann, Chapter 9). These non-Pueblo symbols "became pueblo" in a process similar to what Hartman Lomawaima (1989) calls "Hopification" and what Eric Hobsbawm and Terence Ranger (1983) call "the invention of tradition." This process was not stable and, over time, these same symbols came to be invested with yet new meanings that were themselves reproduced by new material practices. Current examples of such semiotically charged practices that layer and interweave indigenous, Spanish, and Mexican symbols are Santiago's Day Celebration (Lange 1959) and the Matachines Dance (Rodriguez 1996). In their resistance to the Spaniards, the Pueblos remade themselves.

The volume is organized into three sections. The first section addresses the constitutive roles of architecture and settlement in the objectification of Puebloan social and political identities. In Chapter 2, T. J. Ferguson examines the "architecture of resistance" in the Zuni district. Between 1680 and 1692, the Zuni people experienced a profound social transformation that saw the consolidation of their six villages into a single settlement on Dowa Yalanne. Ferguson argues that the architecture and spatial patterning of the new settlement can be interpreted as a physical record of the social processes affecting the Zuni, including patterns of resistance, residence, and ritual. The settlement consists of two large roomblocks with smaller isolated roomblocks distributed across the south end of the mesa. Using a space syntax approach, he suggests that the diversity in the sizes of the roomblocks indicates that different types of social units were being replicated, most of which involved a direct correspondence between social and spatial groupings. He regards this as evidence of a high degree of social experimentation involving the unification of households, clans, kiva groups, medicine societies, and priesthoods.

In Chapter 3, Michael Elliott addresses two unresolved problems in Jemez archaeology using historical data from the newly retranslated journals of Diego de Vargas by the University of New Mexico Vargas Project. These problems are the identification of the various missions established by the Spaniards and the mesatop refuges occupied by Jemez and Keres people during the Revolt period. Elliott discusses Giusewa, Patokwa, Walatowa, Astialakwa, and Boletsakwa. He also reviews the debate regarding the identifications of the missions of San José de los Jemez, San Diego de la Congregación, San Diego de los Jemez, San Diego del Monte, and San Juan de los Jemez. He then analyzes the distance information given

in the Vargas journals and concludes that the Kubler-Bloom-Scholes thesis is the most accurate. One of his findings is that Boletsakwa is the refuge village occupied by Jemez and Santo Domingo people on San Juan Mesa mentioned by Vargas.

In Chapter 4, Mark Lycett foregrounds the relationships of community and place. Adopting a historical ecological approach, he poses a series of questions that focus upon how Spanish missionization created, legitimized, and perpetuated novel social relationships. His case study involves a study of the occupational history of the missionized pueblos in the Galisteo Basin. In three cases, he shows that a new and more restricted residence was created within the confines of an older larger village. He observes that social space and claims of ownership were being remade just as physical space was being reconstructed. One of his most important conclusions is that residential abandonment does not necessarily denote a loss of place, but rather a reconfiguration of its role and historical associations.

The second section focuses on how material culture meanings legitimized and mobilized social groups. In Chapter 5, Jeannette Mobley-Tanaka explores the use of ritual imagery as a means of resistance during the period prior to the 1680 Revolt. She notes that because the early revolt attempts often had tragic consequences, Pueblo people quickly implemented more passive, less visible forms of resistance of the sort that Scott (1990) has called hidden transcripts. She identifies two techniques that came to characterize the "Pueblo style of resistance." The first technique was feigned acceptance, outwardly by obeying the missionaries, while continuing traditional practices in secret. The second technique was to manipulate information flows through rumor and innuendo in order to exert control. Her analysis focuses on elucidating the character of the hidden transcript through the study of the cross motif, which carried meaning in both native and Spanish religious contexts, and was represented on ceramics, kiva murals, jewelry. She suggests that the cross's polyvalent and ambiguous character (meaning simultaneously bird, dragonfly, star, and Christian cross) was intentionally exploited by the Pueblo people to preserve aspects of their traditional ritual practices, while outwardly suggesting conversion to Christianity.

In Chapter 6, Barbara Mills explores the gendering of resistance by arguing that Pueblo women actively used ceramics to objectify and signal new social identities and beliefs. Her work builds upon the literature on colonialism that shows that the women's production was reorganized as demands for tribute increased. This suggests that women may have expressed their resistance in the technological choices they made. She argues that "sudden or punctuated shifts" in technology may be interpreted as a strategy to intentionally manipulate ideological symbols in a complementary process of resistance and identity formation. In her analysis of pre- and post-Revolt Zuni ceramics, she documents a shift from glaze-paint to matte-paint pottery that she interprets as a deliberate act of breaking with the Spanish associations of the earlier tradition. She also notes there is a marked increase in representation of textile designs and the use of feather motifs. This latter motif may be evidence for the intentional creation of a region-wide stylistic horizon linking peoples of different languages and social statuses.

Similarly, in Chapter 7, Patricia Capone and I emphasize the agency of Pueblo women during the Revolt through our study of ceramics from Kotyiti Pueblo. Our study of pottery designs and motifs reveals that some women used the medium of their pottery to objectify the popular revitalization discourse. In particular, we identify the use of specific archaic motifs, such as the double-headed key, that would have signified a commitment to "living in accordance with the laws of the ancestors." We also find evidence that women were experimenting with novel designs and motifs, some of which may be associated with an "iconography of resistance." Our petrographic analyses of the Kotyiti glazewares provide tentative confirmation of the "refugee effect" and the presence of families from San Felipe Pueblo within the predominantly Cochiti community. However, we have not so far found evidence for San Marcos people who are also said to have been living in the community. Our results are grounded in a Peircian semiotics that specifies different kinds of sign-object relations. This approach offers a new perspective on the style/function debates and implies that style and function are best understood not as essential qualities of material culture, but rather as moments in the interpretive process.

In Chapter 8, Kurt and Cindy Dongoske examine the success of the Spanish missionization effort at Hopi by comparing Spanish documentary sources with Hopi oral historical accounts and rock art. They take as their case study the village of Awatovi because of its reputation as the most receptive Hopi village to the Spanish efforts at conversion. They regard rock art as a form of "written history," and propose that the rock art panels on the cliff faces below the village should reveal evidence of this conversion by the use of Christian symbols. Their findings, however, contradict this thesis and call into question the degree to which the people at Awatovi were receptive to the return of the Catholic church. They suggest, following Hopi historical accounts, that the Hopi maintained their traditional religious practices but performed them away from the view of the friars. They also argue that this strategy of passive resistance enabled the Hopi to select those elements of Spanish culture that improved their own quality of life. The implications here are that social factors, other than the reintroduction of Catholicism, may have been operative in the destruction of Awatovi by their Hopi neighbors.

In Chapter 9, Matthew Liebmann considers the meaning of the persistence of Christian imagery during the Revolt era. One possible reading might view it as evidence of false consciousness that the Pueblo people were converted to the dominant Spanish ideology and that this persisted even in the absence of the Spaniards. According to Liebmann, this view denies Pueblo people agency and presumes that such imagery was static and monolithic. As an alternative, he argues that Christian symbols were appropriated and reinterpreted by Pueblo peoples and given new meanings that actively aided in the creation of new identities. For example, he interprets a rock art "Mary" image in M-100, a cavate in Group M in Frijoles Canyon that was re-occupied during the Revolt period. He shows that this image combines elements of Spanish and traditional Pueblo elements to create a new form that itself can be seen as an example of "Pueblofication." He also discusses the practice of resistance through inversion and suggests that this is represented by the construction of new kivas at Abó and Quarai in the "sacred ground" of the mission, the incorporation of wood from the "hermitage" at Cebollita into a new kiva, and the use of a room in the convent at Sandia for the storage of katsina masks. For him, the Revolt era is an unique liminal time when identities of all sorts were in flux, and the kinds of resistance that were in play run the gamut from public transcripts to hidden transcripts to somewhere in between.

The third section focuses on social and political dynamics focusing particularly upon identity, alliance formation, and patterns of warfare. In Chapter 10, Peter Whiteley explores the meanings of Awatovi in Hopi historical consciousness. His "re-imagination" has two dimensions. It articulates with and extends the notions of the "historical imagination" discussed by Marshall Sahlins and the "imagined community" of Benedict Anderson in a study of Hopi oral history and cultural form. Whiteley emphasizes that political resistance to Spanish authority was partly structured in terms of a "ritually configured social imaginary of pan-Pueblo proportions." The direct transfers of ideas and people, from the Rio Grande to Hopi and within the Hopi district resulted in a wholesale transformation and revitalization of Hopi society. He then proposes that this revitalization movement was centered upon the celebration of *Wuwtsim* at Awatovi. This movement appears to have been led by Francisco de Espeleta, a charismatic ritual leader, and possibly involved the use of peyote. The implication of his analysis is that the form and structure of contemporary Hopi society is not so much the outcome of environmental adaptation, but rather an intentional, historical product crafted in the context of resistance to the Spanish crown.

In Chapter 11, Michael Wilcox offers a critical evaluation of the dominant discourses of Southwestern archaeology and borderlands history from the perspective of postcolonialism. Following the lead of Gayatri Spivak and Homi Bhabha, he suggests that these two fields have contributed to a colonial narrative that portrays Native cultures as passive recipients of colonial conquests, diseases, and technologies. He argues that the discursive practices of both fields have materially contributed to the contemporary conditions of Pueblo people. Wilcox singles out the focus on disease in processual archaeology as a kind of "microenvironmental determinism" that denies the agency of native peoples and advocates a more nuanced approach based upon ethnicity and the diacritica of race in the colonial encounter. He argues that the common experience of discrimination and marginalization motivated a pan-ethnic movement that attempted to remove the source of inequality and restore equilibrium and group autonomy. At the local level, this was accomplished by the establishment of new settlements in a regional aggregation event, which implies a restructuring of communal identities, kin, and clan affiliations and communal relations.

In Chapter 12, Rick Hendricks describes and analyzes the battles at Black Mesa, Kotyiti, and Astialakwa as part of the "last act" of the Spanish-Pueblo war. His analysis reveals that there was a consistent Spanish plan of attack that was ultimately successful in capturing these mesa villages. The Pueblo strategy was not successful because it was less coordinated and appears to have depended upon the prowess of individual warriors. Hendricks poses an intriguing question—Why were these battles so decisive when they produced so few casualties and most of the warriors escaped? One of the answers he offers is the warriors had little maneuverability because their families had been taken captive. A second answer is that the loss of the mesa and village likely had profound symbolic meaning. It revealed that there were no safe havens in the face of the combined use of advanced weaponry, military tactics, and Pueblo auxiliaries by the Spaniards.

In Chapter 13, Curtis Schaafsma explores Apache-Pueblo interaction during the seventeenth and early eighteenth centuries. He provides an exhaustive review of the ethnohistoric literature to challenge the notion, made popular by Benavides, that the relations between the

Apache (and Navajo) and the Pueblos were uniformly adversarial. He shows that there is, in fact, strong evidence that they routinely colluded and conspired with the Pueblos against the Spaniards. The first reliable documentation of this appears almost immediately after the founding of the New Mexico colony in 1598. His research indicates that there were special relations between certain Apache and Pueblo groups and that the Apache (Navajo) were involved in all of the major revolt attempts up to and including the Revolt of 1696.

In the final chapter (Chapter 14), Joseph Henry Suina argues that the high degree of ritual secrecy in Eastern Pueblo society can be seen as a legacy of the colonial encounter. He begins his essay with an autobiographical account of his first visit to Hopi where he witnessed the open performance of a katsina ceremony that he considered to transgress the boundaries of what he knew as proper behavior at his home village. Further reflection upon his strong reaction caused him to appreciate some of the differences between Eastern and Western Pueblos with respect to their distinctive relationships with the Spaniards. He notes that the average size of the western Pueblos is nearly 10 times that of those of the east. He identifies several reasons for this including demands for land by missionary and civil institutions, encroachment by colonists and settlers, disease, and emigration. He then discusses how the effects of religious persecution still govern relations with outsiders. "For us, religion was not then and is not today just a casual one-hour Sunday affair. It is all encompassing and regulates all aspects of our lives." He suggests that Pueblo people used the celebration of Christian events and individual saints as a vehicle to perpetuate their native forms of worship.

Conclusions

The story of the Pueblo Revolt has been dominated by the frontier perspective of Borderlands historical scholarship. From this perspective, the Revolt was a unique response to specific economic and religious practices associated with the colonizing activities of Spanish crown and church in New Mexico. Abuses occurred because the

distances from Spanish centers of authority made communication slow and the enforcement of the Law of the Indies difficult. It is undeniable that the Spanish secular and religious institutions, such as encomienda and the mission, provided the context for Pueblo resistance. Yet, by focusing on this as simply a frontier problem, historical studies have failed to explore the social and ideological mechanisms by which the Pueblos were able to marshal effective resistance and the ways in which the process of resistance itself transformed the Pueblo people.

Anthropological studies have tended to interpret the Revolt from an acculturationist perspective. This view emphasizes the dynamic interrelationships between the Pueblos and Spaniards, but because this relationship is asymmetrical, the focus is usually upon the cultural traits and practices that the Pueblos borrowed from the Spaniards. There is an assumption here of evolutionary progress whereby Spanish technology is assumed to be superior to that of the Pueblos and therefore both inherently desirable and easily assimilated. This approach, however, has been sharply critiqued within anthropology because of its failure to recognize the agency and power of native peoples.

Recent anthropological studies have identified the Revolt as part of a millenarian movement designed to unify the Pueblo world in opposition to foreign beliefs and values. This view explicitly acknowledges the active roles of Pueblo religious leaders in shaping a response to religious persecution, economic oppression, Apache raiding, drought, and disease. It also reveals the power of rhetoric and discourse in the public sphere.

However, both historical and anthropological approaches share a common limitation in that they typically neglect the "materiality of meaning." They are largely silent upon the ways in which Pueblo people used material culture to materialize group identities and objectify social relations as they lived out their lives in the context of the colonial encounter. As we demonstrate in this volume, material culture established, subverted, and transformed a set of meanings that served in the seventeenth century, and still serve today, as vital cultural resources for Pueblo people. Archaeology, by virtue of its disciplinary focus upon material culture, can thus be used to repatriate the materiality of meaning to discourses about resistance and identity formation.

In the end, we must recognize that writing the Revolt is not the same as living it. Pueblo people today are the heirs to the actions and beliefs of their ancestors and the Revolt remains an important part of their contemporary identity. In 1980, the Tricentennial of the Pueblo Revolt was celebrated by a series of events including a run linking the Rio Grande Pueblos to the Hopi (Agoyo 1980). It is commemorated on an annual basis by the Popay run at the Eight Northern Pueblos craft fair. But the Revolt is also signified by the persistence of Puebloan cultural traditions and practices in the face of Spanish, Mexican, and now American political and economic control. As Joseph Suina reminds us, this complex juxtaposition of meanings is publicly performed on each village's feast day when the village's patron saint is honored and traditional dances are held for the renewal of the world.

Notes

1. The terms "rebellion" and "revolt" incorporate a Western bias. For Pueblo people, what the Spanish called a "revolt" was in fact a "war of independence," or, as Herman Agoyo points out in his preface, "a holy war." Notwithstanding, I use the terms here as a shorthand to refer simultaneously to specific events and to the processes of resistance to Spanish rule during the seventeenth century.

2. The first historian of the Pueblo Revolt is Fray Agustín Vetancurt who published his *Teatro Mexicana* in 1697 (Vetancurt 1971 [1697]). Other important Spanish sources include Don Carlos Sigüenza y Góngora (Leonard 1932), and Fray Sylvestre Vélez de Escalante (Twitchell 1914).

3. There were several uprisings following the 1680 Revolt. These include most notably the Revolts of 1694 and 1696 (Espinosa 1988; Jones 1989; Kessell et al. 1998).

4. See Parmentier (1979) for a discussion of Poheyemu (Poseyemu).

5. For other refutations, see Riley (1999).

6. Other scholars who have regarded the Revolt as a millenarian movement include Gutierrez (1991:131) and Riley (1999:214). Examples of millenarianism in New Spain are the Acaxee Rebellion of 1601 (Deeds 1998), the Tepehuan Revolt of 1616 (Reff 1995), and the Yaqui Rebellion of 1740 (Deeds 1998).

7. This practice recalls a Cochiti story in which a priest is killed by dropping chili seeds down a chimney (Benedict 1931:190).

8. There is, at present, no comprehensive summary of Mission archaeology in New Spain and this overview simply highlights some of the more important projects.

9. Mission sites tested and stabilized during this period include: Giusewa (Bloom 1923, Lambert 1979, Reiter 1938), Abó (Toulouse 1938, 1949), Quarai (Ely 1935, Hurt 1990, Senter 1934), and Las Humanas (Gran Quivira) (Hayes et al. 1981).

10. Wimaya:wa and Koliwa both appear to date to the eighteenth and early nineteenth centuries (Ferguson 1996:58, Spier 1917:233, 265).

11. Ferguson (1996:56) considers the Kyaki:ma refuge sites to date to the eighteenth century.

12. Indeed, the use of some Spanish-style features, such as hooded fireplaces, seems more likely to be due to Pueblo immigrants than a local Navajo adoption.

13. See also Fray Carlos Delgado's account of the atrocities committed by the Spanish against the Pueblos during his forty years of service at San Agustín de Isleta (Hackett 1937:427–430).

14. See Levine (1989) for a popular overview.

References Cited

Adams, Eleanor B., and Fray Angélico Chávez (editors translators)

1956   *The Missions of New Mexico, 1776: A Description by Francisco Atanasio Domínguez, with Other Contemporary Documents.* University of New Mexico Press, Albuquerque.

Adams, E. Charles

1989   Passive Resistance: Hopi Responses to Spanish Contact and Conquest. In *Columbian Consequences: Vol. 1. Archaeological and Historical Perspectives on the Spanish Borderlands West,* edited by D. H. Thomas, pp. 77–91. Smithsonian Institution Press, Washington, D.C.

Adler, Michael A., and Herbert Dick (editors)

1999   *Picuris Pueblo through Time: Eight Centuries of Change in a Northern Rio Grande Pueblo.* William P. Clements Center for Southwest Studies, Southern Methodist University, Dallas.

Agoyo, Herman

1980   The Tricentennial Year in Pueblo Consciousness. *El Palacio* 86:27–31.

Applegate, Frank G.

1932   *Native Tales of New Mexico.* J. B. Lippincott Co., Philadelphia.

Ayers, James E. (compiler)

1995   *The Archaeology of Spanish and Mexican Colonialism in the American Southwest.* Guides to the Archaeological Literature of the Immigrant Experience in America, No. 3. Society for Historical Archaeology.

Bailey, Jessie B.

1940   *Diego de Vargas and the Reconquest of New Mexico.* University of New Mexico Press, Albuquerque.

Baldwin, Louis

1995   *Intruders Within: Pueblo Resistance to Spanish Rule and the Revolt of 1680.* Franklin Watts, New York.

Bancroft, Hubert H.

1889   *History of Arizona and New Mexico 1530–1888.* The History Company, San Francisco.

Bandelier, Adolph F. A.

1881   *Report on the Ruins of the Pueblo of Pecos.* Papers of the Archaeological Institute of America, America Series Vol. I. A. Williams and Co., Boston.

1890   *Final Report of Investigation among the Indians of the Southwestern United States, Carried on Mainly in the Years from 1880 to 1885. Part I.* Papers of the Archaeological Institute of America, American Series, Vol. III. University Press, Cambridge, Mass.

1892   *Final Report of Investigation among the Indians of the Southwestern United States, Carried on Mainly in the Years from 1880 to 1885. Part II.* Papers of the Archaeological Institute of America, American Series, Vol. IV. University Press, Cambridge, Mass.

1937   Documentary History of the Rio Grande Pueblos. In *Indians of the Rio Grande Valley,* by A. F. A. Bandelier and E. L. Hewett, p. 115–241. University of New Mexico Press, Albuquerque.

Bannon, J. F.

1974   *The Spanish Borderlands Frontier, 1513–1821.* University of New Mexico Press, Albuquerque.

Benedict, Ruth

1931   *Tales of the Cochiti.* Bureau of American Ethnology Bulletin No. 98. Washington, D.C.

Beninato, Stefanie

1990   Popé, Pose-yemu, and Naranjo: A New Look at Leadership in the Pueblo Revolt of 1680. *New Mexico Historical Review* 65:419–435.

Bloom, Lansing B.

1923   The Jemez Expedition of the School. *El Palacio* 14:14–20.

Bloom, Lansing B., and Lynn B. Mitchell

1938   The Chapter Elections in 1672. *New Mexico Historical Review* 33:85–119.

Bolton, Herbert E. (editor)

1916   *Spanish Exploration of the Southwest, 1542–1706.* C. Scribner's Sons, New York.

Carlson, Roy L.

1965   *Eighteenth Century Navajo Fortresses of the Gobernador District: The Earl Morris Papers, No. 2.* University of Colorado Studies, Series in Anthropology, No. 10. University of Colorado Press, Boulder.

Chávez, Fray Angélico

1967   Pohé-yemo's Representative and the Pueblo Revolt of 1680. *New Mexico Historical Review* 17:85–126.

Comaroff, John, and Jean Comaroff

1992   *Ethnography and the Historical Imagination.* Westview Press, Boulder, Colo.

Cushing, Frank Hamilton

1890   Preliminary Notes on the Origin, Working Hypotheses, and Primary Researches of the Hemenway Southwestern Archaeological Expedition. *Congres International des Americanistes. Compte-Rendu de la Septieme Session, Berlin 1888,* pp. 151–194. W. J. Kuhl, Berlin.

1896   Outlines of Zuñi Creation Myths. *Thirteenth Annual Report of the Bureau of American Ethnology for the Years 1891–1892,* pp. 321–447. Washington, D.C.

Daifuku, Hiroshi

1961   *Jeddito 264: A Report on the Excavation of a Basketmaker III-Pueblo I Site in Northeastern Arizona with a Review of Some Current Theories in Southwestern Archaeology.* Papers of the Peabody Museum of American Archaeology and Ethnology, Harvard University, Vol. 33(1). Cambridge, Mass.

Davis, W. W. H.

1869   *The Spanish Conquest of New Mexico.* Doylestown, Penn.

Deeds, Susan M.

1998   Indigenous Rebellions on the Northern Mexican Mission Frontier: From First-Generation to Later Colonial Responses. In *Contested Ground: Comparative Frontiers on the Northern and Southwestern Edges of the Spanish Empire,* edited by Donna J. Guy and Thomas E. Sheridan, pp. 32–51. University of Arizona Press, Tucson.

Dick, Herbert, and Michael A. Adler
1999   Introduction. In *Picuris Pueblo Through Time: Eight Centuries of Change in a Northern Rio Grande Pueblo,* edited by Michael A. Adler and Herbert Dick, pp. 1–15. William P. Clements Center for Southwest Studies, Southern Methodist University, Dallas.

Dittert, Albert E., Jr.
1958   *Preliminary Archaeological Investigations in the Navajo Project Area of Northwestern New Mexico.* Museum of New Mexico, Papers in Anthropology No. 1. Museum of New Mexico and School of American Research, Santa Fe.

Dozier, Edward P.
1970   *The Pueblo Indians of North America.* Holt, Rinehart and Winston, New York.

Ely, Albert G.
1935   The Excavation and Repair of Quarai Mission. *El Palacio* 39:133–148.

Espinosa, J. Manuel
1940   *First Expedition of Vargas into New Mexico, 1692.* University of New Mexico Press, Albuquerque.

1942   *Crusaders of the Rio Grande: The Story of Don Diego de Vargas and the Reconquest and Refounding of New Mexico.* Institute of Jesuit History, Chicago.

Espinosa, J. Manuel (editor and translator)
1988   *The Pueblo Indian Revolt of 1696 and the Franciscan Missions in New Mexico: Letters of the Missionaries and Related Documents.* University of Oklahoma Press, Norman.

Ferguson, T. J.
1992   Zuni Settlement Patterns during the Pueblo Revolt. In *Current Research on the Late Prehistory and Early History of New Mexico,* edited by Bradley J. Vierra, pp. 85–92. New Mexico Archaeological Council, Special Publication No.1. Albuquerque.

1996   *Historic Zuni Architecture and Society: An Archaeological Application of Space Syntax.* Anthropological Papers of the University of Arizona, No. 60. University of Arizona Press, Tucson.

Ferguson, T. J., and Robert W. Preucel
in press Signs of the Ancestors: An Archaeology of the Mesa Villages of the Pueblo Revolt Period. In *Structure and Meaning in Human Settlement,* edited by Tony Atkin, University of Pennsylvania Press, Philadelphia.

Fetterman, Jerry
1996   Radiocarbon and Tree-Ring Dating at Early Navajo Sites: Examples from the Aztec Area. In *The Archaeology of Navajo Origins,* edited by Ronald H. Towner, pp. 71–83. University of Utah Press, Salt Lake City.

Folsom, Franklin
1973   *Red Power on the Rio Grande: The Native American Revolution of 1680.* Follet Publishing, Chicago.

Guy, Donna J., and Thomas E. Sheridan
1998   On Frontiers: The Northern and Southern Edges of the Spanish Empire in the Americas. In *Contested Ground: Comparative Frontiers on the Northern and Southwestern Edges of the Spanish Empire,* edited by Donna J. Guy and Thomas E. Sheridan, pp. 3–15. University of Arizona Press, Tucson.

Gutiérrez, Ramón A.
1991   *When Jesus Came, the Corn Mothers Went Away: Marriage, Sexuality and Power in New Mexico, 1500–1846.* Stanford University Press, Stanford.

Hack, John T.
1942a   *The Changing Physical Environment of the Hopi Indians of Arizona.* Papers of the Peabody Museum of American Archaeology and Ethnology, Harvard University, Vol. 35(1).

1942b   *Prehistoric Coal Mining in the Jeddito Valley, Arizona.* Papers of the Peabody Museum of American Archaeology and Ethnology, Harvard University Vol. 35(2).

Hackett, Charles W.
1911   The Revolt of the Pueblo Indians of New Mexico in 1680. *Quarterly of the Texas State Historical Association* 15:93–147.

1912   The Retreat of the Spaniards from New Mexico in 1680, and the Beginnings of El Paso. *The Southwestern Historical Quarterly* 16:137–168, 259–276.

Hackett, Charles W. (editor)
1937   *Historical Documents relating to New Mexico, Nueva Vizcaya, and Approaches Thereto, to 1773.* Vol. III. Collected by A. F. A. Bandelier and F. R. Bandelier. Carnegie Institution of Washington Publications No. 330. Washington, D.C. Hackett, Charles W., and Charmion C. Shelby (editor and translator)
1942   *Revolt of the Pueblo Indians of New Mexico, and Otermín's Attempted Reconquest, 1680–1682.* Coronado Cuarto Centennial Publications, 1540–1949. 2 Vols. University of New Mexico Press, Albuquerque.

Hall, Thomas D.
1989   *Social Change in the Southwest, 1350–1880.* University Press of Kansas, Lawrence.

Hayes, Alden C. (editor)
1981   *Contributions to Gran Quivira Archeology: Gran Quivira National Monument, New Mexico.* National Park Service Publications in Archaeology No. 17. Washington, D.C.

Hayes, Alden C., Jon Nathan Young, A. Helene Warren (editors)
1981   *Excavation of Mound 7: Gran Quivira National Monument, New Mexico.* National Park Service Publications in Archaeology No. 16. Washington, D.C.

Hendricks, Rick, and John P. Wilson (editors)
1996   *The Navajos in 1705: Roque Madrid's Campaign Journal.* University of New Mexico Press, Albuquerque.

Hewett, Edgar L., and Reginald Fischer
1943   *Mission Monuments of New Mexico.* University of New Mexico, Press, Albuquerque.

Hobsbawm, Eric J., and Terence O. Ranger
1983   *The Invention of Tradition.* Cambridge University Press, Cambridge, UK.

Hodge, Frederic W.
1918a   Administrative Report. *32nd Annual Report of the Bureau of American Ethnology for the Years 1910–1911.* Washington, D.C.

1918b   Excavations at the Zuni Pueblo of Hawikuh in 1917. *Art and Archaeology* 7:367–379.

1937   *History of Hawikuh, New Mexico: One of the So-Called Cities of Cíbola.* Ward Ritchie Press, Los Angeles.

Hogan, Patrick

1991   *Navajo-Pueblo Interaction During the Gobernador Phase: A Reassessment of the Evidence.* Cultural Resources Series No. 8. Bureau of Land Management, Albuquerque.

Hooton, Earnest Albert

1930   *The Indians of Pecos Pueblo: A Study of their Skeletal Remains.* Papers of the Phillips Academy Southwest Expedition No. 4. Yale University Press, New Haven, Conn.

Hurt, Wesley R.

1990   *The 1939–1940 xcavation Project at Quarai Pueblo and Mission Building.* National Park Service, Southwest Cultural Resources Center, Profession Paper No. 29. Santa Fe.

James, Harry C.

1974   *Hopi History.* University of Arizona Press, Tucson.

John, Elizabeth A. H.

1975   *Storms Brewed in Other Men's Worlds.* Texas A&M University Press, College Station.

Jones, Oakah L.

1989   The Pueblo Indian Revolt of 1696—*Una Rebelión Desconocida:* A Review Essay. *New Mexico Historical Review* 64:361–371.

Josephy, Alvin

1958   *The Patriot Chiefs.* Viking Compass Books, New York.

Kessell, John L.

1992   Return to a Previous Century: Gov. Juan Ignacio Flores Mogollón's Campaign Against Pueblo Indian Kivas, 1719. In *The Native American and Spanish Colonial Experience in the Greater Southwest I: Introduction to the Documentary Records,* edited by D. H. Snow, pp. 409–414. Garland Press, New York.

Kessell, John L., and Rick Hendricks (editors)

1992   *By Force of Arms: The Journals of Don Diego de Vargas, New Mexico 1691–1693.* University of New Mexico Press, Albuquerque.

Kessell, John L., Rick Hendricks, and Meredith D. Dodge (editors)

1995   *To the Royal Crown Restored: The Journals of Don Diego de Vargas, New Mexico 1692–1694.* University of New Mexico Press, Albuquerque.

1998   *Blood on the Boulders: The Journals of Don Diego de Vargas, New Mexico 1694–97.* 2 Vols. University of New Mexico Press, Albuquerque.

Keur, Dorothy L.

1944   A Chapter in Navajo-Pueblo Relations. *American Antiquity* 10:75–86.

Kidder, Alfred V.

1916   Archaeological Exploration at Pecos, New Mexico. *Proceedings of the National Academy of Science* 2:119–123.

1917   *The Old North Pueblo of Pecos: The Condition of the Main Pecos Ruin.* Archaeological Institute of America, Papers of the School of American Archaeology, No. 38. Santa Fe.

1924   *An Introduction to the Study of Southwestern Archaeology with a Preliminary Account of the Excavations at Pecos.* Yale University Press, New Haven, Conn.

1926a   *The Excavations at Pecos in 1925.* Archaeological Institute of America, Papers of the School of American Research, n.s., No. 14. Santa Fe.

1926b   *Early Pecos Ruins in the Forked Lightning Ranch.* Archaeological Institute of America, Papers of the School of American Research, n.s., No. 16. Santa Fe.

1932   *The Artifacts of Pecos.* Papers of the Phillips Academy Southwest Expedition No. 6. New Haven, Conn.

1958   *Pecos, New Mexico: Archaeological Notes.* Phillips Academy, Papers of the Robert S. Peabody Foundation for Archaeology, No. 5. New Haven, Conn.

Kidder, Alfred V., and Charles Amsden

1931   *The Pottery of Pecos, Vol. 1.* Papers of the Phillips Academy Southwest Expedition No. 5. New Haven, Conn.

Kidder, Alfred V., and Anna O. Shepard

1936   *The Pottery of Pecos, Vol. 2.* Phillips Academy Papers of the Southwest Expedition No. 7. New Haven, Conn.

Kidder, Madeline A., and Alfred V. Kidder

1917   Notes on the Pottery of Pecos. *American Anthropologist* 19:325–360.

Knaut, Andrew L.

1995   *The Pueblo Revolt: Conquest and Resistance in Seventeenth-Century New Mexico.* University of Oklahoma Press, Norman.

Kubler, George

1940   *The Religious Architecture of New Mexico in the Colonial Period and since the American Occupation.* Taylor Museum, Colorado Springs Fine Arts Center, Colo.

Lambert, Marjorie F.

1979   Mural Decorations in San Jose de los Jemez Mission Church, Jemez State Monument, New Mexico. *Papers of the Albuquerque Archaeological Society* 6:215–236.

Lange, Charles H., and Carroll L. Riley

1996   *Bandelier: The Life and Adventures of Adolf Bandelier, American Archaeologist and Scientist.* University of Utah Press, Salt Lake City.

Lange, Charles H., and Carroll L. Riley (editors)

1966   *The Southwestern Journals of Adolph F. Bandelier, 1880–1882.* University of New Mexico Press, Albuquerque.

1970   *The Southwestern Journals of Adolph F. Bandelier, 1883–1884.* University of New Mexico Press, Albuquerque.

Lange, Charles H., Carroll L. Riley, and Elizabeth Lange (editors)

1975   *The Southwestern Journals of Adolph F. Bandelier, 1885–1888.* University of New Mexico Press, Albuquerque.

Lawrence, B.

1951   *Part I. Mammals Found at the Awatovi Site, Part II. Post-Cranial Skeletal Characteristics of Deer, Pronghorn, and Sheep-Goat with notes on Bos and Bison.* Papers of the Peabody Museum of American Archaeology and Ethnology, Harvard University, Vol. 35(3).

Leonard, Irving (translator)

1932   *The Mecurio Volante: An Account of the First Expedition of Don Diego de Vargas in 1692,* by C. de Sigüenza y Góngora, The Quivira Society, Los Angeles.

Levine, Frances

1989   Down Under an Ancient City: An Archaeologist's View of Santa Fe. In *Santa Fe: History of an Ancient City,* edited by David Noble, pp. 9–26. School of American Research, Santa Fe.

Lomatuway'ma, Michael, Lorena Lomatuway'ma, and Sidney Namingha, Jr. (narrators)

1993   *Hopi Ruin Legends: Kiqötutuwutsi.* Collected, translated, and edited by Ekkehart Malotki, published for Northern Arizona University by the University of Nebraska Press, Lincoln.

Lomawaima, Hartman H.

1989   Hopification: A Strategy for Cultural Preservation. In *Columbian Consequences: Vol. 1. Archaeological and Historical Perspectives on the Spanish Borderlands West,* edited by D. H. Thomas, pp. 93–99. Smithsonian Institution Press, Washington, D.C.

Lycett, Mark T.

1997   *Preliminary Report of Archaeological Surface Documentation and Test Excavations at LA 162, Bernalillo County, New Mexico, conducted by Northwestern University Archaeological Field Studies Program, between 17 June and 8 August, 1996, under permit SP-269.* Report to the State Historic Preservation Office, Santa Fe, and the Board of Archaeologists, University of New Mexico, Albuquerque.

1998   *Report of Archaeological Excavations at LA 162, Bernalillo County, New Mexico, conducted by the University of Chicago Archaeological Field Studies Program, between 21 June and 19 August, 1997, under permit SE-120.* Report to the State Historic Preservation Office, Santa Fe, and the Board of Archaeologists, University of New Mexico, Albuquerque.

1999   *Report of Archaeological Excavations at LA 162, Bernalillo County, New Mexico, conducted by the University of Chicago Archaeological Field Studies Program, between 21 June and 18 August, 1998, under permit SE-134.* Report to the Historic Preservation Division, State of New Mexico, Santa Fe.

2000   *Report of Archaeological Excavations at LA 162, Bernalillo County, New Mexico, conducted by the University of Chicago Archaeological Field Studies Program, between 21 June and 12 August, 1999, under permit SE-144.* Report to the Historic Preservation Division, State of New Mexico, Santa Fe.

Marshall, Michael P.

1991   *The Pueblito as a Site Complex: Archaeological Investigations in the Dinetah District: The 1989–1990 BLM Pueblito Survey.* Cultural Resources Series No. 8. Bureau of Land Management, Albuquerque.

Mera, H. P.

1940   *Population Changes in the Rio Grande Glaze-paint Area.* Laboratory of Anthropology Technical Series, Bulletin No. 9.

Montgomery, Ross G., Watson Smith, and John O. Brew

1949   *Franciscan Awatovi: The Excavation and Conjectural Reconstruction of a 17th Century Spanish Mission Establishment at a Hopi Indian Town in Northeastern Arizona.* Papers of the Peabody Museum of American Archaeology and Ethnology, Harvard University Vol. 36. Cambridge, Mass.

Nelson, Nels C.

1914   *Pueblo Ruins of the Galisteo Basin, New Mexico.* Anthropological Papers of the American Museum of Natural History. Vol. 15, Part 1. New York.

1916   Chronology of the Tano Ruins, New Mexico. *American Anthropologist* 18:159–180.

Ortiz, Alfonso

1969   *The Tewa World: Space, Time, Being and Becoming in a Pueblo Society.* University of Chicago Press, Chicago.

1980   Popay's Leadership: A Pueblo Perspective. *El Palacio* 86:18–22.

1994   The Dynamics of Pueblo Cultural Survival. In *North American Indian Anthropology: Essays on Society and Culture,* edited by R. J. DeMallie and A. Ortiz, pp. 296–306. University of Oklahoma Press, Norman.

Parmentier, Richard J.

1979   The Mythological Triangle: Poseyemu, Montezuma, and Jesus in the Pueblos. In *Handbook of North American Indians, Vol. 9: Southwest,* edited by A. Ortiz, pp. 609–622. Smithsonian Institution Press, Washington, D.C.

Paynter, Robert, and Randall H. McGuire

1991   The Archaeology of Inequality: Material Culture, Domination and Resistance. In *The Archaeology of Inequality,* edited by Randall H. McGuire and Robert Paynter, pp. 1–27. Blackwell, Oxford.

Powers, M. A., and B. P. Johnson

1987   *Defensive Sites of Dinetah.* Cultural Resources Series No. 8. Bureau of Land Management, Albuquerque.

Preucel, Robert W.

2000a   Living on the Mesa: Hanat Kotyiti, a Post-Revolt Cochiti Community in Northern New Mexico. *Expedition* 42:8–17.

2000b   Making Pueblo Identities: Architectural Discourse at Kotyiti, New Mexico. In *An Archaeology of Communities in the Americas,* edited by J. Yaeger and M. Canuto, pp. 58–77. Routledge, London, UK.

Reff, Daniel T.

1995   The Predicament of Culture and Spanish Missionary Accounts of the Tepehuan and Pueblo Revolts. *Ethnohistory* 42:63–90.

Reiter, Paul

1938   *The Jemez Pueblo of Unshagi, New Mexico, with Notes on the Earlier Excavations at "Amoxiumqua" and Giusewa.* 2 Pts. Monographs of the School of American Research 5–6. Santa Fe.

Riley, Carroll L.

1995   *Rio Del Norte: People of the Upper Rio Grande from Earliest Times to the Pueblo Revolt.* University of Utah Press, Salt Lake City.

1999   *The Kachina and the Cross: Indians and Spaniards in the Early Southwest.* University of Utah Press, Salt Lake City.

Rodríguez, Sylvia

1996   *The Matachines Dance: Ritual Symbolism and Interethnic Relations in the Upper Rio Grande Valley.* University of New Mexico Press, Albuquerque.

Sanchez, Jane C.

1983   Spanish-Indian Relations during the Otermín Administration, 1677–1683. *New Mexico Historical Review* 58(2):133–151.

Sanchez, Joseph P.

1989   Twelve Days in August: The Pueblo Revolt in Santa Fe. In *Santa Fe: History of an Ancient City,* edited by David Noble, pp. 39–52. School of American Research, Santa Fe.

Sando, Joe S.

1979   The Pueblo Revolt. In *Handbook of North American Indian: Southwest Vol. 9,* edited by A. Ortiz, pp. 194–197. Smithsonian Institution, Washington, D.C.

1982   *Nee Hemish: A History of Jemez Pueblo.* University of New Mexico Press, Albuquerque.

1992   *Pueblo Nations: Eight Centuries of Pueblo Indian History.* Clear Light Publishers, Santa Fe.

1998   *Pueblo Profiles: Cultural Identities Through Centuries of Change.* Clear Light Publishers, Santa Fe.

Scholes, France V.

1935   Civil Government and Society in New Mexico in the Seventeenth Century. *New Mexico Historical Review* 10:51–111.

1936   Church and State in New Mexico, 1610–1650. *New Mexico Historical Review* 11:297–349.

1942   *Troublous Times in New Mexico, 1659–1670.* University of New Mexico Press, Albuquerque.

Schroeder, Albert H.

1972   Rio Grande Ethnohistory. In *New Perspectives on the Pueblos,* edited by A. Ortiz, pp. 41–70. University of New Mexico Press, Albuquerque.

Scott, James C.

1990   *Domination and the Arts of Resistance: Hidden Transcripts* Yale University Press, New Haven, Conn.

Seifert, Donna

n.d.   Archaeological Excavations at the Palace of the Governors, Santa Fe, New Mexico: 1974 and 1975. Ms. on file, Museum of New Mexico, History Bureau, Santa Fe.

Senter, Donovan

1934   The Work on the Old Quarai Mission, 1934. *El Palacio* 37:169–174.

Silverberg, Robert

1970   *The Pueblo Revolt.* Weybright and Talley, New York.

Simmons, Marc

1980   The Pueblo Revolt: Why Did it Happen? *El Palacio* 86:11–15.

Smith, Watson

1952   *Kiva Mural Decorations at Awatovi and Kawaika-a, with a Survey of Other Wall Paintings in the Pueblo Southwest.* Papers of the Peabody Museum of American Archaeology and Ethnology, Harvard University, Vol. 37. Cambridge, Mass.

1971   *Painted Ceramics of the Western Mound at Awatovi.* Papers of the Peabody Museum of American Archaeology and Ethnology, Harvard University, Vol. 38. Cambridge, Mass.

Smith, Watson, Richard B. Woodbury, and Nathalie F. S. Woodbury

1966   *The Excavation of Hawikuh by Frederick Webb Hodge.* Contributions from the Museum of the American Indian, Heye Foundation, Vol. 20. New York.

Snead, James, and Robert W. Preucel

1999   The Ideology of Settlement: Ancestral Keres Landscapes in the Northern Rio Grande. *In Archaeologies of Landscape: Contemporary Perspectives,* edited by Wendy Ashmore and A. Bernard Knapp, pp. 170–197. Blackwell, Oxford, UK.

Snow, Cordelia Thomas

1974   A Brief History of the Palace of the Governors and a Preliminary Report on the 1974 Excavation. *El Palacio* 80:1–21.

1979   The Evolution of a Frontier: An Historical Interpretation of Archeological Sites. In *Archeological Investigations in the Cochiti Reservoir, New Mexico Volume 4: Adaptive Change in the Northern Rio Grande Valley,* edited by Jan V. Biella and Richard C. Chapman, pp. 217–233. Office of Contract Archeology, Department of Anthropology, University of New Mexico, Albuquerque.

Snow, David

1973a   *Cochiti Dam Salvage Project: Archaeological Excavation of the Las Majadas site, LA 591, Cochiti Dam, New Mexico.* Laboratory of Anthropology Notes No. 75. Santa Fe.

1973b   *Cochiti Dam Salvage Project: Archaeological Excavation of the Torreon Site, LA 6178, Cochiti Dam, New Mexico.* Laboratory of Anthropology Notes No. 76. Santa Fe.

Spicer, Edward

1962   *Cycles of Conquest.* University of Arizona Press, Tucson.

Spielmann, Katherine A.

1993   The Evolution of Craft Specialization in Tribal Societies: Preliminary Report for the 1992 Excavation Season at Quarai Pueblo, New Mexico. Ms. on file, National Park Service, Southwestern Regional Office, Santa Fe.

1994   The Evolution of Craft Specialization in Tribal Societies: Preliminary Report for the 1993 Excavation Season at Quarai Pueblo, New Mexico. Ms. on file, National Park Service, Southwestern Regional Office, Santa Fe.

Spier, Leslie

1917   *An Outline for a Chronology of Zuñi Ruins.* Anthropological Papers of the American Museum of Natural History, Vol. XVIII, Part III. New York.

Stevenson, Matilda Cox

1904   *The Zuni Indians: Their Mythology, Esoteric Fraternities, and Ceremonies.* Twenty-third Annual Report of the Bureau of American Ethnology. Smithsonian Institution, Washington, D.C.

Thomas, Alfred B. (editor and translator)

1935   *After Coronado: Spanish Exploration Northeast of New Mexico, 1696–1727: From the Original Documents in the Archives of Spain, Mexico, and New Mexico.* University of Oklahoma Press, Norman.

Thomas, David Hurst

1999   Mission San Marcos Archaeological Project: Phase II—
        Defining the Architectural Sequence, Proposed Fieldwork
        (1999–2000). Research Proposal, American Museum of
        Natural History, New York.

Toulouse, Joseph H., Jr.

1938   The Mission of San Gregorio de Abó. *El Palacio* 45:103–107.

1949   *The Mission of San Gregorio de Abó.* Monographs of School
        of American Research, No. 13, Santa Fe.

Towner, Ronald H.

1992   Dating the Dinétah Pueblitos: The Tree-Ring Data. In
        Interpreting the Past: Research with Public Participation,
        edited by L. Jacobson and J. Piper, pp. 55–72. Cultural
        Resource Series, Vol. 10. New Mexico Bureau of Land
        Management, Albuquerque.

1996   The Pueblito Phenomenon: A New Perspective on Post-Revolt
        Navajo Culture. In *The Archaeology of Navajo Origins,*
        edited by Ronald H. Towner, pp. 149–170. University of
        Utah Press, Salt Lake City.

Towner, Ronald H. (editor)

1996   *The Archaeology of Navajo Origins.* University of Utah Press,
        Salt Lake City.

Towner, Ronald H., and Jeffery S. Dean

1992   LA 2298: The Oldest Pueblito Revisited. *The Kiva*
        59:315–331.

1996   Questions and Problems in Pre-Fort Sumner Navajo
        Archaeology. In *The Archaeology of Navajo Origins,* edited
        by Ronald H. Towner, pp. 3–18. University of Utah Press,
        Salt Lake City.

Twitchell, Ralph Emerson

1914   *The Spanish Archives of New Mexico.* 2 Vols. The Torch
        Press, Santa Fe.

Tyler, S. Lyman

1952   The Myth of the Lake of Copala and Land of Teguayo.
        Utah Historical Quarterly 20:313–329.

Vetancurt, Augustín de

1971   [1697] *Teatro Mexicano: Description breve de los sucesos
        exemplares, historicos, politicos . . . de los sucesos ejemplares del
        la Nueva-España en el Nuevo Mundo Occidental de las Indias.*
        Cronica de la Provincia del Santo Evangelio de Mexico,
        Editorial Porrúa, Mexico City.

Vierra, Bradley. J. (editor)

1992   *Current Research on the Late Prehistory and Early History of
        New Mexico.* New Mexico Archaeological Council, Special
        Publication No. 1. Albuquerque.

Weber, David J.

1992   *The Spanish Frontier in North America.* Yale University
        Press, New Haven, Conn.

Weber, David J. (editor)

1999   *What Caused the Pueblo Revolt of 1680?* Bedford/St.
        Martins, Boston.

Wiget, Andrew

1982   Truth and the Hopi: A Historiographic Study of
        Documented Oral Tradition Concerning the Coming
        of the Spanish. *Ethnohistory* 29:181–199.

1991   Oral Tradition: A People's Shared Memory. In *Zuni History:
        Victories in the 1990s,* Section II, p. 19. Zuni History
        Newspaper Project, Institute of the North American West,
        Seattle.

Wilcox, David. R.

1981   Changing Perspectives on the Protohistoric Pueblos, A.D.
        1450–1700. In *The Protohistoric Period in the North
        American Southwest a.d. 1450–1700,* edited by D. R.
        Wilcox and W. B. Masse, pp. 378–409. Arizona State
        University Anthropological Research Papers No. 24. Tempe.

Wilcox, David R., and W. B. Masse

1981   A History of Protohistoric Studies in the North American
        Southwest. In *The Protohistoric Period in the North
        American Southwest a.d. 1450–1700,* edited by D. R. Wilcox
        and W. B. Masse, pp. 1–27. Arizona State University
        Anthropological Research Papers No. 24. Tempe.

Willey, Gordon R., and Jeremy A. Sabloff

1980   *A History of American Archaeology.* Second edition. W. H.
        Freeman and Co., San Francisco.

PART TWO
Place, Settlement, and Architecture

Figure 2.1. The mesa of Dowa Yalanne seen from the rooftops of Zuni Pueblo. Photograph by John K. Hillers, 1879.
Courtesy of National Anthropological Archives, Smithsonian Institution, Neg. 2267-e.

Chapter 2

Dowa Yalanne:
The Architecture of Zuni Resistance and Social Change during the Pueblo Revolt

T. J. Ferguson

Introduction

The archaeology of the Pueblo Revolt is preserved at Zuni in the settlement occupied on the top of Dowa Yalanne, a mesa 5 kilometers southeast of Zuni Pueblo (Figure 2.1). This settlement, occupied from 1680 to 1692, constitutes a transition in the settlement pattern of the Zuni people from the occupation of a cluster of six permanent villages to that of a single year-round pueblo (Bandelier 1892:112–115; Hodge 1907:544–545). For the first time, on Dowa Yalanne, the entire Zuni tribe gathered to live in a single settlement. The archaeology of Dowa Yalanne provides a physical record of the social processes affecting Zuni during the tumultuous years of the Pueblo Revolt, including patterns of resistance, residence, and ritual (Ferguson 1992, 1996:47–55). The archaeological record thus provides data about Zuni responses to the Pueblo Revolt that complement the information available in oral traditions and documentary history.

In the Zuni language, *dowa* means "corn" and *yalanne* means "mountain" so Dowa Yalanne is often translated as Corn Mountain. According to Hodge (1907:544), the name for the settlement on top of Dowa Yalanne is *Heshoda Ayahltona*, which Hodge translated as "ancient buildings above." Cushing (1896:429) recorded another Zuni name for the settlement as *Tâaiyá'hltona Hlúelawa*, which he translated as "Towns-all-above of-the-seed-all." This name is thus conceptually related to Corn Mountain. Cushing (1896:429) also referred to Dowa Yalanne as "Thunder Mountain," and this appellation was used by many non-Zuni in the late nineteenth and early twentieth centuries.

Architecture, Praxis, and Social Structure

Architectural remains in the archaeological record are well-suited to analyses of social structure, defined as an analytical conceptualization of the arrangements that link the elements of social life together into a functioning, cohesive unit. Social structure is not static; it depends on the repetition of behavior that can and does change through time in response to the social and technological context in which behavior occurs (Firth 1963:30–40). The genesis, reproduction, and change of form and meaning in particular sociocultural systems stems from praxis, i.e., the intended and unintended actions of individual actors (Karp 1983; Merrill 1988:53–58; Ortner 1984:144–160). Architecturally defined space, as recorded by archaeologists, is the result of a series of actions taken by individuals performing as architects, builders, and occupants. In social

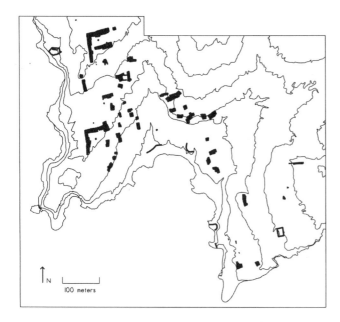

Figure 2.2. Archaeological remains on Dowa Yalanne
(contour interval: 3 meters).

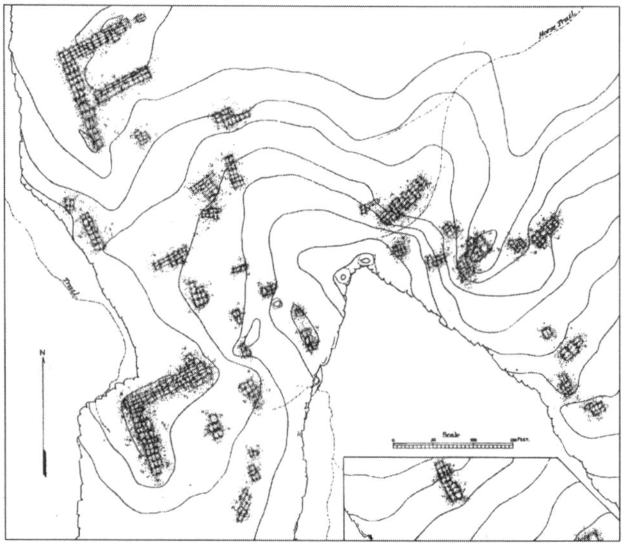

Figure 2.3. The 38 major buildings on Dowa Yalanne
as mapped by the Mindeleffs (1891:Plate LX).

theory, architecture does more than simply *represent* society; it is one of the primary means by which society is directly *constituted* (Giddens 1984). The space created by architecture incorporates society by physically enabling and constraining social interaction in recurrent patterns. In this way, architecture gives form to social structure by unifying spatial and social configurations.

Space syntax offers a set of techniques for representing, quantifying, and interpreting the spatial arrangements found in buildings and settlements (Hanson 1998; Hillier 1996; Hillier and Hanson 1984). The formal analysis of these spatial arrangements using graph theory reveals how space influences modes of social interaction, and thus structures society. As a bounded space, the simplest building can be viewed as a single cell. There are two pathways of growth from the elementary cell: (1) subdividing or accumulating cells so their internal permeability is maintained, and (2) aggregating cells independently so permeability is maintained externally. The first pathway produces a building, the second a settlement. Buildings physically separate categorical social groups from the outside world, using spatial segregation to define and control the relations of their occupants with other people. Settlements contain buildings in a grid of open space that

is the interface between the people dwelling in buildings and the world outside the settlement. This open space structure determines how easy it is for people to gain entry into and move around a settlement.

In applying theories of social structure and space syntax, architecture is analyzed as the material manifestation of dynamic social processes associated with the recursive application of socio-spatial constructs by individuals. The spatial structure of architecture in archaeological contexts provides information about the social structure of the society housed by that architecture. Stripped to its barest elements, space syntax only requires the recognition of closed and open architectural spaces, i.e., buildings and the space that surrounds them. This approach can thus be productively applied to unexcavated archaeological sites such as Dowa Yalanne to yield information about resistance, residence, and ritual during the Pueblo Revolt.

The Archaeological Record of Dowa Yalanne
Sixty-two architectural units are situated around the southwestern edge of Dowa Yalanne, covering about 51 hectares (Figure 2.2). These units include roomblocks, enclosures, walls, dams, and rubble areas. These architectural units are located in several clusters on the low rolling hills of

the mesatop. Fourteen of these units are inferred to have been occupied during use of the mesa as a refuge between 1540 and 1680, during several incidents of hostility involving the Spaniards (Hodge 1937:29–33,91–107). For instance, during the revolt of 1632, when the Zuni first destroyed the Catholic missions that had been established in their villages, the Zuni occupied Dowa Yalanne for several years. Many of the early roomblocks were stone-robbed, apparently during the construction that took place after 1680, and other early roomblocks were probably rebuilt, obscuring their original configuration (Ferguson 1996:49).

Disregarding the units occupied before 1680, there are 48 architectural units associated with the Pueblo Revolt, including roomblocks, enclosures, and walls. Early maps of Dowa Yalanne, such as those illustrated in the Mindeleffs (1891:89–91) classic study of Pueblo architecture in the 1880s, focused on the standing walls of the 38 major buildings (Figure 2.3). The architectural enclosures and walls found in the settlement, generally situated at the mesa edge, were not included on these maps. The major buildings in the Pueblo Revolt settlement contain 433 ground floor rooms. The height of the rubble at the two largest roomblocks indicates that many rooms in these units were at least two stories in height. This is confirmed by photographs taken in the late nineteenth century that depict remnant walls with a second-story (Ferguson 1996:52).

Taking into account two-story architecture, there were at least 559 rooms occupied on Dowa Yalanne during the Pueblo Revolt. If two people occupied each room then a population estimate of 1,120 is derived from archaeological data. This estimate seems low, and it may be that Dowa Yalanne had a higher population density per room than earlier Zuni villages. If a historically documented population estimate of 2,500 during the Pueblo Revolt is accurate, there would have been about 4.5 people per room (Hart 1991).

Mindeleff (1891:90) described buildings on Dowa Yalanne as roughly built, with dry-laid masonry walls displaying hasty and careless construction. Close examination of the remaining architecture, however, reveals that

Figure 2.4. Cholla cacti are clustered in and around the masonry roomblocks on Dowa Yalanne (photograph by Cosmos or Victor Mindeleff, ca. 1885. Smithsonian Institution, National Anthropological Archives, Neg. No. 89-22110).

many roomblocks have walls constructed with mud mortar; some of them are using heavily dressed elements with chinking between courses of masonry. Most of the mortar has eroded from the standing walls, giving them the appearance described by Mindeleff.

Although some of the land on top of Dowa Yalanne is arable, the area that can be farmed is too small to have supported more than a fraction of the Zuni population (Kroeber 1916:29). During the Pueblo Revolt, the Zunis thus continued to farm lands in the valley bottoms surrounding Dowa Yalanne. Many observers have noted that the ruins on Dowa Yalanne are associated with a heavy growth of cholla cacti (Fewkes 1891:110–111; Mindeleff 1891:90). Stands of cholla this thick do not commonly occur in the Zuni area, and their presence may indicate that wild foods were also important in the subsistence economy associated with the Pueblo Revolt (Figure 2.4).

There is a large, diffuse artifact scatter extending over the entire surface of the Pueblo Revolt village, and the major roomblocks all have discrete middens adjacent to them. These middens contain a profuse amount of animal bone, ash, charcoal, lithics, and ceramics. Pottery types represented in the Pueblo Revolt assemblage include small traces of Cibola Whiteware and gray corrugated utility ware, and more numerous amounts of blackware, Kechipawan Polychrome, Matsaki Brown-on-buff,

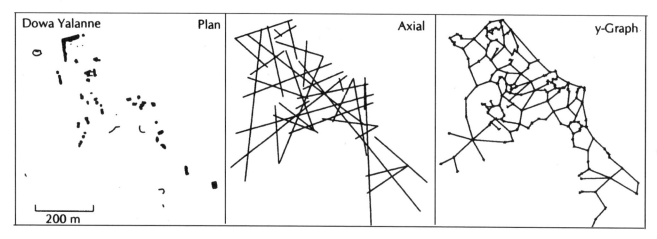

Figure 2.5. Space syntax analysis of Dowa Yalanne showing axial and y-Graph analyses.

Matsaki Polychrome, Hawikuh Glaze-on-red, Hawikuh Polychrome, Ashiwi Polychrome, plain buffware, red-on-buffware, and plain redware.

Resistance

Zuni resistance to an anticipated military reprisal of the Spaniards is evident in the construction of the settlement on top of Dowa Yalanne, a sheer-sided mesa standing more than 300 meters above the valley floor. There are few trails to the top of the mesa, and only one of them, following a sandy bench on the east side of the mesa, can be traversed with horses. The last segment of most of the trails entails a vertical climb, and where the trails breach the top of the mesa there are low walls defending the position. Next to these walls are piles of stones that nineteenth-century Zuni Indians interpreted as defensive stockpiles (Stevenson 1904:286–289). The Zuni said their ancestors were prepared to protect themselves behind these walls, and use the stones as missiles to bombard the Spaniards.

Two low masonry dams were constructed to impound water in reservoirs within the 1680 settlement. These dams are situated at the southern edge of Dowa Yalanne, where they captured water from the largest drainage on the mesatop. A third reservoir, located to the north of the settlement, captured water in a smaller drainage. Impounded water was supplemented by springs at the base of the mesa, accessed via steep trails traversing slickrock

pecked with hand-and-toe holds. These water sources provided an essential resource important to the long-term occupation of Dowa Yalanne as a defensive stronghold.

The architectural layout on top of the mesa is characterized by a well-integrated network of open space (Figure 2.5). The axial lines defined in an analysis of the site's space syntax represent lines of sight between buildings (Hillier and Hanson 1984:90–108). The y-Graph illustrates that the open space within the site approximates a grid, with irregularly spaced lines crossing one another at various angles. These graphs indicate there was relatively open and unimpeded access between the buildings that comprise the settlement. It is the topography of Dowa Yalanne, and not the architecture of buildings that created a fortress that was virtually impregnable. The defensive posture of the settlement thus derived from its position atop the mesa. Once a person gained access to the top of the mesa, movement within the settlement was relatively unimpeded by architectural barriers.

The military effectiveness of the mountain citadel was not tested during the Pueblo Revolt. In November of 1692, Diego de Vargas returned to Zuni with Catholic priests and sixty soldiers but they did not attack Dowa Yalanne (Kessell et al. 1995:206–208). The Zuni allowed the Spaniards to climb up the mesa and enter their village in peace. Some Zuni oral traditions about the Pueblo Revolt recount how the priests of the *Tsu'thlanna* (Great Shell Society) poisoned the springs by placing shells in

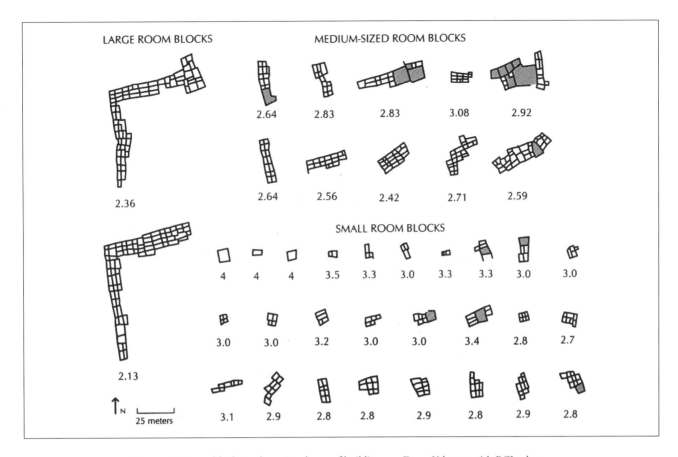

Figure 2.6. Roomblocks in three size classes of buildings on Dowa Yalanne, with RCI values.
Unroofed, open space within room blocks is denoted with hatching.

them, so that the Spaniards arrived bloated and unable to fight (Wiget 1991). Spanish accounts do not contain any reference about this; instead they recount how the Zuni met them at the springs east of Dowa Yalanne, bearing gifts of mutton, melon, and tortillas.

The Zuni convinced Vargas to camp at some distance from Dowa Yalanne, ostensibly to protect Zuni pastures and farms at the base of the mesa from damage from Spanish livestock (Kessell and Hendricks 1992:547; Kessell et al. 1995:208). That night, during a storm, Vargas records that the "Faraón Apache" raided a group of 16 to 18 cattle that had wandered off from the herd the Spaniards brought to provision the expedition. Due to the harsh weather, the fatigue of his horses, and the impending campaign against the Zuni and Hopi, Vargas decided not to pursue the stolen cattle. Given the silences of documentary history, one wonders if the Zuni acted in concert with the Apache or whether, in a fashion analogous to the Boston Tea Party, the Zuni impersonated "wild Indians" in order to attack foreign oppression.

Residential Patterns and Social Change

The buildings on Dowa Yalanne vary substantially in size, configuration of room spaces, and incorporation of unroofed areas. About half the population lived in two large, multi-storied pueblos. Including second-story rooms, one of these large pueblos contained 123 rooms, the other 148 rooms (Figure 2.6). Slightly less than one third of the population lived in 10 buildings, each encompassing from 10 to 30 rooms. The remaining population resided in 26 buildings, each containing between 1 and 10 rooms. About 25 percent of the buildings on Dowa Yalanne incorporate unroofed enclosures in their roomblocks, splitting the configuration of rooms into different room sets or houses.

The contiguity of rooms in buildings has social

implications because the occupants of large, densely packed buildings have different patterns of social interaction than people who live in small, relatively isolated buildings. People living in large buildings have a greater chance of regularly encountering, and thus interacting with, their neighbors. In addition, the occupation of large pueblos and small buildings probably signified membership in different types of social groups.

Room contiguity is measured with an index developed by Clark (1997:240–241), generated by dividing the number of walls by the number of rooms. Low Room Contiguity Index (RCI) values represent high contiguity, that is, many rooms adjacent to one another. As Clark has demonstrated in the Tonto Basin, different social groups can be differentiated based on the RCI values of their settlement plans. The large roomblocks on Dowa Yalanne have low RCI values, ranging from 2.13 to 2.36, indicating they contain many contiguous rooms (Figure 2.5). The RCI values of medium-sized buildings, with values between 2.4 and 3.08, indicate their rooms are less contiguous than the large roomblocks. Small buildings have RCI values between 2.8 and 4.0, indicating they have the fewest contiguous rooms.

Analysis of room contiguity and unroofed space indicates that the occupants of some buildings were in close contact in tightly packed blocks of rooms, while other residents of the settlement lived in less coterminous arrangements. The small size of many roomblocks, and the small size of room sets in sites containing unroofed enclosures, suggests most of the structures were built and occupied by small social groups. These small roomblocks were probably occupied by single lineages or groups of closely related lineages and clan segments. The two largest roomblocks probably represent remnant communities maintaining the spatial order of two earlier seventeenth-century Zuni pueblos. Dowa Yalanne thus seems to incorporate both families living in individual houses and larger social groups of various sizes living in communal structures. This residential pattern is significantly different from the sites occupied immediately before and after Dowa Yalanne.

The diversity in the size of the roomblocks suggests different types of social groups were being replicated. Slightly more that half of the rooms are distributed in the smaller roomblocks with substantial open space around them, suggesting much of the community was organized around a direct correspondence between social and spatial groups. The two large roomblocks had to have been organized with social groups characterized by a transpatial system (Hillier and Hanson 1984:40–41) that crosscut the local residence units incorporated into the roomblocks. The combination of both correspondence and transpatial systems on Dowa Yalanne suggests there was a considerable amount of social experimentation going on in the settlement as the members of six pre-Revolt pueblos sought to reorganize themselves into a single community. This social experimentation included the incorporation of some refugees from the Rio Grande, since Dowa Yalanne was a multi-ethnic community during at least part of its occupation. In 1696, for instance, Vargas reported there were twenty Tanos and two families of Tewa from Santa Clara residing at Dowa Yalanne (Kessell et al. 1998:968–970).

In the Durkheimian terms used as explanatory postulates in the theory of space syntax, this experimentation appears oriented toward balancing the mechanical and organic solidarity of the community (Durkheim 1964; Hillier and Hanson 1984:142). Mechanical solidarity is integration accomplished through similarities in group belief and structure, while organic solidarity stems from an interdependence of structural units based on their differences. Mechanical solidarity requires a segregated and dispersed space that separates the constituent social groups and helps maintain their individual identity as discrete social entities. This element of the settlement on Dowa Yalanne can be seen in the replication of many small buildings dispersed throughout the open space of the community. Organic solidarity, in contrast, requires an integrated and dense space to facilitate the numerous social encounters needed for the exchange of information and material that ties together the mutually interdependent social entities. This element of the community can be seen in the two large pueblo roomblocks and the high degree of integration apparent in the open space structure of the settlement.

The dispersion of roomblocks is an important component of the site structure. Each of the architectural units on Dowa Yalanne is a freestanding entity in the midst of a very grid-like, well-integrated open space. This spatial structure served to maximize face-to-face encounters and social interaction as people moved around the settlement. The encounter space provided in this arrangement must have been useful in fostering the social interaction needed to integrate the diverse social groups that constituted the settlement. The consolidation of what had been six villages into a single community entailed a fundamental reorganization of Zuni society in order to accommodate the unification of households, clans, kivas, medicine societies, and priesthoods. This reorganization required regular and substantial social interaction to forge new community relations.

Formal Aspects of Architecture

Cushing (1888, 1896:330) and Bandelier (Lange and Riley 1970:47–50) suggested the buildings on Dowa Yalanne were constructed in six clusters, corresponding to the six Zuni pueblos occupied before the Pueblo Revolt. Cushing posited these six clusters replicated a sevenfold division of Zuni social organization that symbolically corresponded to the six cardinal directions (cardinal points along with the zenith and nadir). The seventh division was the totality of the settlement, which represented "the middle or mother and synthetic combination of them all" (Cushing 1896:367). It is not clear whether Cushing's notion that the "mythico-sociologic" organization of Zuni was replicated in six clusters of buildings on Dowa Yalanne represented his own thought or an idea shared with him by the Zuni.

Whatever the case, archaeologists who have subsequently investigated Dowa Yalanne have disputed Cushing and Bandelier's assertion that buildings are grouped in clusters corresponding to the six earlier pueblos (Kroeber 1916:28–30; Mindeleff 1891:89–90; Spier

Figure 2.7. Hemenway Expedition Map, ca. 1888, with Frank Hamilton Cushing's notes showing the purported location of kivas ("a") and house clusters (dashed lines) (courtesy of the Brooklyn Museum, Culin Archival Collection, Cushing Series, Box 23: Drawings [Southwest], folder 6).

1917:231). While many people see clusters of buildings on Dowa Yalanne, different analysts intuitively define these clusters in different ways. As Fewkes (1891:110–111) concluded, maps of Dowa Yalanne do not show an arrangement of houses as clearly as might be wished in support of Cushing's theory.

Ritual on Dowa Yalanne

Cushing thought the key to understanding the distribution of the house clusters he saw on Dowa Yalanne was the occurrence in each of an isolated, square four-room chamber or kiva, which he identified on a map prepared for the Hemenway Expedition in 1888 (Figure 2.7). Investigation of Cushing's map during fieldwork in 1989 indicated that his "kivas" are actually roomblocks that range in size from 1 to 12 rooms. None of these buildings can be identified as a kiva using contemporary standards of archaeological classification.

Nonetheless, the historical record suggests there were multiple kivas on Dowa Yalanne. On his visit to the summit in 1692, Diego de Vargas described three kivas (estufas) in the plaza of the pueblo he visited. Vargas wrote:

I reached the said Rock, its front being crowded with the multitude of the said village, and the way up being so difficult and long, I was forced, on account of its bad places, to mount it on foot and, although it cost considerable effort, I succeeded, and . . . being up there, saw the said table land to be very broad and spacious, extending apparently two Leagues, and I mounted my horse to go and enter said village where the natives received me with all its inhabitants whom I saw to be numerous; and having dismounted, I saluted them all, giving them Greeting . . . and being in their Square which contains three estufas, I ordered that a great Cross be placed in it [Vargas 1914:304–305].

The pueblo Vargas described had to have been one of the two largest roomblocks, since they are the only multistoried buildings enclosing plazas. However, no indication of any kivas or subterranean features was discerned in these open areas during recent fieldwork. Archaeological survey of Dowa Yalanne only identified one partially subterranean building that may be a kiva, located in the cluster of buildings between and to the east of the two large pueblos. Zuni kivas apparently underwent architectural change during the Pueblo Revolt. Prior to 1680, Zuni kivas were subterranean rooms located in plazas, and they were thus spatially segregated from habitation rooms (Hodge 1939). After the Revolt, kivas in Zuni Pueblo were constructed as aboveground chambers, fully integrated into roomblocks adjacent to habitations. If kivas were incorporated within the roomblocks on Dowa Yalanne, it will be difficult to recognize them using survey data. Although the archaeological identification of kivas on Dowa Yalanne remains ambiguous, it is unimaginable that the Zuni did not continue to practice their kachina religion during the Pueblo Revolt.

There are a number of enigmatic enclosures and wall segments on Dowa Yalanne that may delineate ritual areas. The two largest buildings have what appear to be small plaza shrines in the ell formed by their roomblocks. There are also two large open enclosures, one of which

has a shrine-like feature abutted to it, and several walls that partition off segments of the cliff edge. It is possible that these areas represent places where kiva or society members could congregate during ceremonies. These features, along with the historically reported kivas, indicate the Zuni maintained their ritual practices during the Pueblo Revolt.

At the same time the Zuni continued to practice their native religion, at least part of the population on Dowa Yalanne also apparently maintained some practice of the Catholic religion. After the missionary fathers with Vargas had performed the acts of absolution and baptism, Vargas was taken to a room where he found the Zuni had curated a number of religious artifacts associated with the Catholic church. As Vargas wrote:

Once this was finished, I heard that the holy vessels, a monstrance, and effigies of Christ Our Lord were on the terraced roof of a house of the governor of that pueblo who had died. Rushing to that house, I went up a wooden ladder to the roof. On the terrace, which had a small panel as a door, I entered and found a small room with an altar arranged in the following manner: On the floor two tallow candles weighing more than a pound and white as snow were burning in two candlesticks. Some painted mantas as a frontal, some altar cloths, and four very large silver chalices with their patens were on a table. In the middle was a gold-plated silver monstrance with its crystal, just like new. This was covered with pieces of cloth from the sacred vestments that had fallen to pieces. Also on the table were three images of Christ Jesus, two excellent ones of cast bronze and the third painted on a very well made cross with a Capuchin St. Francis at His feet. In order to remove the scraps with which it was covered and uncover it, I knelt before these barbarians. With special tenderness about my good fortune in successfully finding such a divine treasure, I kissed the images a thousand and one times. I turned to my companions so that they could consider the risks and travail suffered as well worth it, with the reward of having rescued Christ Jesus.

—[KESSELL ET AL. 1995:207]

Zuni was the only pueblo Vargas visited in 1692 that had curated Catholic religious paraphernalia. The Catholic artifacts he described, along with a missal and 20 other books were collected to take to El Paso, where they could be reconsecrated.

Hodge (1937:102, 1953:2) and other historians (Crampton 1977:40) have suggested that these relics may be related to the Zuni oral tradition about Fray Juan Greyrobe, a Catholic priest who is said to have abjured his faith during the Pueblo Revolt. In this tradition, the Catholic priest was given the choice of being martyred or being adopted into the tribe and dressing in native clothing (Cushing 1896:330–331; Stevenson 1904:286–289). Having chosen the latter, the Catholic priest was taken to Dowa Yalanne, where he resided with the Zuni. In the Zuni tradition, when Vargas approached with his soldiers, Fray Juan Greyrobe wrote a message in charcoal on an animal hide, and peace was restored when this was thrown down the mesa to the Spaniards.

Wiget (1991) notes there are 18 recorded accounts of this tradition, some of which include two attacks by the Spaniards: the first which is repelled by the supernatural means of Great Shell Society, and the second which is prevented by the message delivered by Fray Juan Greyrobe. Wiget thinks that the best hypothesis to reconcile the violence of the Pueblo Revolt with the presence of curated Catholic artifacts is that there was a sizeable minority of Zuni who had converted to the Catholic faith. He suggests this faction could not be destroyed during the Revolt, and their personal allegiance to a young priest resulted in his being spared and preserving some of his religious paraphernalia. As Wiget suggests, if this priest was absorbed into Zuni society, taking a wife, he would probably not have wanted to present himself to Vargas in 1692. This would explain why there is no record of his existence in documentary sources.

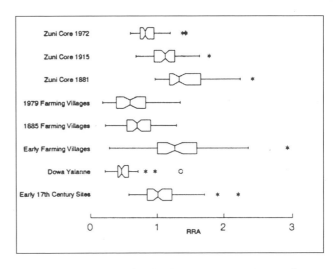

Figure 2.8. Box plots of Real Relative Asymmetry (RRA) values for historic Zuni settlements.

After the Revolt

After peace with the Spaniards was established in 1692, the Zuni moved off of Dowa Yalanne and settled into a single pueblo at Halona:wa, one of the pre-Revolt Zuni villages. This settlement, on the banks of the Zuni River, subsequently became known as Zuni Pueblo (Cushing 1896:331; Kintigh 1985:70). Zuni Pueblo was expanded at this time, and new roomblocks were constructed to the south and east of the original pueblo, eventually enclosing the rebuilt Catholic church in a large plaza. The church that had originally been constructed outside of Zuni Pueblo on a trash mound came to occupy a central position in the settlement plan (Ferguson and Mills 1988:245–247).

Room contiguity and the structure of open space in Zuni Pueblo are substantially different than that found in the Pueblo Revolt settlement on Dowa Yalanne. One means to gauge this is through the syntactic measurement of relative asymmetry, which calculates the segregation of space (Hillier and Hanson 1984:15–16). Box plots of Real Relative Asymmetry (RRA), standardized to control for differences in the size of settlements, demonstrate that the Pueblo Revolt village on Dowa Yalanne has a more integrated open space structure than any of the historic Zuni settlements (Figure 2.8). The pueblos occupied before the Pueblo Revolt in the seventeenth century, and

Figure 2.9. *Victory on Top of Dowa Yalanne—1680*
(cartoon by Phil Hughte, 1991, courtesy of Dru Anne Hughte).

Zuni Pueblo in the nineteenth century, have higher RRA values, indicating their spatial structures are more segregated. In human terms, this means that access within these settlements was more restricted than it was on Dowa Yalanne. The segregated spatial structure of Zuni Pueblo in the eighteenth and nineteenth centuries was due to both to the need for defense, and the orientation of the village around kivas, plazas, and sacred pathways that have highly controlled access. In the years following the Pueblo Revolt, the architectural hallmarks of pueblo life were fully reconstituted at Zuni Pueblo, where a unified population maintained a well-integrated social structure.

Political trouble continued at Zuni Pueblo after the Revolt, and in 1702, Spanish officials conducted an investigation of Indians from Acoma, Laguna, and Zuni who were urged to rebel by the Apaches. The next year, in 1703, three Spaniards illegally residing in Zuni were killed by the Zuni in response to their aggressive and overbearing behavior. These three "exiles" from Santa Fe had accompanied the priests and soldiers sent to reestablish the mission in Zuni after 1692. During this incident, part of the Zuni population sought refuge on Dowa Yalanne, while the remainder the tribe sought refuge with the Hopi. How long the Zuni remained on top of Dowa Yalanne during this occupation is not known, but the stay was probably brief (Hodge 1954:3; Woodbury 1979:472). The 1703 incident was the last documented use of Dowa Yalanne as a place of refuge.

Even though the occupation of the village on Dowa Yalanne ceased, the mesa was never "abandoned." The imposing landform of Dowa Yalanne dominates the eastern horizon at Zuni Pueblo, and the mesa continues to play a vital role in Zuni life as a sacred area. Many active shrines are located along its base and on its crest, providing a link between the past and present at Zuni Pueblo (Culin 1907:5; Parsons 1918; Stevenson 1904:61, 234).

Depictions of Dowa Yalanne are prominent icons in the artistic repertoire that defines the contemporary identity of Zuni. A cartoon by Zuni artist Phil Hughte, for instance, depicts the Zuni victory during the Pueblo Revolt (Figure 2.9). Although contemporary Zuni can today find humor in the events of the Pueblo Revolt, the archaeology and history of the insurrection indicate that it was no laughing matter at the time. It took a substantial effort to construct and live in the settlement on top of Dowa Yalanne, and the Zuni worked hard to reconstitute a society based on multiple villages into a single, tightly knit community. The descendents of the Zuni who lived on Dowa Yalanne today appreciate a rich social life that stems in part from the actions taken by their ancestors during the Pueblo Revolt.

Acknowledgments

This chapter is based on field research in 1989 funded in part through a National Science Foundation Grant (BNS-8720491). The research was undertaken with the approval of the Zuni Tribal Council, and conducted under the auspices of the Zuni Archaeology Program. During the course of research and publication, Roger Anyon, E. Richard Hart, Theodore Jojola, Robert Leonard, Barbara Mills, Robert Preucel, and Wirt H. Wills provided critical comments that improved many of the ideas expressed in the chapter. Dru Ann Hughte graciously allowed the late Phil Hughte's illustration to be used in this publication. Thanks are due to Tom Kennedy and his staff at the A:shiwi A:wan Museum and Heritage Center for their assistance in obtaining permission to use this illustration.

References Cited

Bandelier, Adolph F. A.
1893   An Outline of the Documentary History of the Zuni Tribe. *A Journal of American Ethnology and Archaeology* 3(1):1–115.

Crampton, C. Gregory
1977   *The Zunis of Cibola.* University of Utah Press, Salt Lake City.

Culin, Stewart
1907   Zuni Notes. Ms. on file, The Brooklyn Museum Archives, New York.

Cushing, Frank Hamilton
1888   Preliminary Notes on the Origin, Working Hypothesis, and Primary Researches of the Hemenway Southwestern Archaeological Expedition. *Proceedings of the International Congress of the Americanists* 7:151–194.
1896   Outlines of Zuni Creation Myths. In *Thirteenth Annual Report of the Bureau of Ethnology,* pp. 321–447. Government Printing Office, Washington, D.C.

Clark, Jeffrey J.
1997   Migration and Integration: The Salado in the Tonto Basin. Unpublished Ph.D. dissertation, Department of Anthropology, University of Arizona, Tucson.

Durkheim, Emile
1964   [1893] *The Division of Labor in Society.* Free Press, New York.

Ferguson, T. J.
1992   Zuni Settlement Patterns during the Pueblo Revolt. In *Current Research on the Late Prehistory and Early History of New Mexico,* edited by Bradley J. Vierra, pp. 85–92. New Mexico Archaeological Council, Albuquerque.
1996   *Historic Zuni Architecture and Society, An Archaeological Application of Space Syntax.* Anthropological Papers of the University of Arizona 60. University of Arizona Press, Tucson.

Ferguson, T. J., and Barbara J. Mills
1988   Settlement and Growth of Zuni Pueblo. *Kiva* 52(4):243–266.

Fewkes, Jesse Walter
1891   Reconnaissance of Ruins In or Near the Zuni Reservation. *A Journal of American Ethnology and Archaeology* 1(3):93–133.

Firth, Raymond
1963   *Elements of Social Organization.* Beacon, Boston.

Giddens, Anthony
1984   *The Constitution of Society: Outline of the Theory of Structuration.* University of California Press, Berkeley.

Hanson, Julienne
1998   *Decoding Homes and Houses.* Cambridge University Press, Cambridge, Mass.

Hart, E. Richard
1991   Appendix I, Zuni Population, 1539–1989. In "A History of Zuni Water Use" by E. Richard Hart. Expert testimony submitted to the United States Claims Court in behalf of the Zuni Indian Tribe in *City of Gallup v. USA,* No. Civ. 84–0164, District Court, McKinley County, New Mexico.

Hillier, Bill
1996   *Space is the Machine.* Cambridge University Press, Cambridge, UK.

Hillier, Bill, and Julienne Hanson
1984   *The Social Logic of Space.* Cambridge University Press, Cambridge, UK.

Hodge, Frederick W.
1907   Heshota Ayahtona. In *Handbook of American Indians North of Mexico,* edited by Frederick Webb Hodge, Part 1, pp. 544–548. Government Printing Office, Washington, D.C.
1937   *History of Hawikuh.* Ward Richie Press, Los Angeles.
1939   A Square Kiva at Hawikuh. In *So Live the Works of Men,* edited by Donald D. Brand and Fred E. Harvey, pp. 195–214. University of New Mexico Press, Albuquerque.
1954   *Towayalane, A Mesa with a History.* Privately published.

Karp, Ivan
1983   Agency and Social Theory: A Review of Anthony Giddens. *Ethnologist* 3:131–137.

Kessell, John L., and Rick Hendricks (editors)
1992   *By Force of Arms, The Journals of Don Diego de Vargas, 1691–1693.* University of New Mexico Press, Albuquerque.

Kessell, John L., Rick Hendricks, and Meredith D. Dodge (editors)
1995   *To the Royal Crown Restored, the Journals of Don Diego de Vargas, New Mexico, 1692–1694.* University of New Mexico Press, Albuquerque.

Kintigh, Keith
1985   *Settlement, Subsistence, and Society in Late Zuni Prehistory.* Anthropological Papers of the University of Arizona 44. University of Arizona Press, Tucson.

Kroeber, Alfred E.
1916   Zuni Potsherds. *Anthropological Papers* 18(2):39–205. American Museum of Natural History, New York.

Lange, Charles H., and Carroll Riley (editors)
1970   *The Southwest Journals of Adolph F. Bandelier, 1883–1884.* University of New Mexico Press, Albuquerque.

Merrill, William L.
1988   *Rarámuri Souls.* Smithsonian Institution Press, Washington, D.C.

Mindeleff, Victor
1891   A Study of Pueblo Architecture in Tusayan and Cibola. In *Eighth Annual Report for the Bureau of American Ethnology for the Years 1886–1887,* pp. 3–228. Government Printing Office, Washington, D.C.

Ortner, Sherry B.
1984   Theory in Anthropology since the Sixties. *Comparative Studies in Society and History* 26(1):126–166.

Parsons, Elsie Clews
1918   War God Shrines of the Laguna and Zuni. *American Anthropologist* 20:381–405.

Spier, Leslie
1917   An Outline for a Chronology of Zuni Ruins. *Anthropological Papers* 18(3):207–331. American Museum of Natural History, New York.

Stevenson, Matilda Coxe
1904   The Zuni Indians, Their Mythology, Esoteric Fraternities, and Ceremonies. In *Twenty-third Annual Report of the Bureau of American Ethnology for the Years 1901–1902,* pp. 3–634. Government Printing Office, Washington, D.C.

Vargas, Zapata Lujan Ponce de Leon, Diego de

1914   Re-Conquest of New Mexico, 1692: Extracts from the
        Journal of General Don Diego de Vargas Zapata Lujan
        Ponce de Leon. *Old Santa Fe Magazine* 1:288–307.

Wiget, Andrew

1991   Oral Tradition: A People's Shared Memory. In *Zuni History,
        Victories in the 1990s,* Section II, p. 19. Institute of the
        North American West, Seattle, and Pueblo of Zuni, New
        Mexico.

Woodbury, Richard B.

1979   Zuni Prehistory and History to 1850. In *Handbook of
        North American Indians: Southwest,* Vol. 9, edited by
        Alfonso Ortiz, pp. 467–473. Smithsonian Institution,
        Washington, D.C.

Chapter 3

Mission and Mesa:

Some Thoughts on the Archaeology of Pueblo Revolt Era Sites in the Jemez Region, New Mexico

Michael L. Elliott

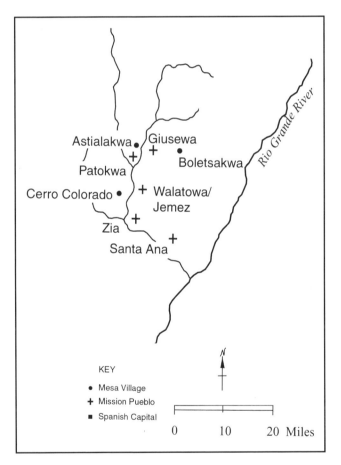

Figure 3.1. Map of the Jemez region.

Introduction

In my chapter, I review some persistent questions regarding the identities and locations of the missions and villages occupied during the seventeenth century in the Jemez district. Historical documents provide us with five mission names: San José de los Jemez, San Diego de la Congregación, San Diego de los Jemez, San Diego del Monte, and San Juan de los Jemez. However, there is considerable scholarly debate as to locations of these missions and some of these names may refer to the same mission. Related to this, there is some confusion with respect to the identities of the villages visited by Don Diego de Vargas including Astialakwa, Patokwa, Boletsakwa, and Walatowa. My analysis makes use of the distance data provided in the Vargas journals recently retranslated by the Vargas project of the University of New Mexico. By clarifying some of these issues, I hope to shed new light on the processes of settlement change and population movements during the Revolt and Reconquest periods.

Historical Background

The Jemez, a Towa-speaking people, developed a distinctive material culture and settlement system in the upper Rio Jemez, Rio Guadalupe, and Rito Vallecitos drainages during the fifteenth and sixteenth centuries (Figure 3.1). The key elements of this distinctive culture area are the high elevation to which they adapted, the size and number of their villages, and the prevalence of small structures and other agriculture-related sites.

Early Spanish explorers, such as Coronado and Espejo described the Jemez people as occupying a number of large villages between 1540–1580 (Hammond and Rey 1940, 1966). In 1598, Don Juan de Oñate established the first permanent Spanish colony in New Mexico near San Juan Pueblo. He soon assigned a Franciscan missionary to the Jemez, Fray Alonso de Lugo. Lugo probably established a small mission at Giusewa, but did not remain for long, having left New Mexico by 1601 (Scholes 1938:62). However, the process of missionization and reduction (the policy of combining the native residents of several smaller villages into large ones to make them easier to control) had begun in the Jemez area. Little information is available for the Jemez region from 1601–1621. The Jemez mission built by Lugo was probably abandoned sometime between 1601 and 1610. In 1614 the Jemez were reported to be *infieles* (Scholes 1938:63).

Fray Gerónimo de Zárate Salmerón continued the missionization process in 1621. He reestablished a mission called San José de los Jemez and later had another mission built called San Diego de la Congregación at a village he founded anew. Salmerón attempted to bring the Jemez down off the mesas and into the two mission villages. He listed the large village of Amoxiumqua, near the rim of Jemez Canyon and over-looking the San José mission as a *visita* of San José. Salmerón claimed to have baptized 6,566 individuals at Jemez during his service there (Milich 1966). Salmerón left Jemez in 1626. The two memorials of Fray Alonso de Benavides, the Custodian of the New Mexico missions, his memorial of 1630 (Ayers 1965 [1916]) and his revised memorial of 1634 (Hodge et al. 1945), provide important information about these two early Jemez missions. In 1623 the Jemez people revolted, burning the San Diego mission and reoccupying their mesatop villages. They were pacified three years later and Fray Martín de Arvide reestablished the San Diego mission. The San José mission seems to have been permanently abandoned sometime during 1632–1639. After that time, the San

Diego de la Congregación was the only active mission.

Only scattered references to the Jemez missions exist for the period between 1630 and 1680. One of the most interesting references is to "the baths of San José de los Jemez." Governor Manso visited the baths (probably the Jemez Hot Springs) seeking relief from illness (Scholes 1938:96). He reported the area as *"despoblado."* He also took a priest with him, suggesting that the mission of San José was not staffed. Another important source on the Jemez missions is the documentation of the 1672 Chapter Elections (Bloom and Mitchell 1938). The elections took place at San Diego de Jemez, apparently the San Diego de la Congregación of the 1620s. San Diego is described as "the center of missionary work for the whole province" (Bloom and Mitchell 1938:109).

The 1600s were a time of great turmoil in the region. There was continual strife among the religious and civil authorities in New Mexico. The natives were often caught in the middle of these battles, and resisted the imposition of the Catholic religion and other Spanish institutions in any way they could (Scholes 1937, 1942). Great famines, epidemics, and warfare with the Spanish and other Native American tribes drastically reduced Pueblo populations. The Jemez conspired with other Pueblos and tribes during this period to drive out the Spaniards, but were found out and punished (see Schaafsma, Chapter 13). These conflicts culminated in the Pueblo Revolts of 1680 and 1696.

Jemez mission history may thus be summarized as follows. The first mission may have been established in 1598 by Fray Lugo. Lugo left New Mexico in 1601 and the mission he built was probably abandoned shortly thereafter. Fray Salmerón ministered among the Jemez from 1621 to 1626. He either rebuilt or built anew San José and San Diego de la Congregación mission. The Jemez revolted and burned San Diego in 1623. Fray Arvide rebuilt San Diego in 1626 but left the area in 1629. The San José mission was abandoned and is not mentioned as being active after 1639. San Diego was apparently the only active mission in the Jemez area from 1640 to 1680.

Events of the Pueblo Revolt Period

The Jemez were important participants in the Revolt of 1680, and martyred one of their two missionaries, Fray Juan de Jesús, on August 11 at San Diego de la Congregación (Hackett and Shelby 1942:31). The other Jemez missionary, Fray Francisco Muñoz, escaped with Luis de Granillo, *alcalde mayor* of the Jemez, Zia, and Santa Ana Pueblos after being warned of the revolt.

Espinosa relates a story of Fray Juan de Jesús's death:

> At Jemez, when the alcalde mayor and the guardian of the mission fled, Fray Juan de Jesus remained in his convent cell. That night a group of Jemez rebels entered the cell and took Fray Juan to the cemetery, where the lit many candles, stripped him naked, mounted him on a pig, and beat him cruelly as they ridiculed him and led him about the cemetery. Then they took him off the pig, made him get down on all fours, and took turns mounting his back and whipping him. Fray Juan suffered all of this with only the words, "Do with me as you wish, for this joy of yours will not last more than ten years, after which you will consume each other in war." This angered the tormenters, and they killed him with war clubs and threw his body in the rear of the pueblo.
>
> —[ESPINOSA 1988:35]

Diego de Vargas later found what he believed were the remains of Fray Juan de Jesús, and removed them to Santa Fe for burial (Kessell et al. 1998:342). After the Pueblo Revolt, the Spanish abandoned New Mexico for 12 years. Governor Otermín tried to reconquer New Mexico in 1681, but failed, as did Governors Reneros and Jirónza. Governor Diego de Vargas returned to New Mexico to reclaim it for the Spanish king and for God in 1692. He planned two entries. His first expedition was to reconnoiter and assess the situation. He performed ritualized repossessions of a number of pueblos, including Jemez of San Diego Mesa.

Vargas discovered that many changes had occurred. Many of the native pueblos in the river valleys were abandoned, with the former residents having moved to more defensible locations on high mesas. Although we may never know exactly what transpired during the 12-year interregnum of Spanish rule in New Mexico, one may speculate that the natives moved to these locations because they were afraid of Spanish retribution, conflict with their neighbor pueblos, and raids from nomadic non-puebloan tribes. Vargas met no opposition during his first expedition.

His second expedition, in 1693, was a re-colonizing expedition. Vargas and the Spanish intended to stay in New Mexico this time, and did. Although the Pueblos were not united, many resisted the Spanish attempts to reconquer them, passively at first, then aggressively. The Jemez, though feigning allegiance to Spain and the Catholic Church, continued to rebel and to attack their neighbors, such as Zia, who were cooperating with the Spaniards.

Vargas eventually punished the Jemez for their continued resistance. On July 24, 1694, he attacked Astialakwa, the Jemez refuge village on top of Guadalupe Mesa, killing 84 warriors and taking 361 prisoners. He removed all the provisions and livestock from the village and burned it. The Jemez were forced to participate in a battle against the Tewa rebels on Black Mesa and rebuild the church at San Diego del Monte to get the prisoners back. They also rebuilt the old San Diego de la Congregación church, this time with the name San Juan de los Jemez.

Continued strife occurred between the Jemez and Spanish. Finally, on June 4, 1696, the Jemez and some of their original Indian allies revolted again, and again martyred one of their missionaries at San Diego del Monte, Fray Francisco de Jesús. Fray Francisco de Vargas, *custos* of the New Mexico missions, described Fray Francisco de Jesús's death in a letter to the provincial minister:

> In the Pueblo of San Diego de los Jemez on that day [June 4, 1696] at about eleven in the morning they took the life of the apostolic father preacher Fray Francisco de Jesus, whom they called, deceitful, to go out to confess a sick person, and the Indians,

waiting in advance at the door of the convent, caught him and killed him next to a cross that the said religious had set up in the cemetery; and on many occasions the said religious was heard to say, and I heard him say, that he had it so that they could crucify him on it, and although these wishes were not attained, he succeeded in expiring at the foot of the cross after he had been wounded many times, as they ended his life.

—[ESPINOSA 1988:250]

Luis Cunixu, a native of San Diego del Monte later captured at Pecos with some of Fray Francisco de Jesús's religious paraphernalia, said that the natives had clubbed the priest to death (Kessell et al. 1998:750). Fray de Vargas found Fray Francisco de Jesús's remains, which had been partially devoured by animals. He recovered some of the bones and buried them at Zia Pueblo (Espinosa 1988:212). The other minister to the Jemez, Fray Juan Muñoz of San Juan de los Jemez, was at Pecos Pueblo relieving an ill minister, and thus escaped the wrath of the Jemez.

Vargas and his lieutenants then mounted punitive campaigns against the Jemez. It appears that at first the Jemez returned to their burned-out pueblo on the *peñol* after the 1696 Revolt (Kessell et al. 1998:796). One battle resulted in the deaths of 35 natives of Acoma and five Jemez (Kessell et al. 1998:881). For a number of years, the Jemez lived among the Navajo, Hopi, and possibly other pueblos. It also seems that many Jemez returned to small sites in remote areas of the Jemez Mountains. By 1703, some of the Jemez refugees had moved back to rebuild their mission, while others continued to trickle in from the mountains (Hackett 1937:376). In 1716, a group of 113 Jemez returned from the Hopi Mesas (Bloom and Mitchell 1938:108).

Revolt Period Missions and Villages

The seventeenth-century missions and villages present a difficult and basic problem in the Jemez area. Historical documents provide evidence for five mission names. These

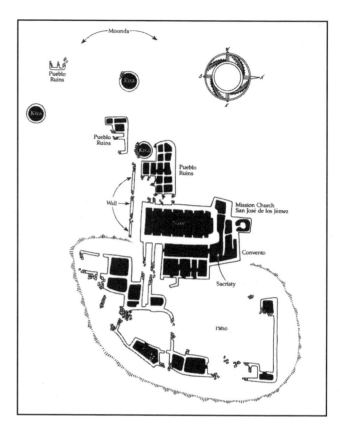

Figure 3.2. Map of Giuséwa (Elliott 1993).

are San José de los Jemez, San Diego de la Congregación, San Diego de los Jemez, San Diego del Monte, and San Juan de los Jemez. Archaeologists have only securely identified three of these. Giusewa is generally regarded to be the site of San José de los Jemez (the mission there having been abandoned by 1639), Patokwa is regarded as the site of San Diego del Monte, and Walatowa is thought to be the location of San Juan de los Jemez.

Similarly, Towa place names are difficult to assign with certainty. Many sites appear to have more than one name. Sites seem to have different names depending upon the direction in which they are approached. Jemez Pueblo now considers place names to be sacred information and not to be divulged. Therefore, the Towa place names assigned to sites by past and present researchers may be considered only provisional and related to what Pueblo sources told researchers in the late eighteenth and early nineteenth centuries. Two other Jemez sites in the area have major Revolt-era components. These are Astialakwa and Boletsakwa.

Giusewa and San José de los Jemez

Giusewa (LA 679) is a large, multi-component site with ruins of a large pueblo village located about half a mile north of the Jemez hot springs (Figure 3.2). The name Giusewa means "at the hot place" in the Towa language and the pueblo is properly called Giusewatowa "pueblo at the hot place" (Harrington 1916:393). The most visible features at the site, however, are the walls and foundations of a seventeenth-century church and *convento* known as San José de los Jemez. This identification was first made by George Kubler (1936, 1940). The mission was built around 1621 on top of the ruins of an earlier church.

Giusewa exhibits several features common to other mission sites and at least one that is unique—an octagonal tower. The long main room in the church is the nave, which in plan-view, is cross-shaped. The transepts that form the nave's crosspiece are near the front of the nave. Entry was by means of the narthex, a raised porch-like platform at the entrance to the nave. On the east side of the narthex was the baptismal font that held holy water. At one time, the nave exhibited a series of pedestals commemorating the saints and the Stations of the Cross. A set of steps on the north end of the nave leads up to the sanctuary. Two more steps lead up to the altar area. East of the sanctuary is the sacristy. At the north end of the church is its most unusual feature, an octagonal tower that at one time may have stood 50 or more feet high. The convento was entered through a long hallway leading out of the sacristy. The *camposanto* was located to the south and southwest of the entry to the nave.

Giusewa has been the focus of a number of excavation and stabilization projects. Edger Lee Hewett conducted the first investigation in 1910 as a joint field school between the School of American Archaeology and the Bureau of American Ethnology (Hodge 1918). Work apparently centered on the cemetery and the artifacts were sent to the National Museum (now the Smithsonian Institution). In 1921 and 1922, Lansing B. Bloom, Wesley Bradfield, and Sam Hudelson directed a series of excavations for the School of American Research in Santa Fe (Bloom 1923). The mission, some of the rooms of the

convento and 24 rooms in the pueblo were excavated. From 1935 to 1937, the University of New Mexico excavated a series of rooms in locations adjacent to the previous work (presumably the southwest corner of the pueblo). In 1936, Francis Elmore excavated eight rooms in the pueblo in the section west and adjoining the mission, a kiva, and one large room in the convento. In 1937, Joseph H. Toulouse, Jr. and Ele Baker continued work on the pueblo and convento. Four rooms and several features were excavated in 1965 under the supervision of Laurens Hammack of the Museum of New Mexico in the context of the construction of the new Visitors Center. Finally, excavations were conducted in 1977 and 1978 in order to alleviate drainage problems and facilitate stabilization.

Archaeologists have recovered more than 100 burials, 100 whole or partial vessels, and over 100,000 sherds, lithics, and faunal remains. The largest collection is held by the Museum of New Mexico and includes the artifacts recovered during the 1921–1922, 1936–1937, 1965, and 1977–1978 excavations. The other major collection of artifacts is at the National Museum of Natural History of the Smithsonian Institution and includes the artifacts recovered during the 1910 excavation. Several smaller collections include the Maxwell Museum at the University of New Mexico, the Southwest Museum in Los Angeles, the Brooklyn Museum in New York, and the National Museum of the American Indian in New York. Human remains recovered from Giusewa are curated at the University of New Mexico, the National Museum of Natural History, and the Southwest Museum.

Patokwa Pueblo and San Diego del Monte

Patokwa (LA 96) consists of a two-plaza enclosed pueblo with a Spanish mission and convento complex, smaller unattached roomblocks, several large depressions, probably kivas, a Coalition period pueblo, and a nearby Developmental period site with pithouses and other features (Figure 3.3). Scholes (1938) identified the mission as San Diego del Monte. Bloom (1931:162 n.5) assigns this site the name "Astialakwa," which most scholars assign to LA 1825, the refuge pueblo atop Guadalupe Mesa to the

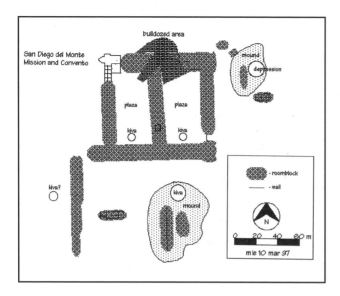

Figure 3.3. Sketch map of Patokwa.

Figure 3.4. Detail of 1779 Miera y Pacheco map
(from Adams and Chavez 1956).

North. The meaning of the place name "Patokwa" is obscure. Bloom (1931:162 n.5) translates the name as "place of the index finger" but does not think it is the correct name for the site, which he calls Mashtiashinkwa, "place of the thumb." Other researchers have not followed Bloom in this matter. Sando (1979:419) translates Patokwa as "turquoise-moiety place." The 1779 Miera y Pacheco map shows the site of Patokwa as a ruin labeled as "S. Diego" and Walatowa is labeled as "Xemes" (Figure 3.4).

The main section of the site consists of a large rectangular pueblo with two enclosed plaza areas located on a low mesa about 100 feet above the Rio Guadalupe and Rio Jemez. The site may be considered defensively located because of the rivers and its elevation. The small Spanish mission building and convento is located in the northwest corner of the pueblo and is integral to the overall plan. This part of the site was constructed mostly of red sandstone slabs. The mounds are quite high, suggesting three or more stories in many areas. Interestingly, there are two small kivas within the plazas, a large kiva near the older section, and two other large depressions, possibly kivas. These may date to earlier components. There are several smaller roomblocks, apparently single-story and constructed after the main part of the site, located outside the central core. I have estimated the total number of

rooms at Patokwa at about 600, including possible second- and third-story rooms (Elliott 1982:17). South of the main mounds of the site lies a large pueblo mound that dates to the Coalition period. South of that mound lies a site with large depressions indicating pithouses, and very early ceramics for this area, dating to circa A.D. 900.

Patokwa has suffered extensive bulldozer damage on the north-central part of the site. Here, a bulldozer made several cuts completely through the mounds, spreading the material over a wide area. Local legends relate that this activity was an attempt to locate a golden mission bell supposedly buried on the site by Spanish priests during the Pueblo Revolt of 1696. This same legend has been told about many seventeenth-century Spanish mission sites in New Mexico. The bulldozer damage dates to when the site was in private ownership. The Forest Service only acquired the land in the 1970s. A site map prepared in the 1930s shows a contiguous roomblock in that area. The State Register nomination form prepared in the 1960s shows the extent of the damage. There are numerous potholes in the mounds as well.

No authorized excavations have been conducted at Patokwa. The Museum of New Mexico has a surface collection made by various archaeologists in its "sherd drawers." In 1984, Rory Gauthier and I analyzed these artifacts in three two-by-two meter sample units on the site. In terms of ceramics, we noted a number of late varieties of Jemez Black-on-white, tradewares from Keres and Tewa villages, a few tradeware sherds from Acoma, and a few Spanish types, including San Luis Blue-on-white majolica (Elliott and Gauthier 1984).

Walatowa, San Diego de la Congregación, and San Juan de los Jemez

Walatowa (LA 8860) is the current Jemez pueblo, so a full exposition of its features and characteristics is beyond the scope of this paper. Nevertheless, a brief summary follows. Walatowa is located at an elevation of about 5,800 feet on the east side of the Rio Jemez a mile south of its confluence with the Rito Vallecitos. Little archaeological work has been done within the pueblo proper. Dodge (1982) describes monitoring done in association with excavation of a waterline trench. There appears to be little evidence of prehistoric components at Walatowa. A large Classic period pueblo, Setoqua (LA 499) lies about two miles south of Walatowa.

The core architecture of Walatowa consists of two plazas between three long roomblocks. We have a sketch of Walatowa by Richard Kern from 1846 (Weber 1987). We have various photos from the turn of the century. Elsie Parsons's (1925) ethnography contains photos and a sketch map of the pueblo (Figure 3.5). Parsons mentioned 143 houses and two kivas. It appears that little changed at Jemez between 1846 and 1925.

Immediately south of the central core of the pueblo lies the present San Diego Catholic Church and camposanto. To the west of the present church is a mound identified as an old church on both Parsons's (1925) map and on Sando's (1979) map of the pueblo. This could be either the mission known as San Diego de la Congregación, or San Juan de los Jemez.

I have already discussed the history of San Diego de la Congregación. The San Juan de los Jemez mission was probably built at Walatowa in late 1694 or early 1695 to minister to the Jemez from the refuge site of Boletsakwa, on the mesa now known as San Juan Mesa and abandoned after the Revolt of 1696.

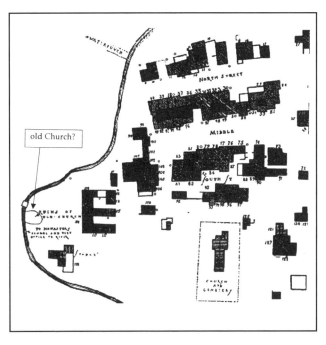

Figure 3.5. Parsons's (1925) sketch map of Jemez Pueblo (Walatowa).

Walatowa was reoccupied after 1703 (Bloom and Mitchell 1938:107). In 1706, a new church was built, with its advocacy changed to San Diego (Hackett 1937:376). This church was destroyed in 1709 (Salpointe 1898:93, cited in Kubler 1940:84). By 1744, a new church had been built (Hackett 1937:405). This was probably the church visited by Dominguez (Adams and Chávez 1956). Simpson visited the site in 1849 (MacNitt 1964). Kern's sketch of the site shows a mission building in about the same location as the present church, though it may have been rebuilt in 1856 (Lamy 1874:25, cited in Kubler 1940:85).

Astialakwa Pueblo

Astialakwa (LA 1825) is a complex, fortified habitation and refuge pueblo with numerous roomblocks, defensive walls, rock art, and agricultural features. The site is located on a high, detached mesa, or peñol, now called Guadalupe Mesa, about 800 feet above the surrounding countryside. The name of the site is disputed, but archaeologists and historians, at least, have agreed on the name Astialakwa. The meaning of the place name "Astialakwa" is obscure. Bloom (1931:162 n.5) translates the name as "place of the index finger" but does not provide a reference.

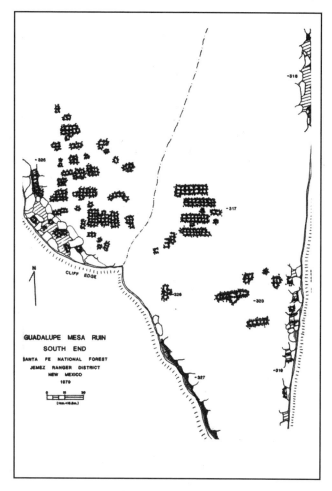

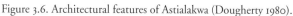

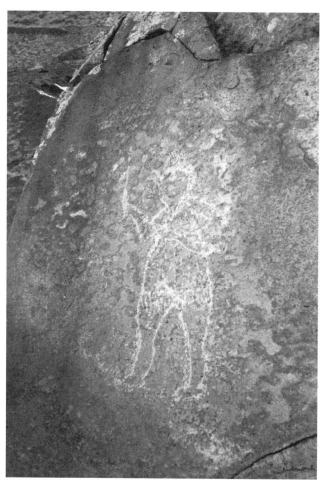

Figure 3.6. Architectural features of Astialakwa (Dougherty 1980).

Figure 3.7. Warrior petroglyph at Astialakwa.

Julia Dougherty (1980) surveyed the top of Guadalupe Mesa in 1979 (Figure 3.6). She recorded the site in groups of architectural and defensive features. Over the years, researchers have noted additional features of the site, including teepee rings to the north of the main architectural concentration, the trails, another defensive wall, and a near life-sized anthropomorphic "warrior" petroglyph (Figure 3.7), holding a bow in one hand and an arrow in the other.

The architectural features at Astialakwa are all single-story masonry construction. The building materials are shaped and unshaped tuff blocks. There are no plazas or subterranean kivas at Astialakwa. The walls of some structures are still standing to five feet or more. The masonry appears to have been hastily constructed. Many rooms have been constructed against cliffs or boulders in places where the cliffs have subsided several meters.

Defensive features at Astialakwa include several low walls or revetments on the southwest and east sides, and at the south and north ends of the mesa. The main trail to the mesatop from the southwest passes through a portcullis-like gap. A poignant reminder of the battles that were waged atop Guadalupe Mesa are piles of even-sized water-worn pebbles about two inches in diameter that most archaeologists have interpreted as slingstones. Vargas's journals mention being pelted with stones during a battle at Astialakwa (Kessell et al. 1998:372).

No authorized excavations have been conducted at Astialakwa. The only artifacts from the site known to lie in collections included two Tewa Polychrome vessels

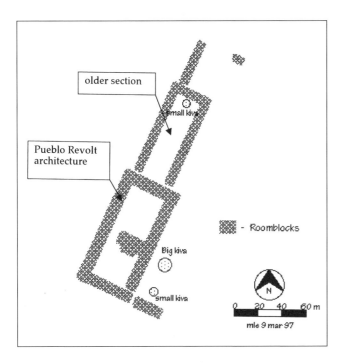

Figure 3.8. Sketch map of Boletsakwa.

illustrated by Mera (1939:58–61), and a Kotyiti Glaze Polychrome bowl in the Museum of New Mexico. The Laboratory of Anthropology type-sherd collection begun by Mera has various sherds collected from Astialakwa, probably by Mera. Rory Gauthier and I systematically analyzed these items in 1984 (Elliott and Gauthier 1984). Artifacts observed includes numerous late varieties of Jemez Black-on-white, a few late Rio Grande glazeware bowl and jar rims, a few tradewares such as Tewa Polychrome, Kapo Gray, and Sankawi Black-on-cream, and two rare forms, a glaze polychrome soup plate rim sherd, and a glazepaint rectangular tray rim sherd. The Santa Fe National Forest has some bags of unprovenienced and unanalyzed sherds, flakes, and other material confiscated from a pothunter.

Boletsakwa Pueblo

Boletsakwa (LA 136) is a complex, multicomponent site occupying a high mesa, part of what is now called San Juan Mesa, north of the village of Ponderosa. This isolated peñol is about 500 feet above the surrounding countryside. Boletsakwa means, "place of the abalone shell," in the Towa language (Bloom 1931). Assignment of

this name to this site is based on ethnographic and historic sources.

Boletsakwa proper consists of a series of low mounds and features dating to the late Coalition/early Classic period (A.D. 1250–1400) adjoining a large, twin-plaza pueblo (Figure 3.8) dating to the Pueblo Revolt period (A.D. 1680–1696). It appears that the builders of the Pueblo Revolt component may have salvaged building materials from the earlier component at the site, and also possibly from LA 135 which lies about 200 meters northeast of Boletsakwa, and also dates to the late Coalition/early Classic period (A.D. 1250–1400). The architectural features at both early sites are highly reduced and exhibit few building stones on the surface.

In addition to the habitation features Boletsakwa exhibits a large, well constructed Rio Grande–style big kiva just to the east of the Pueblo Revolt architecture. A smaller depression, a probable plaza kiva, is located within the earlier architecture at the north end of the site. Another large depression is located just south of the big kiva, which may have been a reservoir. Between LA 135 and LA 136 is another large depression that is likely a reservoir. A few hundred meters south of LA 136 lies a large dam enclosing another reservoir. Near this feature is a small structure, or fieldhouse.

Near the mesa rims on both the southeast and northwest sides are some low walls, possibly defensive. These walls are located near where the two trails that currently lead up to the mesatop emerge on top. There is also a third trail from the north. LA 135 lies on the extreme northeast end of the mesa, and is highly defensive in appearance. Two sides of the triangular-shaped site are sheer cliffs about 40 feet high. The third side of the site is sealed off from the rest of the mesa by a broad wall that is still a meter high. The mesa is also the site of significant concentration of rock art. Lance Trask (1991) has recorded a number of rock art panels. Among other interesting features are numerous bedrock grinding facets on some hard rhyolitic tuff rock near the mesa rims (Figure 3.9). Literally hundreds of grinding facets can be seen.

H. P. Mera of the Laboratory of Anthropology recorded

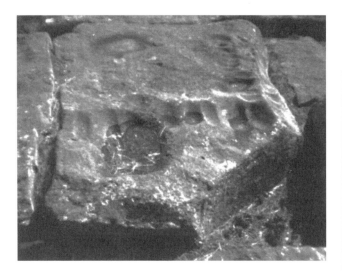

Figure 3.9. Bedrock grinding feature at Boletsakwa.

Table 3.1. Tree-ring Dates from Boletsakwa
(Robinson et al. 1972).

Cat no	Date
RG-379	1492p-1656v
RG-766	1472p-1663v
RG-764	1621p-1680v
RG-763	1646-1680v
RG-765	1647v-1680cG
RG-768	1641p-1681vv
RG-757	1650v-1681r
RG-758	1650p-1682vv
RG-758	1628p-1683v
RG-767	1647p-1683v
RG-758	1658p-1683v
RG-758	1653p-1683r
RG-758	1650p-1683r

The letters after the dates mean:

year alone - no pith ring present
p - pith ring present
v - subjectively near a cutting date
vv - no way of determining actual cutting date
c - outermost ring is continuous around the entire section
G - beetle galleries present
r - outermost ring is not continuous around the entire section

Boletsakwa in the 1930s. He drew a site map, and collected and analyzed ceramics and other artifacts. In the 1930s Benny Hyde and W. S. Stallings, Jr., most likely collected tree-ring samples at the site (Table 3.1). During the 1960s, Girl Scouts from the Eliza Seligman Camp conducted a series of reconnaissance surveys and small-scale excavations in the Jemez area. In 1968, the so-called Girl Scout Archaeological Unit conducted some excavations at LA 136, near the big kiva. Among the more interesting artifacts recovered was a human figurine (Bohrer 1968). Rory Gauthier's and my 1984 analysis of the potsherds in the Laboratory of Anthropology sherd drawers revealed three components, two prehistoric components and a historic component dating to the Pueblo Revolt era.

A History of Thought on the Jemez Missions

There have been three periods of activity in the quest to identify the known mission ruins with their contemporaneous names and the events known to have occurred at them. The earliest attempt was by Adolph Bandelier in his "Final Report" (1892), and in his journals (Lange et al. 1975, 1984). Bandelier's identifications were canonical until the 1920s and 1930s. Three researchers, Lansing Bloom (1922, 1931, 1938) France Scholes (1938), and George Kubler (1936, 1940) published revised mission identifications, all in essential agreement with each other. The work of these

men centered on the interpretations of the Salmerón Relaciones and the two Memorials of Benavides. These identifications are now widely accepted, and are routinely quoted by such Jemez researchers such as Reiter (1938), Ellis (1956), and the author (Elliott 1993).

Several events occurred in the 1990s that have provided new opportunities for reassessment. The first event was the publication of a master's thesis by Robin Farwell in 1991 on the mission at Giusewa. She reviewed documents, archaeological remains from excavations at Giusewa, and architectural details of the mission. She was uncomfortable with the identification of Walatowa as the site of San Diego de la Congregación and suggested that the Giusewa mission could have been both San José and San Diego de la Congregación. Her reasons were the presence of Glaze F pottery at Giusewa, the location of the baptistery outside the entry of the church, and the size and scale of the building itself (Farwell 1991:118–119).

The second event was a research project organized by

Table 3.2. Jemez Mission Identifications
through the Years.

Source	San Jose de los Jemez	San Diego de la Congregación	San Diego del Monte	San Juan de los Jemez
Bandelier 1892	LA 481	LA679		LA 96
Holmes 1905		LA679		LA 96
Hodge 1907-10	LA 96	LA679		LA 1825 / LA 481
Harrington 1916	LA 96	LA679		LA 1825
Bloom 1931		LA679		LA 96
Kubler 1936-40	LA679	LA 8860	LA 96	LA 8860
Bloom and M 1938	LA679	LA 8860	LA 96	LA 8860
Scholes 1938	LA679	LA 8860	LA 96	LA 8860
Reiter 1938	LA679	LA 8860	LA 96	LA 8860
Farwell 1991	LA679	LA679	LA 96	LA 8860
Elliott (2001, infra)	LA679	LA 8860	LA 96	LA 8860

by New Mexico State Monuments and funded by the Museum of New Mexico Foundation on the history of Giusewa, Jemez State Monument. This resulted in the publication of a short, general report on the site (Elliott 1993), and the preparation of a much more detailed "professional" report (Elliott 1991). The final event was the publication of the Diego de Vargas journals in a multivolume series edited by John Kessell, Rick Hendricks, and Meredith Dodge. The availability of the thousands of pages of documents translated into English is invaluable in the present analysis. I have summarized the various attempted identifications of the locations of the Jemez missions in Table 3.2.

Previous Mission Identifications

Although early visitors such as Lt. James Simpson (MacNitt 1964), in 1846, and Oscar Loew, in 1875, mentioned Jemez mission ruins, Bandelier was the first to assign mission names to specific sites. He identified Giusewa as San Diego de Jemez. "In the bottom (of Jemez Canyon) lie the ruins of the old pueblo of Gin-se-ua, with stately old church of San Diego de Jemez (Bandelier 1892:204)." The ruin now called Giusewa in Jemez Springs is LA 679. He also identifies Amoxiumqua as San Joseph de los Jemez. "As to San Joseph de los Jemez I incline to the belief, as above stated, that it was Amoxiumqua" (Bandelier 1892:205 n.1). Although there

is some controversy about which Jemez ruin was actually called Amoxiumqua, a map in his journals clearly confirms that Bandelier considered LA 481 as Amoxiumqua (Lange et al. 1984:164). He identified Patokwa as the location of San Juan de los Jemez. He writes, " . . . I incline to the belief that a village of which the ruins are visible on the delta formed by the junction of the San Diego (Rio Jemez) and Guadalupe, was San Juan de los Jemez" (1892:208). Later researchers, such as Holmes (1905), Hodge (1907–1910), and Harrington (1916) generally relied on Bandelier's identifications, with some variations. Even Lansing Bloom and France Scholes accepted Bandelier's mission identifications in their earlier work. However, Lansing Bloom (1922:25) questioned how the mission at Giusewa could be San Diego as early as 1922.

There are three basic problems with Bandelier's identifications. First, he made only two short trips to Jemez Pueblo, in 1887 and 1891. It appears that he did not visit many of the sites. Second, there is no mission building evident at Amoxiumqua. Unreported excavations there during 1911–1914 revealed no trace of a mission (Chapman 1911; Reiter 1938). Finally, as Kubler (1936, 1940), Bloom (1938), and Scholes (1938) point out, the Benavides Memorials (1630, 1634) mention two early Jemez missions, San José de los Jemez, and San Diego de la Congregación. Of the two, San José was very spacious and *"curiosa."* San Diego de la Congregación was a newly founded *pueblo de reducción.* Giusewa appears to have been occupied before the mission was built (Elliott 1993), and thus was not newly founded when the two missions were built in the 1620s. Giusewa was probably one of the three so-called *"Aguas Calientes"* pueblos mentioned by Coronado's lieutenant Barrionuevo in 1541 (Hammond and Rey 1940). The mission at Giusewa certainly fits the description of spaciousness and unusual design with its large nave and unique octagonal bell-tower.

The Hodge (1907) and Harrington (1916) identifications of Astialakwa as the site of San Juan de los Jemez suffer from the same problem as Bandelier's identification of Amoxiumqua as the site of San José. There simply is no no mission building evident at Astialakwa. Later descriptive references and events at Astialakwa, notably the battle there on July 24, 1694, almost certainly rule it out as a mission site.

The Kubler-Bloom-Scholes identifications all agree. They place San José at Giusewa, San Diego de la Congregación at Walatowa, San Diego del Monte at Patokwa, and finally, San Juan de los Jemez at Walatowa. A recent analysis of the relevant documents, architecture, and archaeology at Giusewa (Farwell 1991) confirms the identification of the mission at Giusewa as San José. I agreed with these conclusions in my reports on Giusewa in 1991 and 1993, and have seen nothing since then to contradict this notion.

The previously cited evidence from the Benavides Memorials appears to place San José securely at Giusewa, but what about San Diego? Researchers distinguish two San Diegos because of the Benavides Memorials, passages in Vargas's journals, and their interpretations of distance data in the journals. Certain critical passages in Vargas's journals confirm this framework, though some problems remain.

Testing the Kubler-Bloom-Scholes Thesis

One of the primary lines of evidence for identifying the post-Revolt Jemez missions has been the distances between various sites as discussed by Vargas. Some of the documents provide distances, in leagues, a variable unit approximately 2.6 miles, or 4.2 kilometers. The biggest problem in identifying Jemez Revolt-era sites is knowing from which village Vargas departs. Usually, he describes distances to the various Jemez sites from Zia. But which Zia village, at what time period, and to which of the four main villages that the Jemez people occupied during the Revolt era did he travel?

The Zia people occupied at least two villages after the Pueblo Revolt, the village they now occupy (LA 28) and the Cerro Colorado Pueblo (LA 2048). They apparently were living at LA 28 in 1689 when Governor Domingo Jirónza Petríz de Cruzate mounted a punitive expedition against them from the Spanish capital in exile in the El Paso/Juarez area. In one of the most egregious of the

Pueblo Revolt–era atrocities, Cruzate destroyed Zia Pueblo in a bloody battle, and burned it. He killed 600 Zias and captured 70, carrying them off to El Paso del Norte for 10 years of virtual slavery. History does not record whether any of them ever returned. After suffering the crushing blow of Governor Jirónza, the Zia apparently moved to Cerro Colorado.

There is little archaeological information about Cerro Colorado, now located on the Jemez tribal lands. Bandelier mentions the Jemez name for the site was Tutiqua (Lange et al. 1984:164). The site was first recorded by Holmes (1905). He described the site as three groups of buildings, irregular in plan. The walls were five to six feet in height. Holmes remarked on the lack of pottery and other refuse. He mentions the presence of "bits of porcelain," perhaps majolica. He described defensive walls along the edges of the mesa. His map is still the only one available for the site. Ellis revisited the site in the 1950s for the Zia land claim. She describes the layout of the site much as Holmes did, remarking on the "pathway on which wall barricades still may be seen" (Ellis 1956:32) on the west side of the mesa leading down to a spring. "Watch stations" guarded the steeper east side. Each plaza held active shrines of rocks outlining the Zia sun symbol. Ellis found a fragment of a seventeenth-century Spanish olive jar (Ellis 1956:33).

It appears from the historical and archaeological record that Zia occupied Cerro Colorado from 1689 until late 1693 or early 1694. Distances from "Zia" or "Zia Pueblo" mentioned in the Vargas journals during this period must therefore be calculated from that site.

The Jemez people occupied at least four main villages during the Revolt era. Most of the Jemez lived at Walatowa (LA 6680) when the Revolt of 1680 occurred. After the 1680 Revolt, they apparently moved to two villages, Patokwa (LA 96), and Boletsakwa (LA 136). They shared the latter village with Santo Domingo refugees. When Vargas arrived, the Jemez of Patokwa moved up to Astialakwa (LA 1825).

I have summarized the distances cited in the Vargas journals, proposed the sites for the departures and

Table 3.3. Distance Data Cited in the Vargas Journals.

date	from	likely site	to	likely dest	dist cited	actual dist	walking dist	ref
10/23/1692	abandoned Zia Pueblo	LA 28	Cerro Colorado Pueblo	LA 2048	3.00	3.00	3.60	RCR 201
10/24/1692	abandoned Zia Pueblo	LA 28	Cerro Colorado Pueblo	LA 2048	4.00	3.00	3.60	BFA 518
10/24/1692	Cerro Colorado Pueblo	LA 2048	old Jemez Pueblo	LA 8860	2.00	0.80	1.20	BFA 520
10/25/1692	near old Jemez Pueblo	LA 8860	Jemez Pueblo on the high mesas	LA 96	3.00	1.70	1.90	BFA 520
10/25/1692	near old Jemez Pueblo	LA 8860	Jemez Pueblo on the high mesas and return	LA 96	6.00	3.40	3.80	BFA 523
10/25/1692	riverbank near Cerro Colorado	LA 8860	mesas of the Jemez canada	LA 96	3.00	1.70	1.90	RCR 201
10/25/1692	Jemez Pueblo on the high mesas	LA 96	abandoned Jemez Pueblo	LA 8860	3.00	1.70	1.90	RCR 203
10/26/1692	near abandoned Jemez Pueblo	LA 8860	abandoned Santa Ana Pueblo	LA 8975	7.00	5.90	6.70	BFA 523
11/24/1693	abandoned Zia Pueblo	LA 28	Cerro Colorado Pueblo	LA 2048	3.00	3.00	3.60	RCR 429
11/25/1693	occupied Santa Ana	LA 8975	where the C. Colorado rises	LA 2048	5.00	5.00	6.00	RCR 434
11/25/1693	Santa Ana?	LA 8975	abandoned Jemez Pueblo	LA 8860	6.00	6.80	8.10	RCR 436
11/26/1693	abandoned Jemez Pueblo	LA 8860	Jemez Pueblo on the mesa of canada (round trip)	LA 96	4.00	3.40	3.80	RCR 442
11/27/1693	abandoned Jemez Pueblo	LA 8860	abandoned Zia Pueblo	LA 28	3.00	2.90	3.40	RCR 446
07/23/1694	mesa of pueblo Jemez abandoned	LA 96	trail at back of peñol	LA 1825	>1.0	0.90	1.10	BB 323
07/24/1694	abandoned Jemez Pueblo	LA 96	path up the peñol	LA 1825	<1.0	0.50	0.50	BB 324
07/24/1694	peñol of the Jemez	LA 1825	S Domingos on the mesa	LA 136	3.00	2.30	2.80	BB 328
07/26/1694	peñol of the Jemez	LA 1825	next mesa where SD were	LA 136	3.00	2.30	2.80	BB 332
08/03/1694	old pueblo that rebels left	LA 8860	this mesa (Patokwa?)	LA 96	1.50	1.70	1.90	BB 338
08/04/1694	mesa of the Jemez	LA 96	Boletsakwa?	LA 136	8.00	6.70	8.00	BB 339
08/05/1694	mesa of the Jemez	LA 96	within sight of	LA 8860	>1.0	1.00	1.00	BB 340
08/11/1694	pueblo of the Jemez	LA 8860	peñol	LA 1825	>3.0	2.10	2.90	BB 346
09/01/1694	Zia, LA 28	LA 28	low spot near peñol of the Jemez	LA 1825	3.00	4.00	5.00	BB 367
09/01/1694	pueblo on the mesa	LA 96	pueblo on the peñol	LA 1825	1.0+	0.50	0.60	BB 367
09/01/1694	pueblo on the mesa	LA 96	pueblo on San Juan mesa	LA 136	3.00	2.40	2.70	BB 372
03/14/1694	Zia	LA 28	San Juan dlj	LA 8860	2.00	2.90	3.50	BB 685
03/14/1694	Zia	LA 28	San Diego dm	LA 96	4.00	4.60	5.40	BB 686

LA 2048=Cerro Colorado; LA 96=Patokwa; LA 8860=Walatowa; LA 1825=Astialakwa; LA 136=Boletsakwa, LA 28=Zia; LA 8975=Santa Ana
BFA=Kessell and Hendricks 1992, RCR=Kessell et al. 1995, BB=Kessell et al. 1998

destinations, and compiled a GIS-derived list of distances to and from the sites mentioned in this chapter (Table 3.3). I recorded two distances; (1) straight line distance, and (2) a speculative, reconstructed walking distance. Per Kessell, I used 4.2 kilometers per league as a conversion factor.

I have based my conjectured departure and destination sites on certain key descriptive phrases Vargas uses to discuss these sites and on the distances and directions and the descriptions of the sites. For example, when he refers to the pueblo of the Jemez on the mesa, or high mesas, or the mesas of the cañada, he seems to mean Patokwa. I base my interpretation on how Vargas describes the pueblo. He writes, "I saw that it has two plazas, one with an entrance that leads to the other . . . and each with four cuarteles" (Kessell et al. 1998:520). Although Vargas describes ascent as "very difficult" (Kessell et al. 1998:519),

he also states that he ascended the cuesta on horseback (Kessell et al. 1998:520). I do not believe that it is physically possible for a horse with a rider to reach the top of Guadalupe Mesa because of the steepness of the trail and the narrowness of the opening to the top. Patokwa lies on a low mesa about 100 feet higher than the river. Boletsakwa also has two plazas, but is too far from Cerro Colorado to be this mesa site. Vargas later states, "they asked me to come up to a second-story room to eat" (Kessell et al. 1998:522). None of the rooms at Astialakwa appears to have had a second-story. Patokwa was obviously two or more stories high.

When he refers to the pueblo of the Jemez on the peñol, he seems to mean Astialakwa. The term peñol is also used to describe the locations of Acoma and Zuni. Boletsakwa could be considered as lying on a peñol, but it does not meet other descriptions of the location, such as the proximity to Patokwa, and the location of the two trails Vargas uses to attack on July 24, 1694.

Vargas seems to be referring to Patokwa and Walatowa when describing the abandoned pueblo of the Jemez. From his description, it appears that Patokwa was deserted by late 1693 or early 1694, leaving one with the impression that Patokwa is abandoned when he is discussing Astialakwa. However, this is one of his most difficult references to interpret. He is certainly referring to Walatowa when he discusses "the old pueblo of the Jemez." Vargas's reference to Walatowa when he visits there to recover the bones of Fray Juan de Jesús, martyred there in 1680 (Kessell et al. 1998:342), helps firm up this identification. The reference to the locations of San Juan de los Jemez, and San Diego del Monte relative to Zia (Kessell et al. 1998:685), certainly seems to confirm the location of San Juan de los Jemez at Walatowa, and San Diego del Monte at Patokwa.

When he refers to the pueblo on the mesa of San Juan or the pueblo occupied by both Jemez and Santo Domingo natives, he means Boletsakwa. Vargas and his lieutenants visited this area several times. He seems to have first gone to the site after the battle at Astialakwa, on August 4, 1694, to look for corn hidden in small caves, or *coscomates,* that a prisoner had told him about (Kessell et al. 1998:339). Vargas later describes the abandoned site as "a strong pueblo with a plaza that has four house blocks" (Kessell et al. 1998:372). This does not perfectly match Boletsakwa, which now has two plazas, but no other pueblo in this area is quite like what Vargas describes either.

Summary and Conclusions

The Jemez people were active participants in the revolts of 1680 and 1696. They exhibited an unusually high degree of residential mobility during this period, moving their villages several times. They even appear to have briefly abandoned their homeland after the 1696 Revolt. However, by 1703, they had returned and began building their current pueblo and mission at Walatowa. The newly retranslated Vargas journals by the University of New Mexico Vargas Project provide a very useful tool for testing previous mission identifications and establishing the locations of the villages visited by Vargas.

The distances cited by Vargas seem to be relatively accurate, although they are usually less than the actual distances, even the direct measures. The margin of error is easily explainable by variations in actual routes or differences in travel times caused by weather, or other factors. I believe that the distance data confirm the basic elements of the Kubler-Bloom-Scholes mission interpretations. Table 3.4 summarizes my interpretation of the available data on the mission names, other Revolt-era pueblos, locations, and dates in the Jemez area.

Table 3.4. Mission and Pueblo
Locations and Dates in the Jemez Area.

Mission/Jemez Name	LA no.	begin	end	begin	end
San Jose de los Jemez/Giusewa**	LA 679	1598	1601	1621	by 1639
San Diego de la Congregación/Walatow	LA 8860	1621	1623	1626	after 1680
San Diego del Monte/Patokwa**	LA 96	after 1680	1694	1694	1696
San Juan de los Jemez/Walatowa	LA 8860	1694	1696		
San Diego/Walatowa	LA 8860	1703	present*		
Astialakwa**	LA 1825	1693	1694	1696	1696
Boletsakwa**	LA 136	1683	1695		

*the present church has been rebuilt several times
**the pueblos have longer occupations than the mission dates indicate

My interpretation of the Vargas journals has refined, more than replaced, the standard view of the movements of the Jemez people during the Pueblo Revolt era. An important result has been the identification of Boletsakwa as the refuge pueblo occupied for a time by both Jemez and Santo Domingo people. The tree-ring data, the distance data, and actual description of the site in the Vargas journals seem to leave no other interpretation. While I am less comfortable with my conclusion that the Jemez were living at Patokwa when Vargas first entered New Mexico, the journal references, when considered in toto, seem to provide no other alternative. Perhaps tree-ring dates or other information will become available to help test this idea.

The events of the Pueblo Revolt era had a profound effect upon the Jemez people. They lost many warriors in a valiant attempt to preserve their freedom and culture. The result of their defeat by the Spaniards was subjugation and religious indoctrination. That they have survived into the present with so much of their culture intact is a testimony to the strength and persistence of their beliefs.

References Cited

Adams, Eleanor B., and Fray Angélico Chávez
1956   *The Missions of New Mexico, 1776: A Description by Francisco Atanasio Dominguez, with Other Contemporary Documents.* University of New Mexico Press, Albuquerque.

Ayers, Mrs. Edward E. (translator)
1965   [1916] *The Memorial of Fray Alonso de Benavides, 1630.* Horn and Wallace, Albuquerque.

Bandelier, Adolph F. A.
1892   *Final Report of Investigations among the Indians of the Southwestern United States, Carried on Mainly in the Years from 1880 to 1885. Part II. Papers of the Archaeological Institute of America, American Series,* Vol. IV. University Press, Cambridge, Mass.

Bloom, Lansing B.
1922   The West Jemez Culture Area. *El Palacio* 12:18–25.
1923   The Jemez Expedition of the School. *El Palacio* 14:14–20.
1931   A Campaign Against the Moqui Pueblos Under Governor Phelix Martinez, 1716. *New Mexico Historical Review* 6:158–226.

Bloom, Lansing B., and Lynn Mitchell
1938   The Chapter Elections in 1672. *New Mexico Historical Review* 13:85–119.

Bohrer, Vorsila L.
1968   Girl Scout Archaeology Unit. Ms. on file, Laboratory of Anthropology Archives, Santa Fe.

Chapman, Kenneth M.
1911   Notes on the Burial Mounds and Rooms, Amoxiumqua. Ms. on file, Maxwell Museum Archives, University of New Mexico, Albuquerque.

Dodge, William
1982   *Archeological Investigations at Jemez Pueblo, New Mexico: The Monitoring of Indian Health Service Waterline Trenches.* Office of Contract Archeology, University of New Mexico, Albuquerque.

Dougherty, Julia D.
1980   Refugee Pueblos on the Santa Fe National Forest. *Cultural Resources Document No. 1.* Santa Fe National Forest. Santa Fe.

Elliott, Michael L.
1982   Large Pueblo Sites near Jemez Springs, New Mexico. *Cultural Resources Document No. 3.* Santa Fe National Forest, Santa Fe.
1991   Pueblo at the Hot Place. Ms. on file, New Mexico State Monuments, Santa Fe.
1993   *Jemez.* Museum of New Mexico Press, Santa Fe.

Elliott, Michael L., and Rory P. Gauthier
1984   Analysis of Jemez Materials in the Sherd Drawers of the Laboratory of Anthropology. Manuscript in possession of the author.

Ellis, Florence Hawley
1956   Anthropological Evidence Supporting the Claims of the Pueblos of Zia, Santa Ana, and Jemez. Ms. on file, University of New Mexico, Department of Anthropology, Clark Field Archive.

Espinosa, J. Manuel (editor and translator)
1988   *The Pueblo Indian Revolt of 1696 and the Franciscan Missions in New Mexico: Letters of the Missionaries and Related Documents.* University of Oklahoma Press, Norman.

Farwell, Robin Elizabeth
1991   An Architectural History of the Seventeenth-Century Mission Church of San Jose de Giusewa, Jemez State Monument, New Mexico. Unpublished Master's thesis, Department of Art History, University of New Mexico, Albuquerque.

Hackett, Charles W. (editor)
1937   *Historical Documents Relating to New Mexico, Nueva Vizcaya, and Approaches Thereto, to 1773.* Carnegie Institution, Washington, D.C.

Hackett, Charles W., and Charmion C. Shelby (editor and translator)
1942   *Revolt of the Pueblo Indians of New Mexico and Otermin's Attempted Reconquest 1680–1682.* Coronado Cuarto Centennial Publications, 1540–1949. 2 Vols. University of New Mexico Press, Albuquerque.

Hammond, George P, and Agapito Rey
1940   *Narratives of the Coronado Expedition.* University of New Mexico Press, Albuquerque.
1966   *The Rediscovery of New Mexico.* University of New Mexico Press, Albuquerque.

Harrington, John P.
1916   The Ethnogeography of the Tewa Indians. *Twenty-ninth Annual Report of the Bureau of American Ethnology for the Years 1907–1908.* Washington, D.C.

Hodge, Frederick Webb
1918   Administrative report. *Thirty-second Annual Report of the Bureau of American Ethnology for the Years 1910–1911.* Washington, D.C.

Hodge, Frederick Webb (editor)
1907–1910 Handbook of American Indians north of Mexico. 2 Vols. *Bureau of American Ethnology Bulletin* 30. Washington, D.C.

Hodge, Frederick Webb, George P. Hammond, and Agapito Rey, editors)
1945   *Fray Alonso de Benavides' Revised Memorial of 1634.* University of New Mexico Press, Albuquerque.

Holmes, William H.
1905   Notes on the Antiquities of the Jemez Valley, New Mexico. *American Anthropologist* 7:198–212.

Kessell, John L., and Rick Hendricks (editors)
1992   *By Force of Arms: The Journals of Don Diego de Vargas, New Mexico, 1691–1693.* University of New Mexico Press, Albuquerque.

Kessell, John L., Rick Hendricks, and Meredith D. Dodge (editors)
1995   *To the Royal Crown Restored: The Journals of Don Diego de Vargas, New Mexico, 1692–1694.* University of New Mexico Press, Albuquerque.
1998   *Blood on the Boulders: The Journals of Don Diego de Vargas, New Mexico, 1694–97.* 2 Vols. University of New Mexico Press, Albuquerque.

Kubler, George

1936   A Critical Study of the Religious Architecture of New
        Mexico. Unpublished Master's thesis, Yale University, New
        Haven.

1940   *The Religious Architecture of New Mexico.* The Taylor Museum,
        Colorado Springs, Colorado.

Lamy, J. B.

1874   Short History of the Pueblo Indians of New Mexico, sent
        to General C. Ewing by the Bishop of Santa Fe, February 25,
        1874. Ms. on file, Archives of the Archdiocese of Santa Fe.

Lange, Charles H., Carroll L. Riley, and Elizabeth M. Lange (editors)

1975   *The Southwestern Journals of Adolph F. Bandelier:
        1885–1888.* The University of New Mexico Press,
        Albuquerque, and the School of American Research,
        Santa Fe.

1984   *The Southwestern Journals of Adolph F. Bandelier:
        1889–1892.* The University of New Mexico Press,
        Albuquerque, and the School of American Research,
        Santa Fe.

McNitt, Frank

1964   *Navajo Expedition: Journal of a Military Reconnaissance
        from Santa Fe, New Mexico, to the Navajo Country in 1849
        made by Lieutenant James H. Simpson.* University of
        Oklahoma Press, Norman.

Mera, H. P.

1939   *Style Trends of Pueblo Pottery 1500–1840.* Memoirs of the
        Laboratory of Anthropology No. 3. Santa Fe.

Milich, Alicia R. (translator)

1966   *Relaciones: An Account of Things Seen and Learned by Father
        Jeronimo de Zarate Salmeron from the Year 1538 to the Year
        1626.* Horn and Wallace, Albuquerque.

Parsons, Elsie Clews

1925   The Pueblo of Jemez. *Papers of the Phillips Academy
        Southwestern Expedition* 3. Yale University Press, New
        Haven, Conn.

Reiter, Paul

1938   The Jemez Pueblo of Unshagi, New Mexico, with Notes
        on the Earlier Excavations at "Amoxiumqua" and Giusewa.
        The University of New Mexico Bulletin, Monograph Series
        1:4., 3:3.

Robinson, William J., John W. Hannah, and Bruce G. Harrill

1972   *Tree-ring Dates from New Mexico, I, O, U: Central Rio
        Grande Area.* Laboratory of Tree-Ring Research, University
        of Arizona, Tucson.

Salpointe, Rev. J. B.

1898   Soldiers of the Cross: Notes on the Ecclesiastical History
        of New Mexico, Arizona, and Colorado. Banning, Calif.

Sando, Joe S.

1979   Jemez Pueblo. In *Handbook of North American Indians,
        Vol. 9, Southwest,* edited by Alfonso Ortiz, pp. 418–429.
        Smithsonian Institution, Washington, D.C.

1982   *Nee Hemish: A History of Jemez Pueblo.* University of New
        Mexico Press, Albuquerque.

Scholes, France V.

1937   *Church and State in New Mexico, 1610–1650.* Historical
        Society of New Mexico, Publications in History VII,
        Albuquerque.

1938   Notes on the Jemez Missions in the Seventeenth Century.
        El Palacio 44:61–71, 93–102.

1942   *Troublous Times in New Mexico, 1659–1670.* Historical
        Society of New Mexico, Publications in History IX,
        Albuquerque.

Trask, Lance K.

1991   Ancient Billboards: The Rock Art of the Lower Jemez
        Mountains, Santa Fe National Forest, Jemez Ranger
        District, Paliza. Ms. on file, Heritage Resources Report
        1991-10-049, Santa Fe National Forest.

Weber, David J.

1987   *Richard H. Kern: Expeditionary Artist in the Far Southwest,
        1848–1853.* Published for the Amon Carter Museum by
        the University of New Mexico Press, Albuquerque.

Chapter 4

Transformations of Place:
Occupational History and Differential Persistence in Seventeenth-Century New Mexico

Mark T. Lycett

Introduction

Even at a time when the concept of community is undergoing significant theoretical and methodological resurgence in Southwestern archaeology (e.g., Kolb and Snead 1997; Varien 1999; Wills and Leonard 1994), the dynamics of seventeenth-century community formation and transformation remain problematic. What is the relationship between community and place? How is it mediated by colonial institutions, power relations, and the emergent political ecology of the New Mexico colony?

The documentary record suggests a number of intriguing possibilities. Within nine months of colonization, Oñate laid siege to the Pueblo of Acoma, killing hundreds of inhabitants, razing and burning the village, and sentencing more than 500 prisoners to mutilation and servitude (Encinas et al. 1992; Hammond and Rey 1953). Yet, by 1629, Acoma had sufficient population to draw a hopeful Franciscan (Scholes and Bloom 1944–45) and by 1652, a new pueblo had been constructed on the site of the original (Robinson 1990). While clearly in the same location, was this newly constructed place the same community?

During the bloodless prelude to his bloody reconquest of 1692, Diego de Vargas found the erstwhile community of Galisteo relocated to the Plaza at Santa Fe (Kessell and Hendricks 1992). Was this a persistent community in a new place?

In 1706, Francisco Cuervo y Valdés, Vargas's successor, resettled 18 Tano-speaking families from Tesuque at the original site of Santa Cruz de Galisteo, re-christening it Santa María de Gracia (Hackett 1937:380). Like the Pueblos of Pojoaque, Alameda, Isleta, and Sandia, what ties this eighteenth-century settlement to its seventeenth-century namesake?

None of these cases is unique. The period between 1680 and 1696, traditionally referred to as the Pueblo Revolt(s) (Espinosa 1988; Hackett and Shelby 1942), and more recently as the Pueblo-Spanish war (Kessell 1989), witnessed historically unprecedented displacement, disruption, and realignment of Pueblo settlement and augured the beginnings of an eighteenth-century Spanish colony that would redefine the socio-economic matrix and spatial scale of the Pueblo world. Once populous and central settlement clusters lying south and east of Santa Fe were abandoned: Pueblo populations reestablished themselves in former colonial settlements; refugee settlements, themselves amalgams of previously occupied villages, were constructed in defensible locales (e.g., Ferguson 1996; Snead and Preucel 1999); other refugees fled to the Hopi Mesas, or the plains; still other Pueblos were forcibly resettled within the remnant Spanish colony at El Paso. Neither the number nor distribution of Pueblo villages would stabilize until after 1706.

The events of August 1680, and the de-coupling of population, community, place, and location that follow, should not obscure the processes attendant on more than a century of colonial conquest, incorporation, and subjugation. In fact, residential instability had been a consistent feature of the Colonial period in New Mexico, as fewer and less populous Pueblo settlements occupied a smaller overall area (Herr and Clark 1997; Lycett 1995; Schroeder 1979). By the mid-seventeenth century, missionized places had become the focus of settlement, incorporating a declining indigenous population into novel systems of production centered on European crops and domestic animals, new technology, and emerging exchange networks. Despite Spanish efforts to maintain frontier missions, many demographically and geographically marginal communities collapsed by the second half of the seventeenth century, their populations becoming incorporated into larger and more central settlements that survived long enough to become objects of historic and ethnographic inquiry. These emergent communities, however, cannot be characterized as wholly indigenous nor wholly colonial, but as transformed places, entailing both continuity and discontinuity.

In ethnographic writing in general and in the northern Southwest in particular, indigenous communities have often been cast as natural empirical and analytical units, rather than as situational and contextual outcomes of historical process (Fabian 1983; Thomas 1989; Wolf 1984). This distinction may be of particular importance in colonial contexts where the power to create group definitions and even definitions of what can constitute a group are shaped by power relations (cf. Williams 1992). To the extent that the differential persistence of communities and places is central to understanding social and spatial transformation, then the occupational history of place and its relationship to collective identity are clearly at issue.

Intensively occupied residential locales have complex and cumulative histories of construction, maintenance, abandonment, and reuse. Architectural and depositional patterns in these contexts are strongly influenced by demographic variables as well as duration of occupation, periodicity of reoccupation, and post-occupational modification (Adams 1983; Cameron 1991, 1992; Cameron and Tomka 1993; Ferguson and Mills 1987). Both demographic and social disruptions of the Colonial period should influence the structure of residential space. As local populations shift, complex patterns of occupied, unoccupied but maintained, and un-maintained architectural space may develop. The forms these patterns take may implicate the scale, tempo, and history of changing place use. Occupational history is key to questions of how residential places were used and transformed through their use.

How, then, do we move from an archaeology of place (Binford 1982), to an understanding of place-making (Basso 1996)? Perhaps one avenue to explore is the framework of historical ecology that views space as,

" . . . a contingent product, a sediment of human practice, a construction in the material and not merely semantic sense of that word—in short, an artifact" (Biersack 1999:9). Environments, at any scale, are produced through the ongoing dialectical engagement of human agents with the social and natural world, anthropogenesis is perpetual, and the landscape is shaped and constrained by past practices (Crumley 1994; Ingold 1993). Such a perspective is congruent with an understanding of archaeological patterning as the cumulative and historical product of natural and human processes operating at a variety of temporal and spatial scales (Wandsnider 1998). As such, the history of places and their changing role in a larger cultural geography, have the potential to not only inform on the substantive past but to index social memory (Alcock 2001) and invoke historical meanings (Basso 1996).

Community, Mission, Place

The concept of community has been employed by archaeologists to define theoretical, analytical, and even observational units. Several scholars have recently discussed the intellectual history of this concept and its application in Americanist archaeology (Kolb and Snead 1997; Thomas 1998; Varien 1999; Wills and Leonard 1994). While it is beyond the scope of this discussion to review these applications in any detail, it may be useful to briefly discuss four senses in which community has been deployed in the anthropological literature. These need not be mutually exclusive definitions so much as matters of emphasis.

The first of these is as a frequently idealized primitive condition that may be counterpoised to modern society within an evolutionary framework. In this sense, the opposition of community (*Gemeinschaft*) and society (*Gesellschaft*) (Tönnies 1957) is only another example of the many social schemas tracing the movement from the ancient and primitive to the civilized and modern (Kuper 1988; Roseberry 1989; Wolf 1982). While these frameworks have been discredited, their depiction of such communities as traditional, stable, bounded, consensual, and coherent entities remain as often-unexamined assumptions about the nature of small-scale societies.

More common is a concern with the operational definition of community and its archaeological correlates (Lipe 1970; Kolb and Snead 1997; Murdock 1949; Wills and Leonard 1994). Following Wills and Leonard (1994:xiii), " . . . southwestern archaeologists understand 'community' to mean a residential group whose members interact with one another on some regular basis." This understanding of community as a combination of place and social action has dominated archaeological studies. Communities may also be conceived, however, as associations based on common interests, shared cultural history, political association, and cultural construction (e.g., Dongoske et al. 1997; Roseberry 1989; Thomas 1998; Wills and Leonard 1994). In this sense, a community may be both an idiom of identity formation and a situated social group; however, its physical, archaeological correlates are more difficult to specify. Finally, communities, like other analytical units, may be conceived of as historical and processual, " . . . not as fixed entities, but as problematic, shaped, reshaped, and changing over time" (Wolf 1990:590). Thus, both the criteria for what constitutes a community and how communities are constituted may be historically contingent and vary under different social and environmental conditions. Asking, "what is a community?" may be less important than understanding how communities form, identify, and dissolve in varying contexts.

For the indigenous inhabitants of seventeenth-century *Nueva México,* the physical context of community formation became increasing constrained by the spread of the mission system. The frontier mission, or *doctrina,* has played a defining role in Borderlands historiography as the seminal institution of the colonial state (Bolton 1917; Sweet 1995). Beyond their role as trans-local institutions for the propagation and control of sacred knowledge and socio-political identity, however, missions were the single most important location of colonial and indigenous contact and the context in which colonialism as a historical process of disruption, incorporation, and transformation was situated. The mission, in practice, is best approached not as a global blueprint for conversion, but as a set of diverse and historically situated institutions, strategies, and practices deployed by diverse agents in diverse contexts over long periods. The mission, then, may be conceived of simultaneously as place, as re-structured indigenous community, and as the institutional logic of the colonial state.

From the perspective of how communities are produced, we may consider the effect of mission, both as institution and as process. How, for example, does the fact of Spanish colonialism create webs of novel relationships and systems of relationships that people are drawn into, and how do these become natural, conventional, everyday life? How are the demographic crises of the Colonial period mediated by these relationships? How does variation in the circumstances of missionization influence the persistence of communities and the places in which they are situated? As a first step in addressing these questions, I consider variation the occupational history of missionized places in the Galisteo Basin.

The Galisteo Basin

The Galisteo Basin, a low lying area drained by the Galisteo Creek and its tributaries, is bounded on the west by the Ortiz Mountains, on the east by Glorieta Mesa, and on the north by the Santa Fe Plateau, and on the South by the Estancia Basin (Figure 4.1). Seven large late prehistoric settlements are located within this area itself, and several more are located in surrounding areas: the Santa Fe Plateau to the north, the Santo Domingo, and Hagan Basins to the west, and the saddle between the Sandia and Ortiz mountains to the southwest. The Galisteo Basin, enlarged to include San Marcos and La Cienega on the Santa Fe Plateau, was consistently recognized by the Spanish as a distinctive settlement cluster or "province" on the basis of linguistic and geographic criteria.

The occupational history of many locations within this area appears to be discontinuous, and several sites were reoccupied following European colonization. As many as twelve of these sites may have been occupied as residences at the time of colonization, however, nine show at least limited evidence of late glaze deposition and five remained

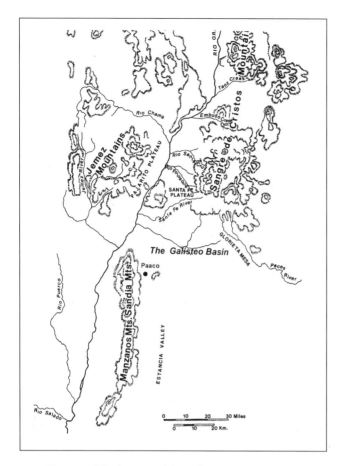

Figure 4.1. The location of the Galisteo Basin and Paaco.

Table 4.1. Late Prehistoric and Historic Pueblo Settlements
in the Galisteo Basin and surrounding areas.
(Modified from Lycett in 1995)

LA NUMBER	CERAMICS (GLAZEWARES)	SIZE
Santa Fe Plateau		
7	A–C, F	450-500 ROOMS
16 (Cieneguilla)	A–C, E–F	1000 ROOMS
98 (San Marcos)	A–F	3098 ROOMS
9154	A–C	75-100 ROOMS
Santo Domingo Basin		
182	A–E	LARGE
412	A–E	LARGE
Arroyo Tonque		
240 (Tonque)	A–F	1500 ROOMS
278	A–D	LARGE
East of Sandias		
24	A–F	UNKNOWN
162 (Paaco)	A–F (B–D in small freqencies)	1500+ ROOMS
Galisteo Basin		
26 (Galisteo)	A–F	1640 ROOMS
40 (Pueblo Blanco)	A–E	1450 ROOMS
62 (Pueblo Colorado)	A–E	881 ROOMS
80 (San Cristobal)	A–F	1645 ROOMS
91, 92 (San Lazaro)	A–F (E in small frequencies)	1841 ROOMS
183 (Pueblo Largo)	A–D	489 ROOMS
239 (Pueblo Shé)	A–E	1543 ROOMS

occupied from the 1620s through 1680. Of these, known mission sites are indicated in Table 4.1.

Of the seven large settlements within the basin proper, three were missionized during the first period of Spanish colonization: Galisteo and San Lazaro between 1610 and 1613, and San Cristobal in 1621. A missionary was resident at San Cristobal in the 1620s, but by mid-century, both San Lazaro and San Cristobal had become *visitas* of Galisteo. Galisteo was the earliest and longest occupied mission in the eponymous basin. San Marcos and its visita, La Cienega, entered the mission system during the 1630s. San Pedro is a poorly documented mission or *visita* occupied intermittently during the seventeenth century. Following the Pueblo Revolt, remaining Pueblo settlements in the Galisteo Basin were abandoned in favor of the former colonial settings of Santa Fe and La Cañada in the Española Basin. Following forced migration from these places, the former inhabitants of the Galisteo

Basin and Santa Fe Plateau were dispersed to a number of other settlements including Laguna and First Mesa at Hopi. In 1706, Governor Cuervo y Valdés resettled the Pueblo of Galisteo with 90 Tano speakers who had been resident at Tesuque (Hackett 1937). Aboriginal habitation in the Galisteo Basin apparently collapsed in the wake of the 1780–1781 smallpox epidemic, when the mission records were transferred to Pecos (Chávez 1957).

San Cristobal and the Tano District

Between 1912 and 1917, Nels Nelson conducted a research program for the American Museum of Natural History aimed at delineating a chronological framework for the Puebloan Southwest and tracing the historical roots of modern Pueblo villages (Nelson 1919a, 1919b). The most notable aspect of this program was Nelson's excavation of several large late prehistoric or Contact period habitation sites in the Galisteo Basin (Nelson 1913, 1914a, 1917). Following an initial six-week reconnaissance that took note of more than 115 sites, Nelson chose the historically Tano-speaking settlement cluster as the basis for his chronological framework (Nelson n.d. a). Excavations focused primarily on San Cristobal, but included Galisteo, San Lazaro, Pueblo Largo, Pueblo Colorado, Pueblo Blanco, and Pueblo Shé (Nelson 1914a). In 1913, Nelson returned to map these sites (Nelson 1914a), and in 1914, he excavated the stratigraphic block in midden B at San Cristobal, which provided the data for *Chronology of the Tano Ruins* (Nelson 1916; Woodbury 1960). Between 1914 and 1920, Nelson extended his excavations to large prehistoric and historic sites located in areas adjacent to the Galisteo Basin, and conducted wide ranging surface surveys in the hopes of generalizing his chronological framework to the Southwest as a whole (Nelson n.d. a, n.d. b; cf. Kidder 1924).

Subsequent excavations at Galisteo Basin sites occupied after A.D. 1400 include work at Pueblo Largo (Dutton 1951, 1953), and Pueblo Blanco (Creamer and Renken 1994). Research at Contact period sites on the Santa Fe Plateau include San Marcos Pueblo (Penman et al. 1998; Reed 1954; Thomas 1999) and Cieneguilla (Creamer and Renken 1994), both apparently mission locations. Tonque Pueblo in the Hagan Basin has been the subject of a number of studies (Barnett 1969; Warren 1970). The most extensive and best-reported excavations in this area are from Paaco on the east side of the Sandias (Lambert 1954; Lycett 2000; Nelson 1915). A number of studies have also been conducted with materials excavated at San Antonio (Cordell 1980).

While his program of research generated a large corpus of information, the vast majority of these data remain unpublished in Nelson's notes, field catalogues, and manuscripts. In addition, both the level of detail and methods of data collection limit the confidence we can place in inferences drawn from this research. Nelson recorded details of architecture and artifact recovery for each excavated room; however, it is not clear that field methods and recording procedures were applied consistently, even within the same site. Despite these limitations, Nelson's notes and collections provide access to formal variation in architecture and artifact distributions at a spatial scale beyond the scope of most modern research projects. These

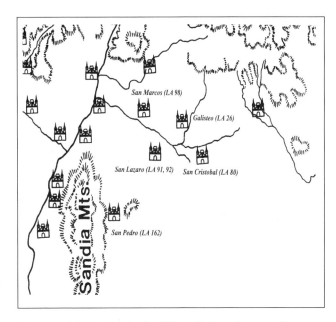

Figure 4.2. Mission sites in the Galisteo Basin and surrounding area.

data make it possible to address the occupational history of Pueblo settlement in relation to other changes in archaeological patterns coincident with European contact (for a complete discussion of these data and their analysis see Lycett 1994, 1995).

As a point of departure, it is useful to begin with San Cristobal, where Nelson (1912a, 1914a) excavated 239 rooms in 1912. This settlement shows evidence of occupation from the time of initial Spanish contact through 1680. San Cristobal, the first large architectural site excavated by Nelson, is a useful starting point because several roomblocks or portions of roomblocks have been completely excavated, providing a large number of contiguous observations. The site consists of 19 roomblocks, 11 plaza areas, eight middens, and associated features including the mission complex, a rock shelter, shrine or watchtower, corrals, and two reservoirs. Many of the currently extant roomblocks were constructed on either trash fill or previously existing structures, suggesting that this location had long been the focus of intensive occupation.

While it is clear that the entire pre-mission pueblo was never occupied contemporaneously, it does appear that this settlement underwent significant spatial reorganization during the period in which its inhabitants had regular access to European artifacts and domesticates.

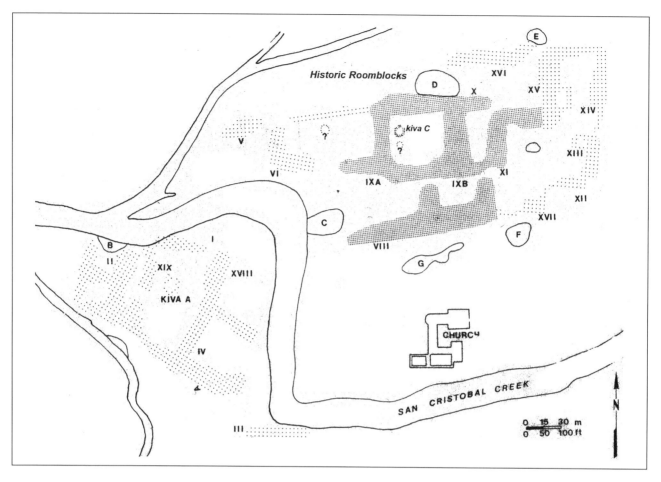

Figure 4.3. San Cristobal (LA 80), location of historic roomblocks indicated by stippling (modified from Nelson 1914a).

These deposits probably date to the last 50 to 60 years of habitation at the site. Rather than a pattern of randomly dispersed abandoned and occupied room complexes, the restructuring took the form of a newly constructed or reconstructed group of roomblocks near the center of the pre-mission pueblo (Figure 4.3).

This site, however, not only shows evidence of a general restructuring at or about the time of Spanish colonization, but patterns of intramural artifact deposition also indicate continuing decline in occupied area following missionization. Of the extensively excavated roomblocks, the highest intramural densities of fauna and ceramics occur in the historic section of the site. Intramural dumping was more common during the final 50 to 60 years of San Cristobal's occupation than in the preceding 200 years. Attrition in the occupied area of this site continued throughout the seventeenth century

as portions of the historic roomblocks continued to be abandoned and filled with domestic trash (Figure 4.4).

Although Nelson's 1912 field season focused on San Cristobal, he also excavated 217 rooms in six other large Galisteo Basin pueblos. Only two of these, San Lazaro and Galisteo, were occupied throughout the seventeenth century. Nelson (1912b) excavated 57 rooms at San Lazaro within both the post-mission and pre-mission pueblos. Again, the late occupation is localized on the east side of the Arroyo Chorro, and shows some evidence of being superimposed over previous structures. Based on ceramic and faunal densities, intramural deposition is significantly higher within the historic section of the site. Again, the latest occupied portion of the site also had the highest levels of intramural trash fill.

Nelson (1912c) excavated 25 rooms at Galisteo in a four-day period, before snow forced an end to the 1912 field season. Like San Cristobal, the late occupation of this site is spatially restricted. Both intramural dumping and localized middens occur within the area of historic occupation. Nevertheless, the most notable thing about the artifact inventory from Galisteo is its poverty.

Excluding Galisteo, which has few extant collections, and Largo, which was probably abandoned earlier, all of the excavated sites exhibit similar pre-mission ceramic assemblages. That is, there is ample evidence of a widespread fifteenth- and sixteenth-century occupation in the Galisteo Basin. Seventeenth-century Rio Grande glazewares occur in large numbers only in association with European domesticates and artifacts. Nevertheless, small and spatially restricted samples of historic glazes at some sites suggest reuse of these locations following their abandonment as residential sites.

Settlements occupied following permanent Spanish colonization underwent substantial spatial contraction This restructuring took the form of newly constructed or refurbished roomblocks in a limited portion of the existing settlements. Both differential distribution of structural wood and catalogued artifacts within San Cristobal are consistent with the dismantling, stockpiling, and recycling of the pre-mission structures and their contents. Nevertheless, the highest intramural densities of both fauna and ceramics occur in the post-mission portions of these settlements. Depositional intensity does not appear to be a direct function of the time since abandonment, but of the conditions under which abandonment occurs.

Peripheral Places: Paaco

In 1914, Nelson (1914b, 1914c, 1915) expanded his research base from the Galisteo Basin, excavating more than 174 rooms at Paaco, a large adobe and masonry settlement on the east side of the Sandia Mountains (Figure 4.4). Subsequent work has added more than 200 rooms to this total (Lambert 1954). More recently, the University of Chicago has carried out a program of surface documentation and extramural excavation in combination with archival and collections research (Lycett 1997, 1998,

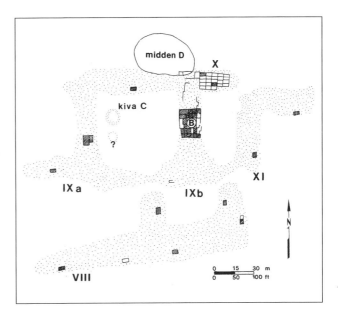

Figure 4.4. San Cristobal, high-density contexts within the historic roomblock indicated by shading (modified from Nelson 1914a).

1999, 2000). Since 1996, our research at Paaco has addressed the relationship between Spanish colonization and the historical transformation of indigenous societies in the northern Southwest. Although we view colonial transformations as a multidimensional process, our research has focused on the interrelationship between occupational history, spatial organization, and the articulation of indigenous social and economic practices with colonial political and economic networks. We are particularly interested in understanding how variation in the duration and intensity of incorporation into colonial networks influences the permanence and stability of seventeenth-century Pueblo villages and structures changes in the organization of local production. Paaco, with its relatively small population, discontinuous occupation, and geographically marginal position within colonial networks, provides an important contrast to mission locations in the nearby Galisteo Basin.

Paaco is a Spanish transcription of an indigenous place name appearing in Oñate's Lists of Obedience and Vassalage (Hammond and Rey 1953). The site was a location of a mission or *visita* occupied sometime during the seventeenth century known as San Pedro. One document suggests that this visita had been abandoned and subsequently resettled during the mid-seventeenth century (Scholes 1929). There is no documentary evidence of indigenous residential occupation later than 1660 (Chávez 1954).

Both surface documentation and excavation suggest that the occupational history and construction sequence of Paaco is complex. Nelson (1914b, 1914c) and Lambert (1954) each recognize two major spatial divisions of architecture within the site. The *South Division,* or *San Pedro Viejo I,* excavated primarily by Nelson, includes at least ten adobe or masonry and adobe roomblocks arranged in four agglutinated plaza groups. These roomblocks are separated from the *North Division (San Pedro Viejo II)* by a low-lying drainage. Both divisions show evidence of a widespread and intensive occupation between the late thirteenth and early fifteenth centuries. Colonial period occupation of the settlement was confined to a single plaza group in the southwest quarter of the North Division. Features associated with this Colonial period occupation include soil and water control facilities, corral enclosures, and a copper smelting facility.

Like San Cristobal, the late occupation at Paaco occurs as a spatially restricted reoccupation of a much larger pre-contact settlement. Four single-story masonry roomblocks were superimposed over previously occupied masonry and adobe structures in a single plaza group. Surface documentation suggests that sixteenth- and seventeenth-century deposition is restricted to this plaza group and its immediate surroundings. Unlike San Cristobal, however, pre-Hispanic occupation was not continuous and it is, at present, not possible to determine at what point in the process of contact and colonization the spatial restructuring of this plaza group took place. Nelson (1914c) excavated 43 rooms in four roomblocks of this plaza group. Later excavations focused on the southern roomblock of this plaza group, exposing 88 rooms in Roomblocks XI and IX (Lambert 1954).

Like San Cristobal, intramural deposition of domestic trash occurs within the Historic plaza group, suggesting continuing decline of occupied and maintained space during the Colonial period. Approximately 26 percent of all excavated rooms have evidence of intramural dumping either in the form of relatively high ceramic or faunal densities or direct indications in the original excavators' notes. At Paaco, high-density contexts are interspersed throughout the historic roomblocks indicating a patchwork of maintained and unmaintained residential space. In Roomblock XI, where the most extensive excavations have occurred, high-density contexts cluster in the western half of the excavated space. In contrast, the easternmost excavated rooms in this roomblock have little evidence of trash fill. During the seventeenth century, maintained space appears to have contracted, shifting eastward within this roomblock and possibly within the settlement as a whole.

It is important to note, however, that the intensity of intramural deposition at Paaco never approaches that of continuously occupied mission sites like San Cristobal. Nor are large, formalized middens associated with the historic occupation of Paaco. Although patterns of spatial restructuring are broadly similar in the two cases, neither the size of the population at Paaco, nor, perhaps, the duration of its residence at the site was sufficient to generate the densities of intramural or extramural artifact and faunal deposition associated with the seventeenth-century occupation at San Cristobal.

Three seasons of excavation on the historic plaza surface indicate a complex sequence of successive resurfacing and reconfiguration of extramural space contemporaneous with shifts in the organization of architectural space in the historic roomblocks (Figures 4.5, 4.6). This sequence includes construction of at least two successive plaza surfaces, followed by conversion of plaza area to animal penning, and construction of two successive barriers to animal movement. Each of these occupations is associated with late Rio Grande glazeware ceramics and radiocarbon dates calibrated to the seventeenth century (Folsom 1999; Lycett 1998, 1999; Lycett et al. 2000; Seddon 1998, 1999).

The distribution and density of structures and features within this area indicates an intensive and varied use of exterior space throughout this period. *Surface* 3, the

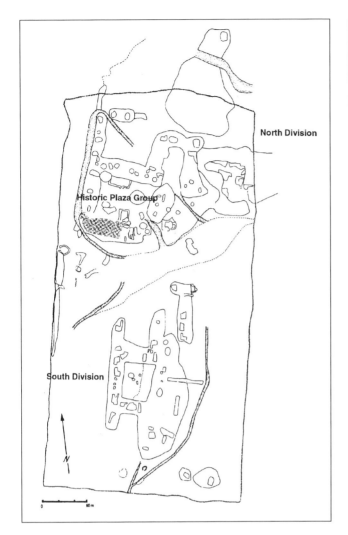

Figure 4.5. Paaco (LA 162).

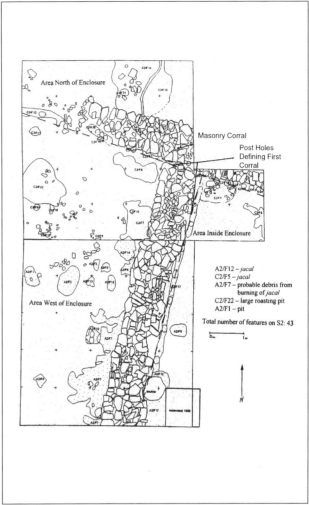

Figure 4.6. Paaco, Plaza Surface 2.

earliest plaza surface exposed, incorporated more than 20 features including architectural foundations, hearths, and several shallow pits (Figure 4.7). A wholesale reconstruction of the plaza occurred sometime during the mid-seventeenth century, creating a new surface with a high density of formal and informal features, including ash-filled depressions, pits, an isolated hearth, and two burned structures. During the period in which historic glazeware ceramics remained in regular use, this space became restructured within a colonial land use system incorporating European domesticates. This restructuring included conversion of plaza space to a complex of corral enclosures located in the southern third of the plaza. Some of these enclosures were constructed to pen animals, while others appear to have been intended to prevent penned animals from entering an enclosed area. Substantial deposits of animal dung had accumulated prior to the construction of the stone enclosures and these constructions superseded an earlier corral represented by lines of postholes. The original wooden corral appears to have been burnt, perhaps deliberately, prior to the construction of the masonry walls. The masonry enclosures lie directly atop the original line of post holes. The construction of these corrals removed nearly one-fourth of the available plaza surface from human use and probably prevented human occupation of the portions of the roomblocks adjacent to the animal pen itself. The final stone enclosures were constructed very late in the occupational sequence and may be part of a post-residential, logistical occupation of Paaco as a pastoral camp.

The post-residential occupation of Paaco is not unusual. There is reason to believe that several formerly occupied settlements became logistical elements in a newly emerging mixed pastoral and agricultural land use system. Small and spatially restricted samples of late ceramics at Pueblo Largo, Pueblo Shé, and Pueblo Colorado probably represent limited reuse of these locations as logistical camps following their abandonment as residential sites. Nelson (1914a) reported that groups from Santo Domingo were believed to have camped at Pueblo Colorado as late as the nineteenth century. Nelson also mapped corral enclosures at each of these pre-mission sites, as well as within the mission period sites. At mission locales, corral enclosures occur both in association with the mission architectural complex and interspersed among the roomblocks. At least some of these structures, like those at Paaco, may post-date residential occupation of these places. Thus, villages abandoned as residential locations in the sixteenth and seventeenth centuries took on new roles as livestock became fully integrated into the emerging land use systems of the eighteenth century. Ferguson (1996) discusses a similar pattern at Zuni, where sites like Hawikuh and Kechiba:wa continued in use as sheep camps long after residential occupation ceased.

The regular reuse of formerly occupied settlements during the Colonial period may have been an important means by which displaced indigenous populations maintained access to and social claims over place. While the incorporation of livestock may have required sheep camps, it did not dictate their location. Residential locales have much to recommend them as sources of raw material, productive facilities, and land, but they also serve as the raw material for social memory and place-making in a transformed landscape.

Discussion and Conclusions

In the disruptions following expulsion of the Spanish colony in 1680 and reconquest of the Northern Southwest between 1692 and 1696, villages broke up, reformed and coalesced into new combinations of community and place that reoriented the Pueblo world. While remarkable for

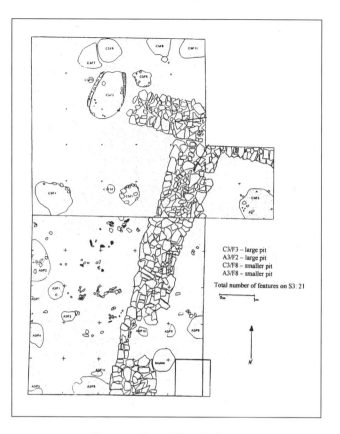

Figure 4.7. Paaco, Plaza Surface 3.

the widespread scale of residential upheaval, the abandonments of the Pueblo Revolt are not a unique historical circumstance, but the continuation of processes that had been ongoing for more than a century. Post-contact settlement shifts in the Rio Grande Valley include contraction in the total area occupied, decrease in the total number of settlements, and decrease in the area occupied within individual settlements. In the Galisteo Basin, habitation sites underwent both spatial reorganization and contraction at or near the time of colonization and continuing attrition of occupied area throughout the seventeenth century. This pattern appears to hold for San Cristobal, San Lazaro, and San Pedro (Paaco), although the intensity of deposition varies across these cases. Data from other important sites such as San Marcos have not been addressed here. Nevertheless, in at least three mission sites in the Galisteo Basin and its immediate vicinity, there appear to be contemporary patterns of spatial reorganization and intramural deposition.

What do these patterns indicate about the history of place use? Pueblo habitation sites have complex and cumulative occupational histories. Architectural and depositional patterns in these contexts are strongly influenced by demographic variables as well as duration of occupation, periodicity of reoccupation, and post-occupational modification. At least two patterns of construction and deposition have been documented ethnographically (Lycett 1995). Over time and coincident with relatively gradual population decline, a complex, discontinuous pattern of occupied, unoccupied but maintained, and un-maintained architectural space may develop in multi-room, agglutinated settlements. Alternately, radical contraction of occupied area and spatial reorganization may occur where the scale of house abandonment is sufficiently broad and its tempo is sufficiently fast (cf. Cameron 1992). Kidder (1958) notes that the increasing tempo of depopulation at Pecos during the eighteenth century led first to a discontinuous pattern of structure abandonment followed by contraction and reconstruction as larger areas became unoccupied. What is remarkable about these seventeenth-century cases is that patterns of structure abandonment begin with contraction and are followed by continued attrition.

These patterns are consistent with occupational instability throughout the Contact period. For many, if not all, settlements this spatial reorganization included individuals or households who had been resident at other locations. While social fluidity and residential mobility may have been long standing elements in the Pueblo world (Naranjo 1995; Ortiz 1994), both the tempo of migration and the constraints upon it are likely to have increased after 1598. Social mechanisms that mediated migration and integration of disparate populations would have been crucial to these communities in the making.

In each case, a new and compact living space was created within the bounds of what was once a much larger settlement. Whether this new space was reclaimed by prior occupants or created anew by migrants from other preexisting communities or both at once, social space

and claims of ownership or access were being remade just as physical space was being reconstructed. This phenomenon appears to have been widespread and certainly would have entailed significant contestation, negotiation, and adjustment as households, individuals, and other scales of social action coalesced into new communities. Occupied area continued to contract as high densities of ceramics and domestic fauna were deposited in historically occupied roomblocks, possibly in an effort to stabilize these abandoned structures. As populations continued to decline, the loss of individuals, households, and the collapse of even larger scales of social organization must have ramified through the web of interconnected social systems that made up the Kingdom of New Mexico. Many settlements, such as Paaco, were entirely abandoned as residential locales during the unfolding of this process.

Residential abandonment, however, does not necessarily denote a loss of place, but rather a reconfiguration of its role and historical associations. For the seventeenth-century residents of the Galisteo Basin, their association with specific places may have shifted from collective to historical, as former residential locations became campsites, corrals, raw material sources, and landmarks in an ongoing cultural geography. Ethnogeographies (e.g., Harrington 1916) are more than descriptive catalogues of place names, they are embodied histories (Ingold 1993); claims about contemporary social, political, and economic relations; and sources with which to resist, contest, and negotiate those relations. In the northern Southwest, the collective and historical identities invoked as expressions of community are often integrally tied to the history of place and may cross-cut both communities as defined by co-residence and archaeological constructions of cultural affiliation (Bayer et al. 1994; Dongoske et al. 1997; Levine 1999). For archaeology, there is significant promise as well as considerable challenge in understanding the changing role of locations within these geographies, and relative to the many, overlapping geographies that have subsumed place.

References Cited

Adams, E. Charles

1983   The Architectural Analogue to Hopi Social Organization
        and Room Use, and Implications for Prehistoric Northern
        Southwestern Culture. *American Antiquity* 48:44–61.

Alcock, S.

2001   The Reconfiguration of Memory in the Eastern Roman
        Empire. In *Empires: Approaches From Archaeology and
        History,* edited by S. Alcock, T. N. D'Atroy, K. D.
        Morrison, and C. M. Sinopoli, in press, Cambridge
        University Press, Cambridge, UK.

Barnett, Franklin

1969   *Tonque Pueblo: A Report of Partial Excavation of an Ancient
        Pueblo IV Indian Ruin in New Mexico.* Albuquerque
        Archaeological Society, Albuquerque.

Basso, Keith H.

1996   *Wisdom Sits in Places: Landscape and Language among the
        Western Apache.* University of New Mexico Press, Albuquerque.

Bayer, L., F. Montoya, and the Pueblo of Santa Ana

1994   *Santa Ana: The Pueblo, and the History of Tamaya.*
        University of New Mexico Press, Albuquerque.

Biersack, A.

1999   Introduction: From the "New Ecology" to the New
        Ecologies. *American Anthropologist* 101:5–18.

Binford, Lewis R.

1982   The Archaeology of Place. *Journal of Anthropological
        Archaeology* 1:5–31.

Bolton, Hubert E.

1917   The Mission as a Frontier Institution in the Spanish
        American Colonies. *American Historical Review* 23:42–61.

Cameron, Catherine M.

1991   Structure Abandonment in Villages. In *Archaeological
        Method and Theory, Vol. 3,* edited by M. B. Schiffer,
        pp. 155–194. University of Arizona Press, Tucson.

1992   An Analysis of Residential Patterns and the Oraibi Split.
        Journal of Anthropological Archaeology 11:173–186.

Cameron, Catherine M., and S. A. Tomka (editors)

1993   *Abandonment of Settlements and Regions: Ethnoarchaeological
        and Archaeological Approaches.* Cambridge University Press,
        Cambridge, UK.

Chávez, Fray Angélico

1954   *Origins of New Mexico Families: In the Spanish Colonial
        Period.* The Historical Society of New Mexico, Santa Fe.

1957   *Archives of the Archdiocese of Santa Fe, 1678–1900.* Academy
        of American Franciscan History, Washington, D.C.

Cordell, Linda S. (editor)

1980   *Tijeras Canyon: Analyses of the Past.* University of New
        Mexico Press, Albuquerque.

Creamer, Winifred, and L. Renken

1994   Testing Conventional Wisdom: Protohistoric Ceramics and
        Chronology in the Northern Rio Grande. Paper presented
        at the 59th Annual Meeting of the Society for American
        Archaeology, April 22, Anaheim, Calif.

Crumley, Carol. L.

1994   Historical Ecology: A Multidimensional Ecological
        Orientation. In *Historical Ecology: Cultural Knowledge and
        Changing Landscapes,* edited by C. L. Crumley, pp. 1–16.
        School of American Research Press, Santa Fe.

Dongoske, Kurt E., M. Yeatts, Roger Anyon, and T. J. Ferguson

1997   Archaeological Cultures and Cultural Affiliation: Hopi and
        Zuni Perspectives in the American Southwest. *American
        Antiquity* 62:600–608.

Dutton, Bertha P.

1951   Girl Scout Archaeological Mobile Camps. *El Palacio* 58:354–369.

1953   Galisteo Basin Again Scene of Archaeological Research. *El
        Palacio* 60:339–351.

Encinias, Miguel, Alfred Rodríguez, and Joseph P. Sanchez (editors
and translators)

1992   *Historia de la Nueva México, 1610.* University of New
        Mexico Press, Albuquerque.

Espinosa, J. Manuel (editor and translator)

1988   *The Pueblo Indian Revolt of 1696 and the Franciscan
        Missions of New Mexico: Letters of the Missionaries and
        Related Documents.* University of Oklahoma Press, Norman.

Fabian, Johannes

1983   *Time and the Other: How Anthropology Makes Its Object,*
        pp. 1–35. Columbia University Press, New York.

Ferguson, T. J.

1996   *Historic Zuni Architecture and Society: An Archaeological
        Application of Space Syntax.* Anthropological Papers of the
        University of Arizona No. 60. Tucson.

Ferguson, T. J., and Barbara J. Mills

1987   Settlement and Growth of Zuni Pueblo: An Architectural
        History. *The Kiva* 52:243–266.

Folsom, H. E.

1999a   Excavation of Block C Addendum (42E/-145N). In *Report of
        Archaeological Excavations at LA 162, Bernalillo County, New
        Mexico, Conducted by the University of Chicago Archaeological
        Field Studies Program, between 21 June and 18 August, 1998,
        under permit SE-134.* Ms. on file, pp. 159–170, with the State
        Historic Preservation Office, Santa Fe, and the Board of
        Archaeologists, University of New Mexico, Albuquerque.

Hackett, Charles W. (editor)

1937   *Historical Documents Relating to New Mexico, Nueva Viscaya,
        and Approaches Thereto, to 1773,* Vol. III, collected by A. F.
        A. Bandelier and F. R. Bandelier. Carnegie Institution of
        Washington Publications No. 330. Washington, D.C.

Hackett, Charles W., and Charmion C. Shelby (editor and
translator)

1942   *The Revolt of the Pueblo Indians and Otermín's Attempted
        Reconquest, 1680–1682.* Coronado Cuarto Centennial
        Publications, 1540–1949. 2 Vols. University of New
        Mexico Press, Albuquerque.

Hammond, George P., and Agapito Rey (editors and translators)

1953   *Don Juan de Oñate, Colonizer of New Mexico 1595–1628.*
        University of New Mexico Press, Albuquerque.

Harrington, John P.

1916   *The Ethnogeography of the Tewa Indians.* Twenty-ninth
        Annual Report of the Bureau of American Ethnology.
        Smithsonian Institution, Washington, D.C.

Herr, S., and J. J. Clark
1997   Patterns in the Pathways: Early Historic Migrations in the
        Rio Grande Pueblos. *Kiva* 62:365–389.

Ingold, Tim
1993   The Temporality of Landscape. *World Archaeology*
        25:152–174.

Lipe, William D.
1970   Anasazi Communities in the Red Rock Plateau,
        Southeastern Utah. In *Reconstructing Prehistoric Pueblo
        Societies,* edited by W. A. Longacre, pp. 84–139. University
        of New Mexico Press, Albuquerque.

Kessell, John L.
1989   Spaniards and Pueblos: From Crusading Intolerance to
        Pragmatic Accommodation. In *Columbian Consequences,
        Vol. I: Archaeological and Historical Perspectives on the
        Spanish Borderlands West,* edited by D. H. Thomas, pp.
        126–138, Smithsonian Institution Press, Washington, D.C.

Kessell, John L., and Rick Hendricks (editors)
1992   *By Force of Arms: The Journals of Don Diego de Vargas,
        1691–1693.* University of New Mexico Press, Albuquerque.

Kidder, Alfred V.
1924   *An Introduction to the Study of Southwestern Archaeology,
        with a Preliminary Account of the Excavations at Pecos.* Papers
        of the Southwestern Expedition 1, Published for Phillips
        Academy by Yale University Press, New Haven, Conn.
1958   *Pecos, New Mexico: Archaeological Notes.* Papers of the
        Robert S. Peabody Foundation for Archaeology, 5.
        Andover, Mass.

Kolb, M. J., and Snead, J. E.
1997   It's a Small World after All: Comparative Analyses of
        Community Organization in Archaeology. *American
        Antiquity* 62:609–628.

Kuper, Adam
1988   *The Invention of Primitive Society: Transformations of an
        Illusion.* Routledge, London.

Lambert, Marjorie F.
1954   *Paa-ko: Archaeological Chronicle of an Indian Village in
        North Central New Mexico.* Monographs of the School of
        American Research 19. Santa Fe.

Levine, Francis
1999   *Our Prayers are in This Place: Pecos Pueblo Identity over the
        Centuries.* University of New Mexico Press, Albuquerque.

Lycett, Mark T.
1994   Structure and Content in Previous Research: Nels Nelson's
        Excavations in the Galisteo Basin. Paper presented at the
        59th Annual Meeting of the Society for American
        Archaeology, April 23, Anaheim, Calif.
1995   *Archaeological Implications of European Contact: Demography,
        Settlement, and Land Use in the Middle Rio Grande Valley,
        New Mexico.* Unpublished Ph.D. dissertation. Department
        of Anthropology, University of New Mexico.
1997   *Preliminary Report of Archaeological Surface Documentation
        and Test Excavations at LA 162, Bernalillo County, New
        Mexico, conducted by Northwestern University Archaeological
        Field Studies Program, between 17 June and 8 August,*
        1996, under permit SP-269. Ms. on file, State Historic
        Preservation Office, Santa Fe, and the Board of
        Archaeologists, University of New Mexico, Albuquerque.
1998   *Report of Archaeological Excavations at LA 162, Bernalillo
        County, New Mexico, conducted by the University of Chicago
        Archaeological Field Studies Program, between 21 June and
        19 August, 1997, under permit SE-120.* Ms. on file, State
        Historic Preservation Office, Santa Fe, and the Board of
        Archaeologists, University of New Mexico, Albuquerque.
1999   *Report of Archaeological Excavations at LA 162, Bernalillo
        County, New Mexico, conducted by the University of Chicago
        Archaeological Field Studies Program, between 21 June and
        18 August, 1998, under permit SE-134.* Ms. on file, Historic
        Preservation Division, State of New Mexico, Santa Fe.
2000   *Report of Archaeological Excavations at LA 162, Bernalillo
        County, New Mexico, conducted by the University of Chicago
        Archaeological Field Studies Program, between 21 June and
        12 August, 1999, under permit SE-144.* Ms. on file, Historic
        Preservation Division, State of New Mexico, Santa Fe.

Lycett, Mark T., H. Folsom, and M. T. Seddon
2000   Occupational History and Extramural Space: Ceramic
        Assemblages and Plaza Surfaces at LA 162 (Paa-ko),
        Bernalillo County, New Mexico. Paper presented at the
        65th Annual Meeting of the Society for American
        Archaeology, Philadelphia, Penn.

Murdock, George P.
1949   *Social Structure.* MacMillan, New York.

Nelson, Nels C.
n.d.a   Field Survey, 1912–1920, Arizona and New Mexico. Unpublished
        field notes. Ms. on file, Department of Anthropology,
        American Museum of Natural History, New York.
n.d.b   General Notes on the Tano Pueblos. Unpublished field
        notes. Ms. on file, Department of Anthropology, American
        Museum of Natural History, New York.
1912a   San Cristobal. Unpublished field notes and catalogue. Ms.
        on file, Department of Anthropology, American Museum
        of Natural History, New York.
1912b   San Lazaro. Unpublished field notes and catalogue. Ms. on
        file, Department of Anthropology, American Museum of
        Natural History, New York.
1912c   Galisteo. Unpublished field notes and catalogue. Ms. on
        file, Department of Anthropology, American Museum of
        Natural History, New York.
1913   Ruins of Prehistoric New Mexico: Extensive Excavations
        of Pueblos in the Rio Grande Valley. *American Museum
        Journal* 13:63–81.
1914a   *Pueblo Ruins of the Galisteo Basin, New Mexico.*
        Anthropological Papers of the American Museum of
        Natural History 15(1).
1914b   San Pedro Viejo I. Unpublished field notes and catalogue
        on file at the Department of Anthropology, American
        Museum of Natural History, New York.
1914c   San Pedro Viejo II. Unpublished field notes and catalogue.
        Ms. on file, Department of Anthropology, American
        Museum of Natural History, New York.

1915   Ancient Cities of New Mexico. *American Museum Journal* 15:389–394.

1916   Chronology of the Tano Ruins, New Mexico. *American Anthropologist* 18:159–180.

1917   Archaeology of the Tano District, New Mexico. *19th International Congress of Americanists,* pp. 114–118. New York.

1919a   General Introduction to the Archaeology of the Southwest. Ms. on file, Department of Anthropology, American Museum of Natural History, New York.

1919b   The Southwest Problem. *El Palacio* 6:132–135.

Naranjo, Tessie

1995   Thoughts on Migration from Santa Clara Pueblo. *Journal of Anthropological Archaeology* 14:247–250.

Ortiz, Alfonso

1994   The Dynamics of Pueblo Cultural Survival. In *North American Indian Anthropology: Essays on Society and Culture,* edited by R. J. DeMallie and A. Ortiz, pp. 278–306. University of Oklahoma Press, Norman.

Penman, S. L., A. F. Ramenofsky, C. Pierce, D. Vaughan, and E. A. Welker

1998   Will the Real San Marcos Pueblo Please Stand Up: An Examination of Bias and Error in Site Maps. Poster presented at the 63rd Annual Meeting of the Society for American Archaeology, Seattle, Wash.

Reed, Erik K.

1954   Test Excavations at San Marcos Pueblo. *El Palacio* 50:65–68.

Robinson, William J.

1990   Tree-Ring Studies of the Pueblo de Acoma. *Historical Archaeology* 24:99–106.

Roseberry, William

1989   *Anthropologies and Histories: Essays in Culture, History, and Political Economy.* Rutgers University Press, New Brunswick, New York.

Scholes, France V.

1929   Documents for the History of the New Mexico Missions in the Sixteenth Century. *New Mexico Historical Review* 4.

Scholes, France V., and Lansing B. Bloom

1944–45 Friar Personnel and Mission Chronology, 1598–1629. *New Mexico Historical Review* 19:319–336; 20:58–82.

Schroeder, Albert H.

1979   Pueblos Abandoned in Historic Times. In *The Handbook of North American Indians, Vol.9: The Southwest,* edited by A. Ortiz, pp. 236–254. Smithsonian Institution, Washington, D.C.

Seddon, M. T.

1998   Excavation of Block A (37E/-150N). In *Report of Archaeological Excavations at LA 162, Bernalillo County, New Mexico, conducted by the University of Chicago Archaeological Field Studies Program, between 21 June and 19 August, 1997, under permit SE-120,* pp. 128–140. Ms. on file, State Historic Preservation Office, Santa Fe, and the Board of Archaeologists, University of New Mexico, Albuquerque.

1999   Excavation of Block C (37E/-145N). In *Report of Archaeological Excavations at LA 162, Bernalillo County, New Mexico, conducted by the University of Chicago Archaeological Field Studies Program, between 21 June and 18 August, 1998, under permit SE-134,* pp. 171–191. Ms. on file, State Historic Preservation Office, Santa Fe, and the Board of Archaeologists, University of New Mexico, Albuquerque

Snead, James E., and Robert W. Preucel

1999   The Ideology of Settlement: Ancestral Keres Landscapes in the Northern Rio Grande. In *Archaeologies of Landscape: Contemporary Perspectives,* edited by W. Ashmore and A. B. Knapp, pp. 169–197. Blackwell Publishers, Oxford, UK.

Sweet, D.

1995   The Ibero-American Frontier Mission in Native America. In *The New Latin American Mission History,* edited by E. Langer and R. H. Jackson, pp. 1–48. University of Nebraska Press, Lincoln.

Thomas, B. W.

1998   Power and Community: The Archaeology of Slavery at the Hermitage Plantation. *American Antiquity* 63:531–551.

Thomas, David Hurst

1999   *Mission San Marcos Archaeological Project, Phase II: Defining the Architectural Sequence.* American Museum of Natural History, New York.

Thomas, N.

1989   *Out of Time: History and Evolution in Anthropological Discourse.* The University of Michigan Press, Ann Arbor.

Tönnies, F.

1957   *Community and Society.* Michigan State University Press, East Lansing.

Varien, M. D.

1999   *Sedentism and Mobility in a Social Landscape: Mesa Verde and Beyond.* University of Arizona Press, Tucson.

Wandsnider, L.

1998   Regional Scale Processes and Archaeological Landscape Units. In *Unit Issues in Archaeology: Measuring Time, Space, and Material,* edited by A. F. Ramenofsky and A. Steffen, pp. 87–102. University of Utah Press, Salt Lake City.

Warren, A. Helene

1970   Tonque: One Pueblo's Glaze Pottery Industry Dominated Middle Rio Grande Commerce. *El Palacio* 76(2):36–42.

Williams, B.

1992   Of Straightening Combs, Sodium Hydroxide, and Potassium Hydroxide in Archaeological and Cultural-Anthropological Analyses of Ethnogenesis. *American Antiquity* 57:60–612.

Wills, Wirt H., and Robert D. Leonard

1994   Preface. In *The Ancient Southwestern Community: Models and Methods for the Study of Prehistoric Social Organization,* edited by W. H. Wills and R. D. Leonard, pp. xiii–xvi. University of New Mexico Press, Albuquerque.

Wolf, Eric R.

1982   *Europe and the People Without History.* University of California Press, Berkeley.

1984   Culture: Panacea or Problem? *American Antiquity* 49:393–400.

1990   Distinguished Lecture: Facing Power—Old Insights, New Questions. *American Anthropologist* 92:586–596.

Woodbury, Richard B.

1960   Nelson's Stratigraphy. *American Antiquity* 26:98–99.

PART THREE
Material Culture Meanings

Chapter 5

Crossed Cultures, Crossed Meanings:

The Manipulation of Ritual Imagery in Early Historic Pueblo Resistance

Jeannette L. Mobley-Tanaka

In this chapter, I explore the use of ritual imagery in Pueblo resistance to religious persecution in the early historic period (that is, prior to the Pueblo Revolt of 1680). In particular, I focus on the contexts of use of the cross motif, which carried meaning in both native and Spanish religion. I argue that the multi-referential nature of the symbol—as bird, dragonfly, stars, or Christian cross—was intentionally manipulated by the Pueblo people to maintain the internal meanings of the ritual system, while simultaneously suggesting a change in that system to the Spanish. The way in which crosses were used is consistent with a broader style of Pueblo resistance that relied on the masking or hiding of native ritual practices and on the deliberate manipulation of information/misinformation in communicating with the Spanish.

Style As a Way of Doing

I follow Hodder's definition of style as "a way of doing" that is historically grounded, structured, and meaningful within cultures (Hodder 1990:45). Style can reinforce, emphasize or mask aspects of information flow (Hodder 1982:125). Because style is historically grounded, stylistic elements may be multi-referential, in that a single morphological form can be involved in a variety of messages depending on the social context of its use (MacDonald 1990:53). Style is therefore a phenomenon likely to be heavily invested with multiple levels of symbolic coding, and the reading of the code is context dependent.

Hodder's definition of style as a "way of doing" allows the application of the concept beyond the material culture realm, to which archaeologists often limit their analyses of style. Such an expansion of the concept is useful, however, when trying to evaluate a social process like resistance through an examination of artistic design. If there was a "way of doing" resistance that structured the actions recorded in the ethnohistoric record, then it likewise should have structured material expressions of resistance in artistic contexts. It is my intention here to identify the style of resistance evident in the ethnohistoric record, and to use that style to begin to uncover more subtle forms of resistance that existed in the everyday lives of Pueblo people, and that were never recognized by the Spanish. To do so requires an understanding of the style of resistance, but also a consideration of the social contexts in which the designs played a part, including traditional religious contexts, both Spanish and Pueblo, that gave meaning to symbols.

The Pueblo Style of Resistance

Spanish colonization and missionary efforts began in the Pueblo region in 1581. From this time until the Pueblo Revolt of 1680, both Spanish colonists and missionaries exacted a heavy toll on Pueblo societies, demanding tribute and labor, and persecuting native religion. The Spanish demand for goods, food, and labor had a severe impact on all aspects of Pueblo life. On the other hand, the missionaries built churches in the Pueblo villages and took up residence there, inserting themselves into the everyday lives of the people. The missionaries demanded labor and goods as well, but their chief concern was the destruction of native religion and the conversion of natives to Catholicism.

In the early historic period armed resistance often had tragic outcomes for the Pueblos, demonstrating that it was not a viable strategy for individual villages. More than one revolt was foiled prior to the successful Revolt of 1680 (Hackett and Shelby 1942), and blatant acts of resistance or rebellion were brutally punished by the Spanish. However, resistance through more passive, less visible means can be traced in ethnohistoric accounts. Not surprisingly, these were of the sort that Scott (1990) has called everyday forms of resistance; the sort of subverted resistance employed by powerless underclasses. Scott (1990) argues that oppressed factions will maintain a subversive discourse in hidden contexts, while masking their resistance in public displays. Ethnohistoric records indicate this was the style of resistance utilized in the Pueblos, and that two such resistance techniques were actively used.

The first technique commonly employed was to mask resistance outwardly by obeying the missionaries, while continuing traditional practices in secret. Spanish friars actively sought out and brutally punished religious leaders, desecrated sacred places, and destroyed ritual items, particularly focusing on items they perceived to be idols, such as masks and katsina dolls, but also prayer sticks and feathers, dance head-dresses, and anything else that the Indians might consider sacred (Dozier 1970:50). The continuance of traditional practices was only possible through carefully concealing ritual spaces and ritual items; as Dozier (1970:50) says, "they did not give up their beliefs or even their sacred rites, but became more careful in concealment and secrecy." At Taos Pueblo, the ritual leader Popé purportedly used an old storage room as a kiva to conceal his ritual performances from the Spanish (Folsom 1973). In the Zuni area, Hodge (1939:211) notes, "whereas the typical Zuni kiva in preceding times was subterranean and occupied a site apart from the domiciles, it later became a part of the house group as at Zuni and Acoma Pueblos today, hardly distinguishable from common dwellings." At the same time that kiva religion continued in a hidden context, the Pueblos consented to baptism, and attended Mass, as the missionaries demanded. In the late 1800s, Matilda Coxe Stevenson noted that the Rio Grande Pueblos:

> are in fact as non-Catholic today as before the Spanish conquest. They have preserved their religion, . . . holding their ceremonials in secret . . . under the very eye of the church. Though professedly Catholic, they wait only the departure of the priest to return to their secret ceremonials.
>
> —[STEVENSON 1894].

Another example of this kind of outward obedience and hidden resistance is in civil government. All of the Pueblos had an imposed set of officers, set in place by the Spanish to enforce the laws and tributes of the conquerors. However, the Pueblos secretly retained their social/ceremonial leaders who were the de facto government, and who guided the civil authorities. This governing structure remains in place today in the eastern Pueblos, where, "the officers of the civil government system are useful in masking the identity and the activities of the native officers who are additionally concerned with ceremonial matters that have, in the past, generated considerable difficulties with Spanish authorities, particularly the missionaries" (Dozier 1970:68).

The second kind of passive resistance that the Pueblos employed successfully was to manipulate information in order to exert some control over situations. A well-documented example of the use of misinformation (which the Spanish fell for repeatedly), was to spread rumors of great riches outside Pueblo territory, usually on the Great Plains to the east. These rumors were repeatedly used to draw the Spanish away from the villages, and at least once into a trap set by Comanches (Silverberg 1970; Terrell 1973). Another carefully placed rumor stopped short an early attempt at reconquest after the Pueblo Revolt. As the Spanish troops advanced up the Rio Grande to Cochiti Pueblo, they were met by the Pueblo leader Alonso Catiti with a group of warriors. Catiti came forward, "remorseful and tearfully asking forgiveness." He received a pardon from the Spanish and begged them to make camp while he brought the other Revolt leaders to them to surrender. The Spanish agreed, but while giving pardons to Catiti's men several whispered to the Spanish that it was a trick to ambush and massacre the Spanish troops, and that thousands of troops were amassing to the north for the attack. This induced the Spanish to withdraw completely without a fight (Folsom 1973:139). It is thought that in fact the rumors were the trick.

Yet another example of manipulation of information flows involves the Hopi response to the Spanish reconquest of New Mexico. After the reconquest of the Rio Grande area, Hopi leaders initiated reconciliatory measures, but then continually stalled in carrying them out. One such incident is described as follows:

> The Moquis [Hopis] . . . sent ambassadors in May 1700 to treat with the governor, professing their readiness to rebuild churches and receive missionaries. At the same time Espeleta, Chief of Oraibe, sent for Padre Juan Garaicoechea to come and baptize children. The friar set out at once . . . and went to Aguatuvi. . . . On account of a pretended rumor that the messengers to Santa Fe had been killed, he was not permitted to visit Oraibe or the other Pueblos at this time; but Espeleta promised to notify him soon when they were ready for another visit.
>
> —[BANCROFT 1889:221–222]

Whiteley (1988:20) notes that this pattern of, "the promise to accept missionaries, the open offer of acceptance and welcome, the unexpected rejection on trumped up grounds . . . all conducted with much diplomacy and overtly conciliatory compromise" was commonly repeated in Hopi interactions with the Spanish and later with the U.S. government.

From these examples, then, the Puebloan style of resistance emerges as one of outward acquiescence, which masked the maintenance of social and religious integrity at a more fundamental level. This false acquiescence was often achieved through hiding or disguising ritual features and paraphernalia and through the deliberate use of misinformation. This style of resistance is one that may well have left material manifestations of resistance in art forms associated with religion.

Most of the resistance centered around protecting native religious systems, which were the one aspect of Pueblo life that were under constant, direct, deliberate attack from the resident missionaries. Despite the fact that starvation and epidemic disease, both brought on by the Spaniards, had decimated the Rio Grande towns in the two years immediately preceding the Pueblo Revolt, the cause of the Revolt that was repeatedly stated by Pueblo captives questioned by the Spanish was religious oppression (Gutierrez 1991; Silverberg 1970). The catalyst for the Pueblo Revolt of 1680 was the imprisonment of a number of ritual leaders, and the Revolt itself was planned by religious leaders, especially Popé, in the kiva and in consultation with three underworld spirits (Folsom 1973; Gutierrez 1991). All of this underscores the central role of Pueblo religion in resistance. Resistance was carried out through religion, as well as to protect religion, and the plans for revolt were legitimated through religion. It is for this reason that the material expressions of this religion are an excellent place to begin an inquiry of everyday forms of resistance in the early historic period. Here I begin that examination through evaluating the use of crosses in Early Historic art. As a multi-referential symbol that carried meaning in both cultures, the cross could have been a motif that was well suited to a style of resistance based on

Figure 5.1. A prehistoric glazeware bowl with double-bar crosses, representing dragonflies. Most crosses on prehistoric vessels appear to represent dragonflies, stars, or birds (redrawn from a photograph courtesy of Maxwell Museum of Anthropology).

Figure 5.2. Prehistoric kiva mural from Pottery Mound. The numerous crosses in the background probably represent insects (photograph courtesy of University of New Mexico).

masking traditional images and misrepresenting religious beliefs to the Spanish.

Crosses, while never a major design element in Pueblo imagery, were certainly not a design motif introduced by the Spanish. Most of the crosses on prehistoric ceramic vessels can be recognized as dragonflies, stars, or as elements of ritual scenes (Figure 5.1). Crosses appear more frequently on prehistoric rock art and kiva murals, where they generally represent stars or insects (Figure 5.2). These prehistoric contexts indicate that crosses had long held ritual meaning for Pueblo people, quite apart from any Christian meanings.

Crosses and Material Culture

Pottery Decoration

Elsewhere, in collaboration with Spielmann and Potter, I have discussed the changes in Rio Grande pottery decoration that we interpret as resistance (Spielmann et al. 1999). In that research, we found that designs on glazeware vessels, made in Pueblos where Spanish missions existed, became simplified and abstracted, masking their potentially ritual meaning. In contrast, designs on

Tabira Whiteware vessels, made in villages that did not have missions, became highly explicit in portraying ritually significant images. We believe that these changes illustrate that pottery designs were being actively used to mask subversive transcripts in public contexts while elaborating them in contexts hidden from dominant classes, as predicted by Scott (1990).

The abstraction of glazeware designs is my focus here, as I believe it represented not only a masking of information, but also the deliberate infusion of multi-referential symbols in order to misinform Spanish viewers. One interesting means of abstraction of bird designs was to replace birds with crosses. While obvious bird motifs become less frequent on glazeware vessels in the historic period, crosses increased in frequency. An examination of 88 whole bowls, Glaze B through Glaze F, in the collections of the Museum of New Mexico, the Western Archeological and Conservation Center, and the Maxwell Museum of Anthropology, revealed crosses and X's on 10 percent (n=52) of prehistoric vessels, and 20 percent (n=36) of historic vessels. Basic design layouts, however, did not significantly change, suggesting that the symbolism was maintained, albeit in an abbreviated form.

While crosses resemble the shape of a bird in flight, they could also represent the central symbol of Christianity. However, their placement where a bird would have been placed within a traditional design indicates a bird to a viewer who knows the design layout and its meaning (Figure 5.3a and b). This may have been an intentional manipulation of a symbol, which the Pueblo people recognized to have different meanings in the Pueblo and Spanish worlds. The replacement of "idolatrous" images with crosses would have satisfied Spanish friars, while retaining a reference to those same images, allowing Pueblo people to maintain the meaning of native imagery.

While the available sample of glazeware bowls is small, it is corroborated by an examination of 525 Zuni polychrome vessels from Hawikuh (illustrated in Smith et al. 1966). On these vessels, crosses are rare on prehistoric types (Heshatauthla, Kwakina, and Kechipawan Polychromes). Crosses first began appearing with any regularity on around 10 percent of Matsaki Polychrome vessels, dating to A.D. 1470–1650, and increase in frequency to 18 percent of vessels of the historic type (Hawikuh Polychrome A.D. 1630–1680).

With the Pueblo Revolt of 1680, the Spanish were driven out of New Mexico, and therefore hidden transcripts of resistance would no longer have been necessary. Therefore, if pottery designs played a part in resistance, dramatic changes in those designs should occur at the time of the Pueblo Revolt. This, of course, did occur, as Adams (1981:325) has documented in the Hopi area, where Spanish vessel forms and design motifs disappear from Hopi ceramics.

The use of the cross on ceramic vessels follows the expected pattern as well. Crosses almost disappear as a motif after the Pueblo Revolt of 1680 throughout the Pueblo region (Frank and Harlow 1974). At the same time, birds reappear, and there is an explosion of the use of feather motifs, across the entire Pueblo area, to the extent that almost every vessel has some form of feather motifs (Frank and Harlow 1974:21; Mills, Chapter 6). These changes further reinforce the idea that crosses were a part

Figure 5.3. Two glazeware bowls with similar design layouts.
(a) A prehistoric vessel showing a common design with bird panels alternating with diagonal bands (photograph courtesy of Maxwell Museum of Anthropology).

(b) An Early Historic glazeware bowl. The design is masked by simplification and abstraction. Alternating with the diagonal bands are crosses rather than birds (photograph courtesy of Western Archeological and Conservation Center, Tucson).

of a strategy of deliberate resistance. Once the resistance was no longer needed, crosses disappear and obvious bird imagery returns in force.

Mural Painting

While the pottery designs are consistent with my expectation for the use of style in resistance, it would be further supported by evidence for a similar pattern of stylistic manipulation in other art forms that are associated with ritual. Murals are one such art form.

The majority of mural paintings known from the prehistoric Southwest has been found in kivas and clearly portrays ritual scenes and sacred iconography (Figure 5.2). Spanish friars routinely destroyed kivas, and their use was forbidden. Because kiva murals were part of a forbidden ritual context, their very existence in the early historic period is clear evidence of resistance. There is no reason to expect the styles to have been manipulated within the context of the kiva, since that is not a context in which the art was visible to the Spanish. However, murals were similarly used to decorate Christian churches at the time, and while there are few extant church murals from before the 1680 Revolt, ethnohistoric descriptions contain some hints that mural painting was manipulated in a way consistent with the Pueblo style of resistance.

Silverberg (1970:69), in his history of the Pueblo Revolt, states that, "on the white-washed walls of the church's interior the [Pueblo] people painted bright murals: birds, flowers, symbols of the sun, the rain, the lightning, abstract forms, the whole lively repertoire of expressive native artists." This statement is intriguing, since rain (or sprinkling water) and lightning are two of the most common non-living designs represented in kiva murals, and birds are the most common zoomorphic depictions (Crotty 1992). This suggests that native artisans, when given some license in painting Christian churches, may have used the opportunity to infuse the space with imagery appropriate to sacred Pueblo places, thus manipulating the meaning of the church itself.

Jewelry

A final art form in which crosses are critically important is jewelry, including the rosaries of the Spanish. Allison Bird (1992) has documented the manipulation of the dual meaning of these crosses in her discussion of crosses in Pueblo silversmithing. She notes that a number of eighteenth- and nineteenth-century descriptions of Pueblo dances describe the dancers wearing crosses, and many of the early photographs (from the late 1800s) likewise show a number of silver crosses on necklaces made by native silversmiths. She suggests that crosses became a popular

motif that was regularly made by natives as well as imposed by the Spanish because of their dual meaning. The preferred style of cross, adopted from the Spanish was the double-bar cross, which resembled native representations of dragonflies. Many of these are designed with a heart at the base. Bird (1992:18) quotes an elderly Pueblo man who remembers that double-bar crosses were a favorite for this reason, and that native silversmiths put a large heart at the bottom of the crosses, "to show what a generous heart the dragonfly has and how much he loves the people." He goes on to say, "it made the priests happy to see the people wear their crosses, because they thought we were wearing the heart of Jesus."

While Bird's informant was speaking of his childhood in the late 1800s, such a use of crosses is likely to have had a much greater antiquity. Pueblo and Plains Indians alike readily received crucifixes on rosaries from missionaries. An illustration of a masked figure from a Tabira Black-on-white vessel (A.D. 1600–1672) indicates that such crosses were put to use in native religious contexts (Figure 5.4).

Conclusion

The archaeological and ethnohistorical evidence for the manipulation of art in the act of resistance is consistent across several pottery types, as well as mural painting and jewelry, and conforms to an overall style of Puebloan resistance evident in the ethnohistoric record. I have suggested that the masking of designs on pottery, the wearing of crosses, and the intentional use of native religious imagery in Christian churches were used to send a message of compliance to the Spanish missionary, while simultaneously maintaining native meanings. The cross, a motif that carried ritual meaning in both cultures, was a particularly useful symbol in this form of resistance. Crosses could be strategically placed in contexts that related to traditional Pueblo meanings without arousing the suspicion of Spanish priests, who attached their own meaning to the motif. Thus, the manipulation of style actively exploited the multiplicity of meanings that style allows.

One question that arises from this interpretation of

A

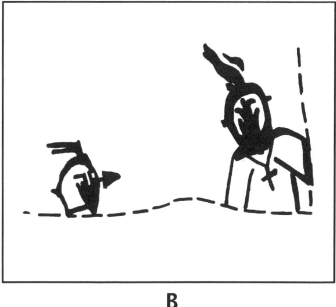

B

Figure 5.4. Ritual figures from two Tabira black-on-white vessels, dating to the late sixteenth or early seventeenth century. Their attire is similar and obviously linked to native religion, but one figure wears a cross (adapted from Hayes et al. 1981).

style is why the Spanish were so easily duped. After all, the Spanish had been waging God's war against native religions in Mesoamerica for years, and were well trained for the job when they reached New Mexico (Gutierrez 1991). They were actively engaged in seeking out and destroying ritual items, and were constantly watching for idolatrous images. In this respect, the Spanish conquerors may have been misled by their own racist preconceptions of native peoples. The Franciscan friars portrayed the Pueblos as "weak and frail" in their writings, referring to them as "children of low intelligence, incapable of leadership or ordination" (Gutierrez 1991:166). Indians who converted to Christianity were never allowed any status in service to the Church, since they were believed to be incapable of understanding the subtleties of the religion (Terrell 1973). Given this attitude, it is not surprising that the Spanish expected no subtleties to the native religion as well. This is clear from the comments of a seventeenth-century governor to New Mexico, who scoffed at the efforts of the friars to ban traditional dances, commenting that they consisted of, "nothing more than something that sounded like hu-hu-hu, and these thieving friars say it is superstitious!" (quoted in Gutierrez 1991:269).

Two other factors may have likewise contributed to the Pueblos ability to deceive their oppressors. First, few of the friars learned native languages, expecting the Pueblos to learn Spanish instead. This could have facilitated the secret retention of ritual information, which the Spanish simply couldn't understand. Second, and perhaps most important, in wearing crosses, presenting gifts to churches, and painting crosses on bowls, the Pueblo people showed the Spanish what they wanted to see. When a painted hide, bearing the image of the sun and moon and above each a cross, was presented to Fray Alonso de Benavides in 1628, he stated that "the symbolism was apparent to me," before any explanation was given. He was quick to read the symbols according to his own belief system as "fruit of the divine word" (Hodge et al. 1945:85). To a Spanish missionary, the idea that a crucifix on the end of a rosary could be a native symbol was simply inconceivable. To the Pueblo people, the crossed meanings across cultures provided a powerful means of passive resistance until the Pueblo Revolt of 1680, and the military defeat of both Crown and Cross.

Acknowledgments

The photographs of glazeware bowls used in this study were taken by Katherine Spielmann and William Graves at The Museum of New Mexico, Santa Fe, the Western Archeological and Conservation Center, Tucson, and the Maxwell Museum of Anthropology, Albuquerque.

References Cited

Adams, E. Charles
1981   The View from the Hopi Mesas. In *The Protohistoric Period in the North American Southwest, a.d. 1450–1700*, edited by D. Wilcox and B. W. B. Masse, pp. 321–335. Arizona State University Anthropological Papers No. 24. Tempe.

Bancroft, Herbert H.
1889   *History of Arizona and New Mexico 1530–1888*. The History Company, San Francisco.

Bird, Allison
1992   *Heart of the Dragonfly*. Avanyu Publishing, Inc., Santa Fe.

Crotty, H. K.
1992   Protohistoric Anasazi Kiva Murals. In *Archaeology, Art and Anthropology: Papers in Honor of J. J. Brody*, edited by M. S. Duran and D. T. Kirkpatrick, pp. 51–62. Papers of the Archaeological Society of New Mexico, No. 18. Albuquerque.

Dozier, Edward P.
1970   *Pueblo Indians of North America*. Holt, Rinehart, and Winston, New York.

Folsom, Franklin
1973   *Red Power on the Rio Grande: The Native American Revolution of 1680*. Follet Publishing, Chicago.

Frank, Larry, and Francis H. Harlow
1974   *Historic Pottery of the Pueblo Indians 1600–1880*. New York Graphics Society, Boston.

Gutiérrez, Ramón A.
1991   *When Jesus Came the Corn Mothers Went Away: Marriage, Sexuality, and Power in New Mexico, 1500–1846*. Stanford University Press, Stanford, Calif.

Hackett, Charles W., and Charmion C. Shelby (editor and translator)
1942   *Revolt of the Pueblo Indians of New Mexico, and Otermin's Attempted Reconquest, 1680–1682*. Coronado Cuarto Centennial Publications 1540–1949. Vols. VIII and IX. University of New Mexico Press, Albuquerque.

Hayes, Alden, Jon Nathan Young, and A. Helene Warren
1981   *Excavation of Mound 7, Gran Quivira National Monument, New Mexico*. Publications in Archaeology 16, National Park Service, Washington, D.C.

Hodder, Ian
1982   *Symbols in Action*. Cambridge University Press, Cambridge, UK.

1990   Style as Historical Quality. In *The Uses of Style in Archaeology*, edited by M. Conkey and C. Hastorf. pp. 44–51. Cambridge University Press, Cambridge, UK.

Hodge, Frederick W.
1939   A Square Kiva at Hawikuh. In *So Live the Works of Men: Papers in Honor of Edgar Lee Hewett*, edited by D. D. Brand and F. E. Harvey, pp. 195–214. School of American Research Press, Albuquerque.

Hodge, Frederick W., George P. Hammond, and Agapito Rey (editors)
1945   *Fray Alonso de Benavides' Revised Memorial of 1634*. Coronado Cuarto Centennial Publications, 1540–1940, Vol. IV. University of New Mexico Press, Albuquerque.

MacDonald, William K.
1990   Investigating Style: An Exploratory Analysis of some Plains Burials. In *The Uses of Style in Archaeology*, edited by M. Conkey and C. Hastorf, pp. 52–60. Cambridge University Press, Cambridge, UK.

Scott, James C.
1990   *Domination and the Art of Resistance: Hidden Transcripts*. Yale University Press, New Haven, Conn.

Silverberg, Robert
1970   *The Pueblo Revolt*. Weybright and Talley, New York.

Smith, Watson, Richard S. Woodbury, and Nathalie F. S. Woodbury
1966   *The Excavation of Hawikuh by Fredrick Webb Hodge*. Museum of the American Indian, Heye Foundation, New York.

Spielmann, Katherine A., Jeanette L. Mobley-Tanaka, and James M. Potter
1999   Style and Resistance in Seventeenth Century Salinas Province. Paper presented at the 64th annual meeting of the Society of American Archaeology, Chicago, Ill.

Stevenson, Matilda Coxe
1894   *The Sia*. Eleventh Annual Report of the Bureau of American Ethnology for the Years 1889–1890, Washington, D.C.

Terrell, John U.
1973   *Pueblos, Gods and Spaniards*. Dial Press, New York.

Whiteley, Peter M.
1988   *Deliberate Acts: Changing Hopi Culture through the Oraibi Split*. University of Arizona Press, Tucson.

Chapter 6

Acts of Resistance:

Zuni Ceramics, Social Identity, and the Pueblo Revolt

Barbara J. Mills

The Pueblo Revolt is one of the best-known examples of a New World indigenous rebellion. Although largely a revolt of Puebloan peoples, it should also be understood in the context of the wider, turbulent times of the late seventeenth century. It encompassed non-Pueblo groups in the Pueblo area, groups in northern Mexico (Deeds 1998; Guy and Sheridan 1998), and other seventeenth-century conflicts between Pueblo and Spanish (Espinosa 1988). As a well-documented rebellion against European colonization (Espinosa 1940; Hackett 1942; John 1975; Kessell 1979; Kessell and Hendricks 1992), the Pueblo Revolt represents an excellent case study in which to investigate the themes of resistance and the impact of a colonial world system on New World populations. Moreover, because the Revolt resulted in widespread changes in community organization and material culture, it is also an ideal time period in which to investigate the interrelationship between ethnogenesis and technological style.

I apply these themes to the analysis of Zuni ceramics, including formal, decorative, and compositional variability. I argue that the process of Zuni ethnogenesis wrought by the Pueblo Revolt resulted in changes in Zuni technological styles that were intentionally manipulated by potters, most likely women, during the late seventeenth through early eighteenth centuries. As such, this study underscores the importance of understanding the relationships between gender, social identity, and technological choice in the construction of new communities that were forged through their resistance to colonialism.

Theoretical Framework

The theoretical framework used in this chapter draws upon models in three separate areas of research: (1) the process of ethnogenesis, (2) women's participation in resistance to the imposition of colonial rule, and (3) the intentional use of material culture as a means of expressing social identity.

As Hill (1996a:1) writes, "ethnogenesis is not merely a label for the historical emergence of culturally distinct peoples but a concept encompassing peoples' simultaneously cultural and political struggles to create enduring identities in general contexts of radical change and discontinuity." Ethnogenesis is an important theme in the literature on European expansion in the Americas (e.g., Anderson 1999; Hill 1996b), but is also applicable wherever indigenous populations were drastically reorganized through colonial processes (e.g., Hudson 1999; Jones and Hill-Burnet 1982; Roosens 1989). Ethnogenesis is a particularly appropriate term for the period of the Pueblo Revolt because this period saw dramatic demographic, social, and political changes as part of the colonial process. Many villages were consolidated and new identities were constructed. This is especially true at Zuni, where multiple villages coalesced into a single village during the Pueblo Revolt.

Women's participation in the process of resistance has been an important part of the anthropological literature on colonialism (Bradford 1996; Etienne and Leacock 1980; Lwyn 1994; Pennell 1987). Archaeological study of the material consequences of colonialism has largely focused on the reorganization of women's labor, especially as demands for tribute production increased. Textiles have been an especially interesting material class because of the ethnohistorically and archaeologically documented changes in gendered relations of production and status (Brumfiel 1996, 1997; Etienne 1980; Webster 1997). When ceramics have been discussed, it is usually in the context of either the introduction of new foods and how labor demands affected cuisines and the scheduling of meals (Brumfiel 1991; see also Beck 2000). Nonetheless, as the primary producers of ceramics in most traditional non-market societies (Mills 2000), women were in a position to express resistance in many different ways, including how they decorated pottery. Few studies have addressed this aspect of women and colonialism and one of my aims here is to see how style changes may have been an intentional part of Pueblo women's resistance to European society in the Southwest.

Ethnoarchaeological, archaeological, and historical research demonstrate that material culture can be a powerful way of expressing social difference and group membership (e.g., Stark 1998). Material culture can be actively or intentionally manipulated to signal identity, but sometimes more passive expressions of identity can also be discerned in artifacts and architecture. Whether active or passive, one concept that is particularly useful is the idea of technological choice in the production of material culture. I use a broad definition of technological choice to include all the decisions that an individual makes during the production of an artifact, whether compositional, formal, or decorative (Schiffer and Skibo 1997:29).

The technological choices that contribute to ceramic variation are constrained by available raw materials, and compromises are made when using these raw materials in the construction of vessels for specific purposes. Within these constraints are a wide variety of options. Some of the choices made are those that cannot be reproduced exactly by potters without seeing a pot under construction, particularly in patterned ways within a particular community. These are most useful for identifying differences in learning frameworks that might relate to more subtle distinctions of social groups in the archaeological record (Lemonnier 1992; Stark et al. 1997; Zedeño 1994). Bourdieu's (1977) theory of *habitus* is often cited as the means by which these systems are reproduced in social terms.

However, other choices are often intentionally manipulated to convey social information. What color slip to apply, what kinds of paints to use, how to shape the pot, and how the vessel will be decorated can be manipulated for political, economic, ideological, and social reasons. Sudden or punctuated changes through time in a suite of these ceramic attributes can be a key to the intentional manipulation of the ceramic medium. In many cases, the reasons for punctuated changes may coincide, such as the manipulation of ideological symbols or styles by political factions (e.g., Bowser 2000; Pauketat and Emerson 1991; Van Keuren 2000; Welbourn 1984; Wonderley 1986). Before these interpretations can be made, however, contextual data are necessary to understand the interplay of different factors (see also Hays 1993).

In this chapter, I use late prehistoric and early historic ceramics from the Zuni area to contextualize the punctuated changes in ceramic form, surface treatment, and decorative styles that occurred after the tumultuous seventeenth century. I argue that this intentional manipulation of ceramic variability was related to the complementary processes of resistance and identity formation following the Pueblo Revolt, and that this was one means by which women participated in the resistance process. In order to look at how these acts of resistance were structured, I take a historical perspective on the ceramic assemblages, beginning with the ceramics made at the time of first European contact.

Historical Context

When Europeans first visited Zuni in the mid-sixteenth century Zunis resided in nine villages (Figure 6.1) (Ferguson 1994; Kintigh 1985, 1990; see also Ferguson, Chapter 2). During the seventeenth century, Zuni was at the outskirts of efforts to colonize the Pueblos. Seventeenth-century routes between Mexico and the Southwest followed the Rio Grande, rather than the earlier routes through eastern Arizona. Nonetheless, missions were established at the two Zuni sites of Hawikku[1] and Halona:wa in 1629. *Visitas* were built shortly afterwards at the sites of Mats'a:kya, Kyaki:ma, and Kechiba:wa (Ferguson 1994:82; Hodge 1937:96). The Zunis did not take well to Spanish authority and violence erupted in 1630, when two priests were killed. Between 1630 and 1680, what were formerly separate villages were consolidated into three villages (Hodge 1937).

The Zuni people used the top of Dowa Yalanne as a retreat several times during the early historic period (Hodge 1937). The Pueblo Revolt was, however, the first extended period of co-residence for the entire population of the tribe (Ferguson 1994). Ferguson (Chapter 2) discusses the distribution of residential groups within this remarkable site, located on the top of Dowa Yalanne. Here, 38 separate roomblocks were occupied during the Revolt, concentrated on the southwestern part of the mesa. A trail led down to the nearby site of Kyaki:ma, where there is still an active spring. After the Revolt, the entire population coalesced at one of the previously occupied

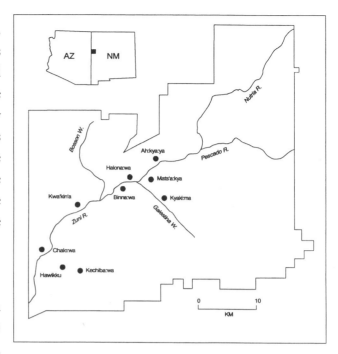

Figure 6.1. Map of the Zuni area, showing locations of sites occupied in the sixteenth century.

sites, Halona:wa. This village is still occupied to the present and remains the ceremonial and population center for the majority of Zunis living on the reservation.

Data Sources

Several archaeological collections must be used to track changes in Zuni ceramics across the historic period. The largest sample of pre-Revolt ceramics, largely whole vessels, is from excavations conducted by Frederick Webb Hodge at Hawikku and now in the collections of the National Museum of the American Indian, Smithsonian Institution. A smaller collection of whole vessels from Hawikku's sister site, Kechiba:wa, was excavated under the direction of Louis Clarke of the Museum of Archaeology and Ethnology, Cambridge University. I analyzed 1,151 decorated vessels from these two sites, including decorative, formal, and surface treatment attributes.

Relatively few Zuni vessels have been excavated from eighteenth-century contexts. Ironically, the best examples of post-Revolt Zuni ceramics, called Ashiwi Polychrome, are the whole and partial vessels excavated by Earl Morris in the Gobernador District of northwestern New Mexico.

Table 6.1

Periods, Collections, and Ceramic Types Used in the Zuni Ceramic Analysis.

	Protohistoric (1450-1630)	Pre-Revolt (1630-1680)	Post-Revolt (1692-1750)
Site Collections Represented in Analysis	Hawikku Kechiba:wa	Hawikku Kechiba:wa	Gobernador Area Zuni Pueblo (Halona:wa)
Decorated Ceramic Wares: Types	**Matsaki Buffware:** Matsaki Brown-on-buff, Matsaki Polychrome **Unnamed Red-on-buff** **Early Zuni Glazeware:** Pinnawa Glaze-on-white Pinnawa Red-on-white Kechipawan Polychrome	**Matsaki Buffware:** Matsaki Brown-on-buff, Matsaki Polychrome **Hawikuh Glazeware:** Hawikuh Polychrome Hawikuh Glaze-on-red	**Matte-paint Polychrome:** Ashiwi Polychrome
Vessel Forms	Globular jars and hemispherical bowls.	Shouldered jars, shouldered bowls, and soup plates.	Jars with elongated necks, mid-body bulge, and concave bases; bowls with bulging zone below rim; hemispherical bowls and globular jars (late), also with concave bases.

These come from the site of Three Corn Ruin (Carlson 1965) and are in the collections of the Museum of Anthropology at the University of Colorado, Boulder. Once interpreted as sites of both Pueblo and Navajo refugees, recent research at Gobernador area sites by Towner (1996, 1999), argues for their more exclusive use by Navajo refugees. Indeed, the Zuni vessels recovered from Three Corn are from Navajo burials at the site. Towner's dendrochronological analyses of these sites unequivocally places occupation in the early to mid-eighteenth century.

Eighteenth-century Zuni ceramics from the Zuni area itself are rare because of limited excavations in contexts dating to this period. However, excavations by the Pueblo of Zuni in the central village have produced several hundred eighteenth-century sherds from intramural and extramural trash deposits (Ferguson and Mills 1982). In addition to these archaeological collections, James and Matilda Coxe Stevenson collected a few eighteenth-century heirloom vessels in the late nineteenth century for the Smithsonian Institution (Bunzel 1972 [1929]:Plate XX, top; Hardin 1989), and in the twentieth century for other museum collections (see especially Batkin 1987; Frank and Harlow 1974; Harlow 1973; and Mera 1939 for

illustrations). In fact, the first vessel collected for the Indian Arts Fund, now part of the collections of the School of American Research, is an eighteenth-century Ashiwi Polychrome vessel from Zuni (Mera 1939:Plate LIX). The post-Revolt Ashiwi Polychrome is the direct antecedent of the more familiar matte-paint Zuni Polychrome of the late eighteenth and nineteenth centuries.

Zuni Ceramics and Technological Choices

To facilitate chronological comparison, I divide my discussion of Zuni ceramics into three periods: (1) the protohistoric or late fifteenth through sixteenth centuries (A.D. 1450–1629), (2) the pre-Revolt period in the seventeenth century (A.D. 1629–1680), and (3) the post-Revolt period, especially the early eighteenth century (A.D. 1692–1750). It is possible to assign most ceramics to one of these periods (Table 6.1) based on technological and stylistic changes that have been identified by researchers at Zuni since the early twentieth century. Richard and Nathalie Woodbury's (Woodbury and Woodbury 1966) excellent summary of protohistoric and early historic Zuni ceramics serves as a baseline, much of which was based on Hodge's notes on his stratigraphic excavations at Hawikku.

Figure 6.2. Kechipawan Polychrome jar from Hawikku
(courtesy, National Museum of the American Indian,
Smithsonian Institution, no. 13/2044, photograph by author).

Figure 6.3. Matsaki Polychrome bowl from Hawikku
showing asymmetrical design (courtesy, National Museum
of the American Indian, Smithsonian Institution,
no. 9/4181, photograph by author).

As the above periods indicate, no ceramic samples are present for the period of occupation during the 12 years of the Pueblo Revolt.

Protohistoric Period

During the fifteenth and sixteenth centuries (ca. A.D. 1450 to 1600), a diversity of wares was made at Zuni. One of the most common in the collections is Matsaki Buffware, decorated with red, black, brown, and occasionally white matte-paints. Early Zuni glazeware (Figure 6.2), decorated with red matte and black, green, or purple glaze paints on a white slip was also made (Bushnell 1955; Mills 1995; Woodbury and Woodbury 1966). Redware vessels, including Salado polychromes and Salado White-on-red, also occur in the assemblages at Hawikku and Kechiba:wa, although it has never been demonstrated that these were actually made at Zuni and I do not include them here. The most common forms of the Matsaki and early glazeware vessels are hemispherical bowls or globular jars with straight necks. By the mid-sixteenth century, both early Zuni glazes and Salado polychromes (if they were ever even made at Zuni) were no longer made. The dominant ware for the remainder of the period was Matsaki Buffware, which

appears to have been made over a long period of nearly 200 years. Previous chemical compositional studies indicate that the ceramics decorated in glaze paints are the most homogeneous, and that varieties of paste recipes (and presumably clay sources) were used in the production of Matsaki Buffware (Mills 1995). The diversity of pastes used for Matsaki Buffware is because of its longer period of production and because it could be fired at a wide range of temperatures, allowing a variety of clays to be used. Glaze painted ceramics in general required higher temperatures and clays were selected appropriately.

Painted designs of the fifteenth- and sixteenth-century Zuni ceramics are diverse. Bichromes are usually painted with bold, geometric designs. Birds, especially parrots, are depicted on several vessels, especially those of the early glazeware. Many of the Matsaki Polychromes are painted with asymmetrical layouts in Sikyatki style, like contemporaneous Yellowware made at Hopi (Figure 6.3).

Masked figures or kachinas are present on several vessels made during the protohistoric period at Zuni (Figure 6.4). Depictions of kachinas are similar to those found on late fourteenth-century ceramics throughout

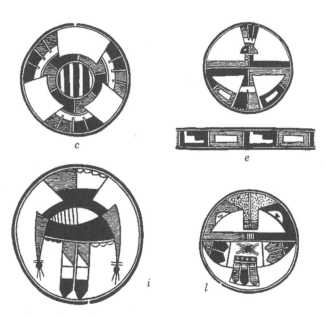

Figure 6.4. Early Matsaki Polychrome bowl interiors
with kachina designs (after Smith et al. 1966:Plate 51c and 51k).

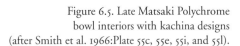

Figure 6.5. Late Matsaki Polychrome
bowl interiors with kachina designs
(after Smith et al. 1966:Plate 55c, 55e, 55i, and 55l).

the Mogollon Rim and Hopi areas (Adams 1991; Ferg 1982; Hays 1994), although they appear to be present slightly later in the Zuni area. Kachina designs occur almost exclusively on bowl interiors, although one rare handled jar form has a kachina face. Not only are bowl interiors a better field of decoration than jar exteriors, bowl interiors are also more private and hidden from the casual observer. By contrast, water jar exterior designs, which would have been more public, are nearly all geometric. The concern for secrecy and the use of bowl interiors for kachina designs predates European contact in the Mogollon Rim area (Van Keuren 2000), and shows continuity with the protohistoric Zuni ceramics.

The diversity of designs, pigments, and paste recipes reflects late prehistoric migrations and the coalescence of different populations at Zuni in the century before European contact. Some of these populations brought with them different mortuary rituals, including cremation burials and the practice of vessel killing (Crown 1994:110; Robinson and Sprague 1965:449). Cremations and inhumations occur in distinct cemeteries at Hawikku (Smith et al. 1966) and Kechiba:wa (Kintigh 2000), supporting the use of these areas by subgroups who sought to maintain different social identities. Kintigh (2000) has recently demonstrated that differences in burial

orientation, categories of grave goods, and the proportions of ceramic wares in mortuary contexts between these two sites are great enough to indicate different population histories and the maintenance of distinctive group identities, perhaps even into the early historic period.

Pre-Revolt Period

A major change occurred in the early decades of the seventeenth century with the re-introduction of glaze painted ceramics. This ware, called Hawikuh glazeware, includes Hawikuh Black-on-red and Polychrome types. The re-introduction of glazeware is associated with the beginning of the Mission period at Zuni, including the re-assignment of friars from the Rio Grande area, where glazeware was continuously made in several districts. One of the friars who moved to Zuni was Fray Francisco Letrado, who had previously been assigned to Las Humanas in the Salinas District (Vivian 1979:23–24). After two years at Las Humanas, Letrado went to Zuni in 1631. He resided there until Zunis killed him in 1632 (Bandelier 1892:96; Hodge 1937:100). Historical sources mention that he had Spanish soldiers with him for protection when he moved to Zuni. Although these sources do not mention that Pueblo people accompanied him from the Rio Grande area, the glazeware that was

d   h

Figure 6.6. Late Matsaki Polychrome bowl interiors with shield designs (after Smith et al. 1966:Plate 55d and 56h).

Figure 6.7. Late Matsaki Polychrome bowl from Hawikku with pendant feather and fringe design (courtesy, National Museum of the American Indian, Smithsonian Institution, no. 8/6819, photograph by author).

made in the early 1630s was clearly inspired by Eastern Pueblo ceramics. Hodge's test pits at Hawikku indicate that glazeware went from zero to over 60 percent of all decorated ceramics from Level 8 to Level 2 (Smith et al. 1966:Figure 36). Based on the association of these levels with artifacts of European manufacture that would have been brought by the seventeenth-century friars, a reasonable estimate for the time span represented by these levels is only 50 to 75 years.

Hawikuh Glazeware and the contemporaneous late Matsaki Buffware show dramatic changes in vessel forms when compared to earlier vessels from the Zuni area (Mills 1995:Figure 8.2). Shouldered bowls and jars were made similar to those of Glaze F in the Rio Grande area and late Hopi Yellowware vessels. These seventeenth-century wares also show several significant changes in design. Kachina iconography becomes less recognizable, but kachinas are still depicted on the interior field (Figure 6.5). Suppression of native religion by the Franciscans was common and potters may have intentionally disguised kachina representation on their vessels. Parrots rarely occur on later Matsaki or Hawikuh vessels, suggesting a disruption of the trade networks supplying these birds to the northern Southwest.

Asymmetrical designs are still found on Zuni ceramics

of the pre-Revolt period, although more rarely of the Sikyatki style. Some of the asymmetrical designs have elements such as stars and feathers with a horizontal dividing panel that appear to be shields (Figure 6.6). These design elements are found throughout the Pueblo area on shields and on rock art depictions of shields in the late prehistoric and historic periods (Schaafsma 2000). That these appear on Zuni ceramics of the Mission period suggests that warfare and the symbolism of conflict may have become more prominent in Zuni lives.

As Hardin (1989) has observed, one of the most common design motifs found on the late Matsaki Polychrome and Hawikuh Polychrome vessels are feathers (Figure 6.7). Many of these appear to be eagle feathers. They often hang vertically in rows, pendant from rims. In other cases, they are used horizontally in band designs (Figure 6.8). Large jars provided two design fields and both vertical and horizontal feathers are present.

All feathers are widely used by Zuni men in the making of prayer sticks. However, Bunzel (1972 [1929]:106) recorded one woman in the early twentieth century as saying that, "women do not prepare prayer sticks, and that is why we always put feathers on the jars." Edmund Ladd's thesis on Zuni ethno-ornithology is particularly useful for specific uses of these feathers. He

Figure 6.8. Hawikuh Polychrome jar from Hawikku (courtesy, National Museum of the American Indian, Smithsonian Institution, no. 9/6374, photograph by author).

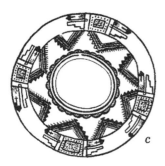 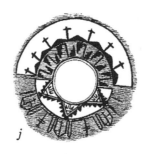

Figure 6.9. Hawikuh Polychrome jar designs with Roman crosses (after Smith et al. 1996: Plate 79c and 79j).

Figure 6.10. Ashiwi Polychrome jar from Zuni Pueblo (Stevenson Collection, no. 41152, Department of Anthropology, Smithsonian Institution, photograph by Margaret A. Hardin).

notes that eagle feathers, especially the asymmetrically tipped feathers of the bald eagle, are among the most valued by Zunis (Ladd 1963:88–89). They are used in the masks of several important deities, including the Shalako. Eagle feathers are a major part of the altars of the Galaxy Society or *Newekwe* to symbolize the breath of the supreme deity, *A'wonawil'ona* (Stevenson 1904:432). Both men and women belong to this society of ritual clowns, which was one of the most powerful medicine societies at Zuni in the later historic period.

Feathers are also associated with brush strokes that suggest the fringe of a textile (seen in Figures 6.3 and 6.7). Textiles were and still are an important part of Pueblo material culture. The production of cotton textiles in the late prehistoric and early historic periods was conducted by men in suprahousehold contexts, especially kivas (Mills 2000; Webster 1997). The frequency of one textile motif, fringing, increases dramatically during the pre-Revolt mission period (Table 6.2), when the use of kivas was being suppressed. Another design element that increases dramatically during this time is the Roman cross (Figure 6.9). Out of 20 vessels with crosses from either Hawikku or Kechiba:wa, 19 date to this period (Table 6.2).

Table 6.2. Design Occurences by Period

Design Element or Motif	Protohistoric (1450-1630)	Pre-Revolt (1630-1680)	Post-Revolt (1692-1750)
Katsinas	5	11	0
Roman Cross	1	19	0
Fringed Elements	3	14	0

Post-Revolt Period

A dramatic break in past technological styles took place at Zuni after the Pueblo Revolt. Neither Hawikuh Glazeware nor Matsaki Buffware vessels were made after this time. Instead, a new ware was made that shows strong similarities with other pueblos, especially Acoma (Dillingham and Elliott 1992). In fact, all the other Pueblos except Hopi, where potters never used glaze-paint, made non-glaze-painted polychromes after the seventeenth century. The new decorated ceramics have been called the matte-paint

Figure 6.11. Ashiwi Polychrome jars (after Mera 1939:Plate LVII, left; Plate LIX, right).
Left, collection of Laboratory of Anthropology cat. no. MNM 7878-12; right, collection of School of American Research cat no. IAF-1.

polychromes because the paint was no longer glazed (Frank and Harlow 1974; Harlow 1978). At Zuni, the earliest of the matte-painted ceramics is called Ashiwi Polychrome (Mera 1939). Changes in vessel form seen throughout the Pueblo area during the early to mid-eighteenth century include elongated necks and the use of concave bases (Figure 6.10). Subtle differences between Pueblos are present in rim and upper body shapes that enable the products of different Pueblos to be distinguished. For example, Acoma vessels of the period have mushroom-shaped upper bodies, whereas Zuni vessel upper bodies are straight. The straight upper body provides a large field of design. At least by the mid-eighteenth century, some Ashiwi Polychrome vessels were also made in a more globular shape, a shape that is found on the Kiapkwa and Zuni Polychromes of later periods.

The designs on Ashiwi Polychrome were predominantly executed with solid red and black paint on white slips. Decoration includes the popular feather motifs of the previous century (Figure 6.11). No kachina imagery is known for any vessel of the period (Table 6.2). Some elements of possible European origin were added, including medallions. During the mid-eighteenth century, the use of hachure is revived from prehistoric usage (Hardin 1989), and it increases in popularity through the latter part of the 1700s. Nonetheless, feather motifs remain popular for jar rims and bowl

exteriors (Figure 6.12). In fact, these become highly standardized decorative elements.

The end of glaze-paint technology in the late seventeenth century has been one of the enigmas of historic Pueblo ceramics. One suggestion in the literature is that lead sources for the manufacture of glaze paints were restricted by the Spanish for their bullets and later by Spanish mining claims (Dillingham and Elliott 1992:128–130; Snow 1982:260). This observation may apply to the Rio Grande Pueblos, but there is no evidence for Spanish exploitation of lead sources in the Western Pueblo area. A long tradition of lead glaze paints is present in the Mogollon Rim and Zuni areas that most likely depended on local lead oxide sources.

Instead, there are several other lines of evidence that support the idea that the end of glaze-paint technology at Zuni was an intentional act to mark a break with earlier ceramic production. One of these lines of evidence is Hodge's observation that the baptismal vessel in the church at Hawikku was a Zuni glazeware pot. If this were the case, then the association of the mission with this vessel type may have been one that the Zunis would want to leave behind them. Another line of evidence is that the reintroduction of glaze-paint technology at Zuni corresponds with the arrival of the missionaries from the Rio Grande in 1630. This would still have been within the memory of aging potters by the time of the Pueblo

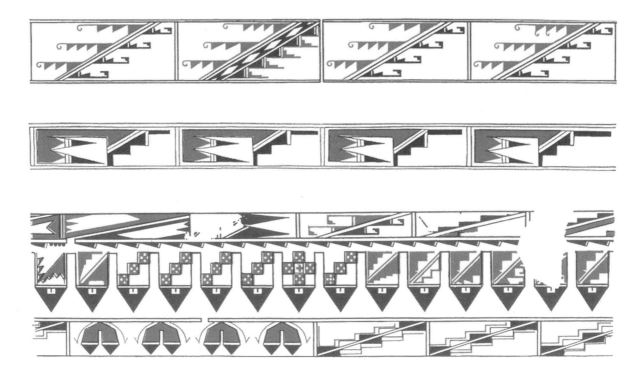

Figure 6.12. Ashiwi Polychrome designs showing diagonal feather motifs on bowls (upper two rollouts) and jar (bottom rollout) (after Mera 1939:Plate 65—top, Plate 66—middle, and Plate 64—bottom).

Revolt. Last, but certainly not least, we should remember that it was not just the glaze-painted Hawikuh Polychrome and Black-on-red that was replaced by the matte-painted Ashiwi Polychrome, but also Matsaki Buffware. Thus, a new ware, with new paint/slip/vessel form combinations was made that replaced what was formerly a much more diverse technological corpus.

I view the more homogenous use of matte-paints and feather motifs as intentional acts of resistance that reinforced a more homogeneous Zuni identity in the period immediately following the Pueblo Revolt. Multiple villages from throughout the Zuni drainage had coalesced for the first time on top of Dowa Yalanne, and then at Zuni Pueblo following the Revolt. The convergent technological and stylistic breaks are ones that enhanced a common ceramic tradition. Rather than multiple traditions that had been the case since the end of the fifteenth century, potters shared a common tradition of vessel painting, slip colors, and especially, common stylistic elements in particular fields.

Discussion

The Pueblo Revolt was an indigenous rebellion against the Spanish that was spurred by three converging conflicts: religious repression, economic oppression, and church-state conflict (Hall 1989:88). Religion was both the target of the Revolt and the source of inspiration for the resisters. Pueblo ritual societies provided the context for planning the Revolt and its leaders held positions of ritual authority within their respective pueblos (Hall 1989:90). Given religious repression, it is not surprising that there was a reduction in the use of obvious religious symbolism on pottery from the earliest period of European contact through the seventeenth century. Recognizable kachina images are rarely present on any vessels made after the seventeenth century. Instead, there is increasing representation of textile designs, illustrating their economic and ritual importance to the Pueblos (Webster 1997), and increasing homogeneity in the use of feather motifs.

Feather motifs may have seemed innocuous to Spanish missionaries and military alike. However, these feathers

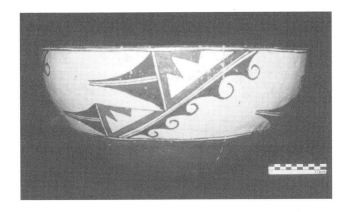

Figure 6.13. Zuni Polychrome bowl exterior (Stevenson Collection, no. E40486, Department of Anthropology, Smithsonian Institution, photograph by Laurie D. Webster).

Figure 6.14. Zuni Polychrome feather designs collected by Ruth Bunzel (after Bunzel 1972 [1929]:Figures 60 and 61).

were an essential part of Pueblo religion associated with the preparation and planting of prayer sticks, Zuni altar decorations, ritual costumes, and even shields. By the nineteenth century, feather motifs had become such important representations of Zuni identity that virtually every potter in the village decorated the outside of her bowls with this design (Figure 6.13). Bowl exteriors are the most visually prominent area of the pot when used in, or carried to, communal feasting events and would have been in active display.

The use of feathers across the Pueblo area is also evidence for a region-wide stylistic horizon. How those feather motifs were incorporated and interpreted by individual Pueblo potters, their families, and within communities was probably quite different across the vast and culturally diverse Pueblo area. Nonetheless, the similarities at the regional scale in the use of feathers is quite striking and suggests a unity that cross-cuts language groups and other important social differences among the Pueblos.

Even to the present day, the use of the exterior feather motif on Zuni ceramics is widespread. The exterior designs of early eighteenth-century through late nineteenth-century Zuni bowls are so similar that it is nearly impossible to assign an accurate date without viewing bowl interiors. These designs were recorded by Bunzel (1972 [1929]; see Figure 6.14) in her corpus of Pueblo pottery elements used at Zuni in the early twentieth

century and were a major part of the revival of Zuni ceramic production in the late twentieth century (Hardin 1983, 1989). This revival continues to the present day, as does the use of the split-feather motif on bowl exteriors.

Conclusion

At Zuni, the relative homogeneity in choice of certain design elements and the sudden or punctuated changes in ceramic technology after the Pueblo Revolt is evidence of women's participation in the construction of new identities. Zuni potters abandoned forms and techniques of ceramic production that were pre-Revolt, especially glazeware technology. Unlike the late prehistoric period when subgroups appeared to have maintained their different identities, eighteenth-century Zuni potters underplayed their social heterogeneity through technological homogeneity. Women, the principal producers of pottery at Zuni, used the medium to express shared social identity. These Pueblo potters were participating in acts of resistance as they helped to construct new social identities during and after the Pueblo Revolt within a process of ethnogenesis. New forms and decorative styles are material evidence of a new Zuni social identity wrought from the processes of settlement aggregation and resistance.

Acknowledgments

I thank Bob Preucel for his kind invitation to participate in the SAA symposium for which this paper was originally written. His comments and encouragement greatly improved the quality of this chapter. I thank T. J. Ferguson for valuable discussions about the Pueblo Revolt and for sharing the results of his own studies at Zuni. I also owe a great debt of gratitude to Margaret Hardin for the many discussions we have had about Zuni ceramics during long hours of looking at vessels in collections and in slides. Susan Hall aided in the recording of vessels at the Museum of the American Indian (now the National Museum of the American Museum, Smithsonian Institution), Laurie D. Webster photographed the collections at the Nation Museum of Natural History of the Smithsonian Institution, and James Vint helped with the database and photograph labeling. The curators and staff at NMAI, NMNH, and Cambridge University are to be thanked for making the collections accessible, especially the late Eulalie Bonar (NMAI), Christopher Chippendale (CU), Deborah Hull-Walski (NMNH), and Mary Jane Lenz (NMAI). My research on the Zuni ceramics was supported through NSF grant BNS-9116686.

Notes

1. I use the spellings for place names that have been adopted by the Pueblo of Zuni in publications and educational materials relating to tribal history. However, ceramic ware and type names retain the published spellings used in the original descriptions. Thus, both Hawikku (for the site) and Hawikuh Polychrome (for the pottery type) are used in this chapter.

References Cited

Adams, E. Charles
1991   *The Origin and Development of the Pueblo Katsina Cult.* The University of Arizona Press, Tucson.

Anderson, Gary Clayton
1999   *Indian Southwest, 1580–1830: Ethnogenesis and Reinvention.* University of Oklahoma Press, Norman.

Bandelier, Adolph A. F.
1892   An Outline of the Documentary History of the Zuni Tribe. *Journal of American Ethnology and Archaeology* 3:1–144. Houghton, Mifflin and Company, Boston.

Batkin, Jonathan
1987   *Pottery of the Pueblos of New Mexico, 1700–1940.* The Taylor Museum of the Colorado Springs Fine Arts Center, Colorado Springs.

Beck, Margaret
2000   Tortillas and Women's Labor in the Hohokam Classic Period. Paper presented at the Sixth Gender and Archaeology Conference, Flagstaff, Ariz.

Bourdieu, Pierre
1977   *Outline of a Theory of Practice.* Cambridge University Press, Cambridge, UK.

Bowser, Brenda J.
2000   From Pottery to Politics: An Ethnoarchaeological Study of Political Factionalism, Ethnicity, and Domestic Pottery Style in the Ecuadorian Amazon. *Journal of Archaeological Method and Theory* 7(3):219–248.

Bradford, Helen
1996   Women, Gender, and Colonialism: Rethinking the History of the British Cape Colony and its Frontier Zones, c. 1806–1870. *Journal of African History* 37(3):351–370.

Brumfiel, Elizabeth M.
1991   Weaving and Cooking: Women's Production in Aztec Mexico. In *Engendering Archaeology: Women and Prehistory,* edited by Joan M. Gero and Margaret W. Conkey, pp. 224–251. Basil Blackwell, Oxford, UK.
1996   The Quality of Tribute Cloth: The Place of Evidence in Archaeological Argument. *American Antiquity* 61:453–462.
1997   Tribute Cloth Production and Compliance in Aztec and Colonial Mexico. *Museum Anthropology* 21(2):55–71.

Bunzel, Ruth L.
1972   [1929] *The Pueblo Potter: A Study of Creative Imagination in Primitive Art.* Columbia University Press, New York.

Bushnell, G. H. S.
1955   Some Pueblo IV Pottery Types from Kechipawan, New Mexico, U.S.A. *Anais do XXXI Congreso Internacional de Americanistas, Sao Paulo . . . 1954,* Vol. 2, pp. 657–665. Editora Anhembi, Sao Paolo.

Carlson, Roy L.
1965   *Eighteenth Century Navajo Fortresses of Gobernador District.* The Earl Morris Papers, No. 2. Series in Anthropology No. 10. University of Colorado Press, Boulder.

Crown, Patricia L.
1994   *Ceramics and Ideology: Salado Polychrome Pottery.* University of New Mexico Press, Albuquerque.

Deeds, Susan M.
1998   Indigenous Rebellions on the Northern Mexican Mission Frontier: From First-Generation to Later Colonial Responses. In *Contested Ground: Comparative Frontiers on the Northern and Southern Edges of the Spanish Empire,* edited by Donna J. Guy and Thomas E. Sheridan, pp. 32–51. The University of Arizona Press, Tucson.

Dillingham, Rick, and Melinda Elliott
1992   *Acoma and Laguna Pottery.* School of American Research Press, Santa Fe.

Espinosa, J. Manuel (editor)

1940   *The First Expedition of de Vargas into New Mexico, 1692.*
        University of New Mexico Press, Albuquerque.

1988   *The Pueblo Indian Revolt of 1696 and the Franciscan
        Missions in New Mexico.* University of Oklahoma Press,
        Norman.

Etienne, Mona

1980   Women and Men, Cloth and Colonization: The Trans-
        formation of Production-Distribution Relations among the
        Baule (Ivory Coast). In *Women and Colonization,* edited by
        Mona Etienne and Eleanor Leacock, pp. 214–238. Praeger,
        New York.

Etienne, Mona, and Eleanor Leacock (editors)

1980   *Women and Colonization.* Praeger, New York.

Ferg, Alan

1982   14th Century Kachina Depiction on Ceramics. In *Collected
        Papers in Honor of J. W. Runyon,* edited by G. X. Fitzgerald,
        pp. 13–29. Papers of the Archaeological Society of New
        Mexico, No. 7. Archaeological Society of New Mexico,
        Albuquerque.

Ferguson, T. J.

1994   *Historic Zuni Architecture and Society: A Structural Analysis.*
        Unpublished Ph.D. dissertation, Department of Anthro-
        pology, University of New Mexico, Albuquerque.

Ferguson, T. J. and Barbara J. Mills

1982   *Archaeological Investigations at Zuni Pueblo, 1977–1980.*
        Zuni Archaeology Program Report 183. Pueblo of Zuni,
        New Mexico.

Frank, Larry, and Francis H. Harlow

1974   *Historic Pottery of the Pueblo Indians, 1600–1880.* New York
        Graphic Society, Boston.

Guy, Donna J., and Thomas E. Sheridan

1998   On Frontiers: The Northern and Southern Edges of the
        Spanish Empire in the Americas. In *Contested Ground:
        Comparative Frontiers on the Northern and Southern Edges
        of the Spanish Empire,* edited by Donna J. Guy and
        Thomas E. Sheridan, pp. 3–15. The University of Arizona
        Press, Tucson.

Hackett, Charles Wilson (editor)

1942   *Revolt of the Pueblo Indians of New Mexico and Otermin's
        Attempted Reconquest, 1680–1682.* Coronado Historical
        Series Vols. 8 and 9. University of New Mexico Press,
        Albuquerque.

Hall, Thomas D.

1989   *Social Change in the Southwest, 1350–1880.* University of
        Kansas Press, Lawrence.

Hardin, Margaret A.

1983   *Gifts of Mother Earth: Ceramics in the Zuni Tradition.* The
        Heard Museum, Phoenix, Ariz.

1989   Zuni Pottery: The Roots of Revival. In *Seasons of the
        Kachina,* edited by Lowell John Bean, pp. 133–163. Ballena
        Press Anthropological Papers 34. Hayward, Calif.

Harlow, Francis H.

1973   *Matte-Paint Pottery of the Tewa, Keres and Zuni Pueblos.*
        Museum of New Mexico, Santa Fe.

Hays, Kelley A.

1993   When is a Symbol Archaeologically Meaningful? In
        Archaeological Theory: Who Sets the Agenda?, edited by
        Norman Yoffee and Andrew Sherratt, pp. 81–92.
        Cambridge University Press, Cambridge, UK.

1994   Kachina Depictions on Prehistoric Pueblo Pottery. In
        Kachinas in the Pueblo World, edited by Polly Schaafsma,
        pp. 47–62. University of New Mexico Press, Albuquerque.

Hill, Jonathan D.

1996a   Introduction: Ethnogenesis in the Americas, 1492–1992.
        In *Ethnogenesis in the Americas,* edited by Jonathan D. Hill,
        pp. 1–19. University of Iowa Press, Iowa City.

Hill, Jonathan D. (editor)

1996b   *Ethnogenesis in the Americas.* University of Iowa Press,
        Iowa City.

Hodge, Frederick W.

1937   *History of Hawikuh, New Mexico: One of the So-Called Cities
        of Cibola.* Southwest Museum, Los Angeles.

Hudson, Mark J.

1999   *Ruins of Identity: Ethnogenesis in the Japanese Islands.*
        University of Hawaii Press, Honolulu.

John, Elizabeth A. H.

1975   *Storms Brewed in Other Men's Worlds.* Texas A&M University
        Press, College Station.

Jones, Delnos J., and Jacquetta Hill-Burnet

1982   The Political Context of Ethnogenesis: An Australian
        Example. In *Aboriginal Power in Australian Society,* edited
        by Michael C. Howard, pp. 214–246. University of
        Queens land, St. Lucia, Australia.

Kessell, John L.

1979   *Kiva, Cross and Crown: The Pecos Indians and New Mexico,
        1540–1840.* National Park Service, U.S. Department of the
        Interior, Washington, D.C.

Kessell, John L., and Rick Hendricks (editors)

1992   *By Force of Arms, the Journals of don Diego de Vargas, New
        Mexico, 1691–1693.* University of New Mexico Press,
        Albuquerque.

Kintigh, Keith W.

1985   Settlement, Subsistence, and Society in Late Zuni Prehistory.
        Anthropological Papers of the University of Arizona 44.
        University of Arizona Press, Tucson.

1990   Protohistoric Transitions in the Western Pueblo area. In
        Perspectives on Southwestern Prehistory edited by Paul E.
        Minis and Charles L. Redman, pp. 258–275. Westview
        Press, Boulder.

2000   Leadership Strategies in Protohistoric Zuni Towns. In
        Alternative Leadership Strategies in the Greater Southwest,
        edited by Barbara J. Mills, pp. 95–116. The University of
        Arizona Press, Tucson.

Ladd, Edmund J.

1963   *Zuni Ethno-ornithology.* Unpublished Master's thesis,
        Department of Anthropology, University of New Mexico,
        Albuquerque.

Lemonnier, Pierre

1992   *Elements of an Anthropology of Technology.* Anthropological Papers of the Museum of Anthropology No. 88. University of Michigan, Ann Arbor.

Lwyn, Tenser

1994   Stories of Gender and Ethnicity: Discourses of Colonialism and Resistance in Burma. *Australian Journal of Anthropology* 5(1–2):60–85.

Mera, H. P.

1939   *Style Trends of Pueblo Pottery, 1500–1840.* Museum of New Mexico, Santa Fe.

Mills, Barbara J.

1995   The Organization of Protohistoric Zuni Ceramic Production. In *Ceramic Production in the American Southwest,* edited by Barbara J. Mills and Patricia L. Crown, pp. 200–230. The University of Arizona Press, Tucson.

2000   Gender, Craft Specialization, and Inequality. In *Women and Men in the Prehispanic Southwest: Labor, Power, and Prestige,* edited by Patricia L. Crown, pp. 301–343. School of American Research Press, Santa Fe.

Pauketat, Timothy R., and Thomas E. Emerson

1991   The Ideology of Authority and the Power of the Pot. *American Anthropologist* 93(4):919–941.

Pennell, C. R.

1987   Women and Resistance to Colonialism in Morocco: The Rif 1916–1926. *Journal of African History* 28(1):107–118.

Robinson, William J., and Roderick Sprague

1965   Disposal of the Dead at Point of Pines, Arizona. *American Antiquity* 30:442–453.

Roosens, Eugene E.

1989   *Creating Ethnicity: The Process of Ethnogenesis.* Frontiers of Anthropology 5, Sage Publications, Newbury Park, Calif.

Schaafsma, Polly

2000   *Warrior, Shield, and Star: Imagery and Ideology of Pueblo Warfare.* Western Edge Press, Santa Fe.

Schiffer, Michael Brian, and James M. Skibo

1997   The Explanation of Artifact Variability. *American Antiquity* 62:27–50.

Smith, Watson, Richard B. Woodbury, and Nathalie F. S. Woodbury

1966   *The Excavation of Hawikuh by Frederick Webb Hodge, 1817–1923.* Contributions from the Museum of the American Indian XX. New York.

Snow, David

1981   The Rio Grande, Matte Paint, and Plainware Tradition. In *Southwestern Ceramics: A Comparative Review,* edited by Albert H. Schroeder, pp. 235–278. The Arizona Archaeologist 15.

Stark, Miriam T. (editor)

1998   *The Archaeology of Social Boundaries.* Smithsonian Institution Press, Washington, D.C.

Stevenson, Matilda Coxe

1904   *The Zuni Indians: Their Mythology, Esoteric Fraternities, and Ceremonies.* Twenty-third Annual Report of the Bureau of American Ethnology, 1901–1902, Government Printing Office, Washington, D.C.

Towner, Ronald H.

1996   The Pueblito Phenomenon: A New Perspective on Post-Revolt Navajo Culture. In *The Archaeology of Navajo Origins,* edited by Ronald H. Towner, pp. 149–170. University of Utah Press, Salt Lake City.

1999   *Dendrochronology of the Navajo Pueblitos of Dinetah.* Unpublished Ph.D. dissertation, Department of Anthropology, University of Arizona, Tucson.

Van Keuren, Scott

2000   Ceramic Decoration as Power: Late Prehistoric Design Change in East-central Arizona. In *Alternative Leadership Strategies in the Greater Southwest,* edited by Barbara J. Mills, pp. 79–94. The University of Arizona Press, Tucson.

Vivian, Gordon

1979   *Gran Quivira: Excavations in a 17th Century Jumano Pueblo.* Archaeological Research Series No. 8. National Park Service, U.S. Department of the Interior, Washington, D.C.

Webster, Laurie D.

1997   *Effects of European Contact on Textile Production and Exchange in the North American Southwest: A Pueblo Case Study.* Unpublished Ph.D. dissertation, Department of Anthropology, University of Arizona, Tucson.

Welbourn, Alice

1984   Endo Ceramics and Power Strategies. In *Ideology, Power and Prehistory,* edited by Daniel Miller and Christopher Tilley, pp. 17–25. Cambridge University Press, Cambridge, UK.

Wonderley, Anthony

1986   Material Symbolics in Pre-Columbian Households: The Painted Pottery of Naco, Honduras. *Journal of Anthropological Research* 42:497–534.

Woodbury, Richard, and Nathalie F. S. Woodbury

1966   Decorated Pottery of the Zuni Area. In *The Excavation of Hawikuh by Frederick Webb Hodge: Report of the Hendricks-Hodge Expedition,* by Watson Smith, Richard B. Woodbury, and Nathalie F. S. Woodbury, pp. 302–306. Contributions from the Museum of the American Indian, Heye Foundation 20. Museum of the American Indian, New York.

Zedeño, Maria Nieves

1994   *Sourcing Prehistoric Ceramics at Chodistaas Pueblo, Arizona: The Circulation of People and Pots in the Grasshopper Region.* Anthropological Papers of the University of Arizona 58. The University of Arizona Press, Tucson.

Chapter 7

Ceramic Semiotics:
Women, Pottery, and Social Meanings at Kotyiti Pueblo

*Patricia W. Capone
and Robert W. Preucel*

The period between the Pueblo Revolt of 1680 and the Spanish Reconquest of 1692 is one of the most intriguing in all of Pueblo history. During this brief 12-year span, Pueblo people were independent of Spanish rule and free to reconfigure their lives on their own terms. The success of the Revolt was facilitated by a cultural revitalization movement carefully crafted by a consortium of Pueblo leaders (Ortiz 1994; Preucel 2000; Reff 1995). This movement, however, did not guarantee political stability and two rival factions emerged. The Keres, Jemez, Taos, and Pecos fought against the Tewa, Tanos, and Picuris (Espinosa 1988:38). Tensions also broke out within the leadership; Popé was deposed by Don Luis Tupatu, only to be reinstated in 1688. After his death, he was succeeded by Tupatu.

In response to this internal warfare, political turmoil, and the anticipated return of the Spaniards, some Pueblo people vacated their mission pueblos and fled to remote locations, taking temporary refuge with the Hopi, Zuni, Acoma, Apache, and Navajo. Among the most prominent of the new villages were Payupki and Tewa Village in the Hopi district and Dowa Yalanne in the Zuni district (see Ferguson, Chapter 2). Others, reluctant to leave the Rio Grande region, established new fortified mesatop strongholds within the rugged Jemez and Sangre de Cristo mountains. These included Black Mesa in the Tewa district, Kotyiti in the Cochiti

district, Cerro Colorado in the Zia district, and Astialakwa and Boletsakwa in the Jemez district (see Elliott, Chapter 3, and Hendricks, Chapter 12). Significantly, many of these villages were socially diverse, composed of people from multiple home-villages and, in some cases, different language groups.

The best known of the Rio Grande strongholds is Kotyiti Pueblo located on Horn Mesa (Figure 7.1). The community consists of two adjacent residential units, a plaza pueblo (LA 295) and a rancheria (LA 84) (Figure 7.2). According to Bandelier (1892:171), the village was established sometime after 1683 and occupied until the spring of 1694 when Diego de Vargas attacked it. In 1912, Nels Nelson (1914a, b) mapped and excavated the entire plaza pueblo and conducted limited testing at the rancheria. In 1995, the second author (RWP) and the Pueblo of Cochiti initiated a collaborative research project to restudy the community (Preucel 1998, 2000).

In this chapter, we focus upon the actions of Pueblo women during this crucial period in Pueblo history using Kotyiti Pueblo as a case study. Previous historical studies of the Revolt and its aftermath have emphasized male leadership, military campaigns, and political alliances. Pueblo women, however, were also active participants in the Revolt and this can be seen archaeologically in how they used ceramics to mediate social and political identities within these new communities (see Mills,

Chapter 7).[1] We begin with a description of the Kotyiti community based upon ethnohistorical data, we then discuss our semiotic approach and, finally, we present the results of our petrographic and stylistic analyses and discuss their implications.

The Kotyiti Community

On August 10, 1692, the twelfth anniversary of the Pueblo Revolt, Diego de Vargas announced his expedition to reconquer New Mexico. His strategy was to march up the Rio Grande Valley and attack Cochiti Pueblo because of its central role in thwarting Antonio de Otermín's reconquest bid in 1681. Vargas writes that, "It was an established opinion that the surrender of the pueblo [Cochiti] would be a victory of greater consequence and triumph than even that of the villa [Santa Fe]" (Kessell and Hendricks 1992:382–383). He was thus distressed when he reached Cochiti Pueblo on September 11, only to find it abandoned and its people taunting him from the protection of the formidable Cochiti Mesa. Vargas chose not to engage the Cochiti people in battle and continued on to take possession of Santa Fe.

Vargas returned to the Cochiti area on October 21, determined to secure the submission of the Cochiti people. He climbed the steep trail up the mesa, entered the plaza, and was peacefully received.[2] Fray Francisco Corvera granted absolution to the Indians and baptized 103 adults and children. Vargas learned that the community was composed of people from the villages of Cochiti, San Felipe, and San Marcos (Kessell and Hendricks 1992:515). He also was told that the people had moved up onto the mesa out of fear of their enemies, the Tewas, Tanos, and Picuris. Vargas entreated them to return to their vacated mission pueblos promising them military protection and a priest. The Pueblo people did not comply with his request.

A year later, Vargas returned to Kotyiti to bring the people down off their mesa. He states that he was greeted by two separate groups of men and women (Kessell et al. 1995:425). By this time, the people from San Felipe had left the community to found their own mesatop village,

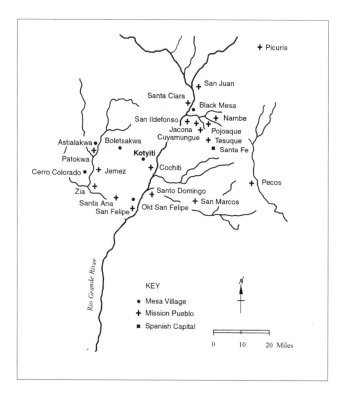

Figure 7.1. Location map of Kotyiti Pueblo in the Northern Rio Grande region of New Mexico.

Old San Felipe, presumably because of disputes with the Cochiti leaders (Hodge et al. 1945:260; White 1932:9). It thus seems likely that the two groups Vargas encountered were the people from Cochiti and San Marcos Pueblos, each under their own leader. Vargas, in fact, named El Zepe as the leader of the Cochiti contingent and Cristobal as the leader of the San Marcos people.

By 1694, factionalism within the community escalated to the point that El Zepe ordered the death of Cristobal and his brother Zue. Their crime was that they had served as Spanish informants. In response to this act and the threat that Kotyiti posed to the friendly villages of San Felipe, Santa Ana, and Zia, Vargas attacked the village on April 17, 1694 (Kessell et al. 1998:192; see also Hendricks, Chapter 12). With him was a combined force of 150 Spanish and Pueblo auxiliaries, the latter composed of warriors from the three allied villages. Although Vargas captured the mesa and village in an early morning attack, most of the warriors escaped into the mountains. Four days later, they counterattacked and succeeded in freeing half of their women and children.

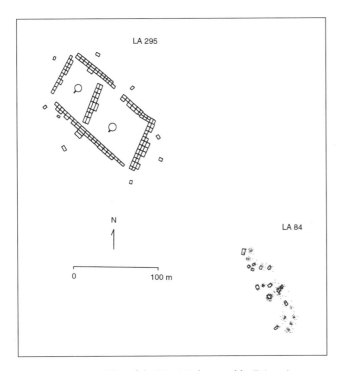

Figure 7.2. Map of the Kotyiti plaza pueblo (LA 295) and rancheria (LA 84).

These accounts, based upon Vargas's journals, reveal a high degree of social and political instability within the Kotyiti community as refugees from several different villages periodically joined and left the community. Bitter disputes broke out regarding how best to respond to the return of the Spaniards. These disputes seem to have been structured along the lines of home-village affiliation; the Cochiti leaders advocated resistance while the San Felipe and San Marcos leaders favored capitulation. These disputes eventually lead to the wholesale emigration of the San Felipe people and caused changes in leadership for the San Marcos people.

Ceramic Semiotics

It is commonly believed in archaeology that material culture embodies two relatively discrete kinds of meanings —function and style (Binford 1965; Dunnell 1978; Wobst 1977). Functional meanings are those features of artifacts that are intended to have an action on the material world. For example, the shape of a pot may be intended to hold water. Stylistic meanings, by contrast, are those that are designed to communicate information. The decorations on the pot may be associated with a specific social identity, such as a membership in a particular ethnic group. Recent studies, however, have shown that this distinction between style and function is difficult to maintain since styles have function and functions have styles (Hodder 1990; Lemonnier 1992).

One response to this problem is to reject the dualism of the style/function debates and focus instead upon the workings of different kinds of meanings in the semiotic process. Most philosophers now agree that knowledge production is a three-place relation (Wylie 2000). This insight is due to Charles Sanders Peirce who considered the sign relation as consisting of the object, the sign, and the interpretant (Buchler 1955; Preucel and Bauer 2001). The *Sign* is something that is understood by the mind as a sign to represent something else, namely the *Object,* or the physical thing or process that exists in the world. The *Interpretant* is thus the semiotic formulation of what the mind has come to know, whether that be some further action or a mental representation. Thus, the Sign acts as a mediator between the Object behind it and the Interpretant in front of it.

Peirce considered one set of signs, those based upon the Sign-Object relation, to be of special importance. These are icons, indices, and symbols. *Icons* are signs whose meaning depends upon a physical likeness. Examples include maps, diagrams, and onomatopoeia. *Indices* are signs whose meaning depends upon spatio-temporal contiguity. Examples include weathervane and wind direction, litmus tests and acidity, smoke and fire, and deictics in language. *Symbols* are signs whose meanings are established by convention. The classic example is the words of a language. For Peirce, these signs are not essentialist categories, but rather dynamic modes in the semiotic process. In addition, they exist in a hierarchical relationship with one another such that a symbol presupposes an index (the object specified) and an index presupposes an icon (the information being signified about that object) (Parmentier 1997:49).

Material culture can thus be interpreted in multiple ways depending upon the kinds of materials involved, the

Figure 7.3. Kotyiti Glaze Polychrome jar (AMNH 29.0/3140, Room 124) and Tewa Polychrome bowl (AMNH 29.0/3052, Room 39) from the Kotyiti plaza pueblo (photograph by Francine Sarin, UPM).

contexts of use, and the audiences in question (Parmentier 1997:51). So for example, pottery analyzed using neutron activation to determine point of origin is functioning as an indexical sign since its material inclusions are indexical of the geology at the place of manufacture. Pottery style studied as a symbol of ethnic or group identity is an indexical sign that is interpreted as functioning indexically. A sequence of pottery styles interpreted as a historical process functions as a symbol, if it is conventional that the sequence has such a meaning.

We use these ideas to explore several interrelated questions with the Kotyiti ceramic data. Our first question is whether it is possible to distinguish the "refugee effect"— the movement of families from San Felipe and San Marcos into the Kotyiti community. Previous studies of glazeware petrography have shown that the potters from San Felipe and San Marcos preferred distinctive inclusion materials—crystalline basalt at the former village and augite latite at the latter (Shepard 1942; Warren 1979a).

We therefore expect that if large numbers of refugees from these villages joined the Kotyiti community, they would have likely brought with them their household ceramics and these should be distinguishable through ceramic petrography. From a semiotic point of view, these inclusion materials function as indexical signs for the analyst.

Our second question is whether we can identify specific social practices such as residential segregation or incorporation. Were peoples from San Felipe and San Marcos restricted to certain areas of the plaza pueblo? Ethnohistorical sources suggest that the people from San Marcos lived in a roomblock on the "second plaza" at the Kotyiti plaza pueblo (Kessell et al. 1995:200). Are the glazewares with distinctive San Felipe inclusions localized within the pueblo? In these cases, we are referring to ceramics functioning as indices that are themselves being interpreted as indices by their makers.

Our third question focuses on the social meanings of

the new corpus of designs and motifs on the decorated ceramics. Did women favor motifs that were consistent with the broader cultural revitalization discourse, for example, by reviving motifs characteristic of earlier pottery. Alternatively, did they contradict it, perhaps by using specific Spanish derived motifs? How widespread were the dominant designs and motifs of this period? Here, we are discussing a pottery style that is functioning as an index (of the revitalization discourse) and is being interpreted by Pueblo people as having some relevant qualitative feature (connection to the kind of life lived by the ancestors).

The Kotyiti Ceramic Assemblage

The Kotyiti ceramic (painted ware) assemblage is dominated by two distinctive ceramic wares—the Kotyiti glazewares and Tewa matte-paint wares (Figure 7.3). In the Mera collection of the Laboratory of Anthropology, the Kotyiti glazewares constitute 61 percent of the assemblage at the plaza pueblo and 70 percent of the assemblage at the rancheria (Table 7.1).[3] The Tewa matte-paint wares are 24 percent of the plaza pueblo assemblage and 16 percent of the rancheria assemblage. Contemporaneous tradewares, including Puname Polychrome and Jemez Black-on-white, account for 6 percent each of the plaza pueblo assemblage and the rancheria assemblage.

The Kotyiti glazewares are a member of the terminal glazeware grouping, Glaze F, in the famous Rio Grande glazeware sequence identified by Nels Nelson (1916), Madeline Kidder and A. V. Kidder (1917) and refined by H. P. Mera (1933). Kotyiti glazewares are usually distinguished from the slightly earlier Glaze E group by an increase in glaze-paint vitrification (Hayes et al. 1981:98). There are two main variants of Kotyiti glazeware: a bichrome and a polychrome formed by the addition of red matte-paint used as a filler in various motifs. Bowls tend to have tall direct rims with pronounced carinations where the rim meets the bowl body. There are two different jar forms—a short-necked globular form that Mera (1939:70, 90–101) considered a local Keresan development and a long-necked form, which he considered to

Table 7.1 Historic Period
Painted Ware Assemblage from Kotyiti
(Mera collection, Laboratory of Anthropology)

	LA 295	%	LA 84	%
Kotyiti Glazewares	97.00	60.63	54.00	70.13
Kotyiti Glaze-on-tan	6.00		2.00	
Kotyiti Glaze-on-red	5.00		7.00	
Kotyiti Glaze-on-yellow	7.00		1.00	
Kotyiti Glaze-on-white	6.00		2.00	
Kotyiti Polychrome glaze-on-tan	14.00		6.00	
Kotyiti Polychrome glaze-on-red	10.00		3.00	
Kotyiti Polychrome glaze-on-yellow	13.00		8.00	
Kotyiti Polychrome glaze-on-white	10.00		8.00	
Tan body	1.00		3.00	
Red body	5.00		9.00	
Yellow body	2.00		2.00	
White body	6.00		3.00	
Kotyiti indet	12.00		0.00	
Tewa matte paint wares	39.00	24.38	12.00	15.58
Sankawi Black-on-cream	2.00		0.00	
Tewa Polychrome	16.00		1.00	
Tewa Red	11.00		4.00	
Pojoaque Polychrome	3.00		1.00	
Tewa Black-on-white	5.00		1.00	
Tewa Black (Kapo)	2.00		5.00	
Tradewares	8.00	5.00	5.00	6.49
Puname Polychrome	4.00		5.00	
Jemez Black-on-white	4.00		0.00	
Unidentified	16.00	10.00	6.00	7.79
Totals	160.00	100.00	77.00	100.00

derive from earlier Tewa forms.

The Tewa matte-paint wares, have been defined by Toulouse (1949), Harlow (1973), and Batkin (1987) and comprise three main types—Tewa Black-on-white, Tewa Polychrome, and Pojoaque Polychrome. Tewa Black-on-white is a bowl form with organic paint black line designs painted on its interior and exterior surfaces.[4] Tewa Polychrome has both bowl and jar forms. The bowl form has a sharp keel with a white slipped decorated band below the rim and a red polished underbody. The jar form has a long neck, which is slipped white and decorated, and a central mid-panel that is slipped and painted. Pojoaque Polychrome is a jar form and is identical to the Tewa Polychrome jar form with the exception that it has an undecorated red slipped and polished neck.

Previous Petrographic Studies

Both Anna Shepard (1942) and Helene Warren (1979a, b, c) have conducted petrographic studies of the Kotyiti glazewares and both researchers have identified a common inclusion type. This is the volcanic rock that

Shepard termed "devitrified tuff" (Shepard 1942:154) and Warren termed "rhyolite tuff" (Warren 1979b:B107). We prefer to use Shepard's terminology because it focuses on the physical characteristics of the rock, rather than Warren's terminology that focuses on chemical compositional characteristics that are not discernible using optical microscopy.

Shepard and Warren, however, have offered conflicting ideas regarding the source of the devitrified tuff. Shepard attributes the tuff to the Northern Pajarito, while Warren associates it with Jemez Mountain volcanics local to Kotyiti and possibly to other villages within the Cochiti area, the Pajarito area, and the Bernalillo area, or less likely to the Northern Pajarito area of Puye. The geographic range of this tuff is extremely broad and this creates certain difficulties in determining the precise location of production. Given this situation, the identification of devitrified tuff, as the primary inclusion material in the glazewares is not sufficient evidence by itself to indicate local production by Kotyiti women.

Geological Survey

In an effort to resolve some of these problems, the first author (PHC) conducted a geological field survey during the summer of 1998. She collected representative samples from the major geological units in and around Kotyiti with special emphasis on: 1) units within the likely collecting range of potters, 2) units that might match the inclusion material in the ceramics, and 3) units that could address Shepard's and Warren's suggestions for inclusion materials. The survey took place following the first author's preliminary petrographic analysis of Kotyiti ceramics and this significantly helped guide the selection of raw material samples.

The areas surveyed for potential inclusion materials were based on Arnold's (1985) cross-cultural exploitable threshold study of distances traveled for clay and temper resources. Arnold found that most potters in traditional societies, who use foot transport, travel up to one kilometer to obtain clay and temper resources (Arnold 1985:57). Only a few potters travel by foot as far as six to nine kilometers for their temper. In this study, potential inclusion resources within a nine-kilometer radius were considered, with the most intensive focus on the resources within the one-kilometer radius. Seventeen samples were described megascopically, and five samples, which appeared to be the best matches to the inclusion materials, were examined and described microscopically in petrographic thin-section.

Kotyiti's location provides ready access to suitable inclusion materials for pottery manufacture. The mesatop is comprised of the Tshirege member of the Bandelier tuff that is part of the Jemez Mountains volcanic series dating to the Quaternary period. The Jemez Mountain volcanic series centers on the Redondo Peak and Valle Grande area and radiates out in a "bulls-eye" pattern. The Tshirege member outcrops at the center of the bulls-eye, Redondo Peak, and forms a ring spanning a radius between 10 to 25 kilometers from the center. The top of Horn Mesa falls within that ring. The lower half of Horn Mesa is comprised of the Otowi member of the Bandelier tuff. The Tshirege and Otowi tuffs are potential inclusion materials that would have been readily available to potters (i.e., they are within one kilometer) and not surprisingly; both tuffs are present in the Kotyiti ceramics. An additional rock unit from the top of Horn Mesa, El Cajete pumice, which could have functioned as suitable inclusion material, does not appear to have been utilized in the ceramics. Additionally, a wide variety of volcanic and sedimentary inclusion materials was available in Cochiti and Bland Canyons, within one kilometer. Some of these appear to have been utilized in minor amounts in the Kotyiti ceramics.

Tshirege tuff was sampled for three reasons: 1) it is the most readily available inclusion material, 2) it is a likely match to the inclusions visible in the ceramics, and 3) it is a possible match to the tuffs that Warren (1979b:B107) and Shepard (1942:154) have described. Our results indicate that Tshirege tuff does indeed match the inclusion materials in the ceramics, but that it only partially matches Warren's and Shepard's descriptions. Thin-sections and hand samples of the tuff show significant variability across the top of Horn Mesa beyond that noted by previous investigators, especially in terms of grain size, weathering, color, and consequently probably chemical composition. This variability is also reflected in the ceramics. We consider it unlikely that this unique combination of rock characteristics would occur in other outcrops of Tshirege tuff across the large area that the general type occurs. This allows us to designate with some confidence the Horn Mesa variety of Tshirege tuff as a source of the inclusions present in the Kotyiti ceramics.

This finding would also appear to reconcile the differences between Shepard's and Warren's descriptions regarding the sources of Kotyiti inclusions. Both researchers were partially correct, but the variability within the single tuff deposit was interpreted by Warren as several different sources. In further support of this idea, it is significant that Shepard's devitrified tuff and Warren's rhyolite tuff, which are notably distinct, co-occur *in the same sherd* in several samples. In sum, our discovery of the co-occurrence of several sub-types of Tshirege tuff in the same sherd and our analysis of the reference rock samples reconcile the contradictions of previous work. They also allow us to designate Tshirege tuff as a major source of local material inclusions in the ceramics from Kotyiti.[5]

Otowi tuff was also sampled because of its close proximity to Kotyiti. It matches a vitric tuff that has been previously identified in the ceramics, and resembles a vitric tuff, previously described by Shepard as deriving from the Northern Rio Grande. One unexpected discovery was that Otowi tuff contains naturally occurring basalt inclusions. This may mean that the presence of basalt in some ceramics is a byproduct of the processing of the tuff and not the result of intentional use of a specific basalt temper. We thus consider Horn Mesa to be the most likely source for those sherds characterized by the co-occurrence of basalt inclusions and Otowi tuff.

We also sampled basalt rocks from the San Felipe area in order to determine the source of the non-local basalt. Shepard (1942:243) originally identified crystalline basalt as the preferred inclusion material for Kotyiti

glazewares made in the San Felipe/Zia district. Our initial petrographic analysis indicated a match between the crystalline basalt of the Kotyiti glazewares from Kotyiti and Shepard's samples of crystalline basalt. Our petrographic analysis of the sampled rock material subsequently confirmed our original interpretation. Significantly, the crystalline basalt is easily distinguishable from the local basalt in the Otowi tuff.

Samples of additional volcanics were collected from Cochiti and Bland Canyons in an attempt to match the volcanic ash inclusions in the Tewa matte-paint wares. According to Shepard, this ash likely derives from the Northern Pajarito area.[6] None of the samples from the canyons matched the material in our sherd samples. Although, we cannot completely rule out the possibility that the ash is present (since there is a wide variety of materials carried in arroyos in Cochiti and Bland canyons), we think it highly likely that this material comes from geological sources in the Española Valley.

Petrographic Analysis

We conducted petrographic analysis on a sample of 128 sherds representing both the plaza pueblo and the rancheria. These sherds are from two different museum collections. The majority (113 sherds), come from the Kotyiti collection at the American Museum of Natural History (AMNH). Nelson took this sample in 1912 during his excavations at the plaza pueblo. His sampling criteria are not known, but presumably, he considered the sherds representative of the ceramics from the individual rooms. Nelson also excavated several rooms at the rancheria, but collected only four sherds. Because of this small sample, we augmented these data with 15 sherds from the Mera collection of the Museum of the Indian Arts and Culture, Laboratory of Anthropology. Mera's sample is the result of a surface collection designed to capture the variability of ceramic types present. This procedure yielded a sample of 109 sherds from the plaza pueblo and 19 sherds from the rancheria.

We have identified the inclusion materials for all sherds in the Kotyiti sample (Figure 7.4a). These include, in

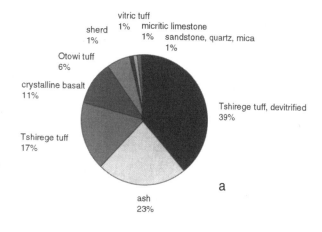

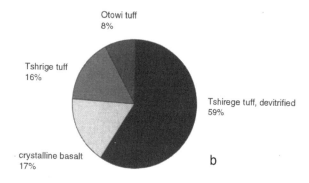

Figure 7.4. Percentages of primary material inclusions:
(a) for all types and, (b) for Kotyiti glazewares
(Glaze F) at LA 295 and LA 84.

decreasing frequency, Tshirege tuff, devitrified (39 percent),
ash (23 percent), Tshirege tuff (17 percent), crystalline
basalt (11 percent), Otowi tuff (6 percent), micritic
limestone (1 percent), sandstone, quartz, mica (1 percent),
sherd (1 percent), and vitric tuff (1 percent). We have also
determined the likely sources of these materials in most
cases. Ceramics locally produced account for 63 percent
of the total assemblage and non-local ceramics account
for 34 percent.

Focusing now on just the Kotyiti glazewares, the
inclusion types in the sample suggest that 83 percent were
locally produced at Kotyiti. This result is substantially
higher than Warren's results which identify locally made,
devitrified tuff in only 50 percent of the glazeware samples
from Kotyiti (Warren 1979b:239). This discrepancy can
perhaps be explained by Warren's unfamiliarity with
the variability in the Tshirege tuff deposit on Horn Mesa
(see above). The glazewares in our sample set contain 59

percent Tshirege tuff, devitrified (this is comparable to
Warren's "devitrified tuff"); along with 24 percent other
local sources (Tshirege tuff, 16 percent, and Otowi tuff,
8 percent) as shown in Figure 7.4b.

Seventeen percent of the glazewares share a single,
non-local inclusion type. This type is crystalline basalt that,
as noted above, is distinctive of the ceramics produced in
the San Felipe/Zia area. The frequency of non-local
glazewares, however, is somewhat low for historic period
sites throughout the Rio Grande, which average around
20 to 30 percent (see Shepard 1942; Warren 1979a, b, c).
This low frequency is consistent with a limited immigra-
tion event associated with refugees from San Felipe Pueblo.

Turning now to the Tewa wares, all of our samples
contained volcanic ash inclusions. This result confirms
the findings of Warren and others. In order to place our
results in a broader context, we examined a sample of 14
Tewa sherds from Black Mesa, a contemporary mesatop
village near San Ildefonso.[7] This village was occupied
historically by people from several different Tewa and Tano
villages.[8] We assumed that the ceramics used at this
village would be representative of those being produced
by Tewa potters during the Revolt period.

Our analysis revealed two inclusion materials, namely
volcanic ash (86 percent) and multi-crystalline quartz
(14 percent). Although the geological map and literature
information (Smith et al. 1970) are inconclusive regarding
the source for the volcanic ash, we think it probable that
Tewa potters were gathering their ash inclusion materials
from traditional use areas below the mesa. We then compared
the Tewa sherds from Black Mesa with the Tewa sherds
from Kotyiti and found that the volcanic ash inclusions
in these two groups were indistinguishable. This
finding strongly suggests that the Tewa ceramics from
both mesatop villages were produced at the same Tewa
villages in the Española Valley.

Residential Segregation and Incorporation
We found no ceramic evidence for residential segregation
between the plaza pueblo and the rancheria. However, we
did find possible evidence for the integration of refugee

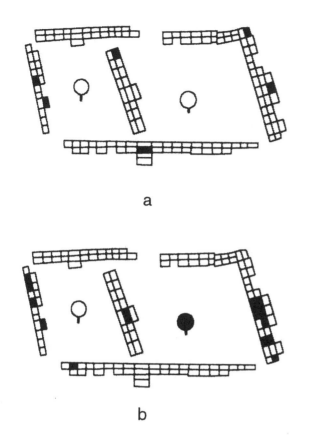

a

b

Figure 7.5. Distribution of sherds with: (a) San Felipe/Zia basalt and,
(b) ash inclusion materials in the Kotyiti plaza pueblo.

Table 7.2. Design Elements on local glazewares.
San Felipe/Zia glazewares and Tewa wares.
(Nelson Collection, AMNH)

Element	Local Glazewares	San Felipe/Zia Glazewares	Tewa Glazewares	Total	Percentage
doubleheaded key	9.00	0.00	0.00	9.00	10.47
hooked triangle	3.00	0.00	6.00	9.00	10.47
triangle	1.00	2.00	3.00	6.00	6.98
feather	2.00	1.00	2.00	5.00	5.81
chevron	4.00	1.00	0.00	5.00	5.81
dotted square	2.00	3.00	0.00	5.00	5.81
dotted clouds	1.00	0.00	4.00	5.00	5.81
zig-zag	1.00	0.00	3.00	4.00	4.65
pendant keys	4.00	0.00	0.00	4.00	4.65
key	2.00	2.00	0.00	4.00	4.65
lunette	0.00	0.00	3.00	3.00	3.49
feather being?	2.00	1.00	0.00	3.00	3.49
line triangle	2.00	1.00	0.00	3.00	3.49
open triangle	2.00	0.00	0.00	2.00	2.33
lozenge	2.00	0.00	0.00	2.00	2.33
corn	2.00	0.00	0.00	2.00	2.33
eye	0.00	0.00	1.00	1.00	1.16
shield	0.00	0.00	1.00	1.00	1.16
slot triangle	0.00	1.00	0.00	1.00	1.16
bird wing	1.00	0.00	0.00	1.00	1.16
medallion	1.00	0.00	0.00	1.00	1.16
bulls eye	1.00	0.00	0.00	1.00	1.16
hook	1.00	0.00	0.00	1.00	1.16
bowtie	1.00	0.00	0.00	1.00	1.16
scallops	1.00	0.00	0.00	1.00	1.16
stepped mountain	0.00	1.00	0.00	1.00	1.16
animal	1.00	0.00	0.00	1.00	1.16
key-tail	1.00	0.00	0.00	1.00	1.16
open square	1.00	0.00	0.00	1.00	1.16
double key cross	1.00	0.00	0.00	1.00	1.16
dotted triangle	0.00	0.00	1.00	1.00	1.16
Totals	49.00	13.00	24.00	86.00	100.00

families within the plaza pueblo. The Kotyiti glazewares with crystalline basalt are predominantly found (66 percent of the cases) in rooms that were added onto older roomblocks (Figure 7.5a). This finding implies that the San Felipe refugees were latecomers and that they were integrated into the village as individual families and not as a discrete social unit.[9] This pattern is in sharp contrast to the ethnohistorical account of the people of San Marcos Pueblo, who are reported to have occupied a roomblock on the "second plaza" and presumably formed their own residentially based political unit. Curiously, we have not yet found any ceramic evidence for the San Marcos people.

The Tewa wares cluster in three roomblocks (I, IV, and VI) and the east kiva (Figure 7.5b). This finding is somewhat unexpected since the ethnohistoric documents do not identify Tewa people as residents of the community. The abundance of Tewa Polychrome was the reason that Hawley (1936:91) defined Kotyiti as the type site for this type. It also appears to be the reason

why Harlow (1973:44) speculated that, "refugee Tewas must have lived at the Kotyiti Pueblo for a while before the village was destroyed in 1694." Although we cannot yet conclusively demonstrate this idea, we consider it a strong possibility.[10] Regardless of whether Tewa people lived in the community, the prevalence of Tewa wares at Kotyiti indicates that not all Keres villages were allied against the Tewa in the post-Revolt period.

Design Element Analysis

In this section, we analyze design element variability as represented by the Kotyiti ceramic assemblage in the Nelson collection (AMNH).[11] Our methodology involves identifying a series of distinct design elements and motifs that were replicated either individually or together with other elements or motifs in registers or panels (see Graves and Eckert 1998; Harlow 1973; Kidder 1915, 1936; Kidder and Amsden 1931).[12] Some of these motifs are identifiable as to their specific referent (e.g., bird wing or

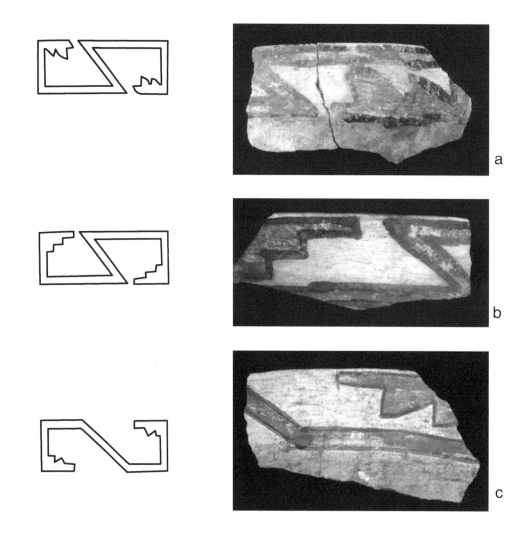

Figure 7.6. Double-headed key motif:
(a) Kotyiti Polychrome Glaze-on-white bowl, 295-C-149; (b) Kotyiti Polychrome Glaze-on-yellow bowl, 295-C-148;
(c) Kotyiti Polychrome Glaze-on-white bowl (295-C-158) (Nelson Collection, AMNH).

animal), but others are considerably more abstract. We identified 31 design elements/motifs on 103 sherds (Table 7.2).

Because of the small sample size, the results of our analyses must be viewed with caution. However, we believe that there is suggestive evidence that Kotyiti women did revive some traditional motifs on their glazeware ceramics. The best example of this is the key motif in its various forms—double-headed, pendant, and crossed. More than a third (36 percent) of all identified designs can be classified as a variant of the key motif. The most common of these forms is the double-headed key (Figure 7.6). Additional examples are known from glazeware vessels from other contemporaneous Revolt

period sites, such as Old San Felipe (Mera 1939:Plate 34).

The double-headed key motif has considerable antiquity in the Rio Grande glazeware sequence. It originated during Glaze B times (A.D. 1400–1450) and continued in use up to Glaze F times (Kidder 1936).[13] Kidder (1936:227) notes, however, that although present, the double-headed key is relatively rare on earlier Glaze E (A.D. 1515–1625) ceramics. During the Revolt period, however, it had an extremely broad regional distribution. Most significantly, it is present on Kotyiti glazeware sherds from three other contemporaneous mesatop villages— Astialakwa, Boletsakwa, and Cerro Colorado.[14] In addition, it is a common motif on related wares such as Puname Polychrome (Carlson 1965:Plate 3c, d, f; Harlow

1973:Plate 23e), Gobernador Polychrome (Carlson 1965:Plate 20b), Hawikuh Polychrome (Smith et al. 1966:Figures 75, 78, 79), and Ashiwi Polychrome (Harlow 1973:Plate 32e). For these reasons, we suspect that at least some women were reviving this motif in order to further the popular revitalization discourse.

Tewa women also used archaic design elements on some of their matte-paint wares. One of the most popular motifs is the hooked triangle (Figure 7.7).[15] This motif accounts for one quarter of all the identified motifs on these wares. The immediate antecedents for this motif can be found on Sankawi and Biscuit wares. The hooked triangle motif has a broad distribution and is occasionally

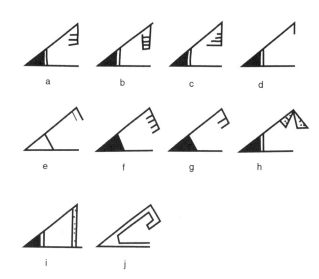

Figure 7.7. Hooked triangle motifs:

(a, b, c, d, i) Tewa Polychrome bowls;
(e) Pojoaque Polychrome jar;
(h) Tewa Black-on-white bowl; and
(f, g, j) Kotyiti Glazeware jars.
All motifs are from sherds from
Kotyiti (Nelson Collection, AMNH)
with the exception of
(d) which is from Black Mesa
(Mera Collection, Laboratory
of Anthropology), and
(i) which is from Astialakwa
(Mera 1935:Plate 14).

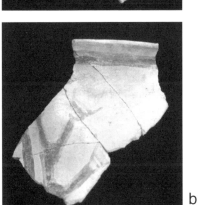

Figure 7.8. "Sacred mountain" motifs:

(a) Kotyiti Polychrome Glaze-on-red jar, (295-C-170);
(b) Kotyiti Polychrome Glaze-on-white jar (295-C-200);
(c) Puname Polychrome jar (295-C-192)
   (Nelson Collection, AMNH).

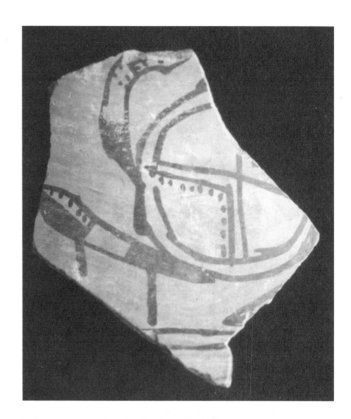

Figure 7.9. Shield motif on a Tewa Polychrome jar (295-C-119) (Nelson Collection, AMNH).

present on contemporaneous Kotyiti glazewares (Figure 7.7f, g, j), Hawikuh Polychrome (Smith et al. 1966:Figures 75e, 781), and Ashiwi Polychrome (Harlow 1973:Plate 32a, b; Mera 1939:Plates 64, 65).

In addition to the revival of some archaic motifs, there is also evidence for considerable experimentation on Kotyiti glazewares involving either combinations of old and new elements, or entirely new expressions. In our sample, this is best illustrated by the "sacred mountain" motif. The "sacred mountain" motif consists of repetitive decorative elements applied to both sides of a triangle. Versions of this motif are present on Kotyiti glazeware and Puname Polychrome sherds (Figure 7.8a, b, c). Somewhat similar motifs, but with "stepped" mountains, are present on some Gobernador Polychrome (Carlson 1965:Plate 19e), and Ogapoge Polychrome vessels (Carlson 1965:Plate 34f).

Similarly, some Tewa matte-paint wares also reveal the introduction of new motifs and design elements. Although our sherd sample is very small (n=4), one Tewa Polychrome jar sherd has a shield motif, which is divided into four quarters with pendant eagle feathers (Figure 7.9).[16] This image is both an unambiguous icon of an actual shield and an index of warfare. In addition, it lends some credence to the idea that an "iconography of resistance" may have been emerging, although additional studies are necessary.

Conclusions

Pueblo women were active agents in the shaping of social and political identities during the post-Revolt period. At this time, many families made the decision to vacate their mission pueblos and establish new multi-ethnic, mesatop communities, like Kotyiti Pueblo in the northern Rio Grande region. Their reasons for leaving the mission villages were likely stimulated by the new revitalization discourse emphasizing "living in accordance with the laws of the ancestors" and the traumatic historical associations of the villages with religious persecution, death, and pollution. Factionalism within these new communities, however, was an ongoing issue as they struggled with new social arrangements and the problem of how to respond to the return of the Spaniards.

Our petrographic analysis provides tentative confirmation of some aspects of the ethnohistorical documents. We have found compelling evidence that refugees from San Felipe lived within the Kotyiti community. However, we have not found evidence for San Marcos people who are mentioned in the same documents. One unexpected result is the evidence for close ties between Kotyiti and the Tewa villages of the Española Valley. This finding challenges the ethnohistorical statements that the Keres were at war with the Tewa during the post-Revolt period. These conclusions depend upon our interpretation of material inclusions in pottery as indexical signs linking pottery to its place of manufacture.

Our analysis of design elements and motifs reveals that women used the medium of their pottery to objectify and shape the popular revitalization discourse. Some women revived archaic design elements and motifs as a means of visually signaling their commitment to "re-turning to tradition." The clearest example of this is the double-headed key motif, which originated in the Rio Grande and quickly spread across the Pueblo World. Other women appear to have experimented with novel design motifs and layouts, and some of these may be associated with an "iconography of resistance." In both these cases, we are interpreting these motifs as indexical signs that Pueblo people themselves recognized as indexical of specific beliefs and meanings.

Finally, our semiotic approach has allowed us to engage with the style/function debates on new terms. Style and function are not essential qualities of material culture; rather they are moments in the interpretive process. Under certain circumstances, an object may have a specific meaning, but in other contexts, the same object may have an entirely different meaning. So, for example, the meaning of the double-headed key motif during the Glaze B period is unlikely to have been identical with its meaning during the post-Revolt period. Similarly, our semiotic approach allows us to rephrase the question of whether we are dealing with "their" meanings or "our" meanings (Conkey and Hastorf 1990). Because semiosis is an ongoing process, we are always producing meanings that implicate different kinds of signs in interpretive narratives. Some of these signs may have been cognized by past actors, while others may not. In the end, a satisfactory account of a particular culture will be one that sensitive to both the interpretive process and the multimodality of signs operative in that culture.

Acknowledgments

We thank David Hurst Thomas for facilitating the loan of ceramics from the Nelson collection of the American Museum of Natural History, Eric Blinman for assisting with the loan of ceramics from the Mera collection of the Museum of New Mexico, Museum of Indian Arts and Culture, Linda Cordell for providing access to the Shepard collection of the University Museum at the University of Colorado at Boulder, Chip Wills for supporting our geological survey, and Michael Bremer for general assistance with the Kotyiti Project. Finally, we wish to acknowledge the help of Michael R. Walsh in our geological fieldwork. Funds for our petrographic analyses were provided by the University of Pennsylvania Museum and the University Research Foundation.

Notes

1. Prior to the Revolt, Spanish demands upon native labor caused substantial changes in the organization of production (Webster 1997:115–116). For example, men appear to have become more actively involved in some traditionally female gendered activities such as tailoring, hide manufacture, and perhaps pottery making. Although the data is sparse, we suggest that even if some men made pottery prior to the Revolt (perhaps soup dishes, cups, and candlesticks for Spanish needs), women likely took this up as their exclusive domain after the Revolt due to the revivalist component of the cultural revitalization discourse (Preucel 2000; Reff 1995).

2. Vargas knew Kotyiti Pueblo as the pueblo of La Cieneguilla de Cochití.

3. The counts for the plaza pueblo do not include the prehistoric wares. These consist of Kwahe'e Black-on-white, Santa Fe Black-on-white, and Glaze A. These types may possibly be associated with an earlier Coalition period architectural component that was taken apart in the building of the plaza pueblo. There are no prehistoric wares associated with the ranchería.

4. We follow Curtis Schaafsma (personal communication) in using the name Tewa Black-on-white to refer to the type called Sakona Black-on white by Harlow (1973:28).

5. Our petrographic analysis of a sample of the utility wares from Kotyiti confirms that Tshirege tuff and Otowi tuff are local inclusion materials.

6. This observation is made by the first author (PHC) based on her inspection of Shepard's petrographic reference collection curated by the University of Colorado Museum, Boulder.

7. These sherds were sampled from Black Mesa (LA 23) in the Mera collection of the Museum of New Mexico, Laboratory of Anthropology.

8. Historical sources indicate that at different times seven different Tewa and two different Tano villages were represented on the mesa (Kessell et al. 1998:116–117). The Tewa villages were San Juan, San Ildefonso, Santa Clara, Nambe, Pojoaque, Cuyamungue, and Jacona; the Tano villages were San Cristobal and San Lazaro.

9. Because of the congruence of the petrographic and historical data, we do not favor the alternative interpretation that these were tradewares.

10. It is quite clear that there were close ties between Tewa people and the people living at Kotyiti. These ties are indicated by several lines of ethnohistoric evidence. Vargas's journals indicate that Juan Griego, a San Juan war captain, was killed in battle at Kotyiti on April 21, 1694. In addition, the Tewa were among the people that fled with the Cochiti into the Jemez Mountains during the Revolt of 1696 (Hackett 1937:351).

11. The sherds in this collection are from excavated contexts and are relatively large compared to those from the Mera collection that were recovered in a surface survey.

12. We make a distinction between design elements and motifs. The former are the discrete units from which motifs are composed.

13. All glazeware date ranges are from Curtis Schaafsma (personal communication).

14. These sherds were identified in the Mera collection of the Laboratory of Anthropology.

15. Kidder (1931:142) calls this motif a "highly conventional bird" and Harlow (1973:141) calls it the "F Figure."

16. Tewa Polychrome jars are an extremely rare form and there are no known whole specimens (Batkin 1987:38).

References Cited

Arnold, Dean E.
1985   *Ceramic Theory and Cultural Process.* Cambridge University Press, Cambridge, UK.

Bandelier, Adolph F. A.
1892   *Final Report of Investigation among the Indians of the Southwestern United States, Carried on Mainly in the Years from 1880 to 1885. Part II.* Papers of the Archaeological Institute of America, American Series, Vol. IV. University Press, Cambridge, Mass.

Batkin, Jonathan
1987   *Pottery of the Pueblos of New Mexico 1700–1940.* The Taylor Museum of the Colorado Springs Fine Arts Center, Colorado Springs.

Buchler, J.
1955   *The Philosophical Writings of Peirce.* Dover Books, New York.

Carlson, Roy L.
1965   *Eighteenth Century Navaho Fortresses of the Gobernador District: The Earl Morris Papers, No. 2.* University of Colorado Studies in Anthropology No. 10. University of Colorado Press, Boulder.

Espinosa, J. Manuel (editor)
1988   *The Pueblo Indian Revolt of 1696 and the Franciscan Missions in New Mexico: Letters of the Missionaries and Related Documents.* University of Oklahoma Press, Norman.

Graves, William M., and Suzanne L. Eckert
1998   Decorated Ceramic Distributions and Ideological Developments in the Northern and Central Rio Grande Valley, New Mexico. In *Migration and Reorganization: The Pueblo IV Period in the American Southwest,* edited by K. A. Spielmann, pp. 263–283. Arizona State University Anthropological Research Papers No. 51. Tempe.

Hackett, Charles W. (editor)
1937   *Historical Documents relating to New Mexico, Nueva Vizcaya, and Approaches Thereto, to 1773. Vol. III.* Collected by A. F. A. Bandelier and F. R. Bandelier, Carnegie Institute of Washington, Washington, D.C.

Harlow, Francis H.
1973   *Matte-Paint Pottery of the Tewa, Keres and Zuni Pueblos.* University of New Mexico Press, Albuquerque.

Hawley, Florence M.
1936   *Field Manual of Prehistoric Southwestern Pottery Types.* University of New Mexico Bulletin No. 291. Albuquerque.

Hayes, Alden C., Jon Nathan Young, and A. H. Warren
1981   *Excavations of Mound 7: Gran Quivira National Monument, New Mexico.* National Park Service, Washington, D.C.

Hays, Kelly A.
1994   Kachina Depictions on Prehistoric Pueblo Pottery. In *Kachinas in the Pueblo World,* edited by Polly Schaafsma, pp. 47–62. University of New Mexico Press, Albuquerque.

Hewett, Edgar Lee
1938   *Pajarito Plateau and Its Ancient People.* University of New Mexico Press, Albuquerque.

Hodder, Ian
1990   Style as Historical Quality. In *The Uses of Style in Archaeology,* edited by M. Conkey and C. Hastorf, pp. 44–51. Cambridge University Press, Cambridge, UK.

Hodge, Frederick W., George P. Hammond, and Agapito Rey

1945   *Fray Alonso de Benavides' Revised Memorial of 1634.*
        University of New Mexico Press, Albuquerque.

Kessell, John L., and Rick Hendricks (editors)

1992   *By Force of Arms: The Journals of Don Diego de Vargas,
        New Mexico 1691–1693.* University of New Mexico Press,
        Albuquerque.

Kessell, John L., Rick Hendricks, and Meredith D. Dodge (editors)

1995   *To the Royal Crown Restored: The Journals of Don Diego de
        Vargas, New Mexico 1692–1694.* University of New Mexico
        Press, Albuquerque.

1998   *Blood on the Boulders: The Journals of Don Diego de Vargas,
        New Mexico 1694–97.* 2 Vols. University of New Mexico
        Press, Albuquerque.

Kidder, Alfred V.

1915   *Pottery of the Pajarito Plateau and of some Adjacent Regions
        in New Mexico.* Memoirs of the American Anthropological
        Association No. 2.

1936   The Glaze-paint, Culinary and other Wares. In *The Pottery
        of Pecos, Vol. II.* edited by A. V. Kidder, pp. 1–383. Yale
        University Press, New Haven.

Kidder, Alfred V., and Charles A. Amsden

1931   *The Pottery of Pecos, Vol. I: The Dull-Paint Wares.* Yale
        University Press, New Haven.

Kidder, Madeline A., and Alfred V. Kidder

1917   Notes on the pottery of Pecos. *American Anthropologist*
        19:329–337.

Lemonnier, Pierre

1992   *Elements of an Anthropology of Technology.* Anthropological
        Papers, Museum of Anthropology, University of Michigan,
        No. 88. Ann Arbor.

Mera, H. P.

1933   *A Proposed Revision of the Rio Grande Glaze Paint Sequence.*
        Laboratory of Anthropology, Technical Series, Bulletin
        No. 5. Santa Fe.

1939   *Style Trends of Pueblo Pottery in the Rio Grande and Little
        Colorado Culture Areas from the Sixteenth to the Nineteenth
        Century.* Memoirs of the Laboratory of Anthropology
        No. 3. Santa Fe.

Nelson, Nels C.

1914a   Excavations of Pueblo Kotyiti, New Mexico. Ms. on file,
        American Museum of Natural History, New York.

1914b   *Pueblo Ruins of the Galisteo Basin, New Mexico.* Anthro-
        pological Papers of the American Museum of Natural
        History 15. New York.

1916   Chronology of the Tano ruins, New Mexico. *American
        Anthropologist* 18:169–176.

Ortiz, Alfonso

1994   The Dynamics of Pueblo Cultural Survival. In *North
        American Indian Anthropology: Essays on Society and Culture,*
        edited by R. J. DeMallie and A. Ortiz, pp. 296–306.
        University of Oklahoma Press, Norman.

Preucel, Robert W.

1998   The Kotyiti Research Project: Preliminary Report of the 1996
        Field Season. Report submitted to the U.S. Forest Service,
        Santa Fe National Forest and the Pueblo de Cochiti.

2000   Living on the Mesa: Hanat Kotyiti, A Post-Revolt Cochiti
        Community in Northern New Mexico. *Expedition* 42:8–17.

Preucel, Robert W. and Alexander A. Bauer

2001   Archaeological Pragmatics. *Norwegian Archaeological Review*
        34:85–96

Reff, Daniel T.

1995   The "Predicament of Culture" and Spanish Missionary Accounts
        of the Tepehuan and Pueblo Revolts. *Ethnohistory* 42:63–90.

Shepard, Anna O.

1942   *Rio Grande Glaze Paint Ware: A Study Illustrating the Place
        of Ceramic Technological Analysis in Archaeological Research.*
        Carnegie Institute of Washington, Contributions to American
        Anthropology and History, No. 39. Washington, D.C.

Smith, R. L., R. A. Bailey, and C. S. Ross

1970   *Geologic Map of the Jemez Mountains, New Mexico.*
        Miscellaneous Investigations Series, Map I-571, 1:125,000.
        United States Geological Survey.

Smith, Watson, Richard B. Woodbury, and Nathalie F. S. Woodbury

1966   *The Excavation of Hawikuh by Frederick Webb Hodge:
        Report of the Hendricks-Hodge Expedition 1917–1923.*
        Contributions from the Museum of the American Indian
        Heye Foundation, Vol. XX. New York.

Toulouse, Joseph H., Jr.

1949   *The Mission of San Gregorio de Abó.* School of American
        Research Monograph No. 13. University of New Mexico
        Press, Albuquerque.

Warren, A. Helene

1979a   The Glaze Paint Wares of the Upper Middle Rio Grande.
        In *Archaeological Investigations in the Cochiti Reservoir, New
        Mexico Volume 4: Adaptive Change in the Northern Rio
        Grande Valley,* edited by Jan Biella and Richard Chapman,
        pp. 187–216. Office of Contract Archaeology, University
        of New Mexico, Albuquerque.

1979b   Historic Pottery of the Cochiti Reservoir Area. In
        *Archaeological Investigations in the Cochiti Reservoir, New
        Mexico Volume 4: Adaptive Change in the Northern Rio
        Grande Valley,* edited by Jan Biella and Richard Chapman.
        Office of Contract Archaeology, pp. 235–245. University
        of New Mexico, Albuquerque.

1979c   The Tempering Materials of Cochiti. In *Archaeological
        Investigations in the Cochiti Reservoir, New Mexico Volume 4:
        Adaptive Change in the Northern Rio Grande Valley,* edited
        by Jan Biella and Richard Chapman, pp. B83–112. Office
        of Contract Archaeology, University of New Mexico,
        Albuquerque.

Webster, Laurie D.

1997   *Effects of European Contact on Textile Production and
        Exchange in the North American Southwest: A Pueblo Case
        Study.* Unpublished Ph.D. dissertation, Department of
        Anthropology, University of Arizona, Tucson.

White, Leslie A.

1932   *The Pueblo of San Felipe.* American Anthropological
        Association Memoir No. 38. Washington, D.C.

Chapter 8

History in Stone:
Evaluating Spanish Conversion Efforts through Hopi Rock Art

Kurt E. Dongoske and
Cindy K. Dongoske

Introduction

The Hopi people live in northeastern Arizona on lands that they have continuously occupied for close to a millennium. Today, there are 12 Hopi villages distributed throughout three mesas, beginning on the east and progressing westward these mesas are called First Mesa, Second Mesa, and Third Mesa. The Hopi Mesas represent three narrow projections along the southern edge of a large geologic basin comprised of Cretaceous period sedimentary rocks known as Black Mesa (Reynolds 1988). Just east of First Mesa and separated by the Polacca Wash Valley is Antelope Mesa, constituting one of the easterly fingers of Black Mesa. Dotted along Antelope Mesa's easterly edge are numerous Hopi ancestral villages, several of which were once large pueblos (Figure 8.1). These pueblos include: Kokopnyama, Nesuftonga, Lululongturque, Chakpahu, Kawaika'a, and Awatovi (Brew 1979:514; Hargrave 1931:95; Smith 1971:1). The Hopi were living at Awatovi when the first Spanish arrived. The Spanish presence at Hopi lasted from 1629 to about 1700 with the destruction of Awatovi with a hiatus of about 12 years immediately following the Pueblo Revolt (Montgomery et al. 1949:18).

This paper examines the success of the Spanish efforts to Christianize the Hopi by comparing Spanish documentary evidence with Hopi ethnohistorical accounts and archaeological evidence in particular Hopi rock art. Specifically, the rock art from the area of the village of Awatovi is examined. The village of Awatovi was selected because it has long been contended (Montgomery et al. 1949:9–12) that this village, of all the Hopi villages, was the most receptive to the Spanish efforts of converting the Hopi to Christianity.

The paper begins with a brief review of the Spanish presence at Hopi, followed by an examination of the three sources of information regarding the effects the Spanish presence had on the Hopi people. Next, the documented rock art panels from below Awatovi are described and a brief examination of how the images depicted there inform on the divergent claims made between Spanish documentary sources and Hopi ethnohistory. Finally, the paper concludes with an evaluation of Adams's (1989) claim that the Hopi response to the Spanish presence in Tusayan was one of "passive resistance."

The Arrival of the Spanish at Hopi

The earliest encounter between the Hopi and the Spanish occurred in 1540 when Pedro de Tovar and Juan Padilla, seeking the province of Tusayan under orders from General Francisco Vásquez de Coronado, arrived at a

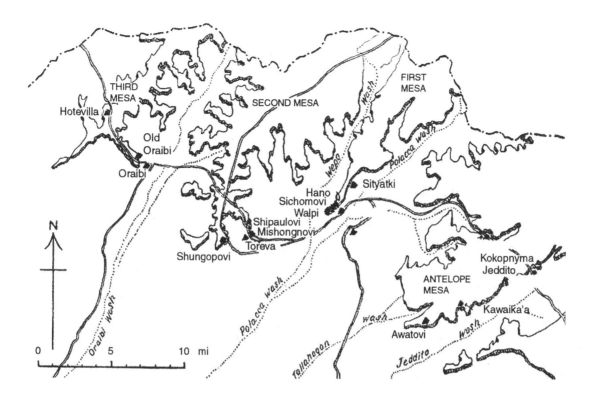

Figure 8.1. Hopi Mesas indicating location of villages (after Smith 1952).

village on Antelope Mesa. Some scholars (e.g., Brew 1979:519) believe that Awatovi was the first Hopi village to encounter the Spanish, because the majority of the other villages on Antelope Mesa had become uninhabited. According to Hopi traditional history (Leigh Kuwanwisiwma, personal communication, 1994) and other scholars (James 1974:36–37; Spicer 1962:189), however, Kawaika'a was the first Hopi village to encounter the Spanish during which a brief skirmish ensued and de Tovar destroyed part of Kawaika'a. The Hopi villagers vacated Kawaika'a partly as a result of de Tovar's destruction and possibly because of previous problems with failing water supplies that made life difficult on Antelope Mesa (Spicer 1962:189). After leaving Kawaika'a, many of the villagers moved to other Hopi towns, while others migrated to Acoma country (Ellis 1979:439). Regardless of which Hopi village first encountered the Spanish, one fact remains consistent: the first meeting between the Hopi and Spaniards appears to have resulted in violence (Brew 1979:519; James 1974:37; Lomatuway'ma

et al. 1993:276; Spicer 1962:189). Later Spanish explorers to visit Antelope Mesa and the Hopi country were Espejo in 1583, Oñate in 1598, and De Vargas in 1692 (Hargrave 1931:95).

The Mission Period at Hopi

The first Spanish mission established among the Hopi was built at the village of Awatovi on Antelope Mesa. Three Franciscans, Francisco Porras, Andrés Gutiérrez, and Cristóbal de la Concepción, arrived at Awatovi on August 20, 1629 and established the mission known as San Bernardo de Aguátubi, named in dedication of the feast day of Saint Bernard of Clairvaux (Brew 1979:519; Montgomery et al. 1949:9). Thus began the Spanish mission program at Hopi and the Mission period that lasted until the Pueblo Revolt of 1680.

In constructing the mission at Awatovi, the Franciscans purposefully chose a location where there was an important Hopi kiva. The Franciscans filled the kiva with clean sand and over the top of the kiva they built the main altar of the church, thereby demonstrating the superposition or superiority of the Christian religion over the Hopi religion (Brew 1979:520; James 1974:47; Montgomery et al. 1949:64, 134–136). The mission of San Bernardo de Aguátubi was built to be an impressive structure with two imposing bell towers, priest quarters, classrooms, sanitary facilities, pens for livestock, as well as quarters for the soldier guards (James 1974:47; Montgomery et al. 1949). There is also evidence suggesting that San Bernardo de Aguátubi served as the headquarters for the entire Franciscan missionary effort at Hopi.

The Franciscans also constructed two other missions at Hopi. The San Miguel Mission was built at Oraibi and the San Bartolomé Mission at Old Shungopavi (James 1974:45; Wiget 1982). Additionally, two visitas were established, one at Kisakovi near Walpi, and one at Mishongnovi (Spicer 1962:191). The two missions were subsequently demoted to visitas with only occasional visits by a priest (Brew 1979:520).

The reason the Franciscans chose the village of Awatovi for the location of their principal mission at Hopi is probably because Awatovi constituted the gateway to the Hopi country, representing, at that time, the largest and most prominent of the Hopi villages, and as such the hub of trade and communication with the outside world. According to Hopi traditions (Courlander 1971:175), Awatovi was founded by the *aawatngyam,* or Bow Clan, from which the village took its name (literally meaning "Bow-High-Place," or "the place of the Bow People"), who were the most prominent and influential of the founding clans (Fewkes 1893:363; Lomatuway'ma et al. 1993:275). Also residing at Awatovi were clans from the pueblos of the Rio Grande region and others from the *Palatkwapi* region to the south (Courlander 1971). The Rio Grande people are believed to have arrived at Awatovi and Sikyatki late in prehistoric times having delayed their arrival by living at Zuni for a period. The descendants of these Rio Grande people are now living in the village of Sichomovi on First Mesa and belong to the Asa or Tansy Mustard Clan (Adams 1991:73; Fewkes 1893:367). Among the many

clans that resided at Awatovi were the *Honanngyam* (Badger), *Pipngyam* (Tobacco), *Tapngyam* (Rabbit), *Taawangyam* (Sun), *Duwangyam* (Sand), *Kyarungyam* (Parrot), *Torsngyam* (Bluebird), *Piqösngyam* (Bearstrap), and *Qaöngyam* (Corn) clans (Courlander 1971:175).

When the Spanish arrived, Awatovi was a very large village with a correspondingly large population. The pueblo consisted of four rows of multi-storied houses, and between them, three large plazas that stretched to the edge of the mesa (Courlander 1971; Fewkes 1893:364). It also contained numerous kivas and shrines (Courlander 1971:175). The historical documents indicate that the people of Awatovi were more accommodating of the Franciscans and their conversion efforts than the other Hopi villages. A report by Father Benavides that characterizes the Hopi as being "rapidly converted" is probably more reflective (although exaggerated) of Awatovi inhabitants than the entire population of Hopi from the other villages (Montgomery et al. 1949:12).

The Pueblo Revolt and Its Aftermath

The Pueblo Revolt occurred at Hopi sometime between August 10 and 13, 1680.[1] The immediate result of the Revolt was that the Hopi effectively drove the Spaniards out of their villages by killing four missionaries; two at Oraibi, and one each at Awatovi and Shungopavi (Brew 1979:521). Fray Joseph de Figueroa died at San Bernardo Aguátubi, and Fray José de Trujillo died at San Bartolome de Xongo Pavi (Shungopavi). At San Miguel de Oraibi, two priests, Fray José de Espeleta and Fray Augustin de Santa Maria were killed (Bancroft 1889:349; Ellis 1974; Wiget 1982). The churches at each of these Hopi villages were destroyed.

Shortly after the Pueblo Revolt, Tewa, Tiwa, Tano, and Keres people immigrated to Hopi, where they took refuge and constructed two new villages: Hano on First Mesa, and Payupki on Second Mesa (Ellis 1974; Mindeleff 1891:39, 59; Spicer 1976:191). The Hopi, fearing Spanish retaliatory military expeditions, moved three villages, Walpi, Shungopavi, and Mishongnovi, which had been located near springs at the base of the mesas, to the safety of the adjacent mesas where attack would be extremely difficult (Brew 1979:522; Dockstader 1985:67; Spicer 1962:192). The Hopi remained independent from Spanish rule until De Vargas's reconquest in the 1690s.

Following re-establishment of the mission at Awatovi, the pueblo was destroyed by other Hopi from the villages of Walpi, Shungopavi, Mishongnovi, and Oraibi, who, according to Hopi tradition, opposed Awatovi's welcoming of the return of the Spanish. After the destruction of Awatovi in 1700, the Spanish never seriously attempted to subjugate the Hopi again partly because of the region's inhospitability to irrigation agriculture and its extreme distance from centers of Spanish authority. From that point on, the Spanish treated the occupants of the Hopi Mesas as more or less an independent nation (Adams 1989:78; Capone 1995).

In evaluating the effectiveness of Spanish Christianizing efforts on the Hopi people, three sources of information are examined: Spanish documents, sources of Hopi traditional history, and archaeological data (Adams 1989:79). To examine only one of these sources of information would provide a biased perspective of Spanish proselytizing efforts at Hopi; however, by examining all three a more holistic perspective of history can be achieved. All sources of history, written or oral, are biased to some degree; the key is to discern in what ways they are biased (Capone 1995:48). In the following discussion, each source of information concerning the Spanish presence at Hopi is examined and the information gleaned from those sources evaluated.

Spanish Documentary Evidence

Spanish documentary evidence regarding the Hopi area for the period from 1630 to 1680 is both scarce and of limited quality (Brew 1949; Wiget 1982). The overwhelming majority of information comes from inquisitional testimony in the case of Governor Bernardo López de Menizábal vs. Fray Alonso de Posadas (Wiget 1982:187). This case reflects a complex jurisdictional conflict between religious and secular authorities for control of Nuevo México (Dockstader 1985:64), and is so highly biased

in nature that it is of limited use as a source of factual evidence (Wiget 1982:187). Yet, these are the primary documentary resources that have been employed to illustrate the relations between the Franciscan priests at Hopi and the Hopi people (Wiget 1982:189); there are no known Spanish documents that originated out of the Hopi area (Brew 1948).

These Spanish documents, although valuable for illustrating Spanish perspectives and chronology, usually do not include detailed information on Hopi culture (Capone 1995:48). The one thing that appears to be consistent throughout these Spanish documents is the claim that the Franciscan priests were very successful in converting the Hopi to Christianity. Father Estévan de Perea describes the conversion of Hopis at Awatovi as, "They [the Hopi] were, however, freed from all their doubts and converted to our holy faith through a great miracle which our Lord brought to pass in that village through the intercession of His servants. . . ." (Brew 1949:9).

Regarding the ability of Father Perea to convert the Awatovian Hopi, a Spanish document contends, "he converted and baptized more than four thousand souls and instructed the Indians with great perfection" (Brew 1949:11). Another Spanish document, this one penned by Fray Gerónimo de Zárate Salmerón, claimed that the "Pueblo of Oraibi had 1,236 souls under its administration, with Aguatobi (Awatovi) having 900 souls and Xongopavi (Shungopavi) having 830 souls" (Brew (1949:17).

Thus, the Spanish documents from this period paint a scene of Franciscan priests successfully converting Hopi to Christianity prior to the Pueblo Revolt. Moreover, most accounts portray the Franciscans as so successful in converting the Hopi at Awatovi to Christianity that during the reconquest of 1692 the Awatovians accepted the return of the Spanish and the accompanying Christian faith. This act precipitated the destruction of Awatovi by other Hopi villages in 1700. However, as presented below, the apparent success of converting Hopi to Christianity as claimed in the Spanish documents can be called into question by Hopi ethnohistorical accounts and the archaeological evidence found in the rock art from the area of Awatovi.

Hopi Traditional Histories

In evaluating the success of Spanish claims of conversion, it is important to consider Hopi traditional histories, which are primarily personal accounts that have been passed down through time. Hopi traditional accounts of the Spanish presence can be viewed as independent sources of information that complement the Spanish documents. However, as with Spanish documents, the Hopi accounts must be read critically, with the potential for biases and special interests kept firmly in mind (Capone 1995:49).

In examining Hopi traditional accounts of the Spanish presence, this paper draws principally from two published sources: *The Truth of a Hopi* by Edmund Nequatewa (1936) and a 1982 study by Andrew Wiget. Wiget (1982:183) evaluated the accuracy of two Hopi oral traditions (from the villages of Shungopavi and Oraibi), represented by four testimonies gathered over a 75-year period, recounting the coming of the Spanish and the Pueblo Revolt. Wiget found that there were several important recurring themes regarding the Spanish presence at Hopi contained within each personal Hopi account. The recurring themes that relate to Spanish efforts at conversion can be grouped as forced Hopi slave labor, suppression of the kiva religion, and enforced church attendance coupled with cruel punishment for violators (Wiget 1982:187). Wiget also identified a high degree of consistency in the Hopi accounts that portray the general motivational and causal patterns underlying the events described in each testimony.

The Spanish exploitation of Hopi labor appears to be tied to efforts at constructing missions. Edmund Nequatewa (1936:42–43), describes Spanish priests as *Tota'tsi,* meaning a tyrant, dictator, demanding person (Hopi Dictionary Project 1998:607) or a grouchy person that will not do anything for himself (childlike), who intimidated the Hopi people into slave labor. In providing an example of this slave labor, Nequatewa recounts that Hopi men were sent to the San Francisco Peaks to get "pine or spruce beams" and under great duress, transported

them back to Shungopavi. Nequatewa specifically describes the Hopi efforts to get beams for Spanish construction of the missions:

> When the Priests started to build the mission, the men were sent away over near the San Francisco peaks to get the pine or spruce beams. These beams were cut and put into shape roughly and were then left till the next year when they had dried out. Beams of that size were hard to carry and the first few times they tried to carry these beams on their backs, twenty to thirty men walking side by side under the beam. But this was rather hard in rough places and one end had to swing around. So finally, they figured out a way of carrying the beam in between them. They lined up two by two with the beam between the lines. In doing this, some of the Hopis were given authority by the missionary to look after these men and to see if they all did their duty. If any man gave out on the way he was simply left to die. There was great suffering. Some died for lack of food and water, while others developed scabs and sores on their bodies.
>
> —[NEQUATEWA 1934:43]

Courlander (1971:160) recounts Hopi traditions that feature forced church attendance and the suppression of the katsina religion. He states that the Spanish were intruding into everything in the village. Franciscans demanded Hopi attendance at the church meetings every Sunday and tried to suppress ceremonies in the kivas and katsina dances. The Franciscans depicted the katsinas as devils working against God, but apparently Hopi elders continued to practice their ceremonies in the kivas in spite of numerous disruptive attempts by the priests.

According to Hopi traditions, the Franciscans were effective at suppressing the kiva religion for a time. However, when the Hopi experienced a period of drought, which lasted for several years, they believed it to be partly caused by the suppression of their traditional religion. In response to the drought, Hopi men would pretend to go hunting, and then visit remote shrines where they would make prayer sticks as they used to in the village (Courlander 1971; Wiget 1982:187).

The Hopi policy toward the Spanish conversion attempts appears to have been one of appeasement and tolerance (or, a passive aggressive response), rather than one of direct confrontation. The logical reason for utilizing this approach is most assuredly because the Hopi had knowledge of the conflict and loss of life that had taken place earlier at Zuni and they probably wanted to avoid a similar disaster (Adams 1989:81). Additionally, the Hopi people had most likely heard of Castaño de Sosa's battle that ended with the defeat of Pecos in 1591, and the Spanish battles with the Acoma people in 1598 and 1599, which resulted in the destruction of the Acoma village with 500 captive Indians who were sentenced as follows: all males over 25 years of age were to have one foot chopped off and serve 20 years of personal servitude, all males between the age of 12 and 25 were sentenced to 20 years of personal servitude, the women over the age of 12 years were sentenced to 20 years of personal servitude, and two Indians from Hopi were sentenced to have the right hand cut off and set free in order to tell the Hopi of their punishment (Dockstader 1985:65; Minge 1991:14). Given this knowledge, there was little doubt left in the Hopi mind concerning the probable results of a direct conflict with the Spanish military or active defiance of the wishes of the Franciscans toward Christianization (Adams 1989:82).

In spite of the outward Hopi appearance of servitude to the Spanish, Hopi history indicates that the traditional religious leadership was maintained and continued to function during the Spanish presence. According to other historical accounts (Bancroft 1889:256; Bolton 1950:228), this Hopi religious leadership insulated the general populace from the Spanish missionaries and even occasionally debated or denounced the padres in public after the priests had spoken.

In comparing these two seemingly contradictory sources documenting the Spanish success of converting Hopi to Christianity, several questions beg consideration. Are the Spanish accounts of conversion correct and the Hopi traditional histories inaccurate? Or, are the Spanish accounts of successfully Christianizing the Hopi inaccurate? Or, are they merely misinterpreting Hopi passive resistance as an acceptance of Spanish dominance and conversion to Christianity? In seeking illumination of these questions a third source of evidence, archaeological data, is examined.

Archaeological Data

Archaeological data provides valuable information on the long-term effects of the Spanish presence at Hopi and the majority of this information come from two sources: the Peabody Museum of Archaeology and Ethnology's excavations at Awatovi (Montgomery et al. 1949), and the Museum of Northern Arizona's excavations at Walpi (Adams 1982). For the purposes of this discussion the archaeological information derived from the Peabody Museum's excavations at Awatovi will be primarily employed. The Peabody Museum's excavations at Awatovi indicate that the Spanish missionaries introduced wheat, cantaloupe, watermelon, chili pepper, peach, apricot, and plum to the Hopi diet (Brew 1949). Before the introduction of Spanish cultigens, the Hopi diet consisted primarily of beans, corn, squash, deer, and rabbit. Based on the faunal remains recovered from Awatovi it is believed that the Spanish introduced the Hopi to sheep, goat, cow, horse, burro, pig, cat, and Greyhound dog (Olsen 1978).

Ceramic evidence indicates there was strong Spanish and/or Eastern Puebloan influence on Hopi pottery production and the design elements employed during the Mission period (A.D. 1625–1680) through the subsequent Pueblo Revolt period (A.D. 1680–1692). Immediately prior to the Pueblo Revolt, the highly stylized Sikyatki Polychromes (A.D. 1375–1625) ceased to be produced by the Hopi and were replaced by San Bernardo Polychromes (A.D. 1625–1740). The Franciscan missionaries encouraged or forced several changes in native ceramics (Adams 1989), discouraging the use of pottery as burial offerings while encouraging the employment of Spanish favored designs, such as flowers, the Maltese cross, and the eight-pointed star (Adams 1989; Capone 1995:82). Flat bottom and ring base vessels became popular, and new forms were introduced, such as candlesticks and everted rim soup plates (Adams 1989:85; Wade and McChesney 1981:44). Some archaeologists (Frank and Harlow 1974:147) have interpreted the shift in pottery production from Sikyatki to San Bernardo to indicate general Hopi cultural decline. From this perspective, the San Bernardo Polychromes are viewed as a stylistically degenerative variety of Sikyatki; however, many of these assumptions regarding Hopi cultural change tend to be grounded in a poor sampling of the ceramic record and the use of simplistic methods of classification (Wade and McChesney 1981:15).

Many of the changes in material culture identified during the Mission period probably reflect the Hopi policy of outward appeasement to the Spanish presence because of the constant threat of Spanish military retaliation. Moreover, the continuation of a outward acceptance and acquiescence to Christian conversion and Franciscan demands by the Hopi would have provided them with continued access to many newly introduced domesticated crops and animals, as well as to metal tools that would have enhanced the quality of day-to-day life.

Rock Art from Antelope Mesa

For the purposes of this analysis, rock art from below the village of Awatovi, is examined for its ability to inform on the efficacy of the Spanish conversion efforts at Hopi. In the context of this analysis, the rock art is conceptualized as a valuable component of the archaeological record that can add a significant and unique dimension to our knowledge of Hopi from prehistoric to historic times. The rock art also serves as an additional line of documentary evidence to evaluate Hopi traditional histories. Moreover, various stylistic differences in rock art can serve to identify cultural relationships, patterns of communication, evidence of trade, and other spheres of social and religious interaction.

In a very general sense, then, the rock art from Awatovi is viewed as a form of "written history" that is broadly comparable with Spanish written documents from the same period. Therefore, an analysis of the rock art

from Awatovi may serve to authenticate or negate the general accounts of Hopi conversion to Christianity related in the Spanish documents. The primary hypothesis utilized in this preliminary study is that if the Spanish were effective at converting the Awatovian Hopi to Christianity, then one should expect Christian iconography to be represented in the various rock art panels located on the rock ledges below the village of Awatovi. The underlying assumption here is that because the creation of rock art is a very labor-intensive endeavor, individuals that create rock art have something important to express. The rock art record of the Southwest demonstrates that before and after the Spanish arrival, rock art was created to mark the territory of religious sodalities or organizations (Olsen 1985; Rohn et al. 1989:132–133). Additionally, rock art pre- and post-Spanish period was used to mark notable events such as the arrival of the railroad, horse (Cole 1990), or celestial events (Burkholder 1994). Therefore, one would expect the presence of the Spanish and the concurrent introduction of Christianity to be a significant enough event to be expressed by the Hopi in their rock art. As our analysis demonstrates, this does not appear to have been the case.

As previously discussed, the village of Awatovi is central to our understanding of the effect of the Spanish presence at Hopi for several reasons. During this period, Awatovi represented the largest and most prominent of the original seven Hopi villages (Redman 1990:1) and was most likely the hub of trade and communication between Hopi and the outside world. Additionally, Awatovi was also the only Hopi village to accept the return of the Spanish presence after the Revolt (Brew 1949).

The village of Awatovi was founded around A.D. 1200 and remained inhabited until the winter of A.D. 1700 when it was destroyed by occupants from other Hopi villages (see Whiteley, Chapter 10). Currently, the visible ruins cover about 23 acres, measuring nearly 400 meters in an east-west direction and 250 meters north-south, and include the remains of a prehistoric pueblo, a historic pueblo, three churches, and associated mission buildings (Redman 1990:1). Brew (1942) estimated the village to contain approximately 5,000 rooms, of which 1,300 were excavated by the Peabody Museum.

The Antelope Mesa Rock Art Survey

Awatovi is situated along the barren, rocky north rim of Antelope Mesa overlooking the Jeddito Wash. The rock art that is associated with the village is located along the first, second, and third terraces of sandstone cliffs immediately below the ruin and extends three miles east to the ruin of Kawaika'a located on Antelope Mesa (Figure 8.1). The exposed rocks in this area range in age from the Precambrian to the recent period and include a majority of the intervening deposits (Cooley et al. 1969; Thornbury 1965). The rocks exposed below Awatovi are primarily Cenozoic, with the earliest being the late Mesozoic (Permian period). The bulk of exposed cliff wall and talus boulders that contain the rock art are comprised of Dakota sandstone and Mancos shale. The cliffs are exposed at varying levels and heights across the study area and are periodically covered by deep, stable sand dunes. Areas within the study area that contain small box-like canyons are usually flanked on either side by sand dunes and narrow bench areas with a smooth cliff face that tends to exhibit the highest amount of rock art sites (Dongoske 2000:212).

The Hopi Tribe's Cultural Preservation Office documented the rock art from Antelope Mesa as part of a multi-phase project to identify for management purposes all the historic properties located between Awatovi and Kawaika'a. Because of increasing vandalism on Antelope Mesa, the Cultural Preservation Office determined that a complete documentation of cultural resources was necessary to successfully manage them now and in the future. The first phase consisted of a Class III inventory of 3.5 sections of land situated between and including the pueblo ruins of Awatovi and Kawaika'a and recorded 128 archaeological sites. During the Phase I inventory it became apparent that the rock art sites, located along the edge of the mesa, were too numerous and complex to be adequately recorded within the scope, time, and funding allocated for the inventory (Dongoske 2000:4).

The Cultural Preservation Office received funding from the National Park Service's Historic Preservation Fund Grant to Indian Tribes and Alaska Natives to support Phase II, which consisted of documenting all the rock art sites located within the previously inventoried 3.5 sections. The primary objective of Phase II was to produce a permanent record of the rock art as a management tool and to chronicle the rich and extensive Hopi occupation and history of the area (Dongoske 2000:5).

For this analysis, rock art includes *petroglyphs,* which are forms of sculpture, and *rock paintings* (monochrome and polychrome) exhibited on natural rock surfaces (Cole 1992:7). Combinations of petroglyph and rock paintings occur on Antelope Mesa. The majority of rock art identified within the Antelope Mesa study area is petroglyphic and is executed in a variety of techniques including, but not limited to, controlled pecking by use of a pecking stone and/or hammerstone, incising and grooving by use of a sharpened stone or other hard material such as bone or metal, and abrading or grinding by a stone rubbed on the host rock. The rock art panels generally face south or east and generally exhibit smoother surfaces as a result of the varying effects of weathering making them well suited for the production of petroglyphs.

The area between the villages of Awatovi and Kawaika'a contain an approximate 1,920 acres of rock cliff surface and talus boulders offering practical surfaces for the execution of rock art. Currently, within this area 302 rock art sites have been documented. Additionally, a single linear mile of cliff escarpment extending to the west from Awatovi and across three terraces is currently being surveyed; the additional rock art sites documented here will contribute to the expanding database of information. The eastern face (edge) of Antelope Mesa is characterized here by three distinct levels: the mesatop, a middle shelf or bench immediately below the mesatop, and a bottom shelf located at the base of the mesa where it meets the Upper Jeddito Valley floodplain (Dongoske 2000:68).

Generally, the cliff wall and talus slope immediately below the mesa edge exhibits few rock art sites because

Figure 8.2. Example of common rock art elements associated with water sources. Portions of Panels I, J, and K
from rock art site AMRAPS S19-13-99 (HCPO).

the exposed rock is generally lightly patinated and rough in texture. When rock art is encountered in this area, it tends to be associated with a water source, and is characterized by areas of heavier patination and often represented by simple geometric figures that are generally in poor condition due to weathering.

The frequency of rock art sites nearly doubles on the cliff walls and boulders that characterize the middle shelf below Awatovi. Here, the exposed sandstone is more deeply patinated and is moderately rough to smooth in texture. Numerous water sources were identified along this shelf as well, and most of these consist of natural water sluices and catchment basins formed by the runoff of rain and snow melt from the mesatop. Water sources continue to be a favored place for rock art along the middle shelf; ogre faces with barred teeth, "water bugs" with antennae, stick arms, and legs, and snakes are common elements

at these locations (Figure 8.2). Though infrequently represented, plumed serpents can occasionally be found in association with a water source as well. Additionally, the rock art along this middle shelf becomes more complex with the appearance of early katsina figures and masks. Of particular note, is that rock art sites datable to the late Pueblo III through V temporal periods tend to be located within a quarter mile or less of the site of Awatovi. These rock art sites tend to be larger, covering numerous panels, and exhibiting katsina forms, masks, shield-like discs, anthropomorphic figures with shield-like disc bodies, and rug/clan motifs (Figure 8.3). Also common at these sites are the juxtapositioning of more recent forms with earlier (Pueblo I to Pueblo III, A.D. 700–1100) figures that include deer/antelope, watch springs, concentric circles, simple unadorned faces, squiggle lines, foot and hand prints, and geometric shapes (Dongoske 2000:66–67).

Figure 8.3. Typical rock art representations from rock art sites dated to the Pueblo III-IV period. Rock art site AMRAPS S24-88-98 (HCPO).

The bottom shelf contains the highest number of rock art sites. The available cliff wall for rendering rock art is greater than that of the middle shelf, and the degree of patination appears more consistent. In general, the host rock is a moderately dark, rust-brown in color and the sandstone cliffs tend to be smooth textured and free from blemishes. Both the cliff wall and talus boulders contain rock art; most of the rock art sites located on cliff walls are far overhead and this is likely the result of hundreds of years of deflating ground soils due to erosion.

The rock art sites located along this bottom shelf are numerous and contain some of the most elaborate and complex figures for the entire Antelope Mesa study area. Similar to the middle shelf, later (Pueblo III-IV, A.D. 1250–1600), datable forms tend to be located near the site of Awatovi, the largest rock art sites with the most complex panels are located within a half mile or less of the village. Katsina figures and masks, two-dimensional faces created by pecking a face across a natural crest in the rock, stylized birds, shields and shield-like discs, diverse and unusual animal forms, and the rug/clan motif are the more prominent figures found here.

In comparison to the western portion of the study area, a more densely forested mesatop characterizes the eastern end with numerous benches located below the rim and extending down to the Jeddito Valley floor. Here there is more available cliff space on which to create rock art, and most of the cliffs are located below the mesa rim on the middle bench, nearest the base of the mesa. Sand dune formations continue in this section, but generally are deflated at the edge of the mesa. The exposed middle and base cliffs contain the majority of rock art; very little rock art was documented on the cliff walls and talus slope immediately below the mesa rim.

The pueblo of Kawaika'a is located within this portion of the study area and is estimated to contain 3,000 to 4,000 rooms constituting one of the largest of the prehistoric pueblos on Antelope Mesa. The rock art documented in proximity of this ruin is distinctly different, both stylistically and thematically, from the rock art inventoried in the rest of the project area. Here, the katsina culture rock art depictions change stylistically from the typical katsina representations found in the majority of the study area. Specifically, katsina and mask renditions appear to be localized; that is, the figures, when found, look different from any other katsina and mask renditions identified in the rest of the project area. Stylistic differences are characterized by katsina figures that are less elaborate or detailed in comparison to those noted below the village. Moreover, the figures tend to be blocky with rectangular

Figure 8.4. Western shield from Kawaika'a.

or square bodies and heads; wavy upright hair is popular with typically unadorned torsos and ears. Other than eyes, facial features are generally not depicted. Shields and shield-like discs are considered to be associated with the later puebloan time periods. Of particular note are two remarkable shield figures, each resembling the other in size and interior design, that are located on either end of Kawiaka'a (Dongoske 2000:186–187). The placement of these shields at the west and eastern ends of the pueblo appears to have been purposeful; each shield can be seen from a distance, as each is located in places where travelers approaching the pueblo must pass. The eastern shield marks the trailhead that runs below the rim of the mesa leading into the village of Kawaika'a, and the western shield is situated near the western trailhead entrance to the village. These two figures may represent the only "true" shields identified throughout the Antelope Mesa study area (Figure 8.4). The occurrence of a

distinctly different localized, and preferential style in rock art representations near the village of Kawaika'a is interpreted as probably representing different Keresan ethnic groups that once resided at Kawiaka'a, but were not present at Awatovi (see Ellis 1979:448–449; Stephen 1936:2:1157). Hopi traditions confirm the presence of Laguna and possibly Zuni clans at Kawaika'a prior to the arrival of the Spanish.

General Observations

A detailed, systematic analysis of the Antelope Mesa rock art has not been completed, however, for the purposes of this discussion general statements regarding several reoccurring images can be presented.

Animal figures are the most common theme and are generally found in groupings or singular depictions of deer/ antelope, butterflies, hummingbirds, stylized birds, cranes, duck-like birds, rodent-like animals, snakes, and dog-like figures. Rock art sites containing primarily animal themes often also exhibit abstract and geometric figures, such as watch springs, concentric circles, lines of dots, simple squares, rectangles and circles. It is rare to find a predominant animal theme on a panel intermixed with katsina and katsina-like forms associated with the later Pueblo III and IV temporal periods. In those unusual circumstances when this does occur, the katsina forms are either superimposed or juxtaposed upon the panel. Shields and shield-like discs, anthropomorphic shields, rug/clan motifs, and checkerboards for example, are believed to be associated with more recent puebloan time periods and are rarely found on panels with simple figures and themes unless superimposed over older figures (Dongoske 2000:213).

One image, the *A'losaka,* is prolific throughout the study area. The western edge of the study area, near Awatovi, contains numerous depictions of *A'losaka,* and they tend to decline in frequency as one moves toward the east, nearer the village of Kawaika'a. In fact only one image of *A'losaka* was documented near Kawaika'a and this was approximately one-half mile west of the village.

The association of *A'losaka* with the village of Awatovi is to be expected and its representation in the rock art here comes as no surprise. *A'losaka,* a horned moisture and fertility deity, has an intimate and historic association with Awatovi. Smith (1952) states that according to the accepted Hopi mythico-biography:

> [T]he original A'losaka, child of the Sun and Earth Mother, lived in the San Francisco mountains, whence he came by means of a rainbow to woo a maid of Awatovi. The results of his successful suit were a group of horned offspring, known collectively as A'losakas, and the cult of his worship flourished particularly at Awatovi, where his children became the cult ancestors or the patrons of the members of the Horn Society.

A'losaka and his wife, *Pavayoykyasi,* are said to have resided at Awatovi and to have provided it with bountiful harvests and plentiful rain (Lomatuway'ma et al. 1993:282). In addition, *A'losaka* is said to have saved the village of Awatovi from a firestorm that burned across the plain (Curtis 1922:88). Given *A'losaka*'s association with the village of Awatovi and his powers over moisture and fertility it is not surprising that his image is represented numerous times in an area below Awatovi that overlooks agricultural fields and gardens.

By far the most ubiquitous figure found in the study area is what is referred to as the "clan" or "rug" symbol. In its most basic form, this symbol is represented as a square or rectangle with the interior treatment including diagonal, vertical, or horizontal lines, hatching, steps, or a combination of these; the interior designs are distinct and as diverse in design as they are numerous (well over one hundred of these figures have been recorded in the study area). When Hopis were asked to view sketch renderings and photographs of these figures, they responded that these are clan symbols probably attributable to the occupants of Awatovi, and may also be rug and/or pottery designs related to the particular clan.

One technological observation regarding the rock art below Awatovi dating to the Pueblo III-IV period is the use of elaborate fine-lined and detailed applications. This shift in technology is interpreted as reflecting the use of metal tools introduced by the Spanish to the Hopi; these tools would have undoubtedly changed many standards in the production of rock art. Metal tools reduce the required labor and permit more detailed and elaborate rock art representations.

Evidence of Spanish Imagery in the Awatovi Rock Art

Evidence of Spanish imagery in the rock art from Antelope Mesa is extremely rare. Only four different types of rock art depictions have been documented that may be associated with the Spanish presence at Hopi. These four different types of rock art depictions consist of two possible versions of a cross, one depiction of a possible Spaniard on a horse, and one depiction of an event that occurred at Hopi during the Spanish occupation.

Figure 8.5. Shield with cross from Panel A, rock art site AMRAPS S24-143-98 (HCPO).

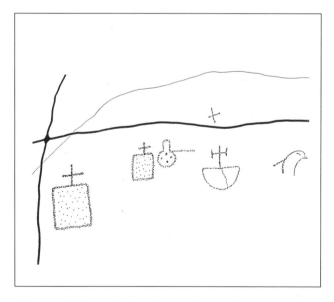

Figure 8.6. Rock art forms with crosses from rock art site AMRAPS S24-156-98 (HCPO).

Possible Renditions of the Cross

At two rock art sites, 24-143-98 and 24-156-98, are depictions of what might be considered stylized versions of a Christian cross. Site 24-143-98 is located very near Awatovi and consists of three conjoined panels (Panels A, B, and C) separated by deep vertical cracks in the cliff wall. Panel A contains the most remarkable and unusual shield identified within the study area (Figure 8.5). The shield is very large at .80 meters in diameter, and unlike other shields depicted in the area, has no head, arms, or legs. The shield is also very distinct in that it resembles a talisman or amulet. The body is circular with triangular fringing encircling the outer edge. The interior is marked prominently by the placement of a large "X" or cross with pendulum-like appendages. Additionally, there are four triangular corners projecting inward from the edge of the shield and in between the arms of the cross. At this time, it is unclear whether this depiction represents a Hopi shield design or a Hopi stylized interpretation of a Maltese cross.

Rock art site 24-156-98 consists of six forms that are fully patinated and geometric in design. This particular rock art site is unusual because three of the six forms represented here are unlike anything else in the study area. Two of these three forms consist of squares with a cross-like form placed on top of the square (Figure 8.6). The interior portion of each square is pecked to create a polka dot effect throughout the interior. The two square and cross forms are located at the left side of the panel.

To the right of the square and cross forms is the third unusual form which resembles a boat with mast and cross-beam (Figure 8.6). Possible interpretations of these three forms are the depiction of a church and steeple for the square and cross forms and a Spanish ship with a mast for the third form; however, when Hopi elders were questioned about the significance of the cross representations their response was that these cross depictions represented stars in the sky.

Rider on Horse

Rock art site 19-13-99 is located approximately 150 meters south of archaeological site AZ:J:08:102 (ASM), a Pueblo

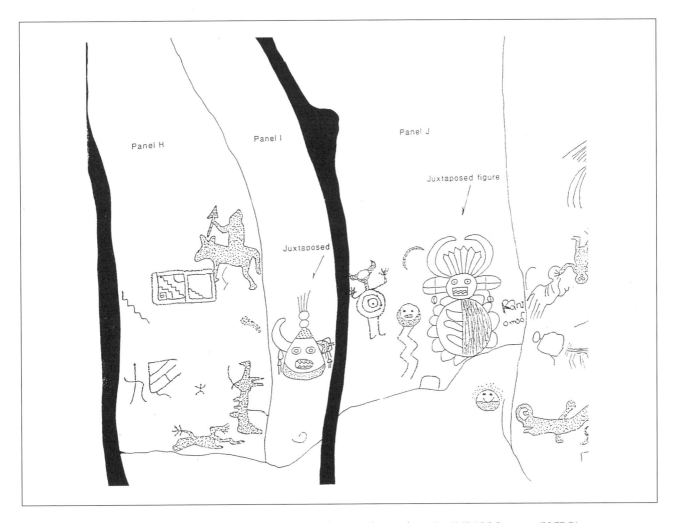

Figure 8.7. Depiction of a Spanish rider on a horse from Panel H, rock art site AMRAPS S19-13-99 (HCPO).

III-IV habitation site. There are 17 panels (A-Q) that comprise this site and the individual panels tend to be separated by natural vertical cracks in the cliff face. For the purposes of this discussion the upper portion of Panel H is of particular interest. Here, two forms are depicted adjacent to one another, the upper form appears to have been created sometime after the execution of the lower form. The lower form consists of a detailed rug/clan motif adjacent to what appears to be a horse and rider (Figure 8.7). The horse and rider depiction is well defined, rendered in left side profile, and the rider is clearly holding what appears to be a staff with a spearhead attached. This form may very well represent a Hopi depiction of a Conquistador on a horse and is the most conclusive documentation in the rock art from Awatovi of a Spanish presence.

Rock Art Corroborating Hopi Traditional History

Rock art site 24-142-98 is a large and complex site with numerous rock art figures rendered in stone through multiple techniques; pecking, incising, and painting. The site is located approximately one-eighth of a mile below and east of Awatovi. The site is located on a stretch of exposed sandstone cliff that terminates at the west end by the presence of a large, stable sand dune formation. The exposed sandstone cliff is approximately 20 to 25 feet in height, is a dark pink to rust color, smooth textured, and easily accessible from Awatovi. The site's rock art is exhibited in 11 panels (A-K).

Panel E is the largest of the panels and the one most relevant to the present discussion. It contains the greatest number of forms and is the most complex and elaborate

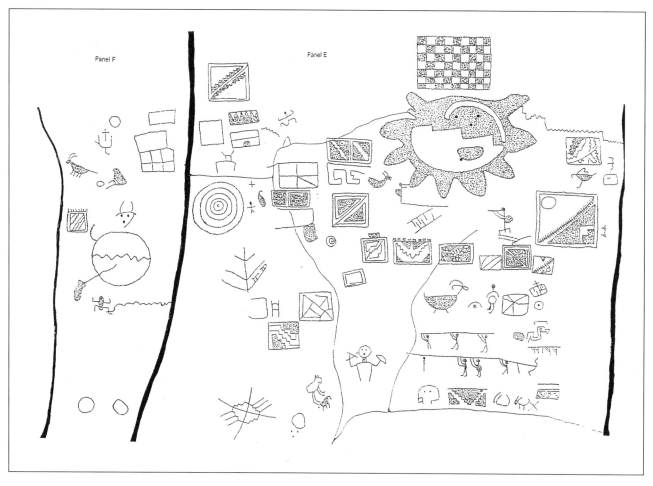

Figure 8.8. Stick figures carrying, above their heads, a long stick or pole that may substantiate the Hopi account of transporting logs from the San Francisco Peaks to the Hopi Mesas. Panel E from rock art site AMRAPS S24-142-98 (HCPO).

of all the panels represented at this site. Of particular interest is the depiction of three, sometimes four, human stick figures walking in a row and carrying above their heads a long, horizontal stick, pole, or log. There are three separate depictions of this activity, placed one above the other, within Panel E (Figure 8.8). This scene may depict the Hopi historical account, as related by Nequatewa (1934:43), of the forced labor of Hopi in transporting logs from the San Francisco Mountains for the construction of the missions.

Hopi Passive Resistance

Based on a preliminary analysis of a portion of the rock art from the vicinity of Awatovi, it appears that Hopi artists did not have a strong interest in portraying Christian iconographic symbols or chronicling the presence of the Spanish. Rather, they appear to be most interested in continuing to depict traditional Hopi religious symbols, clan histories, and clan identity markers. It must be stressed to the reader, that these preliminary interpretations are based only on approximately 60 percent inventory of the rock art from Antelope Mesa. The rock art within the western portion of Antelope Mesa, encompassing the remainder of Awatovi and Talahogan Canyon, is currently being inventoried and may affect the interpretations presented here.

Two scenarios could account for the paucity of Christian symbolism in the rock art. First, the Christianized Hopis may have been prohibited by the Franciscan monks from the practice of depicting Christian (and Hopi) religious symbols in rock. Second, the Hopi may have demonstrated an outward behavior that would indicate conversion to maintain access to the material goods introduced by the Spanish, but retained their adherence to traditional religious practices including the making of traditional rock art. The first scenario is indirectly supported by the Spanish documents that assert the success of the Franciscans in converting the Hopi to Christianity; however, these documents, as demonstrated, are highly suspect because of their propagandistic nature. The second scenario is supported by the Hopi traditional accounts that suggest that traditional religious practices continued during the period of conversion. The rock art evidence, however, is consistent with the second scenario. It provides data for the continuation of traditional rock art images and reveals the virtual absence of Christian iconography.

Adams (1989:88) contends that the Hopi successfully resisted Spanish culture and conversion efforts through their skillful use of diplomacy and "passive resistance." In general, the Hopi policy toward the Spanish was to tell them what they wanted to hear and feign obedience through public demonstrations of the acceptance of the Christian faith and Spanish authority. When the Spanish left, the Hopi quickly returned to their traditional ways.

The preliminary analysis of the rock art data suggests that the Spanish had little effect on the ways in which the Hopi expressed themselves and communicated through the medium of rock art. Moreover, Hopi traditional historical accounts coupled with the rock art from below Awatovi suggest that during the Spanish presence the Hopi maintained adherence to their traditional religious practices, but performed their religious observances away from the view of the Franciscan padres. The Hopi policy of "passive resistance" appears to have been very successful in enabling the Hopi to select elements of Spanish culture that would improve their own day-to-day life, principally subsistence items, while protecting them from the more culturally invasive and threatening elements of Spanish policy (Adams 1989:88).

This policy of "passive resistance" not only worked well in dealing with the Spanish, but according to Leigh Kuwanwisiwma (personal communication, 2000), the Hopi practiced these same tactics in dealing with the United States government's recent historical attempts at assimilation through the missionary programs. In order to minimize the missionaries' invasive presence into Hopi family and ceremonial lives and to gain access to needed materials and goods, the Hopi would attend events (sewing clubs, church services, and special religious observances) held by the local missionaries. This allowed the Hopi access to needed items and provided the missionaries with a sense of success in their proselytizing efforts, all the while the Hopi maintained their traditional ceremonial observances.

In conclusion, the Spanish were unsuccessful in implementing their mission program at Hopi. They not only failed in their effort to establish missions during colonization, they failed in their attempts to reestablish them after the Pueblo Revolt. The special status of the Hopi is indicated by the fact that the Spaniards never attempted to found Spanish settlements at Hopi (Adams 1989:87). It is clear that the failure of Spanish missionary program was due to the remote location of the Hopi and strategies of passive resistance adopted by the Hopi people. To this day, contemporary Hopis tend to be practitioners of traditional Hopi religion and very few have converted to Christianity.

Acknowledgments

We would like to extend our appreciation to Robert Preucel for organizing the symposium in which an earlier version of this paper was presented at the 1998 annual meetings of the Society for American Archaeology and for his support, patience, and constructive comments on the development of this manuscript. We would also like to thank Nancy Coulam and T. J. Ferguson for their review and suggestions on this manuscript. The documentation of the rock art of Antelope Mesa was generously supported by National Park Service Historic Preservation Fund Grant No. 04-97-NA-0412.

Notes

1. The exact date when the Revolt took place at Hopi, or among the other western pueblos (Acoma or Zuni), is unknown. The anticipation and confusion precipitating violence at Tesuque on the night of August 9, 1680 (Hackett and Shelby 1942:[I]:xxviii) may have created delay and confusion in initiating the Revolt among the western pueblos (Wiget 1982:193).

References Cited

Adams, E. Charles

1991   *The Origin and Development of the Pueblo Katsina Cult.* University of Arizona Press, Tucson.

1989   Passive Resistance: Hopi Responses to Spanish Contact and Conquest. In *Columbian Consequences: Vol. 1. Archaeological and Historical Perspectives on the Spanish Borderlands West,* edited by D. H. Thomas, pp. 77–91. Smithsonian Institution Press, Washington, D.C.

1982   Walpi Archaeological Project: Phase II. Volumes 1–9. Museum of Northern Arizona Report Submitted to Heritage Conservation and Recreation Service, Interagency Archeological Services, San Francisco.

Bancroft, Hubert H.

1889   *History of Arizona and New Mexico,* Volume XVII (1530–1888). The History Company, San Francisco.

Bolton, Herbert E.

1950   *Pageant in the Wilderness: The Story of the Escalante Expedition to the Interior Basin, 1776, including the Diary and Itinerary of Father Escalante.* Utah State Historical Society, Salt Lake City.

Brew, John Otis

1942   Preface. In *The Changing Physical Environment of the Hopi Indians of Arizona,* by John T. Hack, pp. v–x. Papers of the Peabody Museum of American Archaeology and Ethnology, Harvard University 35(1). Cambridge, Mass.

1949   Part I: The History of Awatovi. In *Franciscan Awatovi: The Excavation and Conjectural Reconstruction of a 17th-Century Spanish Mission Establishment at a Hopi Indian Town in Northeastern Arizona,* by Ross Montgomery, Watson Smith, and John Otis Brew. Papers of the Peabody Museum of American Archaeology and Ethnology, Harvard University 36. Cambridge, Mass.

1979   Hopi Prehistory and History to 1850. In *Handbook of North American Indians, Volume 9: Southwest,* edited by Alfonso Ortiz, pp. 514–523, Smithsonian Institution, Washington, D.C.

Burkholder, Grace

1994   *Perceptions of the Past: Solar Phenomena in Southern Nevada.* Burkholder, Boulder City, Nev.

Capone, Patricia H.

1995   *Mission Pueblo Ceramic Analyses: Implications for Protohistoric Interaction Networks and Cultural Dynamics.* Unpublished Ph.D. dissertation, Department of Anthropology, Harvard University, Cambridge, Mass.

Cole, Sally

1990   *Legacy on Stone: Rock Art of the Colorado Plateau and Four Corners Region.* Johnson Publishing, Boulder.

1992   *Katsina Iconography in Homol'ovi Rock Art, Central Little Colorado River Valley, Arizona.* Arizona Archaeological Society, Phoenix.

Cooley, M. E., J. W. Harshbarger, J. P. Akers, and W. F. Hardt

1969   Regional Hydrogeology of the Navajo and Hopi Indian Reservations, Arizona, New Mexico, and Utah. *Geological Survey Professional Paper* 521-A, U.S. Government Printing Office, Washington, D.C.

Courlander, Harold

1971   *The Fourth World of the Hopis: The Epic Story of the Hopi Indians as Preserved in their Legends and Traditions.* University of New Mexico Press, Albuquerque.

Curtis, Edward S.

1922   *The North American Indian, Vol. 12, The Hopi.* Plimpton Press, Norwood, Mass.

Dockstader, Frederick J.

1985   *The Kachina and the White Man: The Influence of White Culture on the Hopi Kachina Religion.* University of New Mexico Press, Albuquerque.

Dongoske, Cindy K.

1997   Antelope Mesa Archaeological Survey. Ms. on file, Cultural Preservation Office, The Hopi Tribe, Kykotsmovi, Ariz.

2000   Antelope Mesa Rock Art Documentation Project: 1998–2000. Ms. on file, Cultural Preservation Office, The Hopi Tribe, Kykotsmovi, Ariz.

Ellis, Florence H.

1974   The Hopi: Their History and Land Use. In *Hopi Indians. American Indian Ethnohistory: Indians of the Southwest,* edited by D. A. Horr, Garland Publishing, Inc., New York.

1979   Laguna Pueblo. In *Handbook of North American Indians, Volume 9: Southwest,* edited by Alfonso Ortiz, pp. 438–449, Smithsonian Institution, Washington, D.C.

Fewkes, Jesse Walter

1893   A-wà-to-bi: An Archaeological Verification of a Tusayan Legend. *American Anthropologist,* o.s., VI:363–375.

Frank, Larry, and Francis H. Harlow

1974   *Historic Pottery of the Pueblo Indians, 1600–1880.* New York Graphic Society, Boston.

Hackett, Charles W., and Charmion C. Shelby (editor and translator)

1942   *Revolt of the Pueblo Indians of New Mexico, 1680–92, and Otermin's Attempted Re-conquest.* 2 Vols. University of New Mexico Press, Albuquerque.

Hargrave, Lyndon L.

1931   Excavations at Kin Tiel and Kokopnyama. In *Recently Dated Pueblo Ruins in Arizona,* by Emil W. Haury and Lyndon L. Hargrave, Smithsonian Miscellaneous Collections, 82(11), Smithsonian Institution, Washington, D.C.

Hopi Dictionary Project (compilers)

1998   *Hopi Dictionary, Hopìikwa Lavàytutuveni: A Hopi-English Dictionary of the Third Mesa Dialect.* University of Arizona Press, Tucson.

James, Henry C.

1974 *Pages from Hopi History.* University of Arizona Press, Tucson.

Lomatuway'ma, Michael, Lorena Lomatuway'ma, and Sidney Namingha, Jr. (narrators)

1993 *Hopi Ruin Legends: Kiqötutuwutsi.* Collected, translated, and edited by Ekkehart Malotki, published for Northern Arizona University by the University of Nebraska Press, Lincoln.

Mindeleff, Victor

1891 *A Study of Pueblo Architecture in Tusayan and Cibola.* Smithsonian Institution Press, Washington, D.C.

Minge, Ward Alan

1991 *Ácoma: Pueblo in the Sky.* University of New Mexico Press, Albuquerque.

Montgomery, Ross G., Watson Smith, and John O. Brew

1949 Franciscan Awatovi: The Excavation and Conjectural Reconstruction of a 17th Century Spanish Mission Establishment at a Hopi Indian Town in Northeastern Arizona. *Papers of the Peabody Museum of American Archaeology and Ethnology* Volume 36, Harvard University, Cambridge, Mass.

Nequatewa, Edmund

1936 *Truth of a Hopi and Other Clan Stories of Shung-opavi.* Edited by Mary Russell F. Colton, Museum of Northern Arizona, Bulletin No. 8, Flagstaff, Ariz.

Olsen, Nancy

1985 Hovenweep Rock Art: An Anasazi Visual Communication System. University of California at Los Angeles, *Institute of Archaeology Occasional Paper 14.*

Olsen, Stanley

1978 The Faunal Analysis. In *Bones from Awatovi.* Papers of the Peabody Museum of Archaeology and Ethnology, Harvard University, 70(1). Cambridge, Mass.

Redman, Charles L.

1990 Background to the Project. In *Awatovi Ruins of Antelope Mesa: Preservation and Development Plans, Final Report Presented to The Hopi Tribal Council,* by Charles L. Redman, Steven R. James, and Diane M. Notarianni. Department of Anthropology, Office of Cultural Resource Management Report No. 8, Arizona State University, Tempe.

Reynolds, Stephen J.

1988 *Geologic Map of Arizona.* Arizona Geological Survey, Phoenix.

Rohn, Arthur H., William M. Ferguson, and Lisa Ferguson

1989 *Rock Art of Bandelier National Monument.* University of New Mexico Press, Albuquerque.

Smith, Watson

1952 *Kiva Mural Decoration at Awatovi and Kawaika'a with a Survey of Other Wall Paintings in the Pueblo Southwest.* Papers of the Peabody Museum of American Archaeology and Ethnology, Vol. 37, Harvard University, Cambridge, Mass.

1971 *Painted Ceramics of the Western Mound at Awatovi.* Papers of the Peabody Museum of Archaeology and Ethnology, Vol. 38, Harvard University, Cambridge, Mass.

Spicer, Edward H.

1962 *Cycles of Conquest: The Impact of Spain, Mexico, and the United States on the Indians of the Southwest, 1533–1960.* University of Arizona Press, Tucson.

Stephen, Alexander M.

1936 *Hopi Journal of Alexander M. Stephen.* 2 Vols. Edited by Elsie C. Parsons. Columbia University, Contributions to Anthropology, No. 23. New York.

Thornbury, W. D.

1965 *Regional Geomorphology of the United States.* John Wiley & Sons, Inc., New York.

Wade, Edwin L., and Lea S. McChesney

1981 *Historic Hopi Ceramics: The Thomas V. Keams Collection of the Peabody Museum of Archaeology and Ethnology Harvard University.* Peabody Museum Press, Cambridge, Mass.

Wiget, Andrew O.

1982 Truth and the Hopi: An Historiographic Study of Documented Oral Tradition Concerning the Coming of the Spanish. *Ethnohistory* 29(3):181–199.

Chapter 9

Signs of Power and Resistance:

The (Re)Creation of Christian Imagery and Identities in the Pueblo Revolt Era

Matthew J. Liebmann

Archaeology . . . contributes a detailed picture of the objective conditions and cultural forms inhabited by mass populations, while historical records may tend towards the official records of dominant groups. Archaeology itself therefore becomes an instrument of the limits of dominance by recovering that history which time itself was expected to repress in favour of the state chronicler

—(MILLER 1988:76).

Following the Pueblo Revolt of 1680, leaders of the rebellion encouraged Pueblo peoples to eliminate the Spanish influences from their world and return to "traditional," pre-Hispanic ways of living. Archaeological evidence documents this re-creation of traditional Puebloness in architecture (Ferguson and Preucel 2000; Snead and Preucel 1999) and artifacts (Adams 1981, 1989; see Mobley-Tanaka, Chapter 5 and Capone and Preucel, Chapter 7), and indeed, many Spanish elements were purged from the Pueblo world during the brief period of decolonization from 1680–1692. However, archaeological and ethnohistoric data reveals that even though Pueblo leaders, "ordered the churches burned and holy images broken up" (Hackett and Shelby 1942:251), Catholic characteristics were not completely eradicated during this period. In fact, Christian imagery and material culture continued to be used by Pueblo peoples following the Revolt; upon their reconquest, Spaniards found crosses, altars, chalices, and lamps in use at Pueblo villages. However, these Christian elements were often used in very different ways in the post-Revolt Pueblo world than they had been under Spanish domination.

Pueblo responses to Catholicism following the Revolt were varied and complex. During Antonio de Otermín's unsuccessful reconquest attempt of 1681, the Spaniards found the churches and convents of Sandia, San Felipe, and Santo Domingo destroyed and lying in ruin (Hackett and Shelby 1942:259–260). Yet, at these same villages, they found ecclesiastical objects, such as incensories, censors, and boxes of holy oils, carefully preserved in the homes of the leaders of the Revolt. Pueblo opinions regarding Christianity were multiple, shifting, and contested during this period. The testimonies of Pueblo persons recorded in Spanish court documents attests to this ambivalence within the Pueblos: "some said that if the Spaniards should come [back] they would have to fight to the death, and others said that in the end they must come and gain the kingdom because they were sons of the land and had grown up with the natives" (Hackett and Shelby 1942:235; see also Espinosa 1942:134–135).

What then are we to make of the conspicuous adoption of Catholic imagery by some Pueblo persons in the Revolt period? A straightforward interpretation might suggest that Pueblo use of Christian symbolism is evidence of

Catholic belief and practice, and that these signs simply document the extent of Spanish dominance and influence, even in the Revolt period. This position assumes that the use of Catholic symbols by Pueblo peoples at this time is evidence of false consciousness, that the dominant Spanish ideology had convinced Native persons to believe in the system by which they were subjugated. Such an interpretation not only denies agency to Pueblo peoples in the seventeenth century, but also presumes that Christian symbols meant the same things to all people at all times, ignoring the context in which these signs were employed. Thus, the assumption of the straightforward practice of Catholicism among the Pueblos during the Revolt period (based on the presence of Christian symbols and artifacts) is an oversimplification of the complex relationships that exist between material signs and their interpreters. Following the Revolt, Christian symbols were appropriated and reinterpreted by Pueblo peoples, often imbued with radically different meanings than those endorsed by the Spanish. In fact, Christian imagery was manipulated and invested with new meanings that were not contrary to traditional Pueblo identities, but played a role in the resistance that helped to formulate new Pueblo identities. Pueblo opposition was not only articulated via passive, subversive, and veiled means, but Native persons also made use of Christian symbols as polysemous signs, resisting the Spanish while simultaneously creating and asserting new identities in the wake of the Revolt.

The (Re)Creation of Pueblo Tradition

Identity is a notoriously difficult concept to define. The Oxford English Dictionary characterizes identity as "the sameness of a person or thing at all times or in all circumstances." In fact, Revolt leaders employed this notion of a single, bounded, unchanging Pueblo identity following their victory in 1680 when they encouraged Pueblo peoples to renounce all Spanish beliefs and customs in order to return to traditional ways of life. In practice, however, this notion of immutable identity becomes problematic and untenable. For the purposes of this chapter, I conceive of identities as recursive, constantly

shifting, negotiated strategies of alliance building. They do not remain static at all times or in all circumstances; rather, they constantly shape and are shaped by perceived similarities and differences. To speak of identity (on either the group or individual level) is to examine the complex intersection of social groupings of ethnicity, gender, class, faction, race, etc. Moreover, because these categories are continually negotiated, identities are constantly changing, malleable concepts. Thus it comes as no surprise that the identities formed by Pueblo peoples following the Revolt are new (re)creations, based in notions of traditional Pueblo concepts, but inevitably different from those of their ancestors.

Ethnohistoric documents reveal that following the Revolt of 1680, Pueblo leaders made a conscious effort to create new Pueblo identities based in the revival of traditional beliefs. Popé, Alonso Catiti, and others preached the renunciation of all Spanish beliefs and customs, commanding their people to undergo ritual purification and renewal of traditional ceremonies. According to a declaration made by Pedro Naranjo (San Felipe) in December 1681, Pueblo men were encouraged to, "break up and burn the images of the holy Christ, the Virgin Mary and the other saints, the crosses, and everything pertaining to Christianity, and that they burn the temples, break up the bells, and separate from the wives whom God had given them in marriage and take whom they desired. . . . They did this, and many other things . . . they thereby returned to the state of their antiquity" (Hackett and Shelby 1942:247–248).

Indeed, many Pueblo persons did adopt these ideals, and the archaeological record attests to this re-creation of traditional Pueblo identities. Churches and haciendas were burned and destroyed, while many new refugee villages were constructed on or adjacent to ancient pueblo sites, denoting a return by the people to the ways of their ancestors. The form and plan of some of the Revolt period plaza pueblos has been interpreted as an architectural assertion of these traditions (Ferguson and Preucel 2000; Snead and Preucel 1999). Furthermore, studies of the ceramics of the Revolt period suggest that pottery designs played a part in resistance to the Spanish as well as in the construction of "traditional" Pueblo identities. Spanish motifs and forms abruptly disappear from Hopi ceramics at this time (Adams 1981:325) and the use of crosses on Pueblo ceramics virtually ceases after 1680 (Frank and Harlow 1974; see Mobley-Tanaka, Chapter 5).

However, the development of "traditional" Pueblo identities was *not* simply a return to pristine pre-Hispanic Puebloness. Rather, this was a contemporary construction of new identities, based in notions of traditional Pueblo practice. The native inhabitants of the northern Rio Grande did not completely return to pre-Columbian lifeways following the Pueblo Revolt. They were selective in their rejection of Spanish influence, retaining many Spanish crops and animals, including sheep, cattle, goats, wool (Adams 1981:325), oxen, horses, mules (John 1996:105), wheat, tomatoes, and chiles[1] (Riley 1999:212). In fact, following the Revolt, Popé reportedly assured the people that if they followed the old practices, they would "harvest a great deal of maize, many beans, a great abundance of cotton, calabashes, and very large watermelons and cantaloupes" (Hackett and Shelby 1942:248). The irony of this statement is that melons were originally Old World crops introduced to the Southwest via Spanish contact (Ford 1987:78–79). Here Popé (allegedly) incorporated elements of Spanish influence, albeit unconsciously, into his depiction of "traditional" Pueblo life. By the 1680s, a restoration of pre-Hispanic Pueblo life was impossible; any return to tradition was inevitably and inherently also a new invention, recursively creating and recreating Pueblo identities.

This selective eradication of Spanish influence has led archaeologists and ethnohistorians to theorize that Pueblo peoples of the Revolt era retained the more functional, utilitarian Spanish elements (Adams 1981:326; John 1996:105–106), while simultaneously rejecting the symbolic and religious aspects of colonialism—most notably Catholic signs and practices. While there are drastic changes in symbolic material culture following the Revolt, Christian symbols were not entirely purged from the Pueblo world. But neither were they utilized in a conventional

Spanish Catholic manner. Pueblo appropriation and manipulation of Christian imagery during the Revolt period suggests that Catholic symbols were re-interpreted by Pueblo peoples, and used in new forms of resistance during the Spanish reconquest of New Mexico. This was not an example of typical colonial syncretism; in this case, indigenous peoples appropriated the symbolic weapons of the colonizers in the formation new Pueblo identities, turning those weapons back on their oppressors, and hoisting them with their own petard.

Ethnohistoric Evidence

Multiple examples of the overt appropriation and manipulation of Catholic imagery following the Revolt are found in ethnohistoric documents and oral histories relating to the Spanish reconquest of New Mexico. On October 25, 1692, Diego de Vargas made his first trip to San Diego Mesa and the ancestral Jemez pueblo of Patokwa (Elliot, Chapter 3; Figure 9.1). Upon his arrival, hundreds of armed Pueblo warriors appeared ready for battle. Jemez leaders greeted the Spaniard outside the pueblo, where "their captain and governor" met Vargas with "a cross in his hand." After dismounting his horse in honor of the holy cross, Vargas found himself surrounded by an armed crowd in the plaza, "while others prepared a great war dance" (Kessell and Hendricks 1992:521). Understandably uncomfortable with this situation, he shared a meal with the leaders of the pueblo "so they would not suspect the bad opinion [he] had formed and was forming against them," and left that same day, requesting that they come down from their mesatop fortress to live in the pueblo they had abandoned (Kessell and Hendricks 1992:522).

As this narrative demonstrates, the people of Patokwa actively used Catholic symbols during the period of Pueblo independence and Spanish reconquest. However, the display of this cross was clearly not a straightforward symbol of Pueblo Catholicism. Here the Jemez seem to have employed Catholic imagery as a weapon to take in and reassure the Spaniards. Once Vargas and his men were coaxed off their horses and into the pueblo, the cross was retired in favor of conventional weapons, asserting

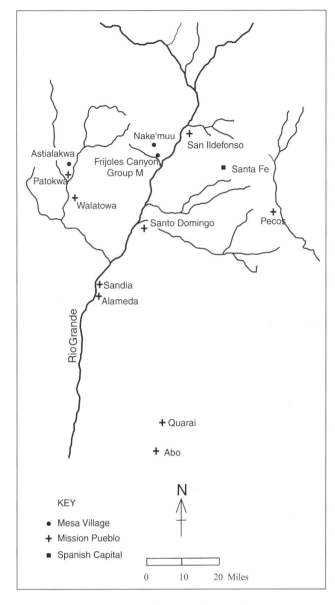

Figure 9.1. Map of Revolt-era sites discussed in chapter.

the Pueblo people's control over the situation. Though the cross was a sign of Christianity and obedience to the Spaniards, the people of Patokwa successfully manipulated these notions, turning the symbolic weapons of colonialism back on their colonizers.

Almost two years later, Vargas returned to San Diego Mesa, attacking the refugee pueblo of Astialakwa on the morning of July 24, 1694 (see Hendricks, Chapter 12). Spanish forces besieged the mesatop pueblo, which sits hundreds of feet above the valley floor. With the pueblo in flames and Spanish forces blocking their escape routes,

Native warriors found themselves trapped. A bloody battle ensued in which 84 Indians were killed; including five burned alive, two executed before a firing squad, and seven warriors who hurled themselves from the edge of the mesa in desperation. Spanish sources attest to the discovery of seven bodies at the base of the mesa following the battle (Espinosa 1942:199). However, according to Jemez legends (Sando 1982:120), just as these men jumped, an apparition of San Diego appeared, and the warriors "floated like butterflies" landing safely in the valley below (Dougherty and Neal 1979). The image of San Diego is still visible today on the side of this mesa, and is visited frequently by the descendents of these warriors (Dougherty and Neal 1979; Sando 1982). The appearance of San Diego is another example of the overt utilization of Christian imagery by Pueblo peoples in resistance to the Spanish during the "Bloodless Reconquest" of the northern Rio Grande. The appropriation of San Diego—a patron saint of the Franciscans—by Pueblo warriors is another example of active manipulated resistance, turning the weapons of the Spanish back on themselves. Here the warriors of Astialakwa were able to exploit a Catholic symbol in the derivation of power for Pueblo peoples, stealing the Spaniards' patron saint and usurping its power for Pueblo use. (Though in the end, the warriors of Astialakwa lost this battle.) Again, this legend is not necessarily indicative of a Christian identity for the people of Astialakwa; rather, it can be viewed as an example of the manipulation of Catholic imagery that characterized the complex negotiation of power and identities during the Revolt period.

Another example of the appropriation of Christian imagery by Pueblo peoples during the Revolt comes from an unpublished translation of Silvestre Vélez de Escalante's *Extracto de Noticias,* which tells of Pueblo warriors wearing Catholic vestments as war trophies following the Revolt. A captain from Alameda Pueblo is said to have worn "an alb and a surplice with a scarlet band over it and a maniple for a crown" (Kessell and Hendricks 1992:16). The same document tells of a Navajo man meeting with Keresan leader Alonso Catiti, wearing

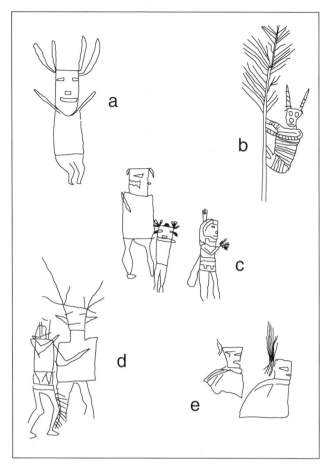

Figure 9.2. Traditional Pueblo images found in cavate M-100, Frijoles Canyon:

(a) east wall, Panel A; (b) east wall, Panel D, clown figure;
(c) east wall, Panel E (from Hewett 1938, now damaged);
(d) east wall, Panel C; (e) east wall, Panel B.

during the Revolt period comes from the cavates of Frijoles Canyon, located today in Bandelier National Monument. Sometime following Spanish contact, a small group of persons reoccupied the homes of their ancestors in a remote and largely inaccessible area (a pattern typical of Revolt period settlements), known today as Group M (Hendron 1943:ii-iv). The presence of Kapo Black, Tewa Polychrome, and a few Glaze F sherds from excavations suggests that the reoccupation of this area of Group M likely took place during or just after the Pueblo Revolt or reconquest (Turney 1948:70). The hidden and protected nature of these dwellings would make this an ideal refuge in the wake of the Revolt/reconquest. In fact, oral histories from San Ildefonso Pueblo recount women and children fleeing their villages to take shelter at Nake'muu, a remote village north of Frijoles Canyon, during the turbulent and violent period following 1680 (Vierra et al. 2000).

The refugees in Frijoles Canyon made incised drawings on the plaster walls of some of the cavates of Group M (Hewett 1938; Toll 1995). Quite often these illustrations exhibit the imagery one would expect to find accompanying a return to tradition, including depictions of katsinas, clowns, snakes, and other customary Pueblo iconography (Figure 9.2). However, there is evidence of Spanish influence represented on these walls as well—an influence that, according to ethnohistoric documents, should be absent from the Pueblo world at this time. On the west wall of M-100, just above and beside the remnants of two mealing bins, one curious image stands out from the rest (Figure 9.3)—a representation bearing evidence of obvious European influence. European-style facial features (the eyes, eyebrows, and nose) and a halo or crown seem to suggest that this may be a Christian figure, similar in many ways to Catholic icons. The figure strongly resembles Spanish colonial depictions of the Virgin Mary, saints, and even the Holy Trinity (see Palmer and Pierce 1992; Figure 9.4). If this is true, it is a surprising image to find in this context, created during the Revolt/Reconquest period and surrounded by traditional Pueblo drawings of katsinas. Yet, upon initial

an alb and chasuble, with an altar cloth tied around his head. Catiti's home was reportedly decorated with carpets, cushions, and a chalice looted from churches. These Christian objects were thought to retain the power of the Spaniards' God, and were appropriated by the Pueblos (and Navajos) in the same way they venerated the scalps of brave enemies, using them in ceremonies to bring rain and other blessings to their people (Kessell and Hendricks 1992:16).

Archaeological Evidence of Catholic Symbols in the Revolt Period

An archaeological example of the appropriation and manipulation of Spanish imagery in Pueblo resistance

Figure 9.3. West wall, Panel B, cavate M-100, Frijoles Canyon.

examination, this appears to be a decidedly non-traditional Puebloan image.

However, this is not a straightforward Christian icon. Comparisons with katsina representations in rock art and on ceramics reveal that this Christian symbol has been manipulated and infused with traditional Pueblo characteristics. The crown/halo may be illustrative of Spanish influence, but similar points are also found adorning katsina masks (often in depictions of the sun katsina), as exemplified on ceramics from Awatovi (Schaafsma 1994: Plate 16), Homol'ovi (Hays 1994:50), and Tsukuvi (Hays 1994:58) and in petroglyphs from the Cochiti Reservoir

District (Schaafsma 1975:77; Figure 9.5). Similarly, the double line surrounding the face in both the petroglyph and the cavate icon image are examples of a stylistic element found in traditional Pueblo art as well as Spanish colonial depictions of the Virgin Mary. Finally, while the eyes and nose of this image are undoubtedly in the European style, the mouth is represented by a rectangle—a characteristic of katsina masks throughout the Pueblo world. This depiction is therefore not simply Catholic—it is an interesting combination of traditional Pueblo and Christian imagery, an illustration of the appropriation and manipulation of European symbols to fit into the formation of traditional Pueblo identities during the Revolt period.

This transformation of colonial imagery can be seen as a strategy for cultural preservation and the re-creation of traditional Pueblo identities, an example of "Pueblofication," to modify a term coined by Hartman Lomawaima (1989). The appropriation and transformation of outside influences in Pueblo spirituality is not unique to the Revolt era; in fact Pueblo people have long pioneered creative solutions to meet new challenges, manipulating and transforming hardships into benefits, and dangers into strengths (Collier 1949:71). It has been argued that ancestral Pueblo people previously adopted outside influences in their spirituality, most famously the Tlaloc from Mesoamerica; but these influences were significantly modified to fit Pueblo culture. The katsina cult itself may have originated to the south of the Pueblo world, but it was undoubtedly adapted to suit Pueblo ceremonial practices (Brew 1943:243; Schaafsma 1994:66). In the same way, Catholic iconography such as that exhibited in cavate M-100 was reconfigured to serve the needs of Pueblo persons during the Revolt era.

Lomawaima states, "The fabric of Pueblo culture was and continues to be tough and flexible, giving wherever and whenever necessary, but scarcely tearing, much less shredding. The Pueblo allowed alien patterns to enter the weave, as they had for many centuries, but incorporated them into a truly Pueblo pattern" (Lomawaima 1989:97; see also Riley 1987:169). In the cases examined here, Pueblo culture was stretched to accommodate Catholic imagery, possibly to assist in bringing Christianized Pueblo peoples back into the fold of traditional Pueblo spirituality. Leaders of the Revolt would not have needed to convince more traditional members of their villages to "return" to traditional ways—it was only those who had adopted Christian beliefs and practices that needed to be recaptured (Robert Preucel, personal communication, 2000). Spanish documents report that Popé and other leaders threatened those who did not purge all Catholic elements from their lives with death (Hackett and Shelby 1942:248). Rules such as this are created only

out of necessity, when people are not behaving in the ways sanctioned by those in authority, and attests to the fact that a significant segment of the Pueblo population was still making use of Christian influences following the Revolt.

Alternatively, the icon in cavate M-100 could be interpreted as an example of resistance through inversion. Catholic imagery may have been infused with Pueblo characteristics explicitly because the Spanish priests viewed "pagan" Pueblo katsina ceremonialism in opposition to Catholicism in the pre-Revolt Southwest. Missionaries viewed katsinas as devils—the opposite of Christian saints—and for this reason, Pueblo people may have infused Catholic images with katsina characteristics in explicit protest of the Spanish—a type of resistance also exhibited through post-Revolt architectural renovations of mission sites.

Resistance through Architecture and Inversion

Pueblo resistance through the inversion of Spanish meanings is exemplified in the architecture of mission sites occupied prior to the Revolt period as well. At some Eastern Pueblo villages, kivas were intentionally placed on the grounds of churches and missions. At Abó and Quarai, kivas were constructed deliberately within the confines of the conventos at a considerable distance from the Pueblo dwellings. Conscious efforts seem to have been made to place traditional Pueblo ceremonial structures in the areas consecrated by Spanish missionaries, even though this was not a conventional location for a kiva (in relation to habitation structures). This type of overt, active resistance appropriates and usurps the sacred ground delineated by the Spanish friars. Indeed, the concept of "holy ground" was almost certainly foreign to a Pueblo population who did not rigidly separate the sacred from the secular—this was a deliberate strategy of resistance on the part of the leaders of Abó and Quarai to reclaim and invert the power usurped by Christianity, reaffirm traditional practices, and recreate new identities for their people.[2]

The practice of resistance expressed in architecture was continued and intensified in the Pueblos after 1680.

Figure 9.4. Spanish colonial art
(after Palmer and Pierce 1992):

(a) *Virgin of Guidance,* detail;
(b) *Virgin of Guadalupe* detail;
(c) cavate M-100 icon, Frijoles
    Canyon, New Mexico;
(d) *Santa Rosa de Lima,* detail;
(e) *The Coronation of the Virgin.*

Spanish documents indicate that following the Revolt at the Pueblo of Cebolleta the "hermitage where the holy sacraments were administered" was destroyed, and the wood was appropriated for the construction of a new kiva (Hackett and Shelby 1942:207). While at Sandia, the fleeing Spaniards reported that cells in the convent of St. Anthony had been converted into "a seminary of idolatry" (Hackett and Shelby 1942:225, 259), with katsina masks hanging on the walls. Leaders of Sandia and Cebolleta utilized, modified, and inverted Christian structures for their own religious practices. This exploitation of Catholicism is very different from the usual colonial syncretism documented elsewhere in the New World (and in other

colonial contexts). At Sandia, there was not a seeping of Christianity into the kiva; instead, traditional Pueblo ceremonialism seems to have overwhelmed Catholicism, making use of the remnants of Christianity that were left behind for Pueblo purposes.

In the above cases, Catholic spaces and architectural elements seem to have been appropriated for the opposite of purposes for which they were intended—"pagan" Pueblo ceremonialism, the contradiction of Christianity (at least to Spanish missionaries). Resistance to the Spanish was here expressed through symbolic inversion, a well-documented strategy in numerous other colonial contexts. Folktales of African-American slaves (such as

Figure 9.5. Katsina images:

(a) mask from an Awatovi Polychrome canteen (Schaafsma 1994:Plate 16);
(b) Sun katsina from Homol'ovi II, Paayu Polychrome (Hays 1994:50);
(c) cavate icon, M-100, Frijoles Canyon;
(d) Jeddito Spattered sherd design (after Hays 1994:58);
(e) petroglyph, Cochiti Reservoir District (after Schaafsma 1975:77).

Br'er Rabbit tales) and festivals such as Carnival turn the world upside down, with actors adopting behavior opposed and contradictory to that expected and intended by dominant forces (Scott 1990:162–182). The same type of resistance was carried out by Pueblo leaders who conducted kiva rituals in churchyards, in convents, and even in kivas literally made from churches. Inversions also occur in modern Pueblos, when on specially sanctioned occasions, tribal members occasionally impersonate priests and imitate Catholic rituals for the entertainment of the crowd (Kenagy 1989:327–328). This inversion of conventional roles is similar to the resistance conducted in the Revolt era (albeit with different meanings in contemporary practice). Resistance through inversion is a type of defiance that typically follows rebellion.

Modes of Resistance

The modes of resistance examined here are very different from the passive forms examined in pre-Revolt contexts by Mobley-Tanaka (see Chapter 5) and made famous by Scott's superb study of Malay resistance, *Weapons of the Weak* (1985). The defiance of Spanish influences prior to the Revolt was largely a passive, subverted resistance, masking traditional beliefs in the symbols of the dominant ideology. Following 1680, Pueblo peoples manipulated Spanish colonial symbols in active, explicit resistance; assuming and transforming the symbols of the colonizer in the liberation of the colonized, and forming distinctive identities in opposition to colonial powers. The explicit adoption of the signs of the dominant ideology by those previously dominated is an inherently different type of resistance than the subversive, everyday defiance employed by powerless underclasses in colonial and postcolonial contexts. This manipulated resistance of appropriation undermines the power of domination once held by these symbols by turning them back on the colonizers. In twenty-first century U.S. contexts, this type of resistance is most closely approximated by the use of the term *nigga* in African-American communities, an appropriation and modification of a word used to dominate that group. Similarly, the use of the terms *queer* and *dyke* by gay

communities manipulates and empowers these groups via words used in their subjugation. Pueblo peoples were able to manipulate Spanish colonial imagery in much the same way following the Pueblo Revolt—not only in obscure, hidden transcripts but often in overt, explicit transformations of resistance.

The Revolt era is a unique liminal stage between discrete periods of colonization; as such, the resistance practiced by Pueblo peoples at this time does not fit neatly into typical categories of defiance. Scott identifies two realms of resistance: *public transcripts,* "the open interaction between subordinates and those who dominate" and *hidden transcripts,* "discourse that takes place 'offstage,' beyond direct observation by powerholders" (1990:2–4). The above examples show Pueblo resistance via Catholic imagery to be sometimes public (use of the cross to deceive Vargas at Patokwa), sometimes hidden (the cavate images in Frijoles Canyon), and sometimes somewhere between the two. The appropriation of mission architecture and Spanish saints are forms of defiance that are not completely open (that is, they were likely not meant to broadcast meaning to the Spanish), but they are not totally offstage, either. This unique liminal position produced many interesting and innovative transcripts of resistance that fall somewhere between the open and clandestine discourses that normally characterize resistance.

Parallel instances of this manipulated resistance of appropriation occur in many post-colonial situations. The Tshidi of the South Africa/Botswana borderland, for instance, appropriate polysemetic biblical metaphors and signs in their resistance to mission Christianity, where "the submission to authority celebrated by the Christian faith was transformed into a biblically validated defiance" (Comaroff 1985:2). Similar re-workings of Judeo-Christian tradition and texts have occurred in the Philippines (Ileto 1979); and among the Rastafarians of Jamaica (Campbell 1987), who relate their post-colonial exile at the hands of Europeans to that of the Israelites in Babylon. In none of these situations, however, do the anthropologists and historians interpreting Judeo-Christian influence mistake resistance via appropriation for the straightforward acceptance of colonial religion (Scott 1990), and neither should archaeologists examining Pueblo uses of Christian symbols following the Revolt.

Comaroff (1985:12) interprets Tshidi Zionism as, "a *bricolage* whose signs appropriate the power both of colonialism and of an objectified Tshidi 'tradition,' welding them into a transcendent synthesis." Yet, while this situation is very much analogous to the use of Christian imagery in Revolt-era pueblos, my interpretation of this resistance is slightly different. Pueblo peoples actively chose to adopt Catholic signs. Viewing this resistance of manipulation and appropriation as syncretism or *bricolage* disregards the importance of agency in the formation of new identities, lending credence to interpretations of Pueblo persons of the Revolt era as manipulated victims of false consciousness. Following the Revolt, Pueblo peoples appropriated symbols useful to them to make an effective response. This is very different from Levi-Strauss's *bricoleur* (1966), which "condemns the dominated to reproduce the material and symbolic forms of a neocolonial system" (Comaroff 1985:261). The application of notions of syncretism and *bricolage* overlooks the nuances of resistance in the post-Revolt Pueblo world. Pueblo peoples were not forced or duped into adopting Catholic signs—this was an intentional strategy employed in the (re)creation of traditional Pueblo identities.

Conclusions

Pueblo identities during the Revolt period were not devoid of Spanish influences, either on a functional/utilitarian level or in the symbolic realm. Christian imagery was appropriated and transformed in the discourses of resistance that formed during the Pueblo Revolt era. However, the assumption that Catholic symbols and traditional Puebloness are mutually exclusive is an over-simplification. As Kopytoff (2000:377) states, "what is significant about the adoption of alien objects—as of alien ideas—is not the fact that they are adopted, but the way they are culturally redefined and put to use." I assert that the Pueblo adoption and redefinition of Spanish imagery in the Revolt period was a form of active resistance

in the formulation of new identities in opposition to colonial structures.

Some persons reading this will no doubt be surprised and perhaps skeptical of the notion that a discourse of Pueblo resistance might incorporate Catholic imagery. However, this reaction may be yet another example of the Euroamerican tendency to expect traditional Indianness to be found in a pristine pre-contact Indian identity. Non-Indians are often surprised when Native peoples incorporate symbolism from outside influences in the construction of their modern Indian identities. But the identities that Native peoples construct and reconstruct for themselves (sometimes based in notions of pre-contact tradition) often adopt external influences without contradiction for those people. Non-indigenous imagery undergoes a transformation during its incorporation into new Native identities. At times, this adoption can include the use of these symbols in differing, opposed, and even contradictory manners. Lomawaima (1989:98) notes that at Hopi, the decision to accept compulsory education was a form of empowerment for the Hopi people, not a sign of defeat: "Not learning English was seen, in effect, as an unwitting way of giving the white man power over Hopi lives." In a similar way, Catholic symbols were adopted and reinterpreted in the Revolt era—not as an assertion of Catholic power, but a refutation of it.

Resistance and revolution are, by definition, responses to force. However, as noted by Hegel and Foucault, power and domination are not one-way streets. The very concept of power asserts the mutuality of the relationship between dominant and dominated. Power is a dynamic association, not merely the force of an active agent (in this case mission Christianity) against a passive (Pueblo) subject. For Pueblo people, the Revolt of 1680 was fundamentally an act of independence, not simply resistance. Just as Americans view the Revolutionary War as more than just a response to British Imperialism, Pueblo people remember 1680 above and beyond the rejection of Spanish colonization. The Pueblo Revolt was a declaration of liberty and sovereignty. Contrary to conventional wisdom, this assertion of independence included reference to and adoption of Christian influences. In fact, the formation of traditional Pueblo identities in the Revolt period sometimes involved the adoption and transformation of Catholic influences, explicitly (re)constructing Pueblo identities through active manipulated resistance to the Spanish.

Acknowledgments

I would like to thank Bob Preucel for his advice in the writing of this chapter, as well as Clark Erickson, Charles Golden, Adam Mohr, Robert Schuyler, Andrew Schwalm, and Miranda Stockett for providing critical comments on the thoughts therein. Any errors are solely my own, however.

Notes

1. Tomatoes and chiles were indigenous to the New World, but were introduced to the Pueblos by the Spanish.

2. James Ivey (1998) hypothesizes that the convento kivas at Abó and Quarai were constructed by Franciscan missionaries to aid in the instruction of Catholic converts. However, I believe that the construction of these kivas by Pueblo persons following the Franciscan abandonment of the missions is a more plausible scenario (based on features such as a sipapu in the Quarai convento kiva).

References Cited

Adams, E. Charles

1981   The View from the Hopi Mesas, in *The Protohistoric Period in the North American Southwest, a.d. 1450–1700,* edited by David. R. Wilcox and W. Bruce Masse, pp. 321–335. Arizona State University Anthropological Research Papers No. 24. Tempe.

1989   Passive Resistance: Hopi Responses to Spanish Contact and Conquest. In *Columbian Consequences: Vol. 1. Archaeological and Historical Perspectives on the Spanish Borderlands West,* edited by David Hurst Thomas, pp. 77–91. Smithsonian Institution Press, Washington, D.C.

Brew, John O.

1943   On the Pueblo IV and on the Kachina-Tlaloc Relations, In *El Norte de Mexico y el sur de Estados Unidos, tercera Reunion de Mesa Redonda sobre Problemas Anthropologicos de Mexico y Centro America,* pp. 241–245. Sociedad Mexicana de Anthropologia.

Campbell, Horace

1987   *Rasta Resistance: from Marcus Garvey to Walter Rodney.* Africa World Press, Trenton, N.J.

Collier, John

1949   *Patterns and Ceremonials of the Indians of the Southwest.* E. P. Dutton & Co., New York.

Comaroff, Jean

1985   *Body of Power, Spirit of Resistance: The Culture and History of a South African People.* University of Chicago Press, Chicago.

Dougherty, Julia D., and William R. Neal

1979   *Guadalupe Mesa.* U.S. Forest Service, Santa Fe National Forest Report, Number 1979-0-018. Santa Fe.

Espinosa, J. Manuel

1942   *Crusaders of the Rio Grande.* Institute of Jesuit History Publications, Institute of Jesuit History, Chicago.

Ferguson, T. J., and Robert W. Preucel

2000   An Archaeology of the Ancestors: Mesa Villages of the Pueblo Revolt. Paper presented at "Structure and Meaning in Human Settlements" conference, University of Pennsylvania, Philadelphia, October 19–21.

Frank, Larry, and Francis H. Harlow

1974   Historic Pottery of the Pueblo Indians, 1600–1880. New York Graphic Society, Boston.

Ford, Richard I.

1987   The New Pueblo Economy. In *When Cultures Meet: Remembering San Gabriel del Yunge Oweenge.* Papers from the October 20, 1984 conference held at San Juan Pueblo, New Mexico, pp. 73–91. Sunstone Press, Santa Fe.

Hackett, Charles Wilson (editor) and Charmion Clair Shelby (translator)
1942   *Revolt of the Pueblo Indians of New Mexico, and Otermin's Attempted Reconquest, 1680–1682.* Volume 2. Coronado Cuarto Centennial Publications, 1540–1940. University of New Mexico Press, Albuquerque.

Hayes, Alden C.
1974   *The Four Churches of Pecos.* University of New Mexico Press, Albuquerque.

Hays, Kelly Ann
1994   Kachina Depictions on Prehistoric Pueblo Pottery. In *Kachinas in the Pueblo World,* edited by Polly Schaafsma, pp. 47–62. University of New Mexico Press, Albuquerque.

Hendron, J. W.
1943   *Group M of the Cavate Dwellings, Rooms 1, 2, 3, 4, and 5, Caves 1, 2, 3, and 4, Frijoles Canyon, Bandelier National Monument, New Mexico.* Ms. on file, Bandelier National Monument, N.Mex.

Hewett, Edgar Lee
1938   *Pajarito Plateau and its Ancient People.* University of New Mexico Press, Albuquerque.

Ileto, Reynaldo Clemeña
1979   *Payson and Revolution: Popular Movements in the Philippines, 1840–1910.* Ateneo de Manila University Press, Manila, Philippines.

Ivey, James E.
1998   Convento Kivas in the Missions of New Mexico. *New Mexico Historical Review* 73:121–152.

John, Elizabeth A. H.
1996   *Storms Brewed in Other Men's Worlds.* University of Oklahoma Press, Norman.

Kenagy, Suzanne G.
1989   Stepped Cloud and Cross: The Intersection of Pueblo and European Visual Symbolic Systems. *New Mexico Historical Review* 64:325–340.

Kessell, John L., and Rick Hendricks (editors)
1992   *By Force of Arms: The Journals of Don Diego de Vargas, New Mexico, 1691–1693.* University of New Mexico Press, Albuquerque.

Kessell, John L., Rick Hendricks, and Meredith D. Dodge
1998   *Blood on the Boulders: The Journals of Don Diego de Vargas, New Mexico, 1694–97.* University of New Mexico Press, Albuquerque.

Kopytoff, Igor
2000   The Cultural Biography of Things: Commoditization as Process. In *Interpretive Archaeology,* edited by Julian Thomas, pp. 377–397. Leicester University Press, London.

Levi-Strauss, Claude
1966   *The Savage Mind.* Wiedenfield & Nicholson, London.

Lomawaima, Hartman H.
1989   Hopification, a Strategy for Cultural Preservation, In *Columbian Consequences: Vol. 1. Archaeological and Historical Perspectives on the Spanish Borderlands West,* edited by D. H. Thomas, pp. 93–99. Smithsonian Institution Press, Washington, D.C.

Miller, Daniel
1988   The Limits of Dominance, In *Domination and Resistance,* edited by Daniel Miller, Michael Rowlands, and Christopher Tilley, pp. 63–79. Unwin Hyman, London.

Montgomery, Ross G.
1949   Part III: San Bernardo de Aguatobi, an Analytical Restoration. In *Franciscan Awatovi: The Excavation and Conjectural Reconstruction of a 17th Century Spanish Mission Establishment at a Hopi town in Northeastern Arizona,* edited by Ross G. Montgomery, Watson Smith, and J. O. Brew. Papers of the Peabody Museum of American Archaeology and Ethnology, Harvard University, vol. 36. Cambridge, Mass.

Palmer, Gabrielle, and Donna Pierce
1992   *Cambios: The Spirit of Transformation in Spanish Colonial Art.* University of New Mexico Press, Albuquerque.

Riley, Carroll L.
1987   *The Frontier People: The Greater Southwest in the Protohistoric Period.* University of New Mexico Press, Albuquerque.
1999   *The Kachina and the Cross: Indians and Spaniards in the Early Southwest.* University of Utah Press, Salt Lake City, Utah.

Sando, Joe S.
1987   *Nee Hemish: A History of Jemez Pueblo.* University of New Mexico Press, Albuquerque.

Schaafsma, Polly
1975   *Rock Art in the Cochiti Reservoir District.* Museum of New Mexico Papers in Anthropology No. 16, Museum of New Mexico Press, Santa Fe.
1994   The Prehistoric Kachina Cult and Its Origins as Suggested by Southwestern Rock Art. In *Kachinas in the Pueblo World,* edited by Polly Schaafsma, pp. 63–79. University of New Mexico Press, Albuquerque.

Scott, James C.
1985   *Weapons of the Weak: Everyday Forms of Peasant Resistance.* Yale University Press, New Haven, Conn.
1990   *Domination and the Arts of Resistance: Hidden Transcripts.* Yale University Press, New Haven, Conn.

Snead, James E., and Robert W. Preucel
1999   The Ideology of Settlement: Ancestral Keres Landscapes in the Northern Rio Grande, In *Archaeologies of Landscapes: Contemporary Approaches,* edited by Wendy Ashmore and A. Bernard Knapp, pp. 167–197. Blackwell, Oxford, UK.

Toll, H. Wolcott
1995   *An Analysis of Variability and Condition of Cavate Structures in Bandelier National Monument.* Intermountain Cultural Resources Center Professional Paper No. 53, Santa Fe.

Turney, John F.
1948   *An Analysis of the Material Taken from a Section of Group M of the Cliffs, Frijoles Canyon, Bandelier National Monument, New Mexico, 1943.* Unpublished master's thesis, Adams State College, Alamosa, Colo.

Vierra, Bradley, Larry Nordby, Gerald Martinez, and John Isaacson
2000   *Long-Term Site Monitoring of the Architecture at Nake'muu.* Poster paper presented at the Southwest Symposium, Santa Fe.

PART FOUR
Social and Politcal Dynamics

Chapter 10

Re-imagining Awat´ovi

Peter Whiteley

*Every society up to now has attempted to give
an answer to a few fundamental questions:
Who are we as a collectivity? What are we
for one another? Where and in what are we?
What do we want; what do we desire; what
are we lacking? Society must define its 'identity,'
its articulation, the world, its relations to the
world and to the objects it contains, its needs
and its desires. Without the 'answer' to these
'questions,' without these 'definitions,' there
can be no human world, no society, no culture—
for everything would be an undifferentiated chaos.
The role of imaginary significations is to provide
an answer to these questions, an answer that,
obviously, neither 'reality,' nor 'rationality'
can provide. . . .*

*The self-transformation of society concerns
social doing—and so also politics, in the profound
sense of the term—the doing of men and women
in society, and nothing else. Of this, thoughtful
doing, and political thinking—society's thinking
as making* itself—*is one essential component*
—(CORNELIUS CASTORIADIS 1987:146–147; 373).

History, Society, and the Imagination

The destruction of Awat´ovi, one of the largest Hopi pueblos, in 1700 is one of the great problems of Hopi historiography. If the Orayvi split, that other watershed event in Hopi history, has been the "Murngin problem" of American anthropology[1]—generating a welter of arguments—explaining Awat´ovi two centuries earlier only appears less thorny by the distance of time. Standard explanations foreground the reappearance of Franciscan missionaries in 1700, after the Hopi churches had all been destroyed and the priests put to death in the Pueblo Revolt of 1680 (e.g., Bandelier 1890–1892:II:371–372; Brew 1949; Brew 1979; Simmons 1979; and see Laird 1977 for additional references). Following De Vargas's reconquest of 1692, Awat´ovi, as the story goes, was willing to re-accept the church, whereas the other Hopi villages remained vehemently opposed. In consequence, when some from Awat´ovi agreed to be baptized by priests visiting from Zuni in 1700 and began to rebuild its church, the other villages got together and sacked Awat´ovi, killing off all the men and capturing women and children who were parceled out to the other villages. Awat´ovi was thenceforth abandoned.

The documentary record is rather thin. A series of testimonials was taken from witnesses in 1702 (Bandelier 1890–1892:II:372, citing a 1713 inventory of documents in Santa Fe), but these evidently went missing, along with many other documents of Pedro Rodríguez de Cubero's governorship, prior to the late nineteenth century (Bandelier 1890–1892:II:372).[2] Father Silvestre Vélez de Escalante's famous *Extracto de Noticias,* which in 1778 synthesized numerous documentary records from the Pueblo Revolt period and thereafter, does not even mention the destruction of Awat´ovi (Vélez de Escalante 1778). The standard historic source is a document written in 1732 at the transplanted Piro settlement of Senecú del Sur (below El Paso) by Father José Narvaez Valverde (Hackett 1937:III:385–386), which indeed cites the reconversions of May 1700 as the precipitating cause of the destruction; but this is an ecclesiastical document, so the inference of cause is hardly surprising. Other explanations include a recent, notorious variant of the reconversion cause, distinguished by anthropophagy. In what we might call the "Toltec Thug Theory" of Pueblo history (Preston 1998; Turner and Turner 1999), the Awat´ovi chief is cast in the role of Adolf Hitler, a Cannibal Dictator left over from so-called Toltec Thugs of Chaco Canyon, who despotically terrorizes his people by chewing them up for their temerity in re-accepting the church.

In view of the imaginative ferment of this explanation, multiculturally mixed metaphors and all,[3] my own recommendation to "re-imagine" must clarify its terms. First, I refer to the *historical imagination* lately of interest in historical anthropology.[4] In particular, Marshall Sahlins's conception of sociocultural form, as historically positioned categorial system, continually wagering and transforming itself in events, provides a powerful way of seeing culture both in and *as* history. In Sahlins's well-known analysis (1981, 1985, 1995) of the Hawaiian encounter with Captain Cook, for example, the categories of Hawaiian culture are put into play, not as some synchronic abstraction, but as a dynamic, self-transforming force. The "structure of the conjuncture"—wherein culture meets, shapes, and is reciprocally shaped by event—points up Sahlins's sense of the continual deformation, transformation, and reformation of sociocultural structures in diachronic process. This approach opens the possibility for a dialectical synthesis of structure and event, an opposition that has long paralyzed anthropological explanations of historical transformations in cultures of the "people without history."[5]

The historical imagination is a contested theoretical zone at present. Keith Basso (1996:154–155, responding particularly to Comaroff and Comaroff 1992) has noted that anthropologists' recent attention to the historical imagination typically reflects Western canons of historicity, and has so far failed to ask *whose* imagination is in question. After a fashion, this is Gananath Obeyesekere's (1992) critique of Sahlins; though Obeyesekere hypothecates a blunt, generic "Native" historical imagination vis-à-vis Western imperialism, rather than a culturally located one (Sahlins 1995). Sahlins interpolates cultural meanings by examining ritual, economic, and other social structures, and their documented historical transformations; Obeyesekere posits a transparent universal intentionalism of blanket indigenous resistance to colonial domination. I find Sahlins's analysis far more persuasive, but seeking to trace *local* (rather than generic) intentionalisms in historical process, I believe, provides an important means to address Basso's question (cf. Whiteley 1988a, 1998). And in the present instance, resistance to the Spanish colonial state and its indigenized surrogates (notably in the church) is unquestionably important. It seems to me that the historical imagination we should be aiming for is one that consciously seeks to *hybridize* (to invoke a favored term from Cultural Studies— e.g., Bhabha 1994) *analysis* across cultural boundaries, but does so through specific attention to local modalities of historical and cultural consciousness.[6]

While the totality of Awat´ovi's significance as event and as historical transvaluation will likely always prove elusive, there is more fertile ground in documents of the Pueblo Revolt period than previously considered (though, alas, nothing like the extent for Sahlins with the Cook documents of the late eighteenth century). The new light we might shed, however, crucially depends on attending to and weighing both Pueblo oral history and cultural form—especially Hopi accounts of Awat´ovi's destruction and the patterning of Hopi social structure. Earlier attempts to recover Hopi history by combining clan migration traditions with archaeology led Jesse Walter Fewkes into some impassable interpretive territory. Ever since, most Southwestern archaeologists have virtually abandoned culture-history for hypothetico-deductive approaches that ignore the oral-historical accounts and ethnographic analogs of contemporary Pueblo cultures. This seems to me very shortsighted.

To build a rigorous, analytically hybrid culture-history in the Southwest requires a full-scale re-imagining of Pueblo pasts. Ethnography has tended, ipso facto, to reify cultural form synchronically. Southwestern anthropology remains vexed by functionalist or materialist models of Pueblo social structures that obscure historical consciousness and transformative agency from the picture.

Let me here introduce my second sense of "imagination," i.e., that involving the "imagined community" and the "social imaginary," which I derive especially from Benedict Anderson and Arjun Appadurai (e.g., Anderson 1991; Appadurai 1996; and see, inter alia, Castoriadis 1987). Appadurai's (1996) focus is displaced transnational population fragments that imagine their community in the contemporary global flux of capital, commodities, and technology. And Anderson is concerned with the emergence of nations, which he would restrict historically to conditions in which the invention of print capitalism enables the circulation of messages of identity and boundary to citizens widely separated in geographic space. Yet, both Appadurai and Anderson are, in effect, working with special cases of the central anthropological problem[7] of the relationship between society, considered as a bounded system of social persons and social relations, and culture, considered as a system of ideas shared among its members. Some form of collective consciousness—Durkheim's *conscience collective,* realized through "collective representations"—articulated especially by key cultural symbols, is the means to understanding how a society imagines itself as a unified form (cf. Castoriadis 1987).

Appadurai's focus on the social imaginary in political process is particularly attached to post-national "culturalist" movements:

> Culturalism . . . is the conscious mobilization of cultural differences in the service of a larger national or transnational politics. . . . Culturalist movements (for they are almost always efforts to mobilize) are the most general form of the work of the imagination and draw frequently on the fact or possibility of migration or secession. Most important, they are self-conscious about identity, culture, and heritage, all of which tend to be part of the deliberate vocabulary of culturalist movements as they struggle with states and other culturalist focuses and groups
>
> —[APPADURAI 1996:15].

Though long before Anderson's print capitalism and

Appadurai's "global ethnoscapes," the Pueblo Revolts of 1680 and 1696 resulted in a diaspora of Rio Grande Pueblo peoples, which threw many of them together in a way that demanded their rethinking of community, identity, and internal boundaries vis-à-vis the Spanish state. With the presence of several substantial Pueblo fragments at Hopi, some of which remained permanently and have been to a greater or lesser degree absorbed into the overall Hopi polity, the revision of the Hopi social imaginary and the re-imagining of Hopi community must of necessity have been rather profound. With the end of Franciscan oppression, which had driven Hopi ritualism underground for half a century, the circumstances were ripe for the consolidation and institutionalization of a culturalist reformation. The rethinking of Pueblo identities, collectivities, and boundaries took multiple forms. Here, I am most interested in how the Awat´ovi holocaust and its indication of conscious, articulate resistance to colonial hegemony represented the re-imagining and restructuring of Hopi community—producing a new Hopi social imaginary, and a new sense of community.

Structure

The typical model of Hopi society and culture that anthropologists use reflects mid-twentieth century ethnography, and the prevailing tendency is to assume a system, a structure, reproducing itself consistently through time. That system comprises an equilibrated arrangement of matrilineal descent groups, religious sodalities, and kiva groups that operated like clockwork in relation to calendrically fixed economic and social demands. However differences, both in clan composition and in the correlations between clans and sodalities, at the several villages arose (e.g., Eggan 1950:65–66; 103), and however Hopis seems to differ with regard to assignations of clan names and eponyms to some individuals and groups (e.g., Titiev 1944:48–58), the conventional wisdom overrides these variations (e.g., Levy 1992). Hopi society is reduced to an equation: clans + sodalities + kivas + the agricultural cycle = immutable Hopi structure.

Hopi ideology does not disagree with that sort of

functionalism, but Hopi historical consciousness also emphasizes cumulative aggregation and transformation. Hopi society is pictured as the product of successive accretions of inmigrating groups and the cultural contributions each brought. For example, before the Snake clan migrated from Tokoonavi (Navajo Mountain) to the Hopi Mesas, there was no Snake society, no ritual performance, no Snake priest as politico-ritual leader, no legitimating charter of group interest—in short a lacuna in the anthropologists' ideal-typical structure. Until the Badger clan arrived from Kiisiwu, there was no *Powamuy* ceremony or society. Before the Flute clan came from Lengya'ovi, there was no Flute ceremony. And so on. Hopis thus frontally characterize their society as a historical amalgamation. Ironically, given the persistent circulation of Whorf's view of the Hopi language, when it comes to structure, it is non-Hopi anthropologists who are into timelessness, whereas Hopis emphasize diachronic and spatial discontinuities: indeed, these are held to explain important structural differences among the three Mesas and their respective villages.

Hopis emphasize that several structural elements derive from Awat'ovi—especially at Walpi, Musangnuvi, and pre-split Orayvi. This refers especially to three of the four *Wuwtsim* or Manhood societies: *Wuwtsimt, Aa'alt* (Two Horn), and *Taatawkyam* (Singers); and two of the women's societies—*Mamrawt* and *Owaqölt*. The first four are not ancillary ritual forms, they are utterly central to the Hopi social system: indeed, one older consultant referred to the *Wuwtsim* societies as "the Hopis' government." Further, several clans or clan segments are regarded as deriving from Awat'ovi: notably Bow, Tobacco, and some Badger, Reed, and Squash segments at Orayvi, Musangnuvi, and Walpi. Bow and Squash/Sparrowhawk at Orayvi, and Tobacco and Reed at Walpi are notably important clans that control the *Wuwtsim* societies (for reasons of simplicity, I focus below mostly on Orayvi and Walpi).

During my fieldwork in the early 1980s, Third Mesa elders made explicit comparisons between the Orayvi split and the destruction of Awat'ovi, suggesting that internal village fission was at work at the latter as much

as exogenous enmity. The second split of Orayvi in November 1909, which precipitated the founding of Paaqavi (Whiteley 1988a, 1988b), occurred in the middle of a *Wuwtsim natnga,* or initiations, at Orayvi's Hawiwvi kiva. These were the first and last initiations into *Wuwtsim* to be held at Orayvi since the split of 1906, and threats were made that several members of the "Hostile" subfaction, which had returned from the new settlement at Hotvela in November 1906, would be killed during the crucial night of the initiations (Whiteley 1988b). Indeed, it is held that those who left Orayvi to found Paaqavi did so to avoid threats by the "Friendly" faction that they would be immolated in the kiva during the *Wuwtsim* initiations—in the identical manner of Awat'ovi. Historical accounts of Awat'ovi's destruction have virtually ignored the temporal reference to *Wuwtsim* in Hopi reports, and typically note that the destruction occurred "sometime" in 1700 or 1701. Yet the association with *Wuwtsim* would pinpoint this to mid-November, or one month after a fateful visit to Santa Fe by Espeleta (see below) and other Hopi leaders who had sought to negotiate their independence from the Spanish regime (Bandelier 1892:371–372).[8] Hopi accounts recorded since the late nineteenth century (Curtis 1922:83–89, 184–188, Fewkes 1898:602, Mindeleff 1891:33–34) agree that Awat'ovi was destroyed during *Wuwtsim,* with all the men in the kivas, where they were suffocated and burned, surprised by a pre-dawn stealth raid into the village. Some accounts (Fewkes 1898:602; Mindeleff 1891:34) are explicit that this occurred during *Wuwtsim* initiations. This would suggest that the destruction concerned more than Christian reconversion *tout court,* and may additionally have had to do with internal ritual issues—again, exactly like the split of Orayvi (Whiteley 1988a, 1988b). What were supposedly Christian converts doing in the kivas during *Wuwtsim*—especially if initiations were involved?

According to some Hopi accounts, the *Wuwtsim* ceremony originated at Awat'ovi—it was an Awat'ovi ceremony (e.g., Curtis 1922:107, 184–188). More explicitly, with the exception of *Kwaakwant,* the One-Horn sodality, the other three societies—*Wuwtsimt* (*Wuwtsim* proper),

Aa'alt (Two-Horn), and *Taatawkyam* (the Singers' society) were from Awat'ovi. *Aawatngyam,* the Bow clan, was the principal clan at "Awat'ovi"—"high place of (the Bow clan)" in Fewkes's translation (1898:594), i.e., the town itself was named for the leading clan.[9] No accounts I have located mention Bear clan presence or leadership (the typical pattern) at Awat'ovi. The Bow clan's preeminence at Awat'ovi was undoubtedly ritually legitimated—and it seems likely this occurred particularly through the *Wuwtsim* system (minus the *Kwaakwant*), and the *Sa'lako* ceremony (which has specific links to *Wuwtsim*). The Bow clan, as I have argued elsewhere (1992) discussing the burning of the Orayvi Two-Horn altar by the chief priest (who was head of the Bow clan) in 1922, was ritually the most powerful of all clans—a fact that would coincide with Awat'ovi's control of the most ritual forms. As noted, Awat'ovi was also the source for two of the three women's societies—*Maraw* and *Owaqöl* (e.g., Curtis 1922:182–183). According to Yoywunu of the Walpi Reed clan, who told this to Edward Curtis in the early twentieth century, Awat'ovi acquired its panoply of ritual knowledge from the Rio Grande Pueblos, where representatives had been sent for the purpose:

> Now the people one day sent the nephew of Tapólo [sic—see below], chief of the Tobacco clan, to pueblos in the Rio Grande Valley to learn their language and make rain songs in that language, so that those outside the fraternity would not understand them. By magic he would go almost instantly to the eastern pueblos, spend the night there, and return in the morning; and when he had learned the language, the people organized the Wuwutsim-wimi [the Wuwtsimt sodality] and the To-wimi [the Singers sodality], and made their songs. These two fraternities were organized from the men of Squash and the Tobacco clans respectively. The men of the Reed clan organized the Al-wimi [the Two-Horn sodality]. . . .
> —[CURTIS 1922:186]

Alexander Stephen (Parsons 1936:718) reported that both

Wuwtsim and Singers society songs were in Keresan. If Yoywunu's temporal reference in the passage above is literal, i.e., that it was Taapalo's (see below) own nephew who was sent, this would have occurred during the Revolt period. If so, his magical speed in going among the Rio Grande Pueblos to acquire ritual knowledge may be a metaphor for the refugee Pueblo presence nearby Awat'ovi. Whether historically true or not in this form,[10] Awat'ovi was certainly the easternmost Hopi town, and more cosmopolitan, with its easier access to the Pueblos farther east.

So far, I have adhered to the pattern of Hopi clan discourse, describing clans as discretely identifiable entities that migrated historically into the villages bringing their private ritual knowledge with them. Much anthropological ink has been spilled to show exceptions to this account and why it should be dismissed as "conjectural history" (in Radcliffe-Brown's terms), in favor of an anthropological interpolation of a social-structural or mental-cultural, but not historical, logic as the axis of clan relationships. Lévi-Strauss (1963:89) has famously taught us that nature arranged by culture into categories—i.e., taxonomically—is "good to think," explaining why it is that so many societies should organize themselves into totemically named groups—like Bear, Eagle, Reed, Tobacco, Sun, etc. As Lévi-Strauss (1966) has also argued, however, a totemic logic opposes history, and directs *consciences collectives* like Hopi to reproduce cultural structures *against* historical consciousness. All events that might prove differentiating are relentlessly absorbed by the "infernal culture machine" (Geertz 1973), endlessly flattening history into the two-dimensional cognitive space of cultural *bricolage*. For some aspects of Hopi clanship, a totemic logic of associations holds true (as Bradfield [1973] has perhaps most successfully shown): clan associations and their ritual symbols in part reflect a praxis of engagement with the natural environment, to correspond with seasonal periodicities. However, there are some notable exceptions to the natural bases of Hopi clan totems: Bow and Flute are the principal ones of concern here. These are two of the only three or four clan names in the total inventory of Hopi clans that derive from a cultural, artifactual domain, rather than from natural models. The Flute clan is only known ethnographically at Walpi, where it has held the principal leadership role since the mid-nineteenth century, providing the Kikmongwi (Village Chief) and ritually underscoring his legitimacy with its ownership of the Flute ceremony. *Lenngyam,* the Flute clan, it is held, migrated to the Hopi Mesas from a village to the north named Lengya'ovi, 'Flute people on top place,'[11] toponymically similar to 'Awat'ovi.'

The idea that clans migrated independently before inclusion into the Hopi ecumene is in part a structural rationalization: obviously if they were unilineal and exogamous, clans must have migrated in moiety pairs at least. Alternatively, they only became unilineal and exogamous after arrival at Hopi. In brief, my hypothesis is this: that the Bow clan and the Flute clan both represent what were once non-clan collectivities characterized by their ritual capacities to transform nature with cultural skills (Bradfield has documented the Bow clan's associations with mastery of game; the Flute society's role in turning back the Sun at and following the summer solstice is transparent, and a mirror of the *Soyalangw* society's concern at the winter solstice).[12] Further, these two clans' ritual capacities to transform nature by cultural means are foregrounded in their respective identities. Both, in short, are *pas pavan-*('very powerful') clans, archetypal culture-wielders and hierarchically important.[13]

Further, both Tobacco and Badger (of the latter, only a segment evidently came from Awat'ovi) are powerful clans too. Curtis (1922:107) records the Tobacco clan leader at Walpi, in his role as Tawmongwi, head of the Singers society, as having a superordinate role in Walpi's *Wuwtsim.* In general, the Tobacco clan controls tobacco curing and distribution, and provides the Tobacco Chief at various ceremonies. The use of tobacco-smoke as transformative and as vehicle of communication to deity is fundamental in Hopi ritual and, again, Lévi-Strauss (1972) has demonstrated its pan-continental significance in this regard.

The Badger clan controls medicines, and is the leading clan in major katsina rituals, likewise highly important in the ritual order. Though I have never heard of the Orayvi Badger clan's *Powamuy* ceremony as introduced from anywhere but Kiisiwu (with no mention of Awat'ovi), the leading protagonists in the Orayvi *Powamuy* at the turn of the twentieth century are strongly reflective of the clan or phratry nexus attributed to Awat'ovi. Voth records the participation of the following named clans in Orayvi's *Powamuy:* "Badger, Reed, Sand, Crow, Bow, Rabbit or Tobacco, Parrot and, perhaps, a few others" (Voth 1901:72). These represent four phratries in turn-of-the-century Orayvi (e.g., Titiev 1944, Whiteley 1985): Badger in one (subdivided, according to some, into Real Badger, Gray Badger, and Navajo Badger, and associated with Butterfly); Bow and Reed (which form a phratry with Greasewood); Rabbit, Tobacco, Parrot, and Crow (which form a phratry with the Katsina clan); and Sand (which forms a phratry with Snake and Lizard). Each of these Orayvi phratries, except Badger, is prominently associated with the key ritual introductions from Awat'ovi noted above: Bow and Reed with *Wuwtsim,* and especially the *Aa'alt* sodality[14]; Parrot (of which Crow is a variant, possibly a sublineage; see Whiteley 1985) with the *Taatawkyam* sodality (again at Walpi, Parrot's phratry mate Tobacco is in charge of *Taatawkyam*); and Sand and Lizard with *Owaqölt* and *Mamrawt,* respectively.

Badger's ritual entitlements are principally concerned with katsinas, especially the great katsina ceremonies of *Powamuy* ("Bean Dance") and *Niman* ("Home Dance"): they do not lie in *Wuwtsim*—at least directly (and Badger has no key involvement in *Maraw* or *Owaqöl*). However, the *Patsavu* ceremony, an elaborate appendix to *Powamuy* performed in certain years, also belongs explicitly to the Badger clan; performance in *Patsavu* is regarded as completing *Wuwtsim* initiation and only occurs following a *Wuwtsim* initiation the previous November. *Sa'lako,* a katsina ceremony, was noted above as a Bow clan ritual prerogative at Orayvi. *Sa'lako* also has a connection with *Wuwtsim,* in that only *Wuwtsim* initiates may perform, especially those who are recently initiated. *Sa'lako* is performed as an (again elaborate) appendix to *Niman,* owned conjointly by the Badger and Katsina/Parrot clans. Through these ritual links, the Orayvi Badger clan has formal associations with the socio-ritual matrix of the *Wuwtsim* ceremonies, even though it is not directly prominent in *Wuwtsim*.

In short, some of the key structural elements associated with Awat´ovi ceremonies are still found, either as direct embodiments or in closely linked forms, within First Mesa and Third Mesa society, where the heirs of Awat´ovi, so to speak, play prominent roles in the socio-ritual structure.

Agents

Who survived Awat´ovi? If significant ritual practices—*Wuwtsim* and the two women's societies—were transferred, when did this occur? Hopi oral history strongly suggests the transfers occurred after the massacre, which means that not only women and children survived. In the case of the *Maraw* ceremony, Saliko, the *Maraw* Chieftess at Walpi in the late nineteenth century, told Fewkes (1898:604) that the life of the Awat´ovi woman who headed *Maraw* was spared when she agreed to introduce the ceremony to Walpi. Similarly, both Curtis's (1922:83, 188) and Courlander's (1982:20–21) informants—more than 50 years apart—unequivocally indicated that the *Wuwtsim* societies were transferred by male survivors of the Bow/Reed[15] and Tobacco clans after the holocaust. Yoywunu told Curtis (1922:188), "Some members of the three fraternities were spared and taken to Walpi, Mishongnovi, and Oraibi, and by them the ceremony of Wuwutsimu was continued." Pautiwa (Ned Zeena) told Courlander in the 1960s:

I'm a Tobacco Clan person. I became a Tobacco chief at one time, around 1932. I was chief till my uncle took me out. So I can tell you something about the Tobacco Clan coming here. When Awatovi was destroyed, the Tobacco clan leader over there took all the sacred tiponi [= *tiiponi*] and brought them here. [Courlander footnotes: "The narrator here refers not only to Tobacco Clan paraphernalia, but to the altars and other sacred

objects of the Two Horn, the Wuwuchim [= *Wuwtsim*], and the Tataukyam [= *Taatawkyam*] kiva societies. Those three fraternities are widely recognized as having originated at Awatovi."] He went clear up to the end of the mesa there, where the Snake Rock is, the Masauwu shrine, brought all the sacred things from the Awatovi kivas. All the sacred things that we have now are from Awatovi. We still use them there. The other villages just copied these things. But the original ones, we still have them in Walpi. The other villages copied these ceremonies too.

—[COURLANDER 1982:20–21]

In another source, Courlander (1971:216) records that both the Tobacco and Bow clan leaders took their people and their key ritual objects (including the Two Horn altar) out of Awat´ovi at night, and hid during the massacre. Though Courlander does not make this inference, according to one of my consultants, the Tobacco clan leader in question was Taapalo (see below). Again, if the rituals were disseminated after the massacre, not all males at Awat´ovi were killed (since males are the principal holders of ritual knowledge—especially of the Manhood societies), and the analogy to the Orayvi split, with its fissile factionalism, gains added significance.

Third Mesa consultants indicate that the Bow clan systematically re-organized *wiimi,* the ritual order, by introducing the *Wuwtsim* ceremonies to Orayvi.[16] This would confirm that the transfer of *Wuwtsim* ceremonies occurred during the post-Revolt period. Further, in light of the broader historical circumstances of the Pueblo Revolts, *Wuwtsim*'s status and practice appear critically connected to Awat´ovi's destruction as part of a culturalist, even a revitalization movement (as Alfonso Ortiz has argued was the purpose of the Pueblo Revolt)—a movement, in short, of re-imagined community. If *Wuwtsim* was practiced at Awat´ovi, or if another version of male initiation was practiced there or at the other villages, prior to the Revolt—and functionally this probably means prior to 1630, since the Franciscans suppressed overt Hopi ritual practices—its meanings may have been constructed according to other social and natural interests. Like the transvaluation of the Tswana, Merina, and Swazi principal rituals under colonialism (Comaroff 1985; Bloch 1986; Lincoln 1989, respectively), or the Hawaiian rethinking of Makahiki rules and meanings when faced with Captain Cook (Sahlins 1981), it is my thesis that Hopi *Wuwtsim* was relocated simultaneously in a context of internal purification and social reorganization, and also of culturalist resistance to the Spanish state. To initiatory aspects concerning sexuality, fertility, adult male identity, and death, was added the principle of revolutionary revitalization. While it is not appropriate to probe into much ritual detail for reasons of Hopi cultural privacy, the strong emphasis on death in *Wuwtsim* initiations seems important here. At a climactic moment of the initiations, terrified initiands are confronted by a representation of Maasaw, who is strongly associated with death and who is here represented as a bloody-headed spirit being, with pieces of flesh torn away from his skull (e.g., Malotki and Lomatuway'ma 1987). Indeed the initiands—as in many male initiation ceremonies globally—are told they will be killed, and rush up the ladder to escape the kiva as fast as possible. However symbolic this communication of death-images to the initiands may be, if the killings at Awat'ovi occurred during or near this phase of the initiation—which would accord with the cultural logic of the ritual's progress—the death-threats and the general ritual import of *Wuwtsim* would certainly have been forever transformed thereafter. No new initiand subsequently can have been in doubt about the potential for catastrophe associated with the ceremony: here was "mere symbolism" fully instrumentalized, and departure from this major incorporation into Hopi society might have results that could be ostensibly shown as devastating. In other words, the threat of death acquires a palpable historical force if it was once enacted upon initiands on a substantial scale. And *Wuwtsim*'s refiguring—at the very least—at Awat'ovi into a ritual of extended internal control and of dramatic resistance to the colonial state transformed some of its basic significances.

Recorded Hopi accounts (e.g., Fewkes 1898:603–605; Voth 1905:246–255; Curtis 1922:83–89,184–188; Yava 1978:88–97; Courlander 1982:55–60; Lomatuway'ma et al. 1993:275–409) agree that planning the destruction was an inside job. Taapalo is the leader credited with seeking the attack—from leaders at Orayvi, Musangnuvi, and Walpi—and with aiding and abetting the attackers.[17] Some accounts (e.g., Lomatuway'ma et al. 1993:406–409; Voth 1905:258) suggest Taapalo allowed himself to be killed in the process, in a manner that conforms paradigmatically with a tradition of chiefly self-sacrifices in Hopi history; indeed, I reported this version in an earlier work (Whiteley 1988a). But in 1995, Taapalo's Tobacco clan descendant showed me the Tobacco clan house in Walpi and the kiva of the *Taatawkyam,* Singers society, noting that both had been built by Taapalo himself when he moved into the newly established mesa-top town of Walpi[18] following the massacre. Edward Curtis's consultants too were explicit that Taapalo survived, and arranged for his clan relatives first to live with Navajos, and then later for their return (Curtis 1922:89). What was Taapalo's office? As a *Pipwungwa,* Tobacco clan member, it is unlikely he was *Kikmongwi* (Village Chief) or *Qaletaqmongwi* (War Chief); the former was likely vested in the Bow clan, the latter possibly in the Badger, Reed/Eagle or Coyote clan. As *Tawmongwi,* head of the Singers' society, he would have had a parallel role to the probable Squash and Bow clan heads of *Wuwtsimt* and *A'alt,* respectively. A First Mesa Reed clan account suggests Taapalo was Awat'ovi's *Tsa'kmongwi,* an advisor and formal announcer for the *Kikmongwi* (Courlander 1982:57–60).

Another important agent was Francisco de Espeleta, though he is known directly only from the Spanish documents. The Spanish (Twitchell 1911:419, n.422) regarded him as the principal Hopi leader, "the cacique of Orayvi," in the post Re-conquest period, and attributed him with leading the warriors from Orayvi to destroy Awat'ovi, after he had led the trip to Santa Fe to negotiate Hopi sovereignty with Governor Cubero in October 1700. Espeleta had been an assistant to Father José de Espeleta, who, as priest, had alternated between Awat'ovi and

Orayvi in the 1660s and 1670s (Brew 1949:17).[19] Francisco was evidently from Awat´ovi (Brew 1949:17). The Spanish credit Francisco with killing Father José at the 1680 Revolt (Espinosa 1942:348, n.11). Father José had taught Francisco to speak and write fluent Spanish,[20] and Francisco had spent time in Mexico (Brew 1949:17–18; Hackett 1937:385). *If* there is an intersection with Third Mesa Hopi accounts, which credit the Badger clan with having killed the priest at Orayvi, Espeleta may have been a member of this clan. Certainly, a Badger segment from Awat´ovi was recognized into the twentieth century as a distinct lineage of this clan at Orayvi (White n.d.), and the Badger clan of Musangnuvi still explicitly cites Awat´ovi as its origin too. So it is evident that there was a significant Badger clan representation in Awat´ovi, some of which, at least, survived. Moreover, if Espeleta was Badger clan, there is a historic pattern of reciprocal exchange and interrelation with the Tobacco/Rabbit clan (at Musangnuvi, Badger and Rabbit/Tobacco belong to the same phratry; at Third Mesa, they are in different phratries, but there is a disproportionately high degree of intermarriage between Badger and the Rabbit/Tobacco/Katsina/Parrot phratry). As noted above, at Third Mesa's *Powamuy* and *Niman,* the principal katsina ceremonies, the Badger clan and the Parrot/Katsina clan provide joint leadership. Parrot/Katsina is a close phratry mate of Tobacco, and the Tobacco clan also holds a priestly role in these two ceremonies. One Third Mesa Badger clan consultant, who is deeply knowledgeable about his own clan, even misidentified a Parrot/Katsina clan elder as Badger—the sort of clan identity error (i.e., crossing phratry lines) that is very rare indeed. I recorded rather numerous Badger-Tobacco/Rabbit intermarriages at Third Mesa, as did Titiev (n.d.). In short, if Espeleta was Badger, the reasons for Taapalo (Tobacco clan) coming to Orayvi to seek his assistance in the destruction, may well have been cast in terms of Tobacco-Badger alliance—of kinship, if the Musangnuvi model applies, or of close affinity if the Orayvi one does. And the strength of their reciprocal ties is certainly confirmed by their conjoint ritual estate. Furthermore, if the Pueblo Revolt and the events surrounding Awat´ovi are re-imagined as a revitalization movement, Espeleta is a likely candidate for charismatic prophet-leader of resistance and reformation (an archetypal element of such culturalist movements). As a prominent subaltern to imperial agency, Espeleta occupied an intermediary, intercultural status, with significantly deeper understanding, presumably, than most Hopis of matters Spanish and Franciscan; he is structurally well situated—like Handsome Lake among the Iroquois a century later (e.g., Wallace 1969)—for prophet-leadership of a reformative movement.

Events

This notion of reformation and revitalization brings me to the events themselves. One feature of Hopi accounts I have heard over the last 20 years has always particularly intrigued me. As one man put it, "You know, the real trouble at Awat´ovi was peyote." (I prefer to preserve the anonymity of Hopi sources, but let me note that this was a Third Mesa account, and derives from the chiefly lineage of Loololma, the Kikmongwi of Orayvi until his death, ca. 1904). But while intrigued, I was very doubtful. Numerous accounts of Awat´ovi's destruction had been published, but not one had mentioned peyote. Neither does this seem to be a part of oral tradition that is widely known by Hopis: there may be rather few Hopis who know about it. There are no mentions at all that I know in the body of Hopi ethnography about peyote use (cf. Beaver 1952 and La Barre 1969:203, who specifically deny evidence of Hopi use[21]). The closest location where peyote is found naturally is in far southwest Texas and northern Mexico along the Rio Grande (Stewart 1987:6), several hundred miles away, and I have never encountered a single record of Hopis collecting it directly. The possibility of an intertribal trade in peyote—say, from the Mansos, Sumas, or Jumano Indians, or, after the Revolt, relocated Piros, Tompiros, or Tiwas (thereby may hang a tale—see below), around El Paso—certainly exists, but again, to the best of my knowledge is unrecorded in the ethnographic or ethnohistoric literature.[22]

Peyote, however, was clearly present in New Mexico in the seventeenth century (Scholes 1935). Omer Stewart argues that peyote spread from northern Mexico to New Mexico and elsewhere in the seventeenth century along with the colonists, "peyote had become an item of contraband commerce by Indians, mestizos and soldiers who participated in the colonization of New Mexico" (1987:24). Peyote use was fairly widespread in northern Mexico, in some areas far beyond its natural occurrence, and continued to spread among Christianized Indians (Stewart 1987:21). In 1631 and 1632, the Inquisition held several trials for individual uses of peyote (for divinatory purposes) among the New Mexico Pueblos (Scholes 1935:216–220). But references to it thereafter in New Mexico largely disappear (see, e.g., the *Documentary Relations of the Southwest* database).

Peyote is evidently used by medicine men at Isleta pueblo, who in recent times have obtained it in trade from Mescalero Apaches, but previously went to gather it themselves. This is a specialized use, unassociated with the Native American Church (Pueblo Transcripts, Roll 7, Tape 495, Part 4; Roll 8, Tape 692).[23] But the only Pueblo interested in Native American Church peyotism seems to have been Taos, where it is known to have caused much friction with traditionalists (Bodine 1979; Stewart 1987:202–208). And Taos's interest is interpreted by anthropologists as the result of its greater influence from the more peyotist Plains (e.g., Bodine 1979:257); other Pueblos are typically described as too religiously conservative to have any interest in such a novel form. While I have conversed with Navajo peyotists, I have never encountered an active Hopi participant in the Native American Church; there may be some, but it is certainly not common practice, as it is among Navajos (e.g., Aberle 1982).

After I first heard this Hopi account, I thought that if any hallucinogen was involved at Awat´ovi, it was most likely datura (Hopi *tsimona*), which grows plentifully around the Hopi Mesas, appears personified in myths (e.g., the Tsimonmamant, 'jimson-weed girls'), figures in place-names (e.g., Tsimontukwi, 'jimson-weed butte') and is ethnographically recorded as used in medically specialized divination (Whiting 1939, cf. Beaver 1952). None of these types of cultural motifs occurs in any Hopi cultural

domains I know of with peyote, and I do not even know of a Hopi word for peyote.[24] But the accounts I encountered indicated the hallucinogen was a foreign introduction (i.e., which datura is not), indeed that it was introduced by the Spanish (or those with them,[25] which would conform with Stewart's account of peyote at the Eastern Pueblos in the 1630s). All in all, while intrigued, for the longest time I found this Hopi account somewhat implausible and certainly unverifiable: it did not fit with any documentary or published oral history of Awat´ovi I knew of, or with any salient Pueblo ethnography.

Then in 1998, while examining some colonial Spanish records of post-Revolt Pueblo population movements, I found a reference (in the Documentary Relations of the Southwest) that piqued my interest (Figure 10.1). Others, it turned out later, had noticed it: Twitchell (1914) indexes it (SANM II: Item 306, 1720), and Slotkin (1951) presents a rather poor translation of it; subsequently, Beaver (1952) and La Barre (1969:203) dismissed Slotkin's interpretation, while Stewart (1987:202) partly relied upon it. But each of these authors had different purposes in mind. The document concerns events at Taos Pueblo in 1720 involving the consumption of peyote. A local brouhaha ensued, and the Spanish civil authorities came from Santa Fe to hold a trial. Six Taos witnesses were deposed, including the cacique and the Pueblo Governor, an edict was signed by New Mexico Governor Antonio de Valverde y Cossio, and the key perpetrator, one Juan del Alamo, was sentenced to 50 lashes and expulsion from the pueblo. Juan del Alamo, the witnesses unanimously agreed, had introduced the peyote, and encouraged two others, Antonio Quara and Cristobal Teajaya to consume it. At this point—and here is a third sense of the imagination alluded to above—they divined, saw visions, and foretold the future:

. . . en el Pueblo de s.n Geronimo de los thaos, un yndio de el llamado quara bevio la yerva, q. llaman Pellote, en que su fortaleza y eficazia, ocasiona Privarse [?] y veer en la Ymajinaz.n fantasías segun se tiene Por experienzia en las ocasiones q. de ella se visa . . .

[. . . in the pueblo of San Geronimo de Taos, an Indian from there named Quara drank the herb which they call peyote,[26] in which one's strength and capacities are deprived; one sees in the imagination fantasies that are taken for experiences . . .]

In a moment that undoubtedly got Governor Valverde's attention, Quara and Teajaya were reported to have convened a gathering of Taos elders, informing them of a vision depicting Valverde and his troops intending to attack Taos and put all its adult population to death (the vision went on that Valverde had in fact been dissuaded from this course by the Governor of Parral). This image of Taos's feared destruction recapitulates discourses heard before the 1696 Revolt,[27] and echoes that of Awat´ovi four years later. It also reflects the ongoing culture of colonial terror, to invoke Taussig (1987), especially since the immolations of the southern Tiwa and Keresan pueblos by Governors Otermín and Cruzate (in 1681–1682 and 1689, respectively), and De Vargas's suppressions of the Revolt of 1696 (e.g., Kessell et al. 1998).

The 1720 document further suggests, in its report of prophetic visionary experiences, that the peyote was not being used for individual divinations (as was the case in the 1630s Inquisition trials). Rather, the visions are associated with an apocalyptic social, even millenarian, discourse. In short, the connection between peyote use and a fledgling social movement is manifest; indeed, it appears to be the principal reason why this was a matter of state, i.e., for the Provincial Governor, rather than a matter for the Church to address. The Spanish authorities were clearly concerned that this seemed to represent a potentially subversive, possibly reawakened revolutionary interest.

Juan del Alamo was serving at Taos as interpreter. He was a Tiwa—though not from Taos, but Isleta. Moreover, he had only recently returned to Isleta from Hopi. Numerous Isletas had taken refuge at Hopi since the 1680s or 1690s. Some made their way back to the Rio Grande in the early years of the eighteenth century and were resettled at Isleta in 1709 (Adams and Chávez 1956:203), but others stayed on. Especially after Vargas's reconquest of 1692 and

Figure 10.1. Item 306, Spanish Archives of New Mexico (courtesy of the Museum of New Mexico Archives).

the 1696 Revolt, as well as Isletas and other southern Tiwas at Hopi, including the Sandias who built Payupki at Second Mesa, there were sizable numbers of other Eastern Pueblos, including Jemez, Tewas, Tanos, Keresans, Taos (perhaps), and also Zunis (Bloom 1931), and probably some Tompiros from the Saline pueblos east of the Manzano Mountains and Piros along with the Isletas. The Spanish regime was concerned about the Rio Grande "irreconcilables" (Brew 1949:20) at Hopi and had launched punitive campaigns over the destruction of Awat´ovi, beginning with Governor Cubero in June or July of 1701 (Espinosa 1942:349). Finally, in 1716, Governor Phélix Martínez, both prior to and during a military campaign to Hopi, persuaded several more Isletas to return from Hopi, as well as 113 Jemez natives (Bloom 1931).

Those from Jemez were the remnant of—"the entire pueblo"—who had been refugees at Hopi since the mid-1690s (Ellis 1964:13–14). Instructively, Ellis reports that the Jemez Tsuntash society migrated as a group in 1694 to First Mesa with its eagle plume fetish: there is an implication of direct ritual exchange. Jemez consultants further told Ellis that it was during this period that they gave the Hopi the Hemis (= Jemez) katsina, which frequently appears at Hopi *Niman,* in exchange for some Hopi katsinas. The presence in significant numbers of Jemez people at Walpi in 1700, and Walpi's prominent role in the attack on Awat'ovi, as well as Jemez's reputation as fiercely resistant to Spanish authority (see Ellis 1964:passim), all suggest that some Jemez warriors may have participated in the attack (again, possibly with other Pueblo refugees). The account of the Tsuntash society migration suggests further that additional ritual incorporations, of Jemez and other Pueblo practices into Hopi structure, occurred at this time.[28]

In any event, it appears that one of the Isletas who accompanied Martínez's returning caravan in 1716 was Juan del Alamo. The six Taos witnesses were unanimous that "Juanillo" had brought the peyote back from Hopi.[29] For example:

> . . . que esta ínquietud havia causado la yerva que Juanillo el ínterpete [sic] truxo de moqui . . . [" . . . that this disturbance had (been) caused (by) the herb which Juanillo the interpreter brought from Hopi . . ."]
>
> . . . dicha yerva, de cuyo conozimy.to la trujo y condujo desde la Provinz.a de Moqui [" . . . said herb, with the knowledge of which he brought back from the Province of Hopi"].

Reading through this document of the Taos trial, it began to dawn on me that the Hopi accounts I had heard years earlier about peyote at Awat'ovi may have been more credible than I had allowed. Each of the witnesses successively related the same information on the source of the peyote—that Juan del Alamo, the interpreter, who had returned from the "Province of Moqui," had brought

back the herb from there. No Hopi villages were mentioned by name, however. Then, towards the end of the document, a brief summary of further testimony does mention one Hopi village—for the first and only time (Figure 10.2). Four additional Taos witnesses approached the Governor's secretary, Miguel Thenorio de Alba, asking that Juan del Alamo be banished from the pueblo for all the trouble he had caused:

> . . . me avian venido a ber y pedirme que Juan del Alamo Ynterprete de dho Pueblo que se allaba fuera de el; *y es de nazíon tíguas fue segun bos comun el que traxo la Yerva de conque se asen locos de Aguatubí* . . . [emphasis added: " . . . they had come to see me to plead that Juan del Alamo, the interpreter of the said pueblo, should depart from it; and he is of the Tiwa nation[.] [I]t was common knowledge that he brought the herb with which they make themselves crazy from Awat'ovi. . . ."]

One archival swallow does not make a summer of interpretation, but Awat'ovi seems to be indexed here as the source of the substance: if not literally—since it had apparently been deserted 20 years earlier—then as what the post-structuralist literary types call a "trace." And it is possible that Awat'ovi was not completely abandoned in 1700. Voth points out, "[I]t is reasonable to suppose—and the Indians are of the same opinion—that the village and what it contained was by no means totally destroyed, that for some time after objects were gotten from the deserted village, and that the priestesses of the Oáqöl Society went and saved from destruction the highly treasured paraphernalia of their sacred cult" (Voth 1903:3, n.1).

Again, if my inference is correct that Juan del Alamo's return from Hopi occurred with Martínez's expedition in 1716, this further suggests that the hallucinogen was still in use at Hopi. If so, who then was using it at Awat'ovi in 1700—killers or killed, or both?

The apocalyptic and millennial components of the

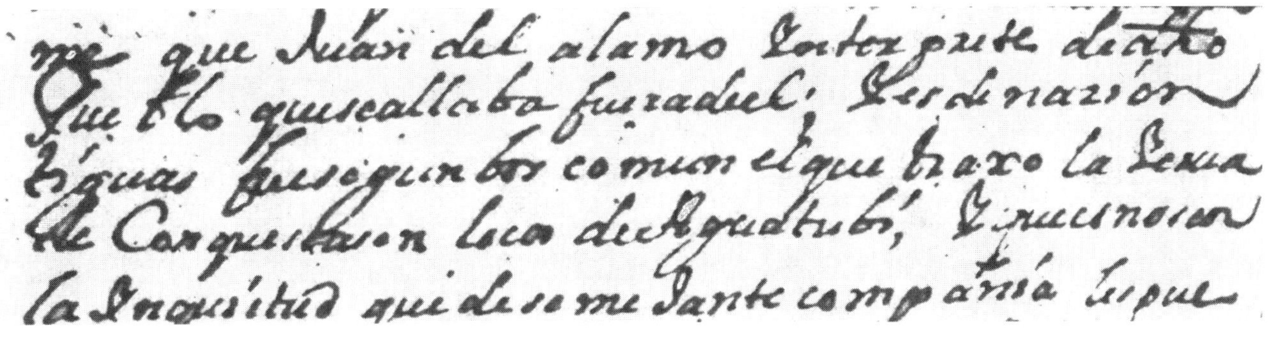

Figure 10.2. Passage in Item 306 mentioning Awat´ovi (courtesy of the Museum of New Mexico Archives).

Taos visionaries' reported prophecies are surely important in this regard. Again, these are visions put to the use of the social imaginary: they are not (or not only—there is one passage which also describes a divinatory use by an aged Taos gardener) techniques for finding lost objects or diagnosing individual afflictions. The implication—either by the Taos witnesses themselves (if the document is read as a transparent record of their avowals), or by the Spanish authorities (who construed these avowals into an official text of judgment and sentence)—is, that, based on his experience with peyote at Hopi, Juan del Alamo had sought to foment a social movement. If that is the case, it follows that something similar was at work in Hopi use of peyote: that it was part of a culturalist movement involving active resistance to the Spanish state, not an interiorist socio-psychological coping-mechanism in response to deprivation, as the "peyote cult" of the nineteenth and twentieth century has largely been interpreted (e.g., Aberle 1982). Further, this would suggest that the known visionary effects of peyote were socially channeled into an organized, conscious re-working of the social imaginary. Although the leads are slender and the documentable connections somewhat tenuous, it turns out that J. Manuel Espinosa—quite independently—has hinted at some parallel suggestions in the Pueblo Revolt of 1680.[30] In a reference I had previously overlooked, Espinosa implies that peyote may have played a role. The Tewa leader of the Revolt, Popé, represented that he had had a visionary experience inside a Taos kiva, in which he encountered, "three devils in the form of Indians. Most horrifying in appearance, shooting flames

of fire from all the senses and extremities of their bodies . . ." (quoted in Espinosa 1988:33). From this account and Scholes's report of the 1630s peyote trials, Espinosa infers that, "the hallucination of seeing flames shooting out of one's body is known to occur to peyote eaters" (Espinosa 1988:34). Again, if there is value in this surmise, a parallel may be inferred with Espeleta at Hopi. We know that he had spent time in Mexico, and I have suggested his general "cosmopolitanism." Although we do not know from the documentary record who the Hopi leaders of the 1680 Revolt were, it certainly follows logically that if Espeleta killed the priest at Orayvi, and in 1700 was the leader of delegations to meet with Cubero in Santa Fe, that he had been in direct contact with Popé and the other Pueblo leaders at Taos in 1680. In short, if Espinosa is correct that Popé's visions were inspired by peyote in 1680, Espeleta may have been directly involved, and may have been a conduit for peyote at Hopi.[31]

While all of this must remain inferential, let me now connect the use of peyote as part of a culturalist movement at Hopi with the critical role of *Wuwtsim* in the destruction of Awat´ovi, and *Wuwtsim*'s subsequent transfer and re-organizing effect at other villages. This nexus of ideas leads, by syllogism in the absence of direct evidence, to the idea that peyote visions were actively utilized as part of a sociopolitical movement of revitalization centered in *Wuwtsim*—i.e., peyote was used in the context of *Wuwtsim*. Now an ethnographic problem immediately arises: if this was in fact the case in 1700, why had it apparently ceased to be so by the late nineteenth century when ethnographers first recorded aspects of *Wuwtsim* ceremonialism? That is a question I cannot answer ethnographically, but Weber's notion of the "routinization of charisma" may help. Weber (and see Wallace 1956) argues that for charismatic leadership to give way to an efficacious transformation of the social order, charisma as the basis of authority must give way to a routinization of ideological and administrative practice—again, similarly to the transformation of Handsome Lake's visions into an organized religious tradition among the Iroquois (Wallace 1969). Structurally speaking, this is a plausible guess about the absence of peyote from later reports of *Wuwtsim,* although there are several possible arguments against it (such as why routinization in the Native American Church has not dispensed with psychotropic experience). The passing of Espeleta (which occurred prior to 1716 [Brew 1949:25])—my candidate for charismatic culturalist prophet—may signal the beginning of a routinization that ultimately dispensed with the use of psychotropic stimulation of the social imaginary. That is the best inference I can make at present.

Existing ethnohistoric interpretations of Awat'ovi predicate that those killed were all Christian converts. However, another aspect of Hopi oral history is troubling in this regard: as noted above, Hopi accounts are unanimous that the attack took place during *Wuwtsim* when all the men were in the kivas. Further, stories of witchcraft surround Awat'ovi's destruction—that it had reached a stage of corruption, or *koyaanisqatsi,* including murder, rape, theft, continual gambling and pleasure-seeking in the kivas, and ritual conflict in the plaza (e.g., Curtis 1922:86; Lomatuway'ma et al. 1993:288)—the classic circumstances that precede destruction or demise of Hopi villages (cf. Lomatuway'ma et al. 1993:passim). The *popwaqt,* witches, or *kwitavit* (literally the 'shits,' a euphemism for sorcerers) had their headquarters in a kiva, the so-called *powaqkiva,* 'sorcerers' kiva.' Guided by elders from Walpi, Fewkes (1893:372–373, 1896:570) believed he located it, and inside he found many bones. This kiva was in the plaza facing the mission church, which would suggest it was a focal point of antithetical imaginaries. Witchcraft, whatever else it may be, is a discourse of the interstices, where pollution

and liminal chaos dwell together (e.g., Douglas 1966). Witchcraft accusations involve an agonistic charge of failure to adhere to the terms of the social contract. Therefore, if Christian reconversion were taken as an index of sorcery, this would suggest its virulently polluting status vis-à-vis a culturalist movement of Hopi revitalization and reformation. Pollution and taboo implicitly entail their corollary of purity, and translated into ritual action, this is realized as purification. Purification, including of the evil of witchcraft, is a central idea in Hopi religious philosophy, and is denoted by the term *naavotsiwni* (see, e.g., Geertz and Lomatuway'ma 1987). Escape from evil circumstances, via the destruction of previous worlds, or villages, and subsequent regeneration of a purified Hopi life is a prominent theme in Hopi historical narratives. The third world (below the present, fourth one), Sikyatki, Palatkwapi, Pivanhonkyapi, and numerous other villages were purified—by flood, fire, or other catastrophe—and then life could be restored anew.[32] The destruction of Awat'ovi thus appears as the instantiation of a paradigmatic purification process and the emergence of a renewed, refigured form of social and cultural structuration throughout Hopi society as a whole.

Conclusion

The events at Awat'ovi in 1700, while susceptible of only circumstantial inference and interpolation, are nonetheless pregnant with structural import. The presence of numerous Rio Grande refugees, many of them implacably hostile to the Spanish, is surely a critical element, despite the fact that Hopi accounts largely fail to mention their presence or their influence in these events. However, it seems evident that this was a time of much cultural exchange among these Pueblo peoples, and it is likely that their conjoint political resistance to the Spanish state was partly framed in terms of a ritually refigured social imaginary of pan-Pueblo proportions. The collective efforts to throw off the Spanish yoke, especially in 1680 and 1696, had forged a new imagined community (where circulating messages did not await the development of print capitalism, but could be manifest in knotted cords, and shared katsina representations, among other symbols). The re-imagining of community at Hopi after the Revolt included direct transfers of ideas and people, both from the Rio Grande and internally among the shifting or rebuilding Hopi villages. Nevertheless, whatever the degree of cause these transfers provided, they appear to be part of a full-blown revitalization and transformation of Hopi culture and society, whose internal structures had been seriously constricted since 1630. Revitalization, pivoting on the axis of the ritual system, was the basis of political resistance, and appears to have centered in *Wuwtsim* at Awat′ovi. Here, *Wuwtsim* served as the specific occasion of radical transformation in 1700, and was the heart of a reborn politico-ritual system that, forged in the sacrificial purification of Awat′ovi's corruption and pollution, restructured the Hopi social and cultural orders in other villages subsequently. The possibility seems strong that this revitalization was led by a charismatic, conjunctural figure like Espeleta. Judging by certain Hopi accounts and circumstantial documentary evidence, the process of revitalization appears to have included the use of peyote, as the imaginative fuel of a re-envisioned cultural and social system. Espeleta's new "magic of the Hopi state," so to speak,[33] may have involved a hallucinogenic lubrication of the social imaginary, transforming the existing sense of Hopi identity, cultural value, and social form. This would suggest that what we know of as Hopi social structure and the system of cultural categories from nineteenth and twentieth century ethnography is not so much the historyless precipitate of continuous structural reproduction in the social engagement with nature (à la Lévi-Strauss), but as a particular, conscious, historic product in which Hopis systemically re-imagined their culture and society in the crucible of resistance to the imperial foe.

Notes

1. As Shuichi Nagata has put it (personal communication).

2. Rick Hendricks has searched long and hard, in Spain and Mexico, for the Cubero period documents, which he infers Cubero took with him when he returned to Mexico at the end of his governorship in 1703 (personal communication). Were they ever to be found, the testimonials of 1702 would undoubtedly be the major historical source on the events at Awat′ovi.

3. *The New Yorker's* (Preston 1998) rendering of Turner's explanation of Awat′ovi includes a lethal mix of Charles Manson, leading a gang of prehistoric psychotics, Genghis Khan, Pol Pot, and Joseph Stalin, in addition to Adolf Hitler, "tinkers," the Toltecs, and Thuggery. One might well wonder what happened to *The New Yorker's* injunction to "Block That Metaphor!"

4. See, for example: Bahr et al. 1994; Basso 1996; Biersack 1991; Bloch 1989; Cohn 1980; Collins 1998; Comaroff and Comaroff 1992; Fowler 1987; Geertz 1980; Hastrup 1992; Hill 1988; Kirch and Sahlins 1992; O'Brien and Roseberry 1991; Price 1983, 1990; Rosaldo 1980; Sahlins 1981, 1985; Schneider and Rapp 1995; Shryock 1997; Tonkin et al. 1989; Vansina 1985; Whiteley 1988a; Wolf 1982. For an excellent discussion of varieties of Native American history, historiography, and historical consciousness, see Nabokov 1996.

5. The paralysis is less apparent in the world-systems-type, materialist historiography of Eric Wolf (1983) and others (e.g., O'Brien and Roseberry 1991; Schneider and Rapp 1995). But here the cause of transformation lies outside culture itself, which is seen as the largely passive, superstructural respondent to material historical forces, in the Marxian tradition.

6. In this regard, I have recently (1999) taken to recommending that Southwestern archaeologists pro-actively reconceive their projects in the mold of Classical Archaeology. Recent archaeological nods to diversity tend to set the "Native" interpretation side-by-side with the archaeological interpretation, rather than seeking analytical conjuncture.

7. This is, of course, a key problem for all social theory, and centrally preoccupies Marx, Weber, and Durkheim, as well as their myriad heirs.

8. From a recent Third Mesa account specifying that the attack occurred on *Wuwtsimtotokya* (the seventh night of the eight-day *Wuwtsim* ceremony), Malotki (1993:291) infers that it took place in the last week of November 1700. He may be correct, although given the historical tumult at Hopi during this period and my sense that *Wuwtsim* was in a process of reformation (below), this account may rationalize the timing a little too closely to the current *Wuwtsim* ceremonial march.

9. The name is a contraction of 'awta,' a bow, and '-ovi,' 'on top,' a place marker. But Fewkes (1898:594) is surely correct when he notes that the village name refers, "to the Bow clan, one of the strongest in the ancient pueblo."

10. In other passages, it is evident that some of Curtis's informants use the name Taapalo generically to refer to a chief who founded Awat′ovi prehistorically (e.g., Curtis 1922:84–85), as well as the chief at the Revolt period, telescoping these events into the same frame. The temporal inference of the borrowing of *Wuwtsim* during the Revolt period may thus be unwarranted, but clearly, other ritual

borrowings were occurring from Pueblo refugees at this period (see below).

11. 'Lengya'ovi' appears to be a contraction. Two lexical possibilities occur: if it is from *'Leenangwya'ovi,'* this would refer directly to the performance of the Flute ceremony occurring in the place on top. If it were *'Lenngyam'ovi,'* that contains a direct reference to the clan: 'Flute clan on top place.' The former seems more intuitively likely to me, but both possibilities are no more than guesses on my part. Anthropologists have frequently confused *Lenngyam,* 'Flute clan,' with *Leengyam,* 'Millet clan,' suggesting that there is no Flute clan per se. Hopi usage (including in English translation) is unambiguous, however, and these are two distinct clan names.

12. The instrumentality of bows and flutes as transducers of masculine power is reported more widely in Hopi culture than just in these clans and sodalities themselves, and at least in the case of flutes is a continent-wide motif, occurring prominently, for example, in the *yurupari* cult in Amazonia.

13. By this, I do not intend that the totemically named clans—especially Bear, Spider, Parrot, Badger, Snake—were any less significant as transformational operators in relation to nature, quite the contrary. However, in their ritual manipulations, these clans borrow from mimetically appropriate forces intrinsic to nature—for example, the Badger clan's mastery of herbal medicines, or the Snake clan's powers with snakes, and thence rain. It is striking that both Bow and Flute were (and the Flute clan still is) notably powerful clans in the Hopi imaginary of ritual hierarchy. I would also include the totemically-named clans as originally non-clan collectivities with different marriage rules before establishment at the Mesas; but this thesis must await development elsewhere.

14. Bow is also associated with the *Wuwtsimt* sodality as well as the total *Wuwtsim* ceremony at Orayvi, although the Sparrowhawk clan held a leading role in the *Wuwtsimt.* Again, there is an Awat'ovi connection here: Sparrowhawk is a close phratry mate of Squash, which organized the *Wuwtsimt* society at Walpi (Curtis 1922:186) and thus logically appears to have been introduced from Awot'ovi. At Hotvela (on Third Mesa), the Squash clan is in charge of Hawiwvi kiva, the kiva of the *Wuwtsimt* society; a kiva of the same name at Orayvi was also the *Wuwtsimt* kiva.

15. My combination of Bow/Reed and farther on of Rabbit/Tobacco is designed to show close connections and infer possible historic identities. There are some circumstances in which the conjoint names may be thought of as referring to the same clan, or as lineages of the same clan, as is the case also with Parrot and Crow, and in some settings with Parrot and Katsina, and Katsina and Crow. Bow, Reed, and Greasewood were different clans at Orayvi and subsequently in Third Mesa society. But they form a phratry together and there are clearly interrelated and partly conjoint ritual roles in certain contexts. The absence at First Mesa of a Bow clan, but the presence there of a Reed clan of Awat'ovi which is regarded as separate from a pre-existing Walpi Reed clan, may reflect an assimilation of Bow to Reed at Walpi, or it may reflect the dying out of a Bow clan group there (Hopi population was still being decimated by smallpox in 1898, not to mention other diseases), and the taking over of its ritual responsibilities by Reed. At Walpi, Reed owns the *Aa'alt*

(Two Horn sodality) as its principal ritual prerogative, as Bow did at Orayvi. So Bow at Orayvi and Reed at Walpi occupy the same socio-ritual sphere—hence my reasoning for inferring an identity.

16. While Third Mesa clan migration narratives situate the Bow clan as arriving from the southwest (e.g., Voth 1905), there is a clear association between the Third Mesa Bow clan and the Bow clan of Awat'ovi.

17. 'Taapalo' is a nickname: it is Spanish for 'shawl' (e.g., Hopi Dictionary Project 1998). The historical import of this, if any, is unclear, but it obscures the possibility of inferring a ritual connection (i.e., with his godfather's clan), were we to know his Hopi name. I am assuming he was fully Hopi: some of the principal Rio Grande Pueblo leaders in the Revolt were mestizos (e.g., Espinosa 1988:34). If there is any possibility that his nickname indicates Taapalo or Espeleta (see below) were of mixed ancestry (Spanish, Black, or Mexican Indian, even possibly the son of a Franciscan priest: abuse of Hopi women by the priests is recounted in Hopi oral history), this would further complicate matters, particularly in light of events discussed below.

18. Pre-Revolt Walpi was located on a bench below the mesatop, in the area Hopis today refer to as Qöötsaptuvela, 'ash slope.'

19. Brew (1949:16–18) speculates that he might have been the same person as "Juan," a boy imprisoned at the Awat'ovi mission who attended the infamous Father Salvador de Guerra, who had a penchant for setting Hopis on fire with burning turpentine. José de Espeleta spared Juan's life when another missionary sought to have him hanged, for reasons unspecified. Francisco was apparently not his first Spanish name (Brew 1949:16–18). But Francisco, or its diminutive 'Panchuelo,' are the only forenames applied to him after the Revolt (Espinosa 1942:348).

20. Interestingly, José de Espeleta was evidently fluent in Hopi; indeed, he was one of a mere three missionaries recorded in 1699 as having been fluent in any Pueblo language—a situation that was inferred as a major cause of Pueblo hostility at the 1680 Revolt (Espinosa 1942:345). The fact that Father José was fluent in Hopi, and that his long-term assistant Francisco was fluent in Spanish, is another index of the latter's conjunctural status (see below).

21. Beaver's negative commentary is in response to Slotkin's translation of the item discussed below.

22. William Merrill (1994; personal communication 1999) has published an account of a multi-ethnic band of peyotists in northern Mexico in the eighteenth century, and it remains possible that Hopis participated in a regional trade for the cactus, but again, if so, this would be a novel piece of information in Hopi ethnology. Slotkin (1955:205) infers peyote use at Hopi from the 1720 document discussed in some detail below, but he offers no elaboration beyond simply including Hopi in a list of places where peyote is recorded. La Barre (1969:203) takes Slotkin to task for this, citing Beaver (1952) to confirm his own negative reading of Slotkin's inferences and specifically repudiating the implication of Hopi use. See below, however.

23. "Our herbs, that's nawar. But the one that the medicine [men] use, the peyote, that's wartur. . . . Some grind it at home and already have it wrapped in a little corn husk, so they'll open up their little corn husk, you know they've got it folded over, and they keep it in their pouch you know, and they'll open it up and take a dab like this and

put it in their mouth. . . . All medicine men use it" (Pueblo Transcripts, Roll 7, Tape 495, Pt. 4 [1967], pp. 20–21).

24. Kimball Romney notes that there is no evidence of a term for peyote in proto-Uto-Aztecan, and infers that "there is no linguistic evidence for any great time depth for the use of peyote among Uto-Aztecan peoples" (quoted in Slotkin 1955:203).

25. The Franciscan missionaries certainly had lay assistants of indigenous Mexican origin. The Hopi word *totaatsim,* 'dictators, tyrants,' used to refer to the priests, is of Nahuatl origin (Hopi Dictionary Project 1998). Malotki (1993:295) infers a direct presence of one or more Nahuas with the priests at Hopi. In Nahuatl, *totahtzin* means "our honored father" (Malotki 1993).

26. The document mostly refers to "pellote/peyote," but one passage suggests it may have been something else—see note 29.

27. For example, Espinosa records this as a motivating narrative for those who participated in the second Revolt. Upon his capture, Xenome, the cacique of Nambé, who had been one of the leaders of the 1696 Revolt, reported:

> At Cochití a Spaniard had told him and other natives that Governor Vargas had decided to massacre within the month all the men of the pueblo, sparing only the small boys. Thereupon the leaders of the Jémez, and the Keres of Santo Domingo and Cochití, joined by partisans from San Felipe, Santa Ana, and Sia, had held a council and decided to join in the uprising. Acting swiftly, Naranjo of Cochití had sent messengers with knotted cords to the different pueblos, as far as Ácoma, Zuñi, and Moqui, and to the Apaches.
>
> —[ESPINOSA 1942:251]

28. Ellis records a Jemez pattern that further reflects the events at Awat'ovi, Sikyatki, and other Hopi villages destroyed during rivalries:

> According to Jemez tradition, the several original villages each consisted of members of a single religious society. These periodically became jealous of another society's apparent "power," which embodied a threat for disapproved competition and also suggested possible dangers from witchcraft should a society decide to use its magic for evil. More than once men from one village are said to have slipped into another, either pretending to be guests or entering while the males of the second village were known to be on some project, the actual object of these visitors being to burn the entire village or at least a society house or kiva. . . . The legends of specific societies record this distrust and turmoil and the integration of survivors and their cults into the conquering villages.
>
> —[ELLIS 1964:11]

29. The only sentence in the document that suggests the herb may not have been peyote (see note 26, above) is ambiguous: " . . . des cubri haver bebido No el peyote sino Una yerva que Juanillo el Ynterprete de naz.n tiguas truxo de moqui" ("I [Alba, Governor Valverde's secretary, hearing the witnesses] discovered that they had drunk not peyote but a herb that Juanillo the interpreter had brought back from Hopi.") In thinking that the two (peyote and "the herb brought back from Hopi") were not identical, Alba may have simply been confused;

in disputing that it was peyote, his purpose seems to be to emphasize its source (Hopi), rather than to identify the plant itself. Since the rest of the document that follows this passage, as well as that which precedes it, continues to refer to peyote, I do not interpret Alba's remark here as a definitive indication it was not peyote. Incidentally, Slotkin's (1951) translation of 'No el peyote' is "Noel peyote" (a Christmas subspecies?!), which makes no sense, but clearly the passage troubled his translator too.

30. Many thanks to Bob Preucel (personal communication, 2000) for bringing this passage in Espinosa (1988) to my attention.

31. In this regard, my inference that Espeleta was Badger clan may gain support from the cultural logic that this clan is associated with the control of powerful medicines (see above).

32. Fewkes (1898:647) specifically discusses the use of fire as a purificatory process.

33. The reference is to Taussig's (1997) argument, though I am taking liberties with his use of "the state."

References Cited

Aberle, David F.
1982   *The Peyote Religion among the Navaho.* University of Chicago Press, Chicago.

Adams, Eleanor B., and Fray Angélico Chávez
1956   *The Missions of New Mexico, 1776.* University of New Mexico Press, Albuquerque.

Anderson, Benedict
1991   *Imagined Communities: Reflections on the Origin and Spread of Nationalism.* Verso, New York.

Appadurai, Arjun
1996   *Modernity at Large: Cultural Dimensions of Globalization.* University of Minnesota Press, Minneapolis.

Bahr, Donald, Juan Smith, William Allison, and Julian Hayden
1994   *The Short Swift Time of Gods on Earth: the Hohokam Chronicles.* University of California Press, Berkeley.

Bandelier, Adolph F. A.
1890–1892 *Final Report of Investigations among the Indians of the Southwestern United States, Carried on Mainly in the Years from 1880 to 1885. Part II.* Papers of the Archaeological Institute of America, American Series, IV. University Press, Cambridge, Mass.

Basso, Keith H.
1996   *Wisdom Sits in Places: Language and Landscape among the Western Apache.* University of New Mexico Press, Albuquerque.

Beaver, William T.
1952   Peyote and the Hopi. *American Anthropologist* 54(1):120.

Biersack, Aletta (editor)
1991   *Clio in Oceania: Toward a Historical Anthropology.* Smithsonian Institution Press, Washington, D.C.

Bloch, Maurice
1989   *Ritual, History and Power: Selected Papers in Anthropology.* Athlone, London, UK.

Bhabha, Homi K.
1994   How Newness Enters the World. In *The Location of Culture,* by Homi K. Bhabha, pp. 212–235. Routledge, New York.

Bloom, Lansing B.

1931   Campaign against the Moqui Pueblos. Annotated by Ralph Twitchell, edited by Lansing B. Bloom. *New Mexico Historical Review* 6(2):158–226.

Bodine, John J.

1979   Taos Pueblo. In *Handbook of North American Indians, Vol. 9, The Southwest*, edited by Alfonso Ortiz, pp. 255–267. Smithsonian Institution, Washington, D.C.

Bradfield, R. Maitland

1973   *A Natural History of Associations: A Study in the Meaning of Community*, Vol. 2. Duckworth, London, UK.

Brew, John O.

1949   The History of Awatovi. In *Franciscan Awatovi: the Excavation and Conjectural Reconstruction of a 17th-Century Spanish Mission Establishment at a Hopi Indian Town in Northeastern Arizona*, by Ross Gordon Montgomery, Gordon Smith, and John Otis Brew. Peabody Museum of American Archaeology and Ethnology, Papers, 36(3). Cambridge, Mass.

1979   Hopi Prehistory and History to 1850. In *Handbook of North American Indians, Vol. 9, The Southwest*, edited by Alfonso Ortiz, pp. 514–523. Smithsonian Institution, Washington, D.C.

Castoriadis, Cornelius

1987   *The Imaginary Institution of Society*. Translated by Kathleen Blamey. Polity Press, Cambridge, UK.

Cohn, Bernard

1980   History and Anthropology: the State of Play. *Comparative Studies in Society and History* 22(2):198–221.

Collins, James

1998   *Understanding Tolowa Histories: Western Hegemonies and Native American Responses*. Routledge, New York.

Comaroff, Jean

1985   *Body of Power, Spirit of Resistance: the Culture and History of a South African People*. University of Chicago Press, Chicago.

Comaroff, John, and Jean Comaroff

1992   *Ethnography and the Historical Imagination*. Westview Press, Boulder, Colo.

Courlander, Harold

1971   *The Fourth World of the Hopis*. Crown, New York.

Courlander, Harold (editor)

1982   *Hopi Voices: Recollections, Traditions, and Narratives of the Hopi Indians*. Recorded, transcribed, and annotated by Harold Courlander. University of New Mexico Press, Albuquerque.

Curtis, Edward M.

1922   *The North American Indian, Vol. 12, The Hopi*. Plimpton Press, Norwood, Mass.

Documentary Relations of the Southwest

n.d.   Database. Arizona State Museum, Tucson.

Douglas, Mary

1966   *Purity and Danger: an Analysis of Concepts of Pollution and Taboo*. Praeger, New York.

Eggan, Frederick R.

1950   *Social Organization of the Western Pueblos*. University of Chicago Press, Chicago.

Ellis, Florence

1964   A Reconstruction of the Basic Jemez Pattern of Social Organization, with Comparisons to Other Tanoan Social Structures. *University of New Mexico Publications in Anthropology*, 11. Albuquerque.

Espinosa, J. Manuel

1942   *Crusaders of the Río Grande: the Story of Don Diego de Vargas and the Reconquest and Refounding of New Mexico*. Institute of Jesuit History, Chicago.

Espinosa, J. Manuel (editor and translator)

1988   *The Pueblo Indian Revolt of 1696 and the Franciscan Missions in New Mexico: Letters of the Missionaries and Related Documents*. University of Oklahoma Press, Norman.

Fewkes, Jesse Walter

1893   A-wa'-to-bi: An Archaeological Verification of a Tusayan Legend. *American Anthropologist*, o.s., VI:363–375.

1896   Preliminary Account of an Expedition to the Cliff Villages of the Red Rock Country, and the Tusayan Ruins of Sikyatki and Awatobi, Arizona, in 1895. *Annual Report of the Smithsonian Institution for the Year ending July 1895*, pp. 557–588. U.S. Government Printing Office, Washington, D.C.

1898   Archeological Expedition to Arizona in 1895. In *Seventeenth Annual Report of the Bureau of American Ethnology, Smithsonian Institution (for 1895–96)*, II:519–752. U.S. Government Printing Office, Washington, D.C.

Fowler, Loretta

1987   *Shared Symbols, Contested Meanings: Gros Ventre Culture and History, 1778–1984*. Cornell University Press, Ithaca.

Geertz, Armin, and Michael Lomatuway'ma

1987   *Children of Cottonwood: Piety and Ceremonialism in Hopi Indian Puppetry*. University of Nebraska Press, Lincoln.

Geertz, Clifford

1973   The Cerebral Savage: on the Work of Claude Lévi-Strauss. In *The Interpretation of Cultures*, by Clifford Geertz, pp. 345–359. Basic Books, New York.

1980   *Negara: the Theatre State in Nineteenth Century Bali*. Princeton University Press, Princeton.

Hackett, Charles Wilson

1937   *Historical Documents Relating to New Mexico, Nueva Vizcaya, and Approaches Thereto, to 1773, Vol. III*. Carnegie Institution, Washington, D.C.

Hastrup, Kirsten, (editor)

1992   *Other Histories*. Routledge, New York.

Hill, Jonathan (editor)

1988   *Rethinking History and Myth: Indigenous South American Perspectives on the Past*. University of Illinois Press, Urbana.

Hopi Dictionary Project (compilers)

1998   *Hopi Dictionary, Hopìikwa Lavàytutuveni: A Hopi-English Dictionary of the Third Mesa Dialect*. University of Arizona Press, Tucson.

Kessell, John L., Rick Hendricks, and Meredith D. Dodge (editors)

1998   *Blood on the Boulders: the Journals of Don Diego de Vargas, 1694–97*. University of New Mexico Press, Albuquerque.

Kirch, Patrick V., and Marshall Sahlins

1992 *Anahulu: the Anthropology of History in the Kingdom of Hawaii.* University of Chicago Press, Chicago.

La Barre, Weston

1969 *The Peyote Cult.* Schocken Books, New York.

Laird, W. David

1977 *Hopi Bibliography: Comprehensive and Annotated.* University of Arizona Press, Tucson.

Lévi-Strauss, Claude

1963 *Totemism.* Translated by Rodney Needham. Beacon Press, Boston.

1966 *The Savage Mind.* University of Chicago Press, Chicago.

1973 *From Honey to Ashes.* Translated by John and Doreen Weightman. Harper and Row, New York.

Levy, Jerrold E.

1992 *Orayvi Revisited: Social Stratification in an "Egalitarian" Society.* School of American Research Press, Santa Fe.

Lincoln, Bruce

1989 *Discourse and the Construction of Society: Comparative Studies of Myth, Ritual, and Classification.* Oxford University Press, New York.

Lomatuway'ma, Michael, Lorena Lomatuway'ma, and Sidney Namingha, Jr. (narrators)

1993 *Hopi Ruin Legends: Kiqötutuwutsi.* Collected, translated, and edited by Ekkehart Malotki, published for Northern Arizona University by the University of Nebraska, Lincoln.

Malotki, Ekkehart, and Michael Lomatuway'ma

1987 *Maasaw: Profile of a Hopi God.* University of Nebraska Press, Lincoln.

Merrill, William B.

1994 Cultural Creativity and Raiding Bands in Eighteenth Century Northern New Spain. In *Violence, Resistance, and Survival in the Americas: Native Americans and the Legacy of Conquest,* edited by William B. Taylor and Franklin Pease, pp. 124–152. Smithsonian Institution Press, Washington, D.C.

Mindeleff, Cosmos

1891 Traditional History of Tusayan. In *A Study of Pueblo Architecture: Tusayan and Cibola,* by Victor Mindeleff, pp. 16–41. Eighth Annual Report of the Bureau of American Ethnology, Smithsonian Institution (for 1886–7). U.S. Government Printing Office, Washington, D.C.

Nabokov, Peter

1996 Native Views of History. In *The Cambridge History of the Native Peoples of the Americas, Vol. I: North America,* edited by Bruce G. Trigger and Wilcomb E. Washburn, pp. 1–60. Cambridge University Press, New York.

Obeyesekere, Gananath

1992 *The Apotheosis of Captain Cook: European Mythmaking in the Pacific.* Princeton University Press, Princeton.

O'Brien, Jay, and William Roseberry (editors)

1991 *Golden Ages, Dark Ages: Imagining the Past in Anthropology and History.* University of California Press, Berkeley.

Preston, Douglas

1998 Cannibals of the Canyon: Christy Turner's Views on Anasazi and Hopi Cannibalism. *The New Yorker* 74(37):76–89.

Price, Richard

1983 *"First-Time": the Historical Vision of an Afro-American People.* Johns Hopkins University Press, Baltimore.

1990 *Alabi's World.* Johns Hopkins University Press, Baltimore.

Pueblo Transcripts

n.d. Microfilm Edition. American Indian Oral History Collection. Center for Southwest Research, University of New Mexico Library, Albuquerque.

Rosaldo, Renato

1980 *Ilongot Headhunting, 1873–1974: A Study in Society and History.* Stanford University Press, Stanford.

Sahlins, Marshall D.

1981 *Historical Metaphors and Mythical Realities: Structure in the Early History of the Sandwich Islands Kingdom.* University of Michigan Press, Ann Arbor.

1985 *Islands of History.* University of Chicago Press, Chicago.

1995 *How "Natives" Think: About Captain Cook, for Example.* University of Chicago Press, Chicago.

Schneider, Jane, and Rayna Rapp (editors)

1995 *Articulating Hidden Histories: Exploring the Influence of Eric R. Wolf.* University of California Press, Berkeley.

Scholes, France V.

1935 The First Decade of the Inquisition in New Mexico. *New Mexico Historical Review* 10:195–241.

Shryock, Andrew

1997 *Nationalism and the Genealogical Imagination: Oral History and Textual Authority in Tribal Jordan.* University of California Press, Berkeley.

Simmons, Marc

1979 History of Pueblo-Spanish Relations to 1821. In *Handbook of North American Indians, Vol. 9, The Southwest,* edited by Alfonso Ortiz, pp. 178–193. Smithsonian Institution, Washington, D.C.

Slotkin, J. S.

1951 Early Eighteenth Century Documents on Peyotism North of the Rio Grande. *American Anthropologist* 53:420–427.

1955 Peyotism, 1521–1891. *American Anthropologist* 57:202–230.

Stephen, Alexander M.

1936 *Hopi Journal of Alexander M. Stephen.* 2 Vols. Edited by Elsie Clews Parsons. Columbia University Press, New York.

Stewart, Omer C.

1987 *Peyote Religion: a History.* University of Oklahoma Press, Norman.

Taussig, Michael

1987 *Shamanism, Colonialism, and the Wild Man: a Study in Terror and Healing.* University of Chicago Press, Chicago.

1997 *The Magic of the State.* Routledge, New York.

Titiev, Mischa

1944 *Old Oraibi: A Study of the Hopi Indians of Third Mesa.* Peabody Museum of American Archaeology and Ethnology, Papers, 22(1). Cambridge, Mass.

n.d. Census Notes from Old Oraibi. Ms. (Courtesy of Margaret Wright.)

Tonkin, Elizabeth, Maryon MacDonald, and Malcolm Chapman, (editors)

1989   *History and Ethnicity.* Routledge, New York.

Turner, Christy G., and Jacqueline A. Turner

1999   *Man Corn: Cannibalism and Violence in the American Southwest.* University of Utah Press, Salt Lake City.

Twitchell, Ralph E.

1914   *The Spanish Archives of New Mexico.* 2 Vols. The Torch Press, Cedar Rapids, Iowa.

Vansina, Jan

1985   *Oral Tradition as History.* University of Wisconsin Press, Madison.

Vélez de Escalante, Fray Silvestre

1778   Extracto de Noticias. Archivo Franciscano, 19/397, 20/428.1. Biblioteca Nacional de México, Mexico City.

Voth, H. R.

1901   *The Oraibi Powamu Ceremony.* Field Museum Publication 61, Anthropological Series Vol. III, No. 2. Chicago.

1903   *The Oraibi Summer Snake Ceremony.* Field Columbian Museum, Publication 83. Chicago.

1905   *The Traditions of the Hopi.* Field Columbian Museum, Publication 96, Anthropological Series 8. Chicago.

Wallace, Anthony F. C.

1956   Revitalization Movements. *American Anthropologist* 58:264–281.

1969   *The Death and Rebirth of the Seneca.* Vintage, New York.

White, Leslie A.

n.d.   Kinship System Charts of the Hopi (Oraibi) [by clan and lineage] noted in the 1932 Field Training Course. Ms. on file, Laboratory of Anthropology, Santa Fe.

Whiteley, Peter M.

1985   Unpacking Hopi "Clans": Another Vintage Model out of Africa? *Journal of Anthropological Research* 41:359–374.

1988a   *Deliberate Acts: Changing Hopi Culture through the Oraibi Split.* University of Arizona Press, Tucson.

1988b   *Bacavi: Journey to Reed Springs.* Northland Press, Flagstaff.

1992   Burning Culture: Auto-da-fé at Oraibi. *History and Anthropology* 6(1):46–85.

1998   *Rethinking Hopi Ethnography.* Smithsonian Institution Press. Washington, D.C.

1999   Can (Pre-)Histories Converge? Meaning, Truth, and Value in the Western Pueblo Past. *Affiliation Conference on Ancestral Peoples of the Four Corners Region,* Vol. 2. Fort Lewis College and the National Park Service. Durango, Colo.

Whiting, Alfred F.

1939   *Ethnobotany of the Hopi.* Museum of Northern Arizona, Bulletin 15. Flagstaff.

Wolf, Eric

1982   *Europe and the People without History.* University of California Press, Berkeley.

Yava, Albert

1978   *Big Falling Snow: A Tewa-Hopi's Life and Times and the History and Traditions of His People.* Edited by Harold Courlander. Crown, New York.

Chapter 11
Social Memory
and the Pueblo Revolt:
A Postcolonial Perspective

Michael V. Wilcox

Studies of what has come to be known as the *Contact period* (ca. A.D. 1492–1800) have long intrigued archaeologists, anthropologists and historians. Broadly defined as both the temporal and geographic location in which interactions between European colonists and Native peoples took place, Borderlands studies have provided the context for a variety of literary, historical, and ethnographic narratives (Weber 1988). Generally, both historians and anthropologists have emphasized the period of contact as a historical moment in which a *Pre-Columbian* or *Indigenous* past is radically transformed through the introduction of European diseases, technologies, social and religious institutions.

Archaeological studies of the Contact period in the Southwest have only reinforced this perception; for many Southwestern archaeologists, interest in Puebloan archaeology ends where colonial history begins. In the search for nomothetic models of human behavior, early practitioners of the "New Archaeology" used the ethnological studies of their intellectual ancestors as a foil. The "scientific" study of the past conceived of Indian prehistory as the *data set* of the remote past. The use of local ethnographic and historical information was rejected as an extension of the Direct Historical Approach (Meltzer 1979, 1983). As a result, remarkably few post-contact

Puebloan sites have been systematically studied (Ayers 1995).

As I argue in this chapter, the adoption of disease-based, conquest and acculturation models by historians and archaeologists has generated a scholarly approach to Contact period studies which simultaneously fails to account for the persistence of Indigenous cultures and traditions and ignores the efforts of Puebloan peoples to resist, manipulate, and transform Spanish cultural practices. While acculturation and disease undoubtedly affected Puebloan communities, the study of Puebloan resistance to Spanish colonists and missionaries during the sixteenth and seventeenth centuries requires the adoption of contextual, interdisciplinary methods and theoretical models.

Unfortunately, traditional divisions between the subjects of historical and anthropological studies have generally hindered this kind of approach. For theoretical, professional, and political reasons, neither archaeologists nor historians have been particularly interested in explaining the persistence of indigenous cultures following contact. For Borderlands scholars and archaeologists, *contact* divides more than the professional domains of each field; contact signals an imminent and inevitable demise and dislocation of Native cultures and communities.

The first challenges to this perspective can be seen in the work of several generations of Native American scholars. From Edward Dozier's early criticisms of acculturation theory (Dozier 1954, 1955, 1962), to Jack Forbes's historical studies (1960, 1963), to Alfonso Ortiz's (1969) ethnological study of Puebloan society, each has offered interpretations of culture change that emphasize the continuity and resistance strategies of Native Peoples. Much of this work anticipates the critical approach to European colonization and domination by Eric Wolf. In *Europe and the People without History*, Wolf questioned the political location of anthropological studies and suggested that the separation of *primitive* and *European* histories marginalized the perspectives of Native Peoples for economic, political and ideological reasons (Wolf 1980:18–19). Further, Wolf suggested that the task of Postcolonial historians should be the recovery of the largely unwritten, unarticulated histories of colonized peoples using interdisciplinary methods, "it is only when we integrate our different kinds of knowledge that the people without history emerge as actors in their own right. When we parcel them out among the several disciplines, we render them invisible—their story which is our story, vanishes from sight" (Schneider and Rapp 1995:6–7).

Wolf's insistence that western scholarship had helped render Native Americans and Africans *a people without history*" foreshadowed the development of what has come to be known as *Postcolonial studies*. Defined as a "discourse of opposition which colonization brings into being" (Ashcroft et al. 1995:117), post-colonialism encompasses a multitude of critical approaches to both the subject and practice of colonization. In critically examining both the processes of colonization, nationalism and ethnogenesis as well as the role of western scholarship in the representation of colonized peoples, post-colonial approaches attempt to articulate the perspectives and resistance strategies of colonial subjects. In deconstructing the monolithic, Eurocentric master-narratives of colonial histories, Postcolonial scholars such as Edward Said (1978), Homi Bhabha (1990), and Gayatri Spivak (1996) have shifted the focus of debate and discussion to the complex interplay of myth, symbol, and memory in the construction of indigenous and national ethnic identities. Located within this context, events such as the Revolt of 1680 offer a unique opportunity to reevaluate traditional narratives of conquest, subordination, and Spanish colonialism.

For archaeologists working in a post-NAGPRA era, where consultation and collaboration with Native communities have become an increasingly common feature of research projects, a series of important questions emerge: 1) To what degree have the theoretical leanings of archaeologists and Borderlands historians unwittingly submerged the histories of Native southwestern peoples? 2) How have studies of diseases been linked to the acculturation model? 3) How did social memory and the processes of resistance transform Pueblo ethnic identities and boundaries?

Postcolonialism and Indigenous Resistance

In New Mexico, both Puebloan and Euro-American accounts of the Revolt demonstrate the degree to which notions of *history* and *the past* are the product of politically situated discursive practices. In the introduction to Folsom's *Indian Uprising on the Rio Grande* (1973) the late Pueblo anthropologist Alfonso Ortiz attempted to locate the Revolt within the larger narrative of North American colonial history, "This revolution was fought for precisely the same reasons that the revolution of 1776 was fought— to regain freedom from tyranny, persecution and unjust taxation. . . . It was a fight for freedom that has never been widely recognized as such, nor accorded the attention by historians that it might have had . . . but it is part and parcel of our common heritage as Americans and it must be made part of our common consciousness" (Folsom 1973:x). Ortiz' account is largely a reaction to earlier celebratory accounts of colonization and conquest and represents the latest in a series of revisionist movements in Contact period history.

Historian Benjamin Keen (1985) has identified three major revisionist trends in Borderlands scholarship. The first occurred between 1880 and the 1930s and is characterized by the work of Herbert Eugene Bolton (1915, 1919, 1930, 1936, 1949, 1964), Charles Lummis (1909, 1956), Adolph Bandelier (1890, 1892, 1910) and John Francis Bannon (1970). Responding to a well-documented legacy of anti-Hispanic sentiments among Anglophile historians, much of this early work renders an adventuresome, "triumphalist" vision of Spanish conquest—simultaneously celebrating the achievements of Spanish colonists and denying or minimizing the oppressive aspects of colonization (Keen 1985:658). Unfortunately, the efforts of early Borderlands scholars to elevate the narrative of Spanish *conquistadores* (vis-à-vis Turner's East to West model), frequently sacrificed the perspectives of Native peoples, mestizos and women (Hurtado 1993, 1995). Rather than viewing conquest, violence and its social consequences as a common feature of colonial regimes, Indigenous, mestizo, and African perspectives were located *outside of and external to* an official transcript of Hispanic colonial history.

Bolton, a student of Fredrick Jackson Turner, was a particularly effective advocate of Borderlands studies and much of his work reveals his persistent efforts to "Parkmanize" the history of the New Mexico. While many of Bolton's students (including Charles W. Hackett, George P. Hammond, J. Manuel Espinosa, and John Francis Bannon) have written extensively on the Revolt, much of this later analysis assumes a fatalistic approach to the less pleasant aspects of conquest and colonization.

The second revisionist tradition is associated with the founding of the "Berkeley School" of demographic studies. Unlike Bolton's early work, this tradition incorporated an interdisciplinary approach to Contact period social change. More neutral in their analysis of colonial violence and its social consequences, the Berkeley scholars directed the attention of historians and archaeologists to European diseases and epidemics as the predominant instruments of colonial destruction (Borah and Cook 1963; Cook and Simpson 1948; Sauer 1935, 1948; Simpson 1952).

Since the 1960s, disease has replaced violence as a more politically neutral, biologically driven agent of social change affecting the Pueblos and their neighbors. Despite the fact that the methods, statistical projections, and conclusions of the Berkeley studies have been widely criticized by historical demographers (Farris 1978; Heinge 1978, 1986; Zambardino 1980), the disease-motivated population crash model has been widely adopted by processual archaeologists, (Dean 1985; Dobyns 1976, 1983; Lycett 1995; Thomas 1989).

The popularity of this approach among Southwestern archaeologists can be attributed to the goal of identifying nomothetic explanations of culture change that could be applied universally to human societies. The adoption of disease-based models supported several of the theoretical claims of the New Archaeology. In emphasizing the discontinuities between a pristine, unacculturated Pueblo prehistory and a "tainted" ethnographic present, processual archaeologists were able to move beyond the theoretical confines of the Direct Historical Approach. The study of epidemic diseases added a universally applicable, empirical dimension to traditional settlement

pattern analysis. The introduction of a "new" bio-medical, technical vocabulary simultaneously enhanced the location of processual archaeology as a nomothetic, "scientific" approach to human prehistory, and helped support a clear disassociation between an Indigenous past and a European dominated historical present.

However, at the same time that archaeologists were using the Berkeley Studies to explain the disappearance of Native peoples, a third revisionist trend gained momentum in the humanities and social sciences. Just as many archaeologists embraced the methods, models and "value-free" scientific claims of the New Archaeology, colonial historians and anthropologists began to approach the subjects of "contact" and colonization from a decidedly different theoretical position. A new wave of interdisciplinary studies attempted to incorporate the perspectives of colonized people, adopting a more critical and self-reflexive approach to the study of colonization and the development of global capitalism. While studies of nationalism (Anderson 1983; Eriksen 1993; Gellner 1983), colonialism (Asad 1973; Cohn 1987; Said 1978, 1993), and resistance (Comaroff 1985; Ong 1987; Scott 1985) have generated substantial interest in the interaction of European colonists and indigenous peoples, studies which integrate these approaches have attracted little attention from Southwestern archaeologists. Among the more promising contributions to the study of the Revolt involves the application of theories of ethnicity, boundary maintenance, and the development of pan-Tribal or "ethnic" conflicts.

Ethnicity and Boundary Maintenance Theory

The most extensive studies of ethnicity and ethnic movements are those associated with the work of British social anthropologists interested in monitoring the development of Pan-Tribal movements in colonial territories. The Copper Belt Studies of the Rhodes-Livingstone Institute were followed in 1969 by Frederick Barth's *Ethnic Groups and Boundaries*. Collectively these works revealed a complex process of cultural interaction, compartmentalization, and resistance to outside influences. Contrary to the acculturation concept, their work suggested that interactions between groups were structured in ways that preserved cultural differences and insulated groups from outside influences. Barth's study of the processes of "boundary maintenance" questioned the assumed premises of acculturation and suggested that all communities have continual contact and relations with other cultures. In examining the social interactions between and among various multi-ethnic or "plural" societies, Barth's synthetic analysis suggested that instead of diminishing cultural distinctions, contacts, and interaction actually *stimulated* a heightened awareness of cultural differences.

The characteristics or diacritica that signaled social differences between ethnic groups were neither uniform, nor limited to the empirically self-evident, signs accepted by anthropologists. In particular, ascriptive categories based upon Western notions of "race" were of little value in determining relationships between members of the same racial category (as defined by Westerners). Instead, social differences were communicated and signaled (both passively and actively) through a whole suite of potential features. Adding a new dimension to the complexity of signification, Barth extended the range of diacritica to include material culture (house forms, clothing) as well as the more traditionally documented somatic features (such as hair texture, skin color etc.). In addition to the more nuanced, behavioral signals such as language, accent, mannerisms, technological choice and "style," individuals actively signaled membership to "insiders" and "outsiders" through social performances and the participation in rituals.

In a dialectical process of integration and segregation, ethnic identities relate the individual to group and the group to the individual. Being a member of a specific group implied an allegiance to the standards of excellence, morality and value orientations specific to that identity (Barth 1969:16). These allegiances allow for the potential diversification and expansion of social relationships to include virtually all sectors and domains of social activity. The opposite was true as well. The identification of outsiders implied the recognition of limitations on shared under-standings, "differences in the criteria for the judgment and

value of performances" and restricted interaction to, "sectors of assumed common understanding and mutual interest"(Barth 1969:15). As a form of identity, ethnicity is superordinal and serves as the basis for any number of social personalities an individual may assume. Provided by the group, ethnicity creates the context in which other facets of identity are expressed, recognized, and given meaning. Linked in this way to status, it provides the context in which other aspects of identity (including gender, age, filial, and clan relations) are evaluated. Group membership implies historically and culturally specific notions of social distance as well as common regional or geographic origins. These common origins invoke fictive or biological kin relations and as the basis for group membership. In this sense, like Benedict Anderson's imagined communities (1985) ethnic identities have a tran-scendent quality and extend the life of the individual into the future and past through descendents and ancestors. Referencing a collective or exclusive past these "cultural memories" are codified in origin myths and oral histories.

Because of these characteristics, ethnic identities have certain organizational capabilities; affiliation with the group conditions social action and provides the basis for collective behaviors and inter-group relations. These col-lective actions include migrations, abandonments, and resettlements as well as the development of ethnic move-ments. While universal models of ethnicity have proven difficult to apply, the processes of boundary maintenance, ethnogenesis, and ethnic conflicts are of particular in-terest to scholars interested in Contact period social in-teraction.

A common theme of these more "processual" discussions of ethnicity is the idea that power imbalances between parallel groups transform these latent, organizational categories into powerful social movements. According to Comaroff (1987:307), ethnic conflicts are generated by the asymmetric incorporation of structurally dissimilar groups within a single political economy. Conflicts result when one group is able to "exert its dominance over another and removes from it the means by which value, labor (and status) are given meaning" (Comaroff 1987:309).

Cohen (1978) argues that "power" rests in the ability to control and restrict access to resources. Defined as "the instrumentalities used to satisfy culturally defined needs and desires" (Cohen 1978:391), resources can include food, water, land, or labor as well as spiritual, technical, or cultural information. Parallel group interactions can be transformed to ethnic conflicts by a number of different processes; expansion, migration, and conquest all have the potential to change the relationships between groups or bring formerly segregated groups in contact with one another.

Colonial expansions involve several factors, which can lead to ethnic conflicts. The process of *ethnic ascription* and *subordination* all help determine the relations between ethnic groups as do the economic and social motives that generate these contacts. Subordination and discrimination against subject populations are justified and maintained through a large-scale process of boundary maintenance. The creation of pan-ethnic ascriptive categories simultaneously denies historical differences between groups and imposes group identities based upon the diacritica relevant to the dominant group.

In the Americas, colonized groups within the Spanish empire were rated in terms of their putative social, geographic, and biological distance from Spain; linguistic discursive practices reinforced the putative symbolic and moral distance between colonizers and colonized. The naming of stigmatized populations as "Indios," for example, simultaneously disregarded the cultural or physical distinctions among colonized peoples, "denying any constituent group a political economic or ideological identity of its own" (Wolf 1980:380). Because the expansion of colonial empires presupposes and depends upon unequal access to resources, racially stigmatized populations are unable to transcend the social boundaries imposed by their own physicality. While conversion allowed for the partial integration of Indians into the colonial social system, ultimately full access to the whole range of social identities and statuses within Spanish society was thwarted by the diacritica of race.

The rigidity of the Spanish colonial system was neither uncontested nor intractable. While some members of stigmatized populations may attempt to emulate the behaviors of the dominant group and improve their own statuses, others feigned acceptance or rejected it outright. The cost of defection was often steep—the new status positions, based in opposition to the interests of their own kin groups are often tenuous (Horowitz 1985:95–141). As is the case with many Pan-ethnic movements, the creation and imposition of subordinate social categories often leads to unintended consequences for the dominant group. The common experience of discrimination, segregation, and persecution helps generate collective responses by subordinate groups. The Pueblo Revolt of 1680 represents one such movement.

Contact and Conquest on the Spanish Borderlands

In colonial New Spain contact between the Pueblos and the Spaniards coincided with the development of Spanish nationalism and the advent of a capitalist world economy. As contact with the known world expanded to include previously unknown geographic regions and peoples, the social categories that defined and divided Europe were projected upon the Americas. The Indian came to symbolize a new kind of person singularly defined by geographic isolation from Europe and Christianity (Williams 1990:13–48). The ascriptive process often creates the conditions in which the use of violence is justified. For many Europeans the presence of peoples outside of the historical religious and philosophical traditions of Europe was symbolic as well. By virtue of his isolation, the Indian was conceived of as a being who required transformation in order to be included within the realm of Europeans. At the same time, the Catholic Church, threatened with defections from a growing movement towards Protestantism, sought to reassert its authority with the aid of Spanish military might.

Spanish notions of social distance and conquest were developed long before contact with the Pueblos. The military conquest of Moorish territories provided the conquering Spaniards with access to slave labor and land holdings of conquered peoples. The justifications for conquest and the terms of social difference were originally based upon religious differences and the consolidation of political power by Spanish monarchs was accomplished through the dispossession and appropriation of Muslim and Jewish wealth in the sixteenth and seventeenth centuries (Kamen 1991:9–57).

Spanish legal authority descended from the monarch whose legal authority in the Americas was uncontested. The Papal donation of 1493 determined that all new territories were a "Papal fief held by the Spanish Crown"(Elliot 1989:7–27). The rights of the crown were subordinate to those of the church and were contingent upon the conversion of Natives to Christianity. This relationship served as a legal and moral justification for the claims of the crown on Indian land and labor. The rewards offered by forcible conquest offer clues to the motives and sensibilities of early explorers. The *Capitulation* was a contract between the crown and the conquistadors that extended rights of property and governance in newly founded territories (Elliot 1969:59). Through this relationship, the leaders of expeditions could acquire titles to land and labor through the crown. Charters for settlements secured the rights of Spaniards to alienate property from Indian communities by force of arms. Spain's presence in the New World was justified theoretically by its missionary efforts. Still the interests of colonists frequently clashed with the mandates of missionary conversion sponsored by the crown and nowhere was this more evident than in the Northern Frontier.

Just as the terms of difference developed in Spain were grounded in the historical interaction of Castilians, Moors, and other Spaniards, Pueblo people came to experience Spanish colonists through a similar historical experience. The economic pressures exerted by Spain's Protestant rivals fueled the drive for silver as well as Indian land and labor. Despite the official pronouncements of Spanish authorities banning the practice of Indian slavery, slave raiding was a frequent and disruptive feature of the frontier economy. As New Spain's northern frontier expanded, acute labor shortages facilitated the development of a substantial, underground slave economy (Powell 1953:64). Native peoples who remained in villages were forced to work in the region's silver mines. The working conditions were often brutal and many native peoples died while working with the toxic agents of silver smelting (West 1949:12). During the 1500s, several Indigenous rebellions raged throughout mining towns in Zacatecas, Guanajuato, San Luis Potosí, and Pachuca (Meyer and Sherman 1991:161). The Mixtón War broke out in 1541 just as Francisco Vázquez de Coronado left Nueva Galicia in search of the Pueblos of Cibola.

Stretching from Guadalajara to Culiacán, the movement presents some striking parallels to the Pueblo Revolt of 1680. Tenamaxtli, a religious leader of the Mixtón urged his followers to, "kill all Spaniards and burn their churches as the first step toward the return to old ways and old gods"(Miller 1985:115). Unable to establish military control, Viceroy Mendoza enlisted the help of 30,000 Aztec and Tlaxcallan allies. Still, control over the region was tenuous. The Chichimeca rebellion began in the 1550s and lasted for nearly 40 years (Weber 1992:212–227). Revolts among Tarahumara, and Acaxee peoples in the sixteenth century were followed by the Xixime Rebellion in 1610 (Salmon 1991:1–51). In 1616, the Tepehuan Rebellion added to the strains between colonists and Native Peoples (Deeds 1998:3–29). Unable to distinguish secular and religious forms of social practice, Spanish colonists interpreted alien ritual behaviors as acts of heresy. In an increasingly familiar pattern, Native religious practices were outlawed and religious leaders were arrested. As the suppression of traditions increased, Native peoples retaliated by defiling Spanish missions and attacking church officials. As the demands for a stable source of Indian labor increased, so did the frequency of slave raiding.

The cycle of violence and retribution were a continual concern of colonial officials. Responding to the crisis, the fourth Viceroy of New Spain, Don Martín Enriquez de Alemanza (1568–1580) issued an order for a War of Fire and Blood, demanding the total elimination of all rebellious natives on the Northern Frontier (Powell 1953:105). Still, there was little agreement among colonial officials regarding these practices. In a confidential letter to King Phillip II, Juan Bautista de Orozco, the military leader appointed to quell the rebellions on the borderlands, stated that the wars waged against native peoples were launched in an effort to secure Indian slaves. Legally, resistance to Spanish colonists was interpreted as a rejection of Christianity. Under the contract of the *Requerimiento,* the doctrine of a *bellum justum* allowed for the legal enslavement of Indios who resisted Spanish authorities. Bautista de Orozco wrote, "In the beginning, this was the easiest solution, but now this right to spoils has become the principle goal of the soldiers and continues to be the cause of great excesses. The capture of free Indians to use in paying off their debts to the merchants will only cause great harm to us" (Naylor and Polzer 1986:46). Faced with few economic opportunities, expensive supplies, and deflated silver prices on the frontier, Spanish adventurers looked for new opportunities along the northern borderlands.

The entradas of the sixteenth century were motivated by a desire to secure access to the resources that fueled the expansion of the Spanish empire. Between 1540 and 1598, the Pueblos encountered four successive waves of disappointed plunderers, adventurers, and profiteers seeking wealth and fortune. Despite the promises and legends of large and wealthy northern cities inspired by Cabeza de Vaca's journey in 1538 and Fray Marcos de Niza's foray in 1539, the pueblos lacked not only the mineral wealth that the Spaniards demanded, but were frequently incapable of providing the levels of tribute required to sustain both the colonists and themselves. From Coronado's failed expedition to find the fabled seven cities of Cibola to the eventual settlement of Oñate at San Juan in 1698, these encounters were characterized by a series of violent confrontations which established the terms and character of the relationships between the two groups throughout the seventeenth century.

Coronado staged violent attacks at several pueblos including Zuni, Acoma, and Hopi. Especially damaging were extended sieges of 13 of the 15 Tiwa communities during the winters of 1540–1542. Both Arenal and Moho were the sites of particularly devastating attacks

(Hammond and Rey 1940:226–230, 333–358). Coronado's demands for food and clothing and shelter as well as his capture of religious leaders at Pecos generated ill feeling towards the colonists. For six months, Coronado's men camped at Tiwa villages and staged expeditions to look for silver, lead, and mercury. As their demands increased, tensions flared between the groups and 200 Tiwa men were burned at the stake (Hammond and Rey 1940:223–234, 330–336). These attacks were followed by a sustained and costly siege at Moho. According to the official testimony provided at Coronado's trial, more than 400 natives were slain (Hammond and Rey 1940:337–393). Ultimately, both Coronado and his men were charged by the Spanish governors for crimes against the Indians.

Coronado's journey was followed by the Chamuscado-Rodriguez, Espejo, and Castaño de Sosa expeditions. In each case, a similar cycle of violence was touched off as demands for tribute, servants, and women pushed the Pueblos to their limits. In those regions especially hard hit by colonial raids, the colonists encountered villages that had been completely abandoned. When they asked where the inhabitants had fled to, they were told that the people had fled into the surrounding hills (Hammond and Rey 1929:71–79). Finally, in 1598, Juan de Oñate established a permanent settlement at the Pueblo of San Juan after reconquering the Pueblos once again in the name of Phillip II.

Oñate's punitive attack on the Pueblo of Acoma was to have lasting consequences. After one of Oñate's nephews was killed in an attack on the pueblo, Oñate ordered a war of *fire and blood*. The Spaniards claim to have killed 800 people in the village (Hammond and Rey 1953:427). The remaining 500 captives were divided among Oñate's party; men over the age of 25 had a foot severed and served 20 years servitude, women over 12 were to serve 20 years. The female children were given to the friars and the boys were given to Oñate's captain, Vicente de Saldívar (Hammond and Rey 1953:21–23). The historical memories of these extreme punishments must have aided Popé in his cause.

The Pueblo Revolt and the Emergence of Pan-Puebloism

The demands for tribute, establishment of missionary programs and the suppression of religious practices placed a continual strain upon the relations between the Pueblos and Spaniards. Despite the fact that different indigenous communities considered themselves distinct culturally, located within their own historical traditions, the Spaniards defined and treated the Pueblos as a single subordinate class. The collective resentment generated by these activities is revealed in the testimony of Pedro Namboa, an 80-year-old Tiwa man from Alameda Pueblo, interviewed following the rebellion. When asked why the Indians had rebelled, he stated that:

> . . . the resentment which all of the Indians have in their hearts has been so strong, from the time this kingdom was discovered, because the religious and the Spaniards took away their idols, and forbade their sorceries and idolatries: that they have inherited successively from the old men the things pertaining to their ancient customs. And that he has heard this resentment spoken of since he was of an age to understand.
>
> —[HACKETT AND SHELBY 1942:61]

Following a pattern typical of ethnic conflicts, the practices of subordination may have unintended consequences for the dominant group. While some individuals may attempt to integrate themselves into the system through the adoption of practices characteristic of the dominant group, eventually the limits of integration are thwarted by the diacritics of the dominant society. While some communities may attempt to remove themselves from the social system through migration or refugee movements, other groups may attempt to coexist with the dominant group. As Horowitz (1985:3–55) documents in his comparative study of ethnic conflicts, eventually the common experience of discrimination and marginalization motivates collective social behaviors or Pan-Ethnic movements which attempt to remove the source of inequality and restore equilibrium and group autonomy. These movements often adopt the shared diacritics of their subordinate group and re-deploy them as symbols of a common identity. Segregation between the groups accelerates and languages and religious practices are cleansed. Group members also characteristically seek a return to orthodox practices that existed prior to contact with the dominant group.

Popé's call to arms was accompanied by a similar set of invocations. Following the failed rebellions at individual pueblos—at Jemez in 1623, at Zuni in 1632, and at Taos in 1639—and the unsuccessful regional rebellions in the Tiwa provinces in 1650, religious leaders were executed or sold into slavery, aggravating a growing discontent among the Pueblos (Knaut 1994:98–99, 169). The evidence for the assertion of orthodox practices is provided by the testimony of Pueblo prisoners following the Revolt. Popé urged the renouncement of Spanish beliefs and customs, called for ritual purification and the reinstatement of traditional ceremonies. Popé ordered, "that all of the pueblos break up and burn the images of the Holy Christ, the Virgin Mary and the other saints, the crosses, and everything pertaining to Christianity and that they burn the temples, break up the bells and separate from the wives whom God had given them in marriage" (Hackett and Shelby 1942:247–248). Ritual purification was necessary in order to reverse the processes of integration into Spanish religious life, "In order to take away their baptismal names, the water and the holy oils, they were to plunge into the rivers and wash themselves with amole, which is a root native to the country washing even their clothing with the understanding that there would thus be taken from them the character of the holy sacraments" (Hackett and Shelby 1942:247–248).

Finally, Popé called for the restoration of Puebloan cultural practices, the rebuilding of the kivas and the desecration of Catholic religious icons. This would allow the Pueblos to, "harvest a great deal of Maize, many beans, a great abundance of cotton calabashes and very large watermelons and cantaloupes; and that they could erect their houses and enjoy abundant wealth and leisure"

(Hackett and Shelby 1942:247–248).

The call for a return to orthodox practices leads to a shift to mesa settlement and the establishment of new multi-Pueblo communities (Ferguson and Preucel n.d.). In 1692, Cochiti people hosted members of San Marcos and San Felipe on Horn Mesa at the new pueblo of La Cieneguilla de Cochiti (Kotyiti) (Kessell and Hendricks 1992:515). In the same year, people from Zia and Santa Ana were living at the new pueblo of La Alameda on Cerro Colorado (Kessell and Hendricks 1992:431). By 1694, members of San Ildefonso, Santa Clara, San Juan, Tesuque, Cuyamungue, Pojoaque, and Jacona Pueblos established a stronghold on the summit of Black Mesa (Kessell et al. 1998:116). In the Jemez Mountains, Jemez and Santo Domingo people established Boletsakwa on San Juan Mesa (Elliott, Chapter 3). Several other ancestral Jemez villages were also reoccupied during the period (Elliot 1982). In 1700, members of San Cristobal and San Lazaro established Tewa Village on First Mesa at Hopi (Dozier 1954).

Ethnographic documents and oral histories offer provocative clues as to how the Pan-Puebloan movement was activated. At the local level, the establishment of new settlements implies a restructuring of communal identities, kin and clan affiliations and communal relations. Choosing to resettle involves a deliberate decision to increase social interaction. With these interactions, however, comes an increased likelihood of social friction. It is instructive then, that the settlement of some of these communities generally parallels linguistic affiliations. At Kotyiti, Cochiti, San Felipe, and San Marcos peoples spoke Keres dialects. At Black Mesa were speakers of Northern Tewa dialects. Tanoan speakers from San Lazaro and San Cristobal migrated to First Mesa at Hopi.

An important strategy of resistance mentioned by Dozier, Ortiz and other Pueblo scholars (see Suina, Chapter 14) was the protection and use of language as a means of insulating Pueblo communities from unwanted outside influences. Following the policies of Franciscan society, few, if any of the Franciscans made efforts to learn the multitude of Puebloan languages (Phelan 1980:86–91). This allowed the Pueblos to interpret Christian doctrine on their own terms. Heavily laden with the thick description of familial relations, cosmology, and religion, language helped affirm communal solidarity and re-establish local identities.

Still, Popé's call for a return to fundamentalist practices and his attempts to assert regional authority had mixed results. While the regional movement was successful, few communities were willing to accede authority to a centralized leadership. As the threat of Spanish domination was removed, the regional system lost momentum. Similar to other pan-ethnic movements, the call for a return to a new fundamentalism invokes different interpretations of orthodox practices. The successful removal of the colonists helped motivate new objectives for individual communities. In the end, local village identities resumed as the ascendant forms of social organization.

In many ways, the Revolt succeeded in its goals by forever changing the balance of power between colonists and pueblos. A higher degree of religious freedom was established and restored. With the re-entry of a new generation of colonists in 1692, the terms and conditions of interaction between the groups were transformed. Once activated, the social memory of the pan-Puebloan identity remained a significant obstacle to missionization and forcible labor.

Conclusions

The Revolt of 1680 offers archaeologists and historians an opportunity to redefine and rethink the origins and application of conquest, disease, and assimilation models. In enabling a more balanced, critical approach to the scholarship and subjects of colonization, ethnogenesis, and resistance, post-colonial approaches raise important questions for Borderlands historians and Southwestern archaeologists alike. While epidemics, droughts, and famines were devastating to Puebloan communities, their impact must be considered in light of the social conditions in which they occurred. Spanish demands for labor and the continual threat of violence were initiated by colonists in an effort to secure their own survival. The cost of these human generated policies was steep; the forcible removal of the Pueblos from more productive and stable modes of agricultural production and the redistribution of fertile farmlands among colonists severely compromised the health of Puebloan communities.

Adding to the complexity of New Mexican social life, the polarization of *Indios* and colonists and the pervasive practice of slave raiding by Spanish colonists created the conditions in which intermediate ethnicities or *castas* such as *genízaros, mestizos,* and *coyotes* developed (Gutiérrez 1991:194–211). The poorly documented presence of these more fluid social categories raises important questions regarding the processes of boundary maintenance and ethnogenesis during the Colonial period. As the events of the Revolt demonstrate, both social practices and the use of cultural and religious symbols helped determine the fault lines between various ethnic groups.

Despite a wealth of anthropological and historical materials, archaeologists have yet to develop adequate theoretical approaches to Contact period studies which account for the development and significance of ethnic categories and their constitutive roles in colonial society. The application of theories of ethnicity and ethnic conflict offer an alternative to processual explanations that rely upon disease and acculturation. For archaeologists, however, the study of ethnicity has been generally limited to the study of diacritica (Lechtman 1977, 1979; Wiessner 1983, 1984, 1985, 1990). A more profitable means of assessing the social interactions between groups involves the examination of ethnicity as a fluid *social process.*

The study of ethnicity also requires a new post-colonial perspective that more thoroughly explores the *articulation* of Indigenous narratives and perspectives. If the *subaltern* is to speak, as Gayatri Spivak argues, new attention must be paid to subjects and topics not traditionally covered by Southwestern archaeologists. The rationalization of social subordination, the use of violence by nation states and the subsequent development of pan-tribal resistance movements are complex social phenomena, which require a critical engagement with both primary and secondary historical materials. Given the current challenges posed by repatriation and collaborative, contextual studies will only be enhanced by the perspectives and criticisms of Indigenous peoples.

References Cited

Anderson, Benedict
1983   *Imagined Communities: Reflections on the Origin and Spread of Nationalism.* Verso, London, UK.

Asad, Talal
1973   *Anthropology and the Colonial Encounter.* Ithaca Press, New York.

Ashcroft, B., G. Griffiths, and H. Tiffin
1995   *The Postcolonial Studies Reader.* Routledge, London, UK.

Ayers, James. E. (compiler)
1995   *The Archaeology of Spanish and Mexican Colonialism in the American Southwest.* Guides to the Archaeological Literature of the Immigrant Experience in America, No. 3. Society for Historical Archaeology.

Bandelier, Adolph F. A.
1890   *Final Report of Investigations among the Indians of the Southwestern United States, Carried on Mainly in the Years from 1880 to 1885: Part I.* Papers of the Archaeological Institute of America, America Series Vol. I. I. A. Williams and Co., Boston.

1892   *Final Report of Investigations among the Indians of the Southwestern United States, Carried on Mainly in the Years from 1880 to 1885: Part II.* Papers of the Archaeological Institute of America, America Series Vol. IV. University Press, Cambridge, Mass.

1910   *Documentary History of the Rio Grande Pueblos of New Mexico,* Papers of the School of American Research 13:1–28. Santa Fe.

Bannon, John F.
1970   *The Spanish Borderlands Frontier, 1513–1821: Histories of the American Frontier.* Holt, Rinehart, and Winston, New York.

Barth, Frederik
1969   *Ethnic Groups and Boundaries: The Social Organization of Culture Difference.* Allen & Unwin, London, UK.

Bhabha, Homi K.
1990   *Nation and Narration.* Routledge, London, UK.

Bolton, Herbert E.
1930   *Spanish Exploration in the Southwest, 1542–1706.* Scribner, New York.

1936   *Rim of Christendom; A Biography of Eusebio Francisco Kino, Pacific Coast Pioneer.* Russell and Russell, New York.

1949   *Coronado, Knight of Pueblos and Plains.* Whittlesey House, New York.

1990   *Coronado, Knight of Pueblos and Plains.* University of New Mexico Press, Albuquerque.

Bolton, Herbert E., and J. F. Bannon
1964   *Bolton and the Spanish Borderlands.* University of Oklahoma Press, Norman.

Bolton, Herbert E., and H. B. Foster
1915   *Explorations on the Northern Frontier of New Spain, 1535–1706.* University of California Press, Berkeley.

Bolton, Herbert E., and T. M. Marshall
1919   *The Colonization of North America, 1492–1783.* The MacMillan Company, New York.

Borah, William W., and Sherburne F. Cook
1963   *The Aboriginal Population of Central Mexico on the Eve of the Spanish Conquest.* Ibero-Americana: 45. University of California Press, Berkeley.

Cohen, Ronald
1978   Ethnicity: Problem and Focus in Anthropology. *Annual Review of Anthropology 7.* Annual Reviews, Inc., Palo Alto, Calif.

Cohn, Bernard S.
1987   *An Anthropologist among the Historians and Other Essays.* Oxford University Press, New York.

Comaroff, Jean
1985   *Body of Power, Spirit of Resistance: The Culture and History of a South African People.* University of Chicago Press, Chicago.

Comaroff, John L.
1987   Of Totemism and Ethnicity: Consciousness, Practice and Signs of Inequality. *Ethnos* 52:301–323.

Cook, Sherburne F., and L. B. Simpson
1948   *The Population of Central Mexico in the Sixteenth Century.* Ibero-Americana: 31. University of California Press, Berkeley.

Dean, Jeffery S., Robert C. Euler, George J. Gummerman, Fred Plog, Robert H. Hevly, and T. N. V. Karlstrom
1985   Human Behavior, Demography, and Paleoenvironment on the Colorado Plateau. *American Antiquity* 50:537–554.

Deeds, Susan
1998   Indigenous Rebellions on the Northern Mexican Mission Frontier: From First-generation to Later Colonial Responses. In *Contested Ground: Comparative Frontiers on the Northern and Southern Edges of the Spanish Empire,* edited by D. Guy and T. Sheridan, pp. 32–51. University of Arizona Press, Tucson.

Dobyns, Harold F.
1976   *Native American Historical Demography: A Critical Bibliography.* Indiana University Press, Bloomington.

Dobyns, Harold F., W. R. Swagerty, and Newberry Library
1983   *Their Number Became Thinned: Native American Population Dynamics in Eastern North America.* University of Tennessee Press, Knoxville.

Dozier, Edward P.
1954   *The Hopi-Tewa of Arizona.* University of California Publications in American Archaeology and Ethnology 44:259–376.

1955   Forced and Permissive Acculturation. *American Indian* VII:38–44.

1962   Differing Reactions to Religious Contacts among North American Indian Societies. *Thirty-fourth International Congress of Americanists,* pp. 161–171. Akten, Wein.

Elliot, J. H.
1969   *Imperial Spain 1469–1716.* Penguin Books Ltd., London.
1989   *Spain and Its World.* Yale University Press, New Haven, Conn.

Elliott, Michael L.
1982   *Large Pueblo Sites near Jemez Springs, New Mexico.* Cultural Resources Report Number 3. U.S.D.A. Forest Service, Santa Fe.

Eriksen, Thomas Hylland
1993   *Ethnicity and Nationalism: Anthropological Perspectives.* Pluto Press, London.

Espinosa, J. Manuel (editor and translator)
1988   *The Pueblo Indian Revolt of 1696 and the Franciscan Missions in New Mexico: Letters of the Missionaries and Related Documents.* University of Oklahoma Press, Norman.

Farris, Nancy M.
1978   Nucleation versus Dispersal: The Dynamics of Population Movement in Colonial Yucatan. *Hispanic American Historical Review* 58:187–216.

1984   *Maya Society under Colonial Rule: The Collective Enterprise of Survival.* Princeton University Press, Princeton.

Ferguson, T. J., and Robert W. Preucel
n.d.   Signs of the Ancestors: An Archaeology of the Mesa Villages of the Pueblo Revolt Period. In *Structure and Meaning in Human Settlement,* edited by Tony Atkin. University of Pennsylvania Press, Philadelphia.

Folsom, Franklin
1973   *Indian Uprising on the Rio Grande: The Pueblo Revolt of 1680.* University of New Mexico Press, Albuquerque.

Forbes, Jack D.
1960   *Apache, Navaho, and Spaniard.* University of Oklahoma Press, Norman.

1963   *The Historian and the Indian: Racial Bias in American History.* Academy of American Franciscan History, Washington, D.C.

Gellner, Ernest
1983   *Nations and Nationalism.* Cornell University Press, Ithaca, New York.

Gutiérrez, Ramón A.
1991   *When Jesus Came, the Corn Mothers Went Away: Marriage, Sexuality, and Power in New Mexico, 1500–1846.* Stanford University Press, Stanford, Calif.

Hammond, George P., and Agapito Rey
1929   *Expedition into New Mexico made by Antonio de Espejo, 1582–1583, as Revealed in the Journal of Diego Pérez de Luxán, a Member of the Party.* Quivira Society, Los Angeles.

1940   *Narratives of the Coronado Expedition, 1540–1542.* University of New Mexico Press, Albuquerque.

1953   *Don Juan de Oñate, Colonizer of New Mexico, 1595–1628.* University of New Mexico Press, Albuquerque.

Hackett, Charles W., and Charmion C. Shelby (editor and translator)
1942   *Revolt of the Pueblo Indians of New Mexico and Otermin's Attempted Reconquest, 1680–1682.* University of New Mexico Press, Albuquerque.

Henige, D.
1978   On the Contact Population of Hispaniola: History as Higher Mathematics. *Hispanic American Historical Review* 58:217–237.

1986   If Pigs Could Fly: Timucan Population and Native American Historical Demography. *Journal of Interdisciplinary History* XVI:700–721.

Horowitz, Donald L.
1985   *Ethnic Groups in Conflict.* University of California Press, Berkeley.

Hurtado, A. L.

1993   Herbert E. Bolton, Racism and American History. *Pacific Historical Review* 62:127–142.

1995   Parkmanizing the Spanish Borderlands: Bolton, Turner and the Historian's World. *Western Historical Quarterly* 26:149–167.

Kamen, Henry A. F.

1991   *Spain, 1469–1714: A Society of Conflict.* Longman, London, UK.

Keen, Benjamin

1985   Main Currents in United States Writings on Colonial Spanish America, 1884–1984. *Hispanic American Historical Review* 65:657–682.

Kessell, John L., and Rick Hendricks (editors)

1992   *By Force of Arms: The Journals of Don Diego de Vargas, New Mexico, 1691–1693.* University of New Mexico Press, Albuquerque.

Kessell, John L., Rick Hendricks, and Meredith D. Dodge (editors)

1995   *To the Royal Crown Restored: The Journals of Don Diego de Vargas, New Mexico, 1692–1694.* University of New Mexico Press, Albuquerque.

1998   *Blood on the Boulders: The Journals of Don Diego de Vargas, New Mexico, 1694–97.* University of New Mexico Press, Albuquerque.

Lechtman, Heather

1977   Style in Technology: Some Early Thoughts. In *Material Culture: Style, Organization and Dynamics of Technology,* edited by H. Lechtman and R. S. Merril. pp. 3–20. West Publishing Co., New York.

Lechtman, Heather, and A. Steinberg

1979   The History of Technology: An Anthropological Point of View. In *The History and Philosophy of Technology,* edited by G. Bugliarello and D. B. Donner, pp. 21–44. University of Illinois Press, Urbana.

Lummis, Charles F.

1909   *The Spanish Pioneers.* Rio Grande Press, Chicago.

1956   *Los Conquistadores Españoles del Siglo XVI; Vindicación de la Acción Colonizadora Española en América.* Editora Latino Americana, Guatemala.

Lycett, Mark T.

1995   *Archaeological Implications of European Contact: Demography, Settlement, and Land Use in the Middle Rio Grande Valley.* Unpublished Ph.D. dissertation, Department of Anthropology, University of New Mexico, Albuquerque.

Meltzer, David J.

1979   Paradigms and the Nature of Change in American Archaeology. *American Antiquity* 44:644–657.

1983   The Antiquity of Man and the Development of American Archaeology. *Advances in Archaeological Method and Theory* 6:1–51.

Miller, R. R.

1985   *Mexico: A History.* University of Oklahoma Press, Norman.

Naylor, Thomas H., and Charles W. Polzer

1986   *The Presidio and Militia on the Northern Frontier of New Spain: A Documentary History.* University of Arizona Press, Tucson.

Ong, Aihwa

1987   *Spirits of Resistance and Capitalist Discipline: Factory Women in Malaysia.* State University of New York Press, Albany.

Ortiz, Alfonso

1969   *The Tewa World: Space, Time, Being, and Becoming in a Pueblo Society.* University of Chicago Press, Chicago.

Phelan, John L.

1980   *The Millennial Kingdom of the Franciscans in the New World: A Study of the Writings of Gerónimo de Mendieta (1525–1604).* Kraus Reprint, Millwood, New York.

Powell, Philip W.

1953   *Soldiers, Indians and Silver: The Northward Advance of Spain, 1550–1600.* University of California Press, Berkeley.

Said, Edward W.

1978   *Orientalism.* Pantheon Books, New York.

1993   *Culture and Imperialism.* Knopf, New York.

Salmon, R. M.

1991   *Indian Revolts in New Spain: A Synthesis of Resistance, 1680–1796.* University Press of America, Lanham, Maryland.

Sauer, Carl O.

1935   *Aboriginal Population of Northwestern Mexico.* Ibero-Americana: 10. University of California Press, Berkeley.

1948   *Colima of New Spain in the Sixteenth Century.* Ibero-Americana: 29. University of California Press, Berkeley.

Schneider, Jane, and Rayna Rapp

1995   *Articulating Hidden Histories: Exploring the Influence of Eric R. Wolf.* University of California Press, Berkeley.

Scott, James C.

1985   *Weapons of the Weak: Everyday Forms of Peasant Resistance.* Yale University Press, New Haven.

Simpson, L. B.

1952   *Exploitation of Land in Central Mexico in the Sixteenth Century.* Ibero-Americana: 36. University of California Press, Berkeley.

Spivak, Gayatri C., Donna Landry, and Gerald M. MacLean

1996   *The Spivak Reader: Selected Works of Gayatri Chakravorty Spivak.* Routledge, New York.

Thomas, David Hurst (editor)

1989   *Archaeological and Historical Perspectives on the Spanish Borderlands West.* Columbian Consequences Vol. 1. Smithsonian Institution Press, Washington, D.C.

Udall, Stewart L., and Jerry D. Jacka

1987   *To the Inland Empire: Coronado and Our Spanish Legacy.* Doubleday, Garden City, N.J.

Upham, Stedman

1987   The Tyranny of Ethnographic Analogy in Southwestern Archaeology. In *Coasts, Plains, and Deserts: Essays in Honor of Reynold J. Ruppé,* edited by S. W. Gaines, pp 265–281. Arizona State University, Anthropological Research Papers, No. 38, Tempe.

Weber, David J.

1988   *Myth and the History of the Hispanic Southwest: Essays.* University of New Mexico Press, Albuquerque.

1992   *The Spanish Frontier in North America.* Yale University Press, New Haven, Conn.

Weissner, Polly

1983   Style and Social Information in Kalahari San Projectile
        Points. *American Antiquity* 48:253–276.

1984   Reconsidering the Behavioral Basis for Style: A Case Study
        among the Kalahari San. *Journal of Anthropological
        Archaeology* 3:190–234.

1985   Style or Isochrestic Variation? A Reply to Sackett. *American
        Antiquity* 50:160–166.

1990   Is there a Unity to Style? In *The Uses of Style in Archaeology,*
        edited by M. W. Conkey and C. A. Hastorf, pp. 105–112.
        Cambridge University Press, Cambridge, UK.

West, Robert C.

1949   *The Mining Community in Northern New Spain: The Parral
        Mining District.* Ibero-Americana: 30. University of
        California Press, Berkeley.

Williams, Robert A., Jr.

1990   *The American Indian in Western Legal Thought: The Discourses
        of Conquest.* Oxford University Press, Oxford, UK.

Wolf, Eric R.

1982   *Europe and the People without History.* University of
        California Press, Berkeley.

Zambardino, R. A.

1980   Mexico's Population in the Sixteenth Century:
        Demographic Anomaly or Mathematical Illusion?
        Journal of Interdisciplinary History XI:1–27.

Figure 12.1. The battle sites, 1694 (map drawn by Jerry L. Livingston).

Chapter 12

Pueblo-Spanish Warfare in Seventeenth-Century New Mexico:

The Battles of Black Mesa, Kotyiti, and Astialakwa

Rick Hendricks

Introduction

It is useful to consider the confrontation between Pueblo Indians and Spaniards in late seventeenth-century New Mexico as a single, protracted struggle, the Pueblo-Spanish War (Kessell and Hendricks 1992:11–12). This war was fought in three acts: the 1680 Pueblo Revolt, the 1681 to 1691 interregnum when the adversaries were separated, and the period from 1692 to 1696 when the Spanish reconquest and second Pueblo Revolt took place. From the standpoint of military history, the 1694 campaigns against three fortified refugee villages on Black, Horn, and Guadalupe Mesas are among the most interesting engagements that took place in the Southwest in the long Spanish period (Figure 12.1). The purpose of this chapter is to examine in detail each of the four military actions that occurred at the three mesas in order to compare and contrast Pueblo and Spanish military strategy. While the focus of the narrative and analysis is on such things as battlefields, armament, and tactics, in keeping with the broad themes of this book, some attention is given to an examination of identity and agency among the combatants, as well as Pueblo resistance and Spanish response.

Spanish Soldiery, Negotiators, and Pueblo Auxiliaries

When Governor Diego de Vargas prepared to go on campaign against the rebellious Pueblos in 1694, he relied on three elements. First, he called on two fighting forces from among the Spanish population, presidial soldiers and militiamen. Second, he gathered intelligence from several sources. Third, he leaned heavily on a shifting grouping of Pueblo allies. In the Spanish world, considerable prestige attached itself to the citizen-soldier. In New Mexico, there was a clear correlation between being a prosperous settler and an officer in the local militia. Frequently, the wealthiest man in a given area would boast the title of militia captain, as did Fernando Durán y Chaves, and when he passed muster, he was invariably the best equipped man with the most spare mounts. Thus, he demonstrated his willingness to defend the province and openly displayed his wealth. At the same time, a reluctance to fight occasionally surfaced. The governor maintained lists of able-bodied men capable of serving in the militia. In time of war, a given number of men from these lists were selected to go on campaign. When Vargas prepared to move against the Jemez on Guadalupe Mesa in 1694, he issued a stern edict threatening dire consequences for failure to pass muster, as was the duty of every loyal vassal of his majesty, the King of Spain (Kessell et al. 1998:317).

By the late seventeenth century, most New Mexicans were, by modern definition, *mestizos,* the products of miscegenation in the New World over the course of several centuries. By their own reckoning, however, most were *españoles,* more of a cultural indication of Spanishness than an ethnic designation. Not a few of these Spanish New Mexicans had Pueblo relatives, especially those individuals who were captured in 1680 and lived among the Pueblos for a dozen years. Many more had relied on Pueblo servants or laborers for generations. Given the bitter experience of the Pueblo Revolt of 1680, however, when so many New Mexicans lost relatives, it is unlikely that the lack of enthusiasm for almost continual campaigning in 1694 was the result of any feeling of kinship with the Pueblos, blood lines and former relationships notwithstanding.

On a number of occasions, Vargas claimed to have recruited 100 Spanish soldiers, their recruitment and service recorded in a journal. This service record has not survived, nor has it proven possible to identify 100 soldiers recruited in 1693. It seems certain that some of the soldiers were former New Mexicans living in El Paso or elsewhere in New Spain. Soldiers also came from such places as Durango, Fresnillo, Sombrerete, Zacatecas, Cuencamé, and Parral (Colligan 1995:169–215). Very few of the men who served under Vargas were peninsular Spaniards, and of the individuals who played prominent roles in the events of 1694, only Vargas (Kessell 1989:11), Antonio de Valverde Cosío (Hendricks 1999:22:148), and Lázaro de Mizquía were from Spain (Kessell and Hendricks 1992:478 n.11). Most of the soldiers considered themselves españoles, but there were mestizos and mulattos as well.

Regardless of how they defined their ethnicity, most of the experienced soldiers had fought alongside Indian auxiliaries, so common was the practice of enlisting them as allies throughout the Spanish empire (Jones 1966:13–23). In the case of the former New Mexican soldiers and the militiamen, they were often more intimately involved with Pueblo Indians. Several of the military leaders in 1694 had grown up among Pueblos, learning their languages and customs. Sergeant Juan Ruiz de Cáceres spoke Tewa and Tano (Kessell et al. 1998:232, 234), and Captain Roque Madrid knew Towa and Keresan (Hendricks and Wilson 1996:114–115), well enough to serve as interpreters. This suggests that both had extended contact with speakers of these difficult languages. Madrid's family lived in the Galisteo Basin. Keresan-speakers from nearby San Marcos Pueblo and Towa-speaking Pecos Indians may have worked on the property.

Former captives were also sources of valuable military intelligence. Lucía, the wife of Pedro Márquez, was taken captive in 1680 and rescued from Nambe Pueblo in 1692. In 1694, she was traveling with rebel Tewas when she provided Vargas with information about the various Pueblo groups living on San Ildefonso Mesa. At the time, she stated that her brother, an Indian from Nambe, had facilitated her escape from the mesa (Kessell et al. 1998:46–47). To the extent that the documentary record accurately reflects the situation, this type of person (and Pueblo allies, especially Spanish-speaking Indians) seems to have assumed the role of negotiator and go-between, which is often ascribed to people of mixed blood. Vargas's attempt to use a *genízaro,* a person of mixed Indian blood, named Juan de la Vega, as a peace emissary to the Pueblos resulted in his death at the hands of the Navajos to whom his captors sent him (Kessell et al. 1998:47–48). Apparently, knowledge of language and custom was more important for the success of the negotiators than whether they were related to specific groups.

Vargas's success as reconqueror of New Mexico rested in no small part on the assistance he received from Pueblo allies. During the campaigns of 1694, Pecos leader Juan de Ye and Zia war captain Bartolomé de Ojeda contributed warriors to the Spanish army. In the case of Ojeda, his leadership and intelligence proved decisive. Vargas had established a fictive kinship relationship with both men, serving as *compadre,* or godparent, at the baptism of their children, which linked him to father and child. Vargas may have been aware that quasifamilial relationships were a part of the Pueblo world, but there is no doubt that his action was a contrivance he used to bind Pueblo leaders to him (Kessell 1994:33–37). Ojeda led warriors from Santa Ana, Zia, and San Felipe against Kotyiti and Guadalupe Mesa. At Kotyiti, his knowledge of the paths up the mesa and his leadership of the assault forces enabled the army to surprise and overwhelm the defenders. Although it is not specifically attributed to Ojeda, at Guadalupe Mesa the Pueblo allies informed Vargas about the trail up the back of the mesa that again made it possible to surprise and defeat the defenders.

Armament

Documentary evidence suggests that the rank and file of the Spanish cavalry wore long, sleeveless leather jackets, called *cueras,* and protective headgear (Secoy 1953:14–15). Vargas mentioned a thick leather hat as being the style worn by the Spaniards, while other soldiers record either the steel morion or a leather hat (Kessell et al. 1998:307).

Gauntlets provided protection for the hands and long boots protected the fighting man's foot and leg to the knee. This type of body armor offered adequate protection for vital areas. Vargas tended to limit description of specific wounds to those of officers. Those he recorded for the battles of 1694 under discussion were not life-threatening ones to extremities or face. In the first siege of Black Mesa, Adjutant Antonio de Valverde Cosío was hit in the face with a stone, resulting in a facial wound that scarred him for life, and Captain Lázaro de Mizquía was wounded in the shoulder. During the second siege of Black Mesa, Captain Antonio Jorge took an arrow in the fleshy part of his arm and suffered severe blood loss but survived (Kessell et al. 1998:150, 379). Even wounds that proved fatal were likely inflicted on exposed areas.

Vargas, his officers, and those soldiers and militiamen with the wherewithal probably had steel cuirasses. When he died, Vargas had eleven such cuirasses in his possession, which would have been available for purchase (Montoya 1704, f.2v). Military leaders in New Mexico in Vargas's day required horses to transport armor, but among those items that they always carried with them, was the leather jacket. They also used leather horse armor, consisting of a sort of apron hanging down to protect the animal's underbelly and flaps to protect its backside. Soldiers carried an oval shield, usually made of leather with metal studs. Hand arms included lances and *media lunas,* or hocking knives, short curved swords and sabers, and what were termed harquebuses, although the frequency of the mention of flints indicates that Vargas's soldiers used flintlocks rather than matchlocks (Kessell et al. 1998:13, 17, 126, 434, 859, 916, 947; Secoy 1953:14).

The most common firearm of Vargas's troops was a short-barreled, flintlock musket, suitable for use on horseback. A seventeenth-century smoothbore musket had a range of approximately 90 meters (Kessell and Hendricks 1992:221 n.87). The short saddle guns were very difficult to aim, and shooting up to the elevation of a mesatop involved more luck than skill (Kessell et al. 1998:160). Vargas had available two bronze cannon and a number of stone mortars with removable chambers. The artillery

he opted to take to the first siege of Black Mesa—the bronze cannon—proved wholly ineffective. There were also blunderbusses and a very few pistols, weapons effective only at close range (Kessell et al. 1998:845, 888). All of these factors taken together dictated the strategy of storming the mesatops.

Indians of the Southwest had a tradition of wearing various sorts of body armor before the arrival of the Spaniards. According to Cushing, the Pueblos wore cuirasses of elk or bison and of cotton and yucca. Melquior Díaz, who reconnoitered Pueblo country before the arrival of Coronado in 1540, reported that the Indians used shields and leather jackets. There is some question as to whether this description was of Apaches rather than Pueblos, but it shows that a Native American leather armor tradition existed prior to the arrival of the leather-jacketed soldiers (LeBlanc 1999:47; Secoy 1953:16–18).

The main offensive weapon of the Pueblos was the bow and arrow. The sinew-backed bow in use in the Southwest (LeBlanc 1999:102; Secoy 1953:18–20), however, had low penetration power, so low that the Spanish leather and metal body armor provided almost complete protection against arrows that struck them in vital areas. Documents record the use of some type of slingshot for hurling smooth river stones. Pueblo warriors became more deadly at close range when they could bring clubs to bear on their enemies. There is also evidence that they used metal-tipped lances made by an Indian blacksmith and what the Spanish called a *garabato* (Kessell and Hendricks 1992:392; Kessell et al. 1998:150), which is either a fork-headed agricultural implement or a meat hook. The tool could have been thrown like a spear or used in close-quarter combat. A meat hook swung on a rope would have been a frightening weapon to use against men trying to scale a mesa. In either case, this is an interesting adaptation of a Spanish item as a weapon. On rare occasions during the conflicts of 1694, the rebel Pueblos captured Spanish firearms and attempted to use them in battle. There is no indication that they inflicted any gunshot wounds on Spaniards or their Pueblo allies.

Supplies

A Spanish soldier in the field in New Mexico needed one sack of biscuit a month made from two bushels of wheat flour or from a half-bushel of maize and a half-bushel of pinole (toasted wheat). One cow provided sufficient jerky for one man for two months. Other items that were also considered necessary were chocolate, sugar, tobacco, and soap. Indian allies needed two bushels of cornmeal for every 100 warriors and a supply of tobacco. The Pueblo allies may also have hunted from to time to add to the larder of the army. The most serious supply problem for Vargas's army in 1694 was securing an adequate amount of gunpowder and lead.

The documents are silent about the provisions a Pueblo warrior required to keep himself in fighting shape. It can be assumed that they were accustomed to living off the land and would have had some dried foodstuffs with them when going off to battle. Doubtless, they supplemented their diet with game they hunted.

Mesatop Refuges

Native Americans in the Southwest have sited their communities atop hills since remote times. The best-known, early example of this practice dates from the period A.D. 200 to 500, when Mogollon pit houses were sited on hills (LeBlanc 1999:136). Rock shelters and cliff dwellings are also early examples of Indians occupying sites that offered defensive potential. The earliest mesatop villages in the Rio Grande Valley date to the Middle to Late Coalition period (A.D. 1250–1325); in the Pajarito District, they are particularly associated with the whole-sale population aggregation of the Classic period (A.D. 1400–1550) (Mera 1940). While there is no question that such locations were defensible, the role they played in strategic considerations regarding warfare is less certain. When Francisco Vásquez de Coronado dispatched Hernando de Alvarado to explore in 1540, he visited Acoma, which he described as "a very strange place built on solid rock" (Garcia-Mason 1979:455). He noted that it was further protected by a wall of stones that could be rolled down on any attackers so that no army would be strong enough

to capture it. Juan de Oñate's men disproved Alvarado's assertion when they overran Acoma in 1599.

The seemingly permanent relocation of pueblos to nearby mesatops among the Eastern Pueblos was probably a direct response to Spanish activities in the 1680s in the aftermath of the Pueblo Revolt, and a demonstrable act of resistance. In the late summer of 1687, New Mexico governor, Pedro Reneros de Posada, led an expedition to attempt the reconquest of the province. The Spaniards traveled upriver and attacked Santa Ana. Reneros burned the pueblo, executed four leaders, and carried off 10 captives to slavery in Nueva Vizcaya. The succeeding governor, Domingo Jironza Petrís de Cruzate, would deal the next blow. Departing on 10 August 1689, the ninth anniversary of the outbreak of the Pueblo Revolt, Jirónza led his troops to Zia Pueblo. There, on 29 August, the Spaniards attacked. According to reports, the battle lasted all day. When it was over, Zia had been burned, 600 of its defenders had perished, and 70 more were taken prisoner (Kessell and Hendricks 1992:24–26).

In September 1692, Vargas arrived at Cochiti and prepared to launch a dawn raid on the pueblo. Much to his surprise, he found it deserted. Traveling on to Santo Domingo, he found it empty as well. There he learned that the Indians from San Felipe had moved up on the mesa, the Cochiti people were on their mesa, and the people of Santa Ana and Zia were living on the Cerro Colorado. Vargas completed his ceremonial reconquest and returned to El Paso. When he returned to settle the province in the fall of the following year, he found Pueblos still living on mesas (Kessell and Hendricks 1992:382–383, 431; Kessell et al. 1995:422).

First Siege of San Ildefonso Mesa, March 4–19, 1694

Site

A basaltic extrusion, San Ildefonso Mesa (Black Mesa) rises to an elevation of about 1,760 meters. It is located north-northeast of the present-day Pueblo of San Ildefonso (Figure 12.2). According to the people of San Ildefonso, the mesa has been used as a temporary refuge and defensible site since remote times, although it was

Figure 12.2. San Ildefonso Mesa (Black Mesa) (photograph by Bill Jack Rogers, courtesy of Museum of New Mexico, No. 58260).

never inhabited for extended periods. Ruins on the mesa indicate the possibility of defensive walls that may date from the Vargas era, particularly those ruins at the otherwise unprotected mesa edge opposite the Giant's Oven, the feature at the southeast end of the mesa (Harrington 1916:294, 297, 298).

The Opposing Forces

On February 25, 1694 in Santa Fe, Governor Vargas gave orders to prepare the troops for the assault on San Ildefonso Mesa.[1] Captain Roque Madrid was to chose 80 soldiers from among the best armed men of the Santa Fe presidio. An additional 30 settlers who had weapons were to be chosen. These militiamen would join the four members of the Santa Fe *cabildo* and accompany Vargas as reinforcements. The total Spanish force at the governor's disposal numbered 115. Vargas also brought along an unspecified number of Pecos warriors as allies (Kessell et al. 1998:1:139).

In December of 1693, 140 warriors from Pecos Pueblo had arrived in Santa Fe and turned the tide of battle in favor of the Spaniards who were besieging the city, which the Tanos had occupied and fortified (Kessell et al. 1995:529). In the eighteenth century, it was common for Pueblo allies to make up 60 to 75 percent of an army in the field in New Mexico (Hendricks and Wilson 1996:3–4). Therefore, it would seem logical that there may have been as many as a hundred or more Pecos warriors with Vargas at the siege of San Ildefonso Mesa in March of 1694.

Vargas observed what seemed to him to be more than a thousand people defending the mesa. It is difficult to evaluate this statement (Espinosa 1942:171–173; Kessell et al. 1998:1:149). While it could be that Vargas literally meant what he said, it is just as likely that he was indicating a large, indefinite or exaggerated number. This latter usage was quite common in the Spanish of the day (Real Academia Española 1979:2:567). Vargas and his contemporaries in New Mexico used it in this sense frequently. Moreover, Vargas doubtless realized that he did not enjoy a numerical advantage almost as soon as he arrived at the mesa.

Regardless of their numbers, the defenders were all Tewas. In January 1694, Pedro Márquez's wife, Lucía, stated that the defenders of San Ildefonso Mesa were from the Pueblos of San Ildefonso, Tesuque, Santa Clara, Jacona, Cuyamungue, and Pojoaque. Two Tewa captives from Ciénega who had been living at Tesuque Pueblo corroborated these statements the following month. One added that he and his brothers had been on the little mesa opposite San Ildefonso Pueblo. Half of the people from Santa Clara, San Ildefonso, Jacona, Cuyamungue, and Pojoaque were on that small mesa; the other half of the people of these pueblos were on the other mesa opposite San Ildefonso Pueblo (Kessell et al. 1998:46–47, 133–134).

Spanish accounts refer to San Ildefonso Mesa as a single feature. Tewa accounts, however, report Indians on two mesas. At the southeastern edge of the mesa, there is a small domed feature that is detached from the main body of the mesa. In Tewa, this feature is called the Giant's Oven. The statement of the prisoner suggests that a physical separation of moieties, the formal divisions of Tewa pueblos for political and ceremonial purposes and for the organization of communal labor, was being observed in 1694. One set of moieties from each of the six pueblos represented would have occupied the Giant's Oven and the other set would have been on Black Mesa proper (Kessell et al. 1998:452, n.81).

Action

On February 26, 1694, the army assembled in the plaza of Santa Fe, and at about two o'clock departed, halting after a march of six leagues. At midnight, it began to rain, and the poor weather continued throughout the following day. With snow threatening, Vargas pushed on the remaining two leagues to the abandoned pueblo of San Ildefonso. Half of the company entered the pueblo, and half remained outside to cordon it off from any attempted enemy attack. Vargas dispatched Roque Madrid and a squadron of 25 men to reconnoiter along the river in the direction of Santa Clara Pueblo. The Spanish army was suffering from a lack of sufficient mounts, and

Madrid was to bring back any horses or mules he found. In the interest of gaining any information he could, Vargas also commanded Madrid to take as many prisoners as possible. After completing his mission, he was to meet the governor and the rest of the army at the base of the mesa (Kessell et al. 1998:139–170).

When Vargas and the company arrived at San Ildefonso Mesa, the Tewas crowded to the edge of the mesa and gave war cries. They shouted down that they were awaiting the arrival of their Jemez, Keres, Apache, Zuni, and Hopi allies. In response to their insults, the Spaniards fired a few shots at them. Given the well-established defensive position of the enemy and the heavy snow, the Spanish army could not advance. Madrid arrived from his reconnaissance with 70 horses and four mules. At about two or three in the afternoon, Vargas withdrew his forces to San Ildefonso Pueblo, where he established his *plaza de armas,* or field headquarters.

By Sunday, February 28, the snowfall had accumulated, preventing any action against the mesa. Vargas sent Sergeant Juan Ruiz de Cáceres on a reconnaissance mission as far as Santa Clara, with the same instructions the governor had given Captain Madrid. When he returned that afternoon, some Tewas attacked him, coming down from the mesa. Rushing to reinforce Cáceres and his men, Vargas found the Tewas and soldiers fighting on the sides of the mesa. When the Indians noticed the reinforcements on their way, they withdrew to the mesatop. The Spaniards continued shooting until evening, but their fire was ineffective because it did not reach the top of the mesa.

The bad weather persisted for the next few days. Vargas continued to send out patrols in search of horses and enemy prisoners. By March 3, the weather began to clear, and Vargas ordered everything readied for the attack. The Indians on the mesa were sending smoke signals, an indication that their allies were nearby or that they were pretending to be in contact with them. The governor was concerned about the effect this might have on his troops' morale. As the army prepared to depart, it began to rain, and the assault was delayed again.

The day dawned clear and cold on March 4, and Vargas ordered his men to prepare for immediate departure. The army soon arrived at the base of the mesa, which they found fortified and defended by an estimated 1,000 people. Apparently, additional warriors had joined the defenders on the mesa under the cover of darkness and the storm of the previous day (Kessell et al. 1998:244). At Vargas's orders, a soldier, Alonso Romero, attempted to fire an artillery piece at the front of the mesa where most of the defenders were congregated. When the cannon went off, it exploded, sending pieces of metal flying among the soldiers. Romero received a facial injury, but no one else was hurt.

Sixty men dismounted and deployed to begin a frontal assault on the mesa. Vargas then prepared a feint. Taking his *alférez* bearing the royal standard and 15 soldiers he went around to the path up the back of the mesa. This maneuver was designed to divert the enemy and cause them to spread themselves out, breaking up their concentrated defense of the principal path up the mesa. The fighting continued for five or six hours. Defenders hurled river stones with slings, threw rocks, shot arrows, and threw hooks. The attacking Spaniards managed to capture the Giant's Oven, but could not cross over to the mesa proper because the gap was protected by walls. Noting that he had 22 men wounded, including some of his ablest officers, Vargas ordered the army to retreat to San Ildefonso Pueblo. He estimated that 14 or 15 of the mesa's defenders were killed. Among the wounded soldiers were Adjutant Antonio Valverde; Sargento Mayor Antonio Jorge; and Captain Lázaro de Mizquía, who was also a member of the Santa Fe cabildo. Vargas's retreat emboldened the defenders and dampened the spirits of his own troops.

The wounds of Captain Mizquía, two militiamen, and two soldiers proved serious, and Vargas evacuated them to Santa Fe the following day, March 5, detailing 10 men to escort them and then return to the siege. He also summoned the squadron he had left guarding the horses up from reserve to consolidate his forces. Finally, the governor ordered more ammunition and provisions. In what was to prove a prophetic statement, only one day into the siege, Vargas voiced the realization that he would need a much larger force to achieve success.

On March 6, Vargas sent two officers and 30 men with 10 pack horses to Santa Clara, San Lázaro, and San Cristóbal. Their mission was to capture an Indian who could tell them where the enemy had hidden their mounts and the cattle they had stolen from the Spaniards. The soldiers were also to gather any provisions they might find and return by nightfall. At midmorning, the Indians on the mesa sent down a force of 200 to try to take some Spaniards as prisoners. They laid an ambush in a nearby barranca. One Indian came riding out on a horse, attempting to lure Spaniards into the barranca. The ruse was spoiled because Vargas and his men could see from the roofs of the house blocks in San Ildefonso Pueblo what the enemy was up to. In the resulting skirmish, the soldiers wounded several Indians. When the detail sent to Santa Clara returned, they reported finding no provisions. They had seen many tracks of Indians who had come to aid the defenders of the mesa.

The horse guard arrived on March 7. The next day, Vargas had the artillery moved to best location for firing on the mesa. Through an interpreter, the governor told the defenders on the mesa to come down and return to their pueblos. Vargas assured them he would do them no harm. In response, the Indians hurled insults, stating that their god was the devil, and he kept them well fed. Realizing he was wasting his time, Vargas reconnoitered all around the mesa, noting new fortifications. In addition to new ramparts, the defenders had raised the height of the existing structures. He set up camp on the bank of the Rio Grande on the side of the mesa and sent a squadron to Santa Clara for maize that the Indians on the mesa had stored there. With his siege headquarters now close to the mesa, Vargas set a watch of three 10-men squadrons. He directed them to guard as much area as possible to prevent the enemy from getting water. He estimated that a force of 300 men would be needed for a siege that would surround the mesa. That night, the soldiers got no sleep. The proximity to the mesa meant that they heard the enemy's shouting through the night.

At dawn on March 9, it began to rain and continued until afternoon. The sentinels remained in camp. Acting on information received from a Pecos ally, Vargas sent a 15-man squadron and 30 to 40 Pecos Indians at midnight to look for the defenders' horse herd. When the patrol returned the next afternoon, they reported that they had found no horses. During his previous reconnaissance, Vargas noted that on one side the mesa was like a wall. Believing it possible to scale that section of the mesa, he sent 15 men to the nearest pueblo for 12 strong ladders for the attack planned for the next day.

On March 11, the army crossed the Rio Grande and approached the mesa. A squadron of 20 men attacked the principal path up, which was heavily fortified. Keeping up continuous fire, they managed to kill several defenders and wound many more. Another squadron went to the side of the mesa and attempted to use the ladders to scale it. This proved impossible because the ground was steep and not sufficiently solid. The defenders countered the Spanish attack by throwing large slabs of rock, hurling stones with slings, shooting arrows, and firing some guns they had captured. After six hours of battle, Vargas realized the futility of trying to climb the mesa and ordered the men to desist. Nine Spaniards had been wounded in this second encounter. Guards manned their posts to try to prevent the defenders from coming down for water.

The next day Vargas took steps to resupply his troops, sending a patrol to Santa Clara to gather maize. Most was to be taken to Santa Fe with the wounded. When the Indians on the mesa saw the packtrain depart, they prepared to attack. Under cover of darkness, they slipped down the mesa and set upon the Spaniards. Some of the militiamen and soldiers had heard war chants. Reasoning that an attack was coming, they were alert, and the attack failed. No pursuit was possible, however, because the soldiers had run low on lead and were awaiting a supply from Santa Fe. In response to the raid of the previous night, on March 13, Vargas ordered the horses brought into the center of camp in the evening. The men were to have their weapons ready to respond to any attack. The next day Vargas again ordered a patrol to go to Santa Clara for maize in order to continue the siege. That night, some of the defenders went down to the river for water, but they were surprised and fled back up the mesa.

On March 15, some of the defenders came part of the way down the mesa. Vargas ordered an artillery piece fired at them. When it was touched off, it exploded as the other one had done. It rained all day and night of the following day, keeping the troops in camp. The rain and dark of night enabled the defenders to replenish their supply of water. Two days later, the stormy weather and darkness again made it possible for the defenders to get more water. Their success discouraged the Spaniards who realized that their siege was ineffective.

During the night of March 18, the rain fell again, and the Indians came down for water without being detected. Vargas and his officers decided that there was little to be gained by staying in the field. Moreover, Vargas was down to half a box of gunpowder and a little lead. More bad news arrived when two soldiers whom Vargas had sent to El Paso for munitions returned empty-handed. They had met a group of Jemez and Cochiti Indians and turned around. Vargas then lifted the siege and returned to Santa Fe.

Battle of the Mesa of La Cieneguilla de Cochití, April 17, 1694

Site

Eleven kilometers northwest of Cochiti Pueblo, the mesa of La Cieneguilla de Cochití (Horn Mesa, Potrero Viejo) ranges in elevation from 1,952 meters to 1,976 meters (Figure 12.3). The pueblo of Hanat Kotyiti (LA 295, LA 84) is located at the highest point of the east end of the mesa (Dougherty 1980:39). The mesa, topped by the Upper Bandelier tuff (Goff et al. 1990:Map 69), sits at the confluence of Bland and Cochiti Creeks and rises approximately 180 meters from the canyon floors (Dougherty 1980:viii). Kotyiti consists of a formal pueblo with two plazas surrounded by houseblocks and a secondary cluster of individual houses approximately 150 meters to the east of the main pueblo (Preucel 2000:10–11). The predominant vegetation is piñon and juniper. A defensive wall of piled volcanic tuff cobbles protects the principal access point on the south side of the mesa (Dougherty 1980:43).

Figure 12.3. The Mesa of La Cieneguilla de Cochití (Horn Mesa) (photograph by John L. Kessell).

The Opposing Forces

Vargas ordered Captain Roque Madrid to select 70 soldiers for the assault on the mesa of La Cieneguilla de Cochití. The addition of 20 militiamen, including three members of the cabildo of Santa Fe brought the total force under the command of Governor Vargas to 90 (Kessell et al. 1998:186). The Keresan leader from Santa Ana, Bartolomé de Ojeda, led a 100-man contingent of warriors from the Pueblos of Santa Ana, Zia, and San Felipe to assist the Spanish assault (Kessell et al. 1998:192).

In April of 1694, Vargas referred to the people occupying the mesa of La Cieneguilla de Cochití as the rebel Indians of the Keres nation. When he visited the Pueblo of Kotyiti on the mesa in October of 1692, he noted that individuals from three pueblos were living there, Cochití, San Marcos, and San Felipe. Two years later, the people from Cochiti and San Marcos were still concentrated on the mesa. After the battle in 1694, an

Indian from San Marcos informed Vargas that the people from his pueblo occupied a house block on the second plaza of Kotyiti (Kessell et al. 1998:199–200). He informed Vargas that the Cochiti were led by El Zepe and that he had put to death Cristóbal, the leader of the people from San Marcos, and his brother, Zue. San Felipe, however, had switched allegiance. It sent a war captain and an unspecified number of warriors to aid the Spaniards (Kessell et al. 1998:204). According to the statements of some of the Keresan allies, the people on the mesa were allied with hostile Jemez, Apaches, and Tewas (Kessell et al. 1998:185). Juan Griego, a San Juan war captain, was killed in the counterattack of April 20 (Kessell et al. 1998:206). Vargas provided no estimate of the number of fighting men he faced on the mesa. In the aftermath of the battle, he accounted for only 363 people, seven who died in battle, one who was burned in his house, 13 captured warriors who were subsequently executed, and

342 noncombatants, presumably women, children, and the elderly (Kessell et al. 1998:193).

Action

On April 12, Vargas noted that Indians from Zia, Santa Ana, and San Felipe had sought his assistance against the Keres on the mesa of Cochiti and their allies the Tewas, Jemez, and Apaches. He therefore ordered his forces readied. The following day the troops left Santa Fe for Cochiti. After a two-day march, the army arrived in San Felipe Pueblo, which was to be the staging area and rendezvous point for the combined forces. There, warriors from Santa Ana and Zia joined those of San Felipe to form the auxiliaries who would fight under the command of Bartolomé de Ojeda (Kessell et al. 1998:185–196).

The army departed San Felipe in the afternoon of March 16, traveling some 15 leagues until almost midnight to be in position for a dawn attack. Vargas halted just beyond the sight of the Indian sentinels whom the Spaniards could see in the light of the fires burning atop the mesa. The moon rose at two o'clock in the morning, and the assault began.

Relying on Ojeda for information about the ways up the mesa, Vargas divided his forces into three main columns. Ojeda knew that the easiest way up was on the southwest side of the mesa where the Cochiti people took their cattle and horses up and down. He led the largest contingent, consisting of 40 Spaniards, under the command of two captains, and 100 Pueblo allies up this trail. Another way up provided access to the funnel canyon and spring. Vargas dispatched 10 men to attack up this path. The main way was straight up and well defended. Captain Roque Madrid led the attack up the main path, but this frontal attack was something of a diversion. He probably only had 20 or 25 men at this point of attack. The plan was for the largest force to catch the defenders unaware from behind. Vargas and an unspecified number of men remained in reserve to guard the horses. Their task was to fight any Indians who tried to escape down the mesa.

The three-pronged attack achieved complete surprise.

The defenders resisted Madrid's repeated charges, but the two captains and Indian allies overwhelmed the defenders, many of whom broke and ran, escaping as best they could. The allied army captured the plaza and pueblo and seized 342 noncombatants and 13 warriors. The latter were absolved and shot. Eight others died in the battle. The Pueblo allies plundered the pueblo and set it on fire. They also carried off unbranded livestock. More than 900 head of sheep and goats were taken. Four hundred were returned to their Spanish owners. Four days after the battle, the warriors staged a bold raid on their captured pueblo. They took the Spaniards and their allies by surprise and managed to free half of their women and children (Kessell et al. 1998:206).

Battle of Guadalupe Mesa, July 24, 1694

Site

The Pueblo of Astialakwa (LA 1825) is located atop Guadalupe Mesa (San Diego Mesa) (Figure 12.4). The elevation of Guadalupe Mesa, which is also capped by the Upper Bandelier tuff, varies from 2,000 to 2,092 meters, with the pueblo sited at about 2,048 meters on a barely noticeable slope (Dougherty 1980:vii, 17). Spanish documents refer to the upper mesa as the *peñol* and to the lower shelf as the mesa, a useful distinction retained herein. The peñol towers 335 meters above the floor of the surrounding valley. The predominant vegetation is piñón, juniper, and several species of *opuntia*. Several intermittent drainages cut across the mesatop, areas of which are cultivable (Elliot 1982:39). Located on the lower mesa or shelf below Guadalupe Mesa was another pueblo called Patokwa (LA 96).

Astialakwa consists of several 1- to 10-room houseblocks. Of particular interest to this discussion is archaeological evidence of defensive fortifications constructed all around Guadalupe Mesa where it is possible to gain access to mesatop. These walls were built by piling up volcanic tuff cobbles and boulders. Piles of river stones suitable in size for use as thrown projectiles are found at the north and south ends of the peñol (Dougherty 1980:19).

Figure 12.4. Guadalupe Mesa (photograph by John L. Kessell).

The Opposing Forces

On July 20, Vargas informed the captain of the presidial company that all of his men, except for the squadron detailed to guard the gates and those who were ill, were to prepare to go on campaign (Kessell et al. 1998:317). Writing in 1778, Fray Silvestre Vélez de Escalante, who had access to documents that have not survived, indicated that Vargas led 120 soldiers and some Indian allies to attack Astialakwa (Vélez de Escalante 1778:Cuaderno 5, Fol. 52r; Jones 1966:51). Since the full complement of the presidial company was only 100, Father Vélez de Escalante must have included the militia in this figure. Vargas had ordered the militia officers to notify all the militiamen on their lists that they were to prepare to go on campaign. From those settlers, he selected 30 men. Therefore, there were 90 presidial soldiers on the campaign.

As he had at La Cieneguilla, Bartolomé de Ojeda led a combined force of Keresan allies consisting of warriors from the Pueblos of San Felipe, Santa Ana, and Zia. The number of Pueblo auxiliaries is not specified, but if it was similar to other campaigns, it would have been around a hundred fighting men (Kessell et al. 1998:322–323).

As for the defenders on the peñol, Spanish reports after the battle indicated that there were some 430 people. One of the captives executed was a Jemez and the other was identified as Apache. He was among other people of his tribe on the mesa. Elsewhere, the Spaniards stated that the Navajo Apaches were allied with the Jemez (Kessell et al. 1998:320, 325), which makes the identities of the executed captive and his brethren uncertain. The Keres of Cochiti were also noted as allies; although there is no evidence they had a presence on Guadalupe. In August, the Spaniards learned that 72 men and women had escaped at the time of the attack on the mesa

(Espinosa 1942:203). Two days after the battle, Vargas's men captured a war captain from Santo Domingo. He had leaped off the peñol during the battle, badly injuring himself. His presence suggests that there was a military alliance between the Jemez and Santo Domingo (Kessell et al. 1998:332).

Action

On July 21, Vargas and his army departed to carry his offensive against the enemy occupying the peñol at Jemez. In the evening following, the troops arrived at Zia Pueblo, where the allies from San Felipe, Santa Ana, and Zia were gathered. A great storm shrouded the peñol and the attackers' movements as they prepared for battle. The Pueblo allies mentioned that there was a trail at the back of the peñol where the defenders had moved, leaving their pueblo on the lower mesa. The Indian allies believed that they could climb the peñol without being seen. Vargas sent 25 soldiers under the command of Eusebio de Vargas to go with them. The rest of the soldiers and the few allies from San Felipe would take the path the Jemez people used to go to their milpas and the pueblo on the lower mesa (Kessell et al. 1998:320–327).

At one o'clock in the morning of July 24, Vargas divided his forces, Eusebio de Vargas departing with his men. Governor Vargas and the rest of the company waited by a hill beside the abandoned pueblo of Patokwa, out of view of the defenders on the peñol, until the morning star came out. Changing to fresh mounts, at dawn Vargas led the troops on the path up the mesa to the peñol, remaining on the slope with the royal standard, a militia captain, and four men, while the vanguard continued up the mesa using the Guadalupe Canyon approach. The men rode as far up the slope as they could and dismounted, meeting resistance.

By that time, the rear attack up San Diego Gorge on the east had put men on the peñol and both attacks were defended. Most defenders barricaded themselves in the pueblo, some fled. Fifty-five were killed in the pueblo. The rear attack killed 12 to 15. By noon, the battle was well over. A total of 84 Jemez defenders were killed.

Seventy died in battle, five were burned in their houses, seven leaped off the mesa to their deaths, and two were executed. There were 361 noncombatants of all ages. The Spaniards took away 172 sheep and goats and some horses. Mopping up operations lasted until four o'clock, when the last of the defenders holed up in their houses were killed.

Second Siege of San Ildefonso Mesa, September 4–9, 1694
The Opposing Forces

Vargas departed Santa Fe for Black Mesa to complete his subjugation of the Tewa rebels on September 4. He stated that he was taking the presidial and the militia companies, and approximately 150 allies from Santa Ana, San Felipe, Zia, Pecos, and Jemez and all available soldiers (Kessell et al. 1998:378). If the presidial company was at full strength, he had a hundred soldiers under his command. The statement regarding the militia company is more difficult to assess. No complete muster of militiamen for this period is known to have survived. More than a decade later, in April 1705, Governor Francisco Cuervo y Valdés ordered a muster of able-bodied men who were capable of bearing arms. Musters took place in Santa Fe, Bernalillo, and Santa Cruz de la Cañada. One hundred ninety-four men turned out, but just over half were suitably equipped for war (Hendricks and Wilson 1996:2). On the previous campaigns against the fortified mesas, Vargas took from 20 to 40 militiamen with him. There is no reason to believe that the militia component of his army was much higher in this instance.

Remarkably, given the importance Vargas attached to the battle for San Ildefonso Mesa, he never commented on the strength of the enemy. He was aware that the Indians living on the mesas represented nine pueblos. There were people from seven Tewa pueblos, Tesuque, Cuyamungue, Nambe, Pojoaque, Jacona, San Ildefonso, and Santa Clara, as well as the two Tano pueblos of San Lázaro, and San Cristóbal (Kessell et al. 1998:232, 235). Although it is impossible to calculate accurately how many people from these pueblos were living on the mesa, there could have been as many as 2,000 individuals, of whom several hundred could have been warriors.

Action

At seven o'clock in the morning of September 4, Vargas and his combined army of soldiers, militiamen, and Pueblo allies departed from Santa Fe. By two o'clock, they arrived within sight of the mesa of San Ildefonso. The men changed mounts and rode on to engage the defenders. Dismounting to lift the spirits of the Pueblo allies, the Spaniards pressed the attack. The skirmishing lasted three to four hours, with the defenders holding the attackers off by throwing rocks and large stone slabs and by shooting arrows. Antonio Jorge received a serious arrow wound to the arm, causing him to lose a lot of blood. Another 10 attackers also suffered wounds. To care for the wounded, Vargas moved his troops to the west end of the mesa (Kessell et al. 1998:378–389).

After a brief respite, at seven o'clock in the evening, 100 of the Pueblo allies, three soldiers, a muleteer, and a militiaman climbed the side of the mesa. Seeing this group separated from the main body of the army, the defenders launched a swift and vigorous attack that drove the allies away, leaving the Spaniards undefended. One soldier and the militiaman were killed, and the other two soldiers were wounded in the action.

The next day, Vargas sent the wounded to Santa Fe under a militia escort. He also summoned from the capital his lieutenant who was to assist him in directing the campaign. The governor then imposed siege discipline on the soldiers, militiamen, and Pueblo allies. No one was to leave his post until he was replaced. In the event a soldier came under attack, he was to be aided. The sounds of shots or a verbal warning were to suffice as a call for assistance. If the troops found themselves in a place that was difficult to defend, they were to withdraw to a more favorable position.

Vargas then sent a squadron to gather maize from the defenders' milpas and bring it within their view. Later in the day, the defenders of the mesa again attacked the Pueblo allies whom the soldiers assisted. Two of the attackers were slain. In the aftermath of the attack, Vargas tightened security, forming a patrol consisting of his officers, three members of the Santa Fe cabildo, two militiamen, and an 11-man squadron to inspect the siege camp. He set the three watches that were to last for the duration of the siege to ensure its success by forcing the Indians to come down from the mesa or attack in desperation resulting from a lack of food and water.

On September 6, the squadron dispatched the previous day returned with their pack mules heavily laden with ears of corn the soldiers had pulled in the milpas in plain view of the defenders on the mesa. The following morning at nine o'clock, they attacked the Spanish sentries. At the sound of gunfire, the rest of the army went out to assist them. In the hour-long skirmish that ensued, six of the defenders of the mesa were killed and many were wounded. When they retreated to the mesa, the Spaniards counterattacked, wounding many more. After the battle, the Pueblo allies began to sing and dance to celebrate their victory, which in Vargas's eyes, frightened the defenders. The governor then doubled the guard so that from the mesa, the defenders could clearly see that they could not go down to gather maize from their milpas or to get water from the river.

At seven in the morning of September 8, a Tewa captain came down from the mesa and told Domingo de Herrera, who spoke Tewa and Tano, that they wanted to make peace. Vargas sent the Tewa back with unconditional demands for the defenders to come down from the mesa. At two o'clock in the afternoon, Vargas went to the slope of the mesa to meet with the war captains and governor. Vargas showed them a banner with the image or Our Lady of Remedies and offered the defenders a pardon. They gave him gifts of buffalo hides, buckskins, and elk hides. The governor told them to come down the next day to talk, but he did not lift the siege; rather he ordered extra vigilance.

The following morning the defenders' captains came down from the mesa and told Vargas that they would spend the winter on the mesa and then come down. There was much work to be done to repair their pueblos. Vargas calmly told them that he could not lift the siege until they came down and went to their pueblos. They could do the needed repairs little by little. The defenders departed. Several hours later, they returned to say that they would remain on the mesa for two weeks. Vargas countered with an offer of one week. The Tewa captain, Domingo, as well as the captains from Nambe and Cuyamungue said they would come down to prepare the pueblos. In their presence, Vargas then ordered the siege lifted. Immediately, the company prepared to return to Santa Fe, and many of the defenders came down from the mesa. They handed over four harquebuses that they captured on September 5. Vargas informed the captains that they were to come to Santa Fe where he would appoint governors and give them the canes of office.

Spanish Strategy

Before every engagement, the Franciscan chaplain prepared the Spaniards for the possibility of death by granting them absolution. Vargas also called on the Virgin of Remedies to watch over them. Considering the space devoted to recording it, such spiritual preparation was evidently an important part of overall strategy. Another basic tenet of Spanish strategy in seventeenth-century New Mexico was divide and conquer. From the outset, Vargas used traditional rivalries among Pueblos, such as that existing between the Towas of Pecos and the Keres of Kotyiti to great advantage. To the extent possible, he also relied on Pueblo auxiliaries to put as many men in the field as possible, trying to add numerical superiority (or at least diminish inferiority) to the considerable technological advantage of firearms. As it turned out, the Spaniards also enjoyed a tactical advantage when it came to confronting a foe on a mesatop.

Vargas's preparations and execution of maneuvers at the first siege of Black Mesa indicate his knowledge of poliocetics, the art of conducting (and resisting) sieges, and his familiarity with classic Iberian siege warfare of the *Reconquista* (Rogers 1992:5, 70, 74–75). From the Middle Ages, the goal of an attacking army was to capture the enemy's fortified places (Parker 1988:7). To the Spanish

soldier, a mesatop was a citadel, a stone fortress defended from behind ramparts and the object of attack. The description of the fighting of Coronado's troops and the Hopi at Hawikuh indicate that the Indians were defending their fortified pueblo in a conventional, European manner. Vargas's experience, however, was quite different. If removal of a pueblo to a mesatop offered protection against the type of destruction that Reneros and Jirónza wreaked, it also confined the defenders, limiting their ability to maneuver. The Apaches, and the Chichimecas before them, had proven that the most effective way to fight the Spaniards was in the open. Hunkering behind the walls atop a mesa was playing into the hands of soldiers who knew the method of assaulting a fortress and had the technology to carry it out successfully, especially with the local knowledge their Pueblo allies supplied.

Vargas attempted to open his attack with cannon fire, designed to strike fear into the hearts of the defenders and soften up the defensives. Unfortunately for Vargas, his cannon exploded. The army then deployed to make a frontal assault, the usual method of attacking a fortress, and Vargas prepared a feint to force the defenders to spread out and weaken their defensive effort. Unable to take the mesa by force, Vargas resolved to conduct a formal siege, clearly locked in his European mindset. Obviously, mobile siege towers and sapping were inappropriate for assaulting a mesa, but he did attempt to scale the mesa with ladders.[2] Silly as it seems today, he was doubtless aware that ladders and artillery had combined to defeat bastions in Spain. He also tried cannon fire again, but the second piece exploded, as had the other one. A number of factors doomed his effort to failure. First, the Spanish army did not have sufficient troops to prevent the defenders from coming down for water. Second, there was not enough gunpowder and lead to keep up steady fire for an extended period. Third, rain and snow made it impossible to discharge firearms. Fourth, the Spaniards took an unacceptably high number of casualties, especially to officers.

In his next engagement, at Kotyiti, Vargas employed a different strategy. Taking advantage of the element of surprise, the combined army attacked at dawn, having moved into position under cover of darkness. Night marches were standard Spanish military practice in the New World. Based on long experience fighting Indians, Spaniards were aware of their reluctance to fight at night (Hendricks and Wilson 1996:142 n.12). Vargas routinely led his army on forced marches all through the night to gain superior position against the enemy. At Kotyiti, Vargas also relied on the intelligence from Ojeda and divided his army into three main columns. A surprise attack from the rear and up a path used for getting water was facilitated by a feigned frontal assault and led to a swift victory.

At Astialakwa, Vargas stuck with this winning formula. He conducted his preparations for the attack under the cover of darkness and a storm. Basing his plans on intelligence the Pueblo allies provided, he divided his forces, sending troops up the back of the mesa and charging up the main path as well. As at Kotyiti, the triumph was swift, although it was much bloodier.

For the return engagement at San Ildefonso Mesa, Vargas took with him every available man. He had noted during the first siege that he lacked sufficient personnel to prevent the defenders from coming down for water. The second move against the rebels took place when their crops were still in the field, although ready for harvest. The larger force was able to keep an effective siege in place, and tight control of the lines was maintained. The army made no attempt to storm the mesa; rather squadrons made sorties to skirmish and counterattacked when the rebels moved against them. After one such encounter, which ended badly for the defenders, the Pueblo allies held a dance to celebrate their victory. Another wrinkle in the Spanish strategy had an element of psychological warfare as well as a practical end, the gathering of the defenders' maize from their fields. These two actions clearly angered and demoralized the Indians on the mesa. The following day they sent emissaries to Vargas and sued for peace.

Pueblo Strategy

Before battle, Indian warriors made their individual spiritual preparations. Their prayers over their weapons prepared them for the coming struggle. Another aspect of religious involvement in warfare may have been priestly control of weather through rituals. The freezing rain and snow that hindered the Spaniards' ability to fight at the first battle for Black Mesa may have been interpreted by Pueblo warriors as evidence of the efficacy of such practices. Archaeological evidence for rainmaking rituals is known from Kotyiti (Preucel 2000:14–15).

Warriors also had more mundane concerns. As did their Spanish foe, Pueblos recognized the power in numbers. Strategic alliances against the enemy were noticeable during the battles for the three mesas. Still, cultural factors may have prevented the various pueblos from forming a cohesive fighting force. Although there is considerable evidence of group maneuvers among Southwestern Indian warriors, such as envelopments, and hierarchical organization into squadrons commanded and coordinated by war captains (Lange 1990:281; LeBlanc 1999:49–51), Indians throughout the Americas displayed a tendency to fight as individuals. Such activities as taking scalps and counting coup were principally activities aimed at enhancing the reputation of the individual warrior. In the Southwest, the use of elaborately decorated, oversize shields may be indicative of the existence of warriors of great renown (LeBlanc 1999:110–111). The presence of warriors and war captains from many pueblos may have presented insurmountable organizational difficulties The archaeological records hints at this lack of cohesiveness in the existence of separate abodes, such as the formal pueblo and haphazard structures at Kotyiti (Preucel 2000:10–13).

The evidence also suggests that Pueblos did not conceive of defense in the same sense as the Spaniards. Piled river stone along the mesa rim is an indication of defensive measures, as are stone walls at vulnerable places. A defensive war, however, implied going on the offensive to prevent the enemy from reaching the pueblo, which would expose the elderly, women, and children to risk. Protection of noncombatants may well have been the primary reason for relocating to the mesatop.

For the warrior, the mesa was a base to return to and

defend if necessary, but war was waged primarily on the offensive. The series of engagements at the mesas demonstrate the basics of Pueblo strategy very clearly: war was carried to the enemy. The Pueblos employed four principal tactics. First, they laid ambushes. The best description of this tactic is of the unsuccessful ambush at the first siege of San Ildefonso Mesa. This elaborate maneuver involved an attempt to lure the Spaniards into a trap in a barranca. Had it not been spotted from the roofs of the pueblo, it might have succeeded to deadly effect. Second, the defenders launched numerous surprise attacks, rushing down the mesa to fall on the unsuspecting Spanish army. At the second siege of San Ildefonso Mesa, the defenders surprised a body of Pueblo allies and Spaniards that was separated from the rest of the army, killing and wounding several men. It seems likely that since these were the only recorded fatalities of the combined army on these campaigns, that they were killed in close combat where the Indians were much more effective. Third, the Pueblos also employed elements of psychological warfare. It was not uncommon for them to send up what the Spaniards considered war cries all through the night. This activity was extremely unnerving and deprived the Spaniards of sleep. The use of smoke signals was also troubling, because it seem to indicate that the defenders on the mesa were communicating with their nearby allies. Fourth, the practice was apparently for the surviving warriors to run away when the tide of battle turned against them, presumably living to fight another day.

Conclusions

Despite the wealth of detail the documentary record contains, a two-part question remains about the strictly military aspects of the campaigns against the mesas. The most obvious is that, since as battles go, these encounters produced remarkably few casualties, why was the loss of life among the defenders so low and yet the defeat so definitive? At the first battle of San Ildefonso Mesa, no more than 20 defenders perished, and an unspecified number were wounded; 31 attackers were wounded. At Kotyiti, Vargas amazingly recorded no casualties for his army, and only 13 defenders died, all of whom were executed. Captured were 342 noncombatants, and days after the battle, returning warriors freed half of them. Only at Guadalupe Mesa were casualties relatively high, 84 defenders killed and 361 noncombatants captured. Seventy-two men and women managed to escape. No one in the attacking army is known to have been harmed. At the second siege of San Ildefonso Mesa, eight defenders died and many were wounded. One soldier and one militiaman were slain, and two soldiers were wounded. Relative to the number of noncombatants, which in the Spanish way of reckoning included elderly, women, and children, it appears that either not all the warriors were defending the mesas or most of them escaped during the course of the battles.

The second part of the question is why was the loss of the mesas so definitive, particularly if most of the warriors had escaped. Several answers suggest themselves. The most practical consideration was that even if the warriors remained free, many of their family members were taken captive. In the event, however, these were offered a pardon on the condition that they return to live in their former pueblos. Another answer is that the loss of the mesas was probably powerfully symbolic. Fortified mesatops were virtually impregnable to attack by stone age weaponry. Unless overwhelmed by sheer numbers, the tradition of seeking temporary refuge (as reported at San Ildefonso and presumably practiced elsewhere), was highly effective and provided security until the danger passed. The congruence of technologically advanced weaponry, tactical superiority, and vital intelligence on the part of the combined Spanish-Pueblo auxiliary army led to the loss of these heretofore safe havens. Whatever the case, the Spanish victory at San Ildefonso in September 1694 concluded the long campaign against the mesas. By the end of the year, the reconquest of New Mexico was complete. The defeated Indians began to return to their former pueblos, abandoning their mesatop refuges. In June 1696, however, many Pueblos reoccupied the sites of their destroyed refuges for a final time as the Pueblo-Spanish moved into its final phase with the outbreak of the second Pueblo Revolt.

Notes

1. Espinosa, Jones, and Forbes provide useful narratives of the campaigns, the first at some length, and the latter two briefly (Espinosa 1942: 168–173, 178–181, 199–201, 204–208; Forbes 1960:253–258; Jones 1966:48–53). While there is general agreement on the basic facts, they differ in some particulars from the reading of the documentary record contained in the volumes of the Vargas Project. In the interest of presenting as accurate a representation of the fine details of these engagements, and as an author of the Vargas series, I have relied on our translations.

2. It is worth noting in this context that Vargas expected to tunnel through the walls of Santa Fe, when he planned his 1693 assault on the town the Tewas and Tanos had fortified (Kessell and Hendricks 1992:87–88).

References Cited

Colligan, John B.

1995   Vargas's 1693 Recruits for the Resettlement of New Mexico. *Genealogical Journal, Society of Hispanic Historical and Ancestral Research* 2:169–215.

Dougherty, Judith D.

1980   *Refugee Pueblos on the Santa Fe National Forest.* Cultural Resources Report 2. Santa Fe National Forest, Santa Fe.

Elliot, Michael L.

1982   *Large Pueblo Sites near Jemez Springs, New Mexico.* Cultural Resources Report 3, Santa Fe National Forest, Santa Fe.

Espinosa, J. Manuel

1942   *Crusaders of the Río Grande: The Story of Don Diego de Vargas and the Reconquest and Refounding of New Mexico.* Institute of Jesuit History, Chicago.

Forbes, Jack D.

1960   *Apache, Navaho, and Spaniard.* University of Oklahoma Press, Norman.

Garcia-Mason, Velma

1979   Acoma Pueblo. In *Handbook of North American Indians, Vol. 9,* edited by A. Ortiz, pp. 450–466. Smithsonian Institution, Washington, D.C.

Goff, Fraser, Jamie N. Gardner, and Greg Valentine

1990   *Geologic Map 69.* New Mexico Bureau of Mines and Mineral Resources, Socorro.

Harrington, John P.

1916   *The Ethnogeography of the Tewa Indians.* Twenty-ninth Annual Report of the Bureau of American Ethnology, Government Printing Office, Washington, D.C.

Hendricks, Rick

1999   Antonio de Valverde Cosío. In *American National Biography,* edited by John A. Garraty and Mark C. Carnes. 24 Vols. Oxford University Press, New York.

Hendricks, Rick, and John P. Wilson (editors)

1996   *The Navajos in 1705: Roque Madrid's Campaign Journal.* University of New Mexico Press, Albuquerque.

Jones, Oakah L., Jr.

1966   *Pueblo Warriors and Spanish Conquest.* University of Oklahoma Press, Norman.

Kessell, John L.

1994   The Ways and Words of the Other: Diego de Vargas and Cultural Brokers in Late Seventeenth-Century New Mexico. In *Between Indian and White Worlds: The Cultural Broker,* edited by M. C. Szasz, pp. 25–43. University of Oklahoma Press, Norman.

Kessell, John L. (editor)

1989   *Remote Beyond Compare: Letters of don Diego de Vargas to His Family from New Spain and New Mexico, 1675–1706.* University of New Mexico Press, Albuquerque.

Kessell, John L., and Rick Hendricks (editors)

1992   *By Force of Arms: The Journals of don Diego de Vargas, New Mexico, 1691–1693.* University of New Mexico Press, Albuquerque.

Kessell, John L., Rick Hendricks, and Meredith D. Dodge (editors)

1995   *To the Royal Crown Restored: The Journals of don Diego de Vargas, New Mexico, 1692–1694.* University of New Mexico Press, Albuquerque.

1998   *Blood on the Boulders: The Journals of don Diego de Vargas, New Mexico, 1694–97.* 2 Vols. University of New Mexico Press, Albuquerque.

Lange, Charles H.

1990   *Cochiti: A New Mexico Pueblo, Past and Present.* University of New Mexico Press, Albuquerque.

LeBlanc, Steven A.

1999   *Prehistoric Warfare in the American Southwest.* University of Utah Press, Salt Lake City.

Mera, H. P.

1940   *Population Changes in the Rio Grande Glaze-Paint Area.* Laboratory of Anthropology Technical Series Bulletin, No. 9, Santa Fe.

Montoya, Antonio

1704   Inventory of Estate of Diego de Vargas, Spanish Archives of New Mexico II:100, 20 April, Santa Fe, New Mexico State Records Center and Archive, Santa Fe.

Parker, Geoffrey

1988   *The Military Revolution: Military Innovation and the Rise of the West, 1500–1800.* Cambridge University Press, Cambridge, UK.

Preucel, Robert W.

2000   Living on the Mesa: Hanat Kotyiti: A Post-Revolt Cochiti Community in Northern New Mexico. *Expedition: The Magazine of the University of Pennsylvania Museum of Archaeology and Anthropology* 42(2):8–17.

Real Academia Española

1979   *Diccionario de autoridades.* 3 Vols. Editorial Gredos, Madrid, Spain.

Rogers, Randall

1992   *Latin Siege Warfare in the Twelfth Century.* Clarendon Press, Oxford, UK.

Secoy, Frank Raymond

1953   *Changing Military Patterns on the Great Plains, 17th Century through Early 19th Century.* Monograph of the American Ethnological Society 21. J. Augustin, Locust Valley, New York.

Vélez de Escalante, Fray Silvestre

1778   Extracto de Noticias. Typescript by Eleanor B. Adams of Biblioteca Nacional de México, document 3:2, Center for Southwest Research, University of New Mexico Library, Albuquerque. Typescript in author's possession.

Chapter 13

Pueblo and Apachean Alliance Formation in the Seventeenth Century

Curtis F. Schaafsma

Introduction

First of all, I am an archaeologist, not a historian. For me, the bottom line evidence for sustaining any interpretation is the empirical archaeological record set in a landscape we can relate to modern U.S.G.S. maps; historical documents are important, but they are not the primary evidence. Nonetheless, for exploring topics such as alliance formation between Apaches and anti-Spanish Pueblos, they are essential. It is only through historical sources that we can address such matters.

I became interested in Apaches around the Rio Grande Pueblos when I found a series of little rock houses in the Piedra Lumbre Valley along the Chama River above Abiquiu, New Mexico on an archaeological survey of Abiquiu Reservoir in October, 1974. Subsequently, I called them and the related archaeological complex, the Piedra Lumbre phase (Schaafsma 1979). The question of "who lived in these little houses" immediately arose. A brief review of the literature in 1974 located a map produced by James J. Hester (1962:Figure 25), which indicated that between about 1600 and 1700 the Navajos lived in the Piedra Lumbre Valley. Therefore, my 1974 interpretation was these houses were built and lived in by the seventeenth-century Navajos, who at that time were called the "Apaches

de Navajo." Currently I am preparing a book called *Apaches de Navajo* that details my evidence for this interpretation (Schaafsma 2002).

My forays into the historical literature were precipitated by the need to evaluate my interpretation that the Piedra Lumbre phase originated with the "Apaches de Navajo" during the seventeenth and early eighteenth centuries (Schaafsma 1974, 1976, 1978, 1981, 1992, 1996). It soon became obvious that one has to avoid those interpretations in the literature that are often based on secondary or tertiary sources and deal as much as possible with the original documents. For a non-historian, certainly not versed in reading hand-written Spanish documents, this poses substantial problems.

While going through some of the available translated and published Spanish documents bearing on the question of Apaches de Navajo living in the Piedra Lumbre Valley, it became clear that there was evidence that Apaches in general in the Rio Grande Valley during the seventeenth and early eighteenth centuries were often in collusion and conspiracy with the Pueblos against the Spaniards and that this topic should be explored. This finding challenges Benavides's view that the Pueblos were in continuous warfare with the Apaches. It also provides a cautionary note on the arguments for conspiracy and intra-village factionalism previously advanced by David Brugge, Al Schroeder, and James Ivey.

Documentary Evidence

It is essential to say something about the availability of documents and the popular notion that other than Benavides there is not much to go on before the 1680 Revolt. This notion may well have begun with historians in the 1920s. For example, in 1928 Lansing B. Bloom said: "Those who are familiar with early Spanish history in the Southwest know how meager is the information which we have as to actual events and conditions in New Mexico during the century which preceded the Pueblo Rebellion of 1680. This is due, of course, to the fact that in that uprising all the government archives in Santa Fe up to that time were completely destroyed" (1928:357). It turns out that in a footnote on the same page, Bloom (1928:357) said that this lack was largely being met by the documentary materials from Spanish archives then being edited by Charles W. Hackett (subsequently published in 1937 [Hackett 1937]), by the "mass of material for this period" secured by France Scholes and by Bloom's own work in Spain (Bloom 1928:357). Scholes in the same volume published a list of the manuscripts he had secured in Mexico City (Scholes 1928:301–323), many of which he later summarized, translated or transcribed in articles in the *New Mexico Historical Review* (Scholes 1936, 1937). This older material together with the new publications of documents for the 1690s (Espinosa 1988; Kessell and Hendricks 1992; Kessell et al. 1995, 1998), make the volume of documentary material potentially available for the seventeenth century almost overwhelming. In other words, even by 1928 Bloom's summation no longer was the case. As historians are well aware, many of the documents survived, often as copies, in Mexico City (Scholes 1928) and in Spain (Hackett 1937).

From at least the September 1598 assignment of the Spanish missionaries to the various Pueblos (Hammond and Rey 1953:345–347) until the August 1680 Pueblo Revolt a wide array of Spanish documents demonstrate

the validity of Benavides's 1634 statement that "the Apaches surround the above mentioned nations [the Pueblos] on all sides" (Hodge, et al. 1945:81). Benavides treated them all as "the great Apache nation" (Forrestal and Lynch 1954:41), as did many other Spaniards during the seventeenth century, who simply called them "Apaches." Benavides described several groups of Apaches by such names as "Apaches del Perillo," "Xila Apaches," "Apaches de Navajò," "Vaquero Apaches," and "Apaches de Quinia" (Ayer 1916; Forrestal and Lynch 1954; Hodge et al. 1945). European mapmakers read Benavides and his account was depicted on maps throughout the seventeenth century (Figure 13.1). Benavides maintained that the Pueblos "have continuous wars" with the Apaches (Hodge et al. 1945:81).

Benavides said all of these Apache groups spoke the same language: "Since they constitute a single nation, they all speak the same language, yet they are so scattered that it varies somewhat in a number of the villages, but not to the extent that they cannot easily understand one another" (Forrestal and Lynch 1954:42). Linguists today are in basic agreement with Benavides regarding the linguistic uniformity of the Apaches surrounding the Rio Grande Pueblos in the early seventeenth century (Foster 1996; Young 1983:393–394).

Many scholars have implicitly followed the lead of Benavides in thinking the relationship between Pueblos and Apaches was uniformly adversarial and they were continuously at war with each other. However, a closer look at the documents indicates that at least some of the time Apaches and anti-Spanish Pueblo people formed alliances against the Spaniards.

Several scholars have advanced the conspiracy interpretation in the past (Brugge 1969; Ivey 1992; Schroeder 1963). Brugge examined this topic (1969) and maintained that factions within the pueblos were often in collusion with the Apaches against pro-Spanish factions in the same pueblos. Ivey subsequently agreed with Brugge and advanced a model that would help explain the, "increase in Apache hostility during the seventeenth century" (Ivey 1992:222). Ivey proposed that, "One group or alliance in

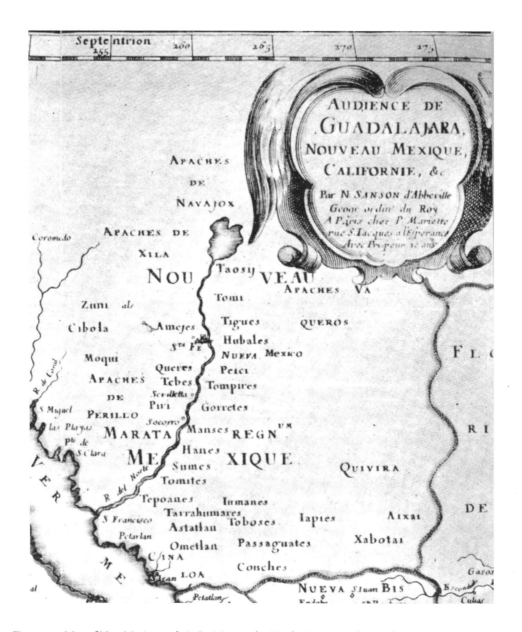

Figure 13.1. Map of New Mexico made in Paris in 1657 by Nicolas Sanson. It depicts the various Apache groups around the Rio Grande Pueblos as described by Benavides in his widely read *Memorial* of 1630 (from the *New Mexico Historical Review* 1936 XI (April) opposite p. 129).

a pueblo would use the Spanish against another group, and the second group would retaliate by arranging an Apache raid that struck at Spanish interest in the pueblo, as well as puebloan members of the opposing group" (Ivey 1992:222).

A consideration of the references cited by Schroeder (1963) and Brugge (1969) will determine that both of them relied heavily upon secondary summaries rather than primary documents. I have made an effort to examine the topic of collusion and conspiracy between Apaches and

anti-Spanish Pueblos utilizing translated and published primary documents and can find nothing that explicitly corroborates the factionalism model proposed by Brugge (1969) and formalized by Ivey (1992) except for a few instances during 1693–1696. On the other hand, there is much documentary material that has not yet been examined for confirmation or rejection of the factionalism model. There is sufficient documentary material readily available to confirm the general picture of Apaches being in collusion and conspiracy with one or a group of pueblos against the Spaniards during the seventeenth century. The available documentary material safely allows rejection of the simple view that the Apaches were always raiders and the Pueblos were always the raided.

Evidence for Apache-Pueblo Alliances

The first reliable indication of a conspiracy between Apaches and hostile Pueblos against the Spaniards and the Christian Pueblos is in an April 9, 1609 Memorial written in San Gabriel by Fray Francisco de Velasco. Fray Velasco had been in New Mexico since Christmas Eve 1600 (Hammond and Rey 1953:24) and at the time of writing the memorial was the prelate of the Franciscans in New Mexico. He was thus in a good position to know intimately what was going on in New Mexico. He was concerned about the fate of the converted Indians near San Gabriel, should the colony be abandoned as was being discussed in Mexico City at that time: "Since those Indians have shown so much friendship for the Spaniards, they have lost the good will of the Picuríes, Taos, Pecos, Apaches, and Vaqueros, who have formed a league among themselves and with other barbarous nations to exterminate our friends. This will happen without fail as soon as the Spaniards leave them and abandon the land" (Hammond and Rey 1953:1094–1095).

Another account of conspiracy between the Apaches and anti-Spanish Pueblos appeared about a year earlier when Fray Lázaro Ximénez arrived in Mexico City from New Mexico and reported to the Viceroy, Don Luis de Velasco (Hammond and Rey 1953:1059). On March 6, 1608 Viceroy Velasco issued an order to Oñate based on Ximénez's report which mentions Apache raids: "Ximénez . . . has reported to me that the Spaniards and the Christian and peaceful natives in New Mexico are frequently harassed by attacks of the Apache Indians, who destroy and burn their pueblos, waylay and kill their people by treachery, steal their horses and cause other damages" (Hammond and Rey 1953:1059).

Apache collaboration with the anti-Spanish Pueblos appears again in the Viceroy's March 30, 1609 instructions to Governor Peralta which is based on Ximénez' second trip to Mexico City (Hammond and Rey 1953:1067): "some of the pueblos and nations are on the frontiers of the Apaches, who are usually a refuge and shelter for our enemies, and there they hold meetings and consultations, hatch their plots against the whole land, and set out to plunder and make war" (Hammond and Rey 1953:1089). This reference indicates that their "enemies" go into Apache territory and hold conspiratorial meetings. Fray Velasco made it clear that these "enemies" are anti-Spanish Pueblo people, who he identified as the Picuris, Taos, and Pecos (Hammond and Rey 1953:1094).

After the move to Santa Fe around 1610 there was a period when meetings with Apaches calmed down and there was little mention of Apache raids. In an order from the Viceroy to Governor Don Juan de Eulate, bearing the date of March 10, 1620, there is no mention of Apache raids on the converted Pueblos (Bloom 1928), or of any conspiracies between Pueblos and Apaches. Documents from the same period summarized by Scholes have the same message (Scholes 1936). The only exception to this is a vague reference to involvement by an Apache in a 1614 incident in which some Jemez people killed a person from Cochiti (Scholes 1938:63). When Scholes first mentioned the incident, he made no mention of Apache involvement: "Meanwhile Father Ordóñez had heard that an Indian of Cochití had been killed by Indians from the Jemez pueblos. Immediately he sent soldiers to seize some of the offenders" (Scholes 1936:44). Later Scholes said that some Apaches were involved (1938:63), and cited as his source a report by Fray Guerta that he had partly transcribed (1936:58–71) but this incident is not in the portion he transcribed and published. Given the fact that this important 1617 report by Fray Guerta has never been otherwise published, it remains vague as to what extent Apaches were involved in this incident.

Speaking of the 1618–1626 period Scholes (1936:145) said: "The Jemez Indians lived in several villages on the frontier between the main Pueblo area and the Navaho country." This position led to the long-standing view that the Jemez were closely allied with the Navajo in the seventeenth century (Brugge 1969). However, there is essentially no documentary evidence for this interpretation since the missionary, Father Fray Alonso Lugo, assigned to Jemez in 1598 (Hammond and Rey 1953:345) produced no documents, left New Mexico in March 1601 (Scholes and Bloom 1944:322) and no other missionaries were at Jemez until Zárate Salmerón arrived in 1621 (Scholes 1938:63). This is especially the case since Salmerón said nothing about Navajos or any Apaches near Jemez during his tenure (1621–1626) (Milich 1966; Scholes 1938:63) and he said that the Navajo country was reached by going up the Chama River (Milich 1966:94). Additionally, Benavides reported the Navajo lived one day's walk from Santa Clara Pueblo (Schaafsma 1981, 2002).

The two memorials prepared by Benavides in 1630 (Ayer 1916; Forrestal and Lynch 1954) and 1634 (Hodge et al. 1945) based on his residency in New Mexico from 1626–1629 remain of major significance. As noted above, he is the primary source of information about the Apaches surrounding the Rio Grande Pueblos. Benavides wrote extensively about the Apaches and regarded them as a prime target for conversion. However, he made so many exaggerations and relied upon hearsay to such an extent, that his accounts constantly have to be evaluated against other documents, archaeological evidence and a consideration of which events he was actually involved with as opposed to events he was merely told about (Reff 1994; Schaafsma 1981, 2002). There is very little hint of any kind of conspiracy and collusion between Apaches and Pueblos in his accounts. He relates a condition of Apaches who raid and converted Pueblos who are raided. He also discussed the trade between the Pueblos and the Plains Apaches.

After Benavides left New Mexico in 1629, there are a number of documents depicting essentially the same conditions through about 1639. The commissary-general of the Franciscan Order Fray Juan de Prada wrote a petition to the King from Mexico City on September 26, 1638 in which he summarized conditions in New Mexico based upon a meeting he held with a number of Franciscan missionaries who had been in New Mexico (Hackett 1937:106–115). He discussed trade in, "buffalo and deer skins which the unconverted Indians are accustomed to bring, who live adjacent to our people and with whom they maintain peace, although always insecure, because these people do not keep their word" (Hackett 1937:108). The "unconverted Indians" were probably Plains Apaches. Subsequently Prada discussed the Spaniards in Santa Fe who "occupy themselves in bearing arms in defense of the reduced Indians against the barbarous and ferocious heathen who are in the habit of making attacks upon them" (Hackett 1937:108). These people evidently were Apaches since he elsewhere specifies Apaches as being a problem: "These *encomenderos* are under obligation to participate with their arms and horses in the defense both of the natives as well as of the religious who are in the frontier pueblos and live in constant danger from the Apache Indians. These are a very war-like people, who live in rancherias in the environs of the converted pueblos, against which that nation makes continuous attacks" (Hackett 1937:110). As in the Benavides's Memorials, there is no suggestion that the Pueblos were in conspiracy with the Apaches at the time of Prada's 1638 petition.

Apache raids increased after 1639, if not earlier since Scholes cited 1632 as the time when "a definite slowing down of the mission program" commenced (1937:105). Scholes summarized an important letter by Friar Andrés Juárez dated October 23, 1647 (1937:99–100). Relying upon this and other documents Scholes summarized the 1640s and mentioned the increasing conspiracy between Apaches and anti-Spanish Pueblos (Scholes 1937:105–106). In a December, 1681 deposition, Juan Domínguez de Mendoza recalled the conspiracies during the administrations of Governor Argüello (1644–1647) and Governor Hernando de Ugarte y la Concha (1649–1653):

He knows particularly that Don Fernando de Arguello in his time had twenty-nine Jemez Indians hanged in the pueblo of Los Jemez as traitors and confederates of the Apaches. . . . And in the time of Señor General Hernando de Ugarte y la Concha there were hanged as traitors and confederates of the Apaches some Tiquas Indians of La Isleta and of the pueblos of La Alameda, San Felipe, Cochití, and Jemez, nine from the said pueblos being hanged.

—[HACKETT AND SHELBY 1942:266]

At the same time (December, 1681) Diego López Sambrana made a deposition in which he recalled the 1650 conspiracy during the time of Governor Concha:

And in the year '50, during the government of General Concha, he discovered another plot to rebel which the sorcerers and chief men of the pueblos had arranged with the enemy Apaches, and for that purpose the Christians, under the pretext that the enemy was doing it, turned over to them in the pastures the droves of mares and horses belonging to the Spaniards, which are the principal nerve of warfare. They had already agreed with the said apostates to attack in all the districts on the night of Holy Thursday, because the Spaniards would then be assembled. The said rebellion was discovered because of Captain Alonso Vaca and other soldiers having followed a drove of mares which the Indians were driving off, and the aggressors being overtaken, they declared that the Christians of the pueblos of Alameda and Sandia had turned them over to them, and that they were all plotting and conspiring with all the said Apaches to rebel and destroy the whole kingdom, and to be left in freedom as in ancient times, living like their ancestors. The Spaniards returned with this news and with a knife belonging to a Christian Indian of the pueblo of Alameda, to the presence of the alcalde mayor of the said district, who was Captain Juan García Olgado. He notified the said governor, and on investigating the case the treason was uncovered, and many Indians were arrested from most of the pueblos of this kingdom. As a result nine leaders were hanged and many others were sold as slaves for ten years.

—[HACKETT AND SHELBY 1942:2:299]

Further demonstration of Apache raids and a continuing and probably growing conspiracy between Apaches and Pueblos in the mid-seventeenth century is found in a September 13, 1653 account of the military expeditions made by Captain Francisco de Ortega against the Apaches in the region south of Albuquerque:

. . . he has participated, in many honorable battles in war with the enemies. One in particular was very opportune and advantageous for halting the many damages and deaths the enemy Apaches were continually carrying out. When they stole and carried off a herd of mares from the jurisdiction of Rio Abajo, the captain went in their pursuit, . . . killing them all.

From signs, knife marks, and other things, he discovered how the Apaches communicated with some of the Christian Indians, which was found to be true. A very large confederation and gathering they had with the Christians was discovered.

—[KESSELL ET AL. 1995:76]

Thus, by the 1650s there is extensive documentary evidence of collusion and conspiracy between Apaches and Pueblos. Many of these references are so general that it is difficult to determine which Apaches were in league with which pueblos, but most indications are to southern Pueblos in league with Apaches. This period soon led to the very unsettled conditions during the 1659—1661 tenure of Bernardo López de Mendizábal (Hackett 1937:131–326; Schaafsma 1994). By Governor Mendizábal's time relationships between Apaches and Spaniards were exacerbated by Spanish slave raids (Worcester 1941:10).

Father Fray Juan Ramírez and others wrote from Santo Domingo Pueblo on September 8, 1659 about the actions of Governor Mendizábal in acquiring slaves and how this was impacting any chance of converting the Apaches, since by "heathen" they almost certainly meant Apaches:

Very great, Sir, has been the covetousness of the governors of this kingdom, wherein they have, under color of chastising the neighboring enemy, made opportunity to send . . . squadrons of men to capture the heathen Indians to send them to the camp and mines of El Parral to sell. . . . For this purpose of making captives, the governor on the fourth of September of this year, 1659, sent out an army of eight hundred Christian Indians and forty Spaniards.

—[HACKETT 1937:186–187]

Evidence of a conspiracy between the southern Pueblos (Piros) and Apaches between 1665 and 1668 is found in the 1681 recollection of Diego López Sambrano: "Later another chastisement was visited upon the Piros here for the same crime . . . when six Indians were hanged and others were sold and imprisoned, for in addition to their crimes and conspiracies they were found in an ambuscade with the enemy Apaches in the Sierra de la Madalena" (Hackett and Shelby 1942:2:299).

On the eve of the 1680 Revolt, Father Fray Francisco de Ayeta provided an extensive account in Mexico City on May 10, 1679 about conditions in New Mexico, with a special focus on the Salinas province which had largely been abandoned by that time, due at least in part to Apache raids. Speaking of New Mexico in general he said: " . . . those provinces were in danger of ruin through the constant attacks made upon them by the Chichimecos of the Apache nation, with whom the rest of the heathen Indians were confederated" (Hackett 1937:296).

For the years leading up to the 1680 Revolt, the documents emphasize Apache raids, and a growing awareness of Pueblos in conspiracy with Apaches against the Spaniards. Most documents from the pre-1680 period are general summaries that only occasionally are specific about place or which Apaches were involved. There are very few military campaign documents from the many raids that must have been involved. Exceptions to this are the Juan Domínguez de Mendoza documents many of which Scholes determined to be forgeries (Miller 1985). Forbes said: "I am indebted to Professor France V. Scholes, of the University of New Mexico, for pointing out

Domínguez de Mendoza's forgeries" (Forbes 1960:143). These documents were submitted along with a *Memorial* by Mendoza to the Viceroy on November 18, 1685 (Hackett 1937:354–356) in an unsuccessful bid to be made governor of New Mexico (Kessell and Hendricks 1992:24). Until some responsible historian clarifies which documents are not forgeries, I do not see how one can rely upon them, as for example Reeve did (Reeve 1956, 1957).

Overall, there is good documentary evidence that Apaches surrounded the Rio Grande settlements during the seventeenth century. As the century wore on, raids by Apaches increased and there were many indications that the anti-Spanish Pueblos were often conspired with neighboring Apaches. This set the stage for the 1680 Revolt and the later collaboration between the Pueblos and various Apache groups after the return of the Spaniards.

The Pueblo Revolt began on August 10, 1680 (Hackett and Shelby 1942:1:5–9) forcing the Spaniard's withdrawal to El Paso where they remained until Governor Diego de Vargas made his "Ritual Repossession" in 1692 (Kessell and Hendricks 1992), followed by the actual recolonization in late 1693 (Kessell et al. 1995).

When Governor Otermín was first informed on August 9, 1680 that a general revolt was imminent he was told that the Pueblos were allied with the Apaches and the combined people were going to attack the Spaniards: "All the nations of this kingdom were now implicated in it, forming a confederation with the heathen Apaches" (Hackett and Shelby 1942:1:3–4). During the siege the Spaniards were threatened by the Pueblos that soon their Apache allies would join them: "On the next day, Saturday, they began at dawn to press us harder and more closely with gunshots, arrows, and stones, saying to us that now we should not escape them, and that, besides their own numbers, they were expecting help from the Apaches whom they had already summoned" (Hackett and Shelby 1942:1:102). However, as the Revolt continued and news came in from throughout New Mexico, there was very little indication that Apaches were actually involved in the attacks. Only the Red River or Acho Apaches at Taos Pueblo were actually reported to have been involved

(Hackett and Shelby 1942:1:71–72).

On November 5, 1681, Governor Antonio de Otermín left El Paso with his army (Hackett and Shelby 1942:2:202) on an attempted reconquest of New Mexico that lasted until February 1682. The Spaniards had expected the Apaches to attack the Pueblos as soon as the protecting Spaniards left and that the Pueblos would welcome their return. This expectation was quickly proven wrong and the Spaniards withdrew to El Paso.

In a December 23, 1681 deposition, Father Fray Francisco de Ayeta examined the fallacious assumptions of the Spaniards about relationships between Pueblos and Apaches:

First, it was the opinion of the whole kingdom without a single exception, founded on knowledge and experience of the country and the Indians of these provinces and of the Apaches who surrounded them, that they would be repentant for the atrocities and iniquities they had committed, and this not from any interest in repentance before God, but for their own convenience, their survival being held impossible in view of their helplessness and lack of spirit and the pitiless warfare that the heathen Apaches would wage upon them, catching them without the protection of the Spaniards, for they have always oppressed them in this manner, because of being both braver and incomparably more numerous. The Spaniards thought that when they entered they would find the greater part of the kingdom destroyed, and that those whom they might find alive would submit most humbly in order to free themselves from the oppression of the Apaches.
—[HACKETT AND SHELBY 1942:2:306–307]

This assumption, "proved to be untrue, for it has been experienced and seen that the Apaches have not destroyed any pueblo or even damaged one seriously" (Hackett and Shelby 1942:2:308). They found that the Pueblos "have maintained themselves without the Spaniards" (Hackett and Shelby 1942:2:308).

Governor Don Diego de Vargas departed with his troops from El Paso on August 21, 1692 for New Mexico and a "Ritual Repossession" (Kessell and Hendricks 1992:357–369) of New Mexico that lasted until his return to El Paso on December 20, 1692 (Kessell and Hendricks 1992:597). Throughout this campaign Vargas maintained a perception of the Apaches that was similar to that summarized in 1681 by Father Ayeta. He seems to have always treated them as "the enemy" and on all occasions treacherous people from whose depredations he had come to protect the Pueblos. He was certainly aware of conspiracies between Apaches and Pueblos, as will be seen, but Apaches always seem to have been incorrigible enemies. His attitude toward Apaches is explicitly imbedded in his exchange with the Tanos fortified in Santa Fe in September, 1692: "They said that when the Spaniards were in the kingdom, they had made peace with the Apaches and later gone out and killed them. They said I would do the same with them, to which I replied that the Apaches were not Christians but traitors who, while at peace, came in to better assure their thefts and killings, as they had done when the Spaniards lived in the land" (Kessell and Hendricks 1992:390). All the way through Vargas's campaign, he basically said the Pueblos should accept him, and he would protect them from the Apaches. However, in many cases the Pueblos were friends with the Apaches living near them.

One of the first incidents in the Vargas era that suggests the involvement of Apaches, in this case, Apaches de Navajo with the Pueblos (northern Tewa) took place in mid-September, 1692 when Vargas was camped outside the Tano fortress at Santa Fe. Vargas was informed on Sunday September 14, "that don Luis of the Picuris nation, governor of all the pueblos of the Tewas and Tanos and to whom they give obedience, has sent word that he will come to see me tomorrow. He had gone to see the Navajo Apaches, who had sent for him" (Kessell and Hendricks 1992:403). Don Luis Picurí did show up on Monday (Kessell and Hendricks 1992:406), after meeting with "the Apaches at his pueblo of San Juan on Sunday night" (Kessell and Hendricks

1992:404). Thus, before meeting with Vargas, don Luis went to visit the Navajo Apaches who were at San Juan Pueblo. This would be quite incomprehensible unless there was some need to obtain their understanding, and perhaps concurrence about his going to meet Vargas in Santa Fe. Don Luis maintained his friendship with the Apaches de Navajo, as will be seen, when Vargas returned with the colony the next year.

At Taos Pueblo on October 8, 1692 Governor Vargas was told about a gathering of rebel Pueblos that included some Apaches, the Faraones: "They told me that two young men, natives of the pueblo of the Taos, had come from the province of Zuni. On the return trip to Acoma they had encountered a large gathering that all the captains from the nations of Zuni, together with those from Moqui, the Jemez, Keres, Pecos, Faraones, Coninas from the Cerro Colorado, and many others from other places had held for three days and nights" (Kessell and Hendricks 1992:454).

Later, on October 25, 1692 Governor Vargas went to the Jemez area and to a village on a high mesa, presumably Guadalupe Mesa, which he ascended on horseback (Kessell and Hendricks 1992:520–521). When he got on top, his reception was not very cordial and he wrote, "I could not help but remember the information of record in these proceedings that the Taos Indians gave me the day of their arrival about the junta they had been at and that these natives of Jemez were the instigators" (Kessell and Hendricks 1992:521). After he entered the village he found himself hemmed in by the crowd, and some had not laid down their weapons. They then asked him to go up to a second-story room to eat. As he left, he met several Apaches: "I inferred from the fact that the Apaches were lodged in the house and that many others were in the houses of the second plaza that the report from the Taos about the aforementioned junta was true" (Kessell and Hendricks 1992:522). This was probably the most dramatic instance on his 1692 trip of Apaches clearly being friendly with the Pueblos, and his correct interpretation was they were all potentially in collusion against him as the Taos people had reported on October 8, 1692.

Governor Vargas with his troops and colonists began

leaving El Paso on October 4, 1693 (Kessell et al. 1995:377). The large party slowly made its way north and after numerous delays caused by rumors of pending Indian insurrection the party entered Santa Fe on December 16, 1693 (Kessell et al. 1995:469). The first suggestion of a pending revolt came with the report of Lorenzo, a Zia Indian who met with Vargas near Socorro on November 10, 1693 (Kessell et al. 1995:399): "He said the Keres Indians from Santa Ana Pueblo and those of San Felipe were very happy about our coming. The people of Santa Ana were going to leave their pueblo if we delayed any longer, because the Jemez, Tewas, and Tanos, who were their enemies, had assured them they were coming to destroy them. . . . The Tewas, Tanos, and Picuris all said they would fight when we went there" (Kessell et al. 1995:403–404). Governor Vargas later wrote to the Viceroy in Mexico City and mentioned the November 10 report by Lorenzo: "The Indian went on to say that many Apaches, whom they had summoned from different rancherias and places, had also prepared" (Kessell et al. 1998:59) to aid the pueblos in resisting the Spaniards. Thus by November 10 Vargas had been told that many Pueblos were allied against him, and that the Apaches were part of the conspiracy waiting to attack him.

This report proved basically true and as events unfolded Vargas learned that the Tewas, Tanos, Picuris, and Taos were allied with the Rio Colorado or "Acho" Apaches and the Apaches de Navajo. Governor Vargas was told of this confederation on November 15, 1693 when the Spaniards were near Santo Domingo Pueblo: "they found an old Indian woman from Cochiti Pueblo who was running toward them. She told them she had gone to her pueblo and on the mesa of Cieneguilla had seen some heavily armed Tewa and Tano Indians on horseback . . . Indians from the Taos and Picuris nations, Apaches from the Río Colorado, and the Navajos were with them" (Kessell et al. 1995:410). This report agreed with the earlier report from Lorenzo and specified that the Acho Apaches and Apaches de Navajo were allied with Tewas, Tanos, Taos, and Picuris against the Spaniards. On November 24, four Pecos Indians confirmed that the Pueblos were allied with these Apaches and waiting to attack the Spaniards: "After asking them about the Tewa and other nations referred to in their district, he said that all of them had gathered opposite the two small hills at the abandoned pueblo of La Cieneguilla with most of the Keres from Cochiti. They also brought with them the Río Colorado Apaches and the Apaches from the province and district of the Navajos to help them fight against my company and me" (Kessell et al. 1995:432).

Eventually these conspirators gave up on the notion of attacking the advancing Spanish party and instead made plans to resist and fight the Spaniards when they tried to enter the Villa of Santa Fe: "They had newly arranged that when I entered the villa of Santa Fe, they would be fortified there, resist, and fight until they killed us" (Kessell et al. 1995:439).

Governor Vargas and his party entered Santa Fe on December 10, 1693 (Kessell et al. 1995:465) and immediately ran into difficulties with the occupants of Santa Fe. By December 17, 1693 Vargas said:

> . . . the evil intentions and treachery meant to achieve the aim of the Indians of the Tano and Tewa nations who are living in this villa of Santa Fe in their walled pueblo have been spread throughout the camp and company . . . I sought to inquire and learn about the evidence. In a short while, the governor of Pecos, don Juan de Ye, came to my tent and told me he was giving me accurate information about the treachery of the Tewa and Tano nations. They were meeting with the Picuris and had many Apaches on the mesa of San Juan Pueblo. They had made a pact with many people to attack the company and me. . . . They were assured of many Apaches in San Juan Pueblo on the mesa, and they were with those who were friends with the Indian cacique, don Luis el Picurí.
> —[KESSELL ET AL. 1995:473]

Vargas summarized the efforts made by the Pueblos in the Santa Fe fortress to fight the Spaniards: "It became known that the Indians of the villa wanted to rebel. They were calling up all the Tewas and Tanos for this. Don Luis el Picurí was coming with the Apaches he had on the mesa of San Juan, the Taos, and the Picuris" (Kessell et al. 1998:67). Given the earlier reports that specified who these "Apaches" were, they must have been Río Colorado (Acho) Apaches and Navajo Apaches. This was the same don Luis el Picurí who had met with the Navajo Apaches at San Juan Pueblo in 1692 (Kessell and Hendricks 1992:403) before he met with Vargas in Santa Fe. Thus in 1693 from all indications the Apaches de Navajo were again on the "mesa of San Juan Pueblo" conspiring with don Luis and the northern Pueblos to attack the Spaniards.

On January 11, 1694, in Santa Fe, Vargas interviewed a Tewa woman named Lucía. In addition to discussing the Pueblo rebels, she was asked about a genízaro named Juan de la Vega: "She said he had arrived at San Juan Pueblo. . . . He went on to Santa Clara, where she knew they handed him over to the Navajo Apaches. They had been at the gathering she said they held, which was in this pueblo. She knew that after the Apaches killed him, they delivered his scalp to two Indians so they could take it to the rancherias of the Navajo Apaches" (Kessell et al. 1998:47–48). This incident shows that in 1694 the Navajo Apaches were deeply involved with Santa Clara and had been at a gathering in Santa Clara Pueblo.

Father Fray José García Marín wrote from Santa Clara Pueblo on December 31, 1694 (Espinosa 1988:135–141). In talking about the geographic setting of Santa Clara he correctly noted that it is on the west bank of the Rio Grande and refers to the sierra of the Navajo Apaches six leagues away: "Santa Clara is contiguous to and on the edge of the Río Grande, isolated on its west bank a distance of six leagues from the sierra of the Navajo Apaches" (Espinosa 1988:140). If the conversion factor of 2.6 miles to the league is used, this means the Navajos were living about 15 miles away. The account can be taken to mean that the Navajos were living about 15 miles from Santa Clara Pueblo somewhere west of the Rio Grande. Taking the position that he did not mean the high Jemez Mountains directly west or southwest of Santa Clara, it appears that his source of information (presumably Santa Clara people) was talking about 15 miles northwest of Santa Clara or up the Chama Valley toward Abiquiu. This would be in the vicinity of "Los Pedernales" where the Santa Clara people stayed with the Apaches de Navajo in 1696 (Figure 13.2; Schaafsma 2002).

By December 1695, the missionaries were beginning to warn of another revolt, perhaps on Christmas Eve 1695 (Espinosa 1988:157). An important letter was written by Father Fray Francisco Corbera at San Ildefonso on December 20, 1695. He was aware of the possible rebellion, knew the Tewa language and did not want to write to Governor Vargas for fear of exposing his people to punishment. Because he knew the Tewa language he learned the San Ildefonso people were making plans among themselves not to flee to Black Mesa as they had before, but to escape to the Navajos: "last night I heard some words that are very suspicious: that if they leave they will not go to the mesa, but rather to the mesas of the Navajos" (Espinosa 1988:158). The Christmas Eve, 1695 rebellion did not happen, but the missionaries continued to be apprehensive.

Governor Vargas received word of the June 4, 1696 Revolt from Roque Madrid that, "the Indians of San Cristóbal had risen up with the Keres, Apaches, Moquinos, and Pecos" (Kessell et al. 1998:727). Vargas later wrote, "On 4 June, at sunset, eleven pueblos rebelled; only five nations are our allies" (Kessell et al. 1998:864). The primary reports for the 1696 Revolt period are in Governor Vargas's campaign journal, Governor Vargas's correspondence with soldiers in the field and interrogations of prisoners (Kessell et al. 1998).

The Navajo Apaches were implicated at the outset. On his initial campaign to assess the damages (Kessell et al. 1998:725–735), Governor Vargas went to San Ildefonso where a grisly scene awaited him: "Found dead there were the two reverend fathers, fray Francisco Corvera, the minister, priest, and guardian of the pueblo, and Fray Antonio Moreno, guardian, minister, and priest of Nambé Pueblo" (Kessell et al. 1998:734) as well as other people. When the Cacique from Nambe was later interrogated (Kessell et al. 1998:751–756), he was asked who killed the

fathers in San Ildefonso, "he said the Apaches, the Indians from that pueblo, a war captain from Santa Clara Pueblo, and another from Jacona were the ones who had killed the reverend fathers" (Kessell et al. 1998:753). Governor Vargas later said, "Some Navajo Apaches were in San Ildefonso Pueblo that day with Indians from Santa Clara Pueblo for the deaths of the two reverend fathers and the people who were with them" (Kessell et al. 1998:966). This was the same Father Fray Francisco Corbera, who in March, 1696 secretly listened to the San Ildefonso people making plans in their kiva to revolt and retreat to the Navajo Apaches (Espinosa 1988:181). This collusion between Santa Claras, San Ildefonsos, and Navajo Apaches followed years of friendship between them documented by the missionaries in those two pueblos and was not a fortuitous situation—it grew out of years of conspiracy between the anti-Spanish Pueblos and the Navajo Apaches.

The Tewa named Diego Xenome or Dieguillo, said Naranjo of Santa Clara:

. . . told them that the Apaches, who had already withdrawn to their land to dance, had agreed to advise them what they decided and determine about what they must do and carry out. . . . Asked about when they expected the decision and report from the Apaches, he said that what he knew was that the Navajo Apaches were in a hurry for all the Apaches and the remaining nations to come together this month to fight. The Zunis, Moquinos, Apaches who live near them, Acomas, Utes, and another nation the declarant was unfamiliar with had said that when the ears of corn appeared in the milpas, which is when the maize was youngest, all these nations were certain to come together with the Apaches, with whom they have been friendly and who were to attack the horses first. They had not done so then, the night the misfortunes occurred, because the river had been high, and some of the Apaches did not know how to swim.

—[KESSELL ET AL. 1998:754]

Figure 13.2. Detail of the Miera y Pacheco map of 1778 showing the Chama River Valley with Abiquiu and the locality of "Los Pedernales" immediately west of Abiquiu. Note also Santa Clara Pueblo on the west side of the Rio Grande. From a photograph taken by the author of the original map when it was on display in 1988 at the Palace of the Governors, Museum of New Mexico, as part of Michael Weber's exhibit on Spanish Cartography (reproduction here courtesy of Dr. Thomas Chavez, Director of the Palace of the Governors, Museum of New Mexico).

In addition to demonstrating Apache involvement in the Revolt, this passage suggests the Pueblos were seeking some kind of advice following the "dance."

Navajo Apache cooperation with the Pueblos is again indicated by accounts of a June 29, 1696 battle at Jemez. The participation of the Navajo Apaches was clearly stated in a letter to Governor Vargas from Bartolomé de Ojeda of Zia dated July 1, 1696: "So as to inform your lordship, that entire gathering was made up of Acomas, Zunis, Moquinos, Navajo Apaches, Cochitis, Tewas, Tanos, and the Jemez of San Juan" (Kessell et al. 1998:798–799). Ojeda mentioned a young captive from Acoma who was subsequently interrogated in Santa Fe who also mentioned Navajo Apaches in the Jemez battle (Kessell et al. 1998:802–803). In addition to the above documents showing Navajo Apache participation in the June 29, 1696 battle at Jemez, other accounts throughout the summer of 1696 consistently relate to Navajo Apaches around the Tewa villages.

On August 27, 1696 Governor Vargas took the statement of Miguel Saxete governor of San Juan de los Caballeros

(Kessell et al. 1998:1001–1004): "Asked where the Indians from Santa Clara were, he said what he knew was that some had gone away to the Navajo Apaches and others to Moqui. All the people had left Santa Clara; no one remained . . . As for all the rest of the pueblos, very few families had stayed. They had all gone away, some to Moqui and others to live with the Navajo Apaches" (Kessell et al. 1998:1003). Another Tewa interrogated later had been with "these from Santa Clara in Los Pedernales" (Kessell et al. 1998:1028), near Abiquiu (Figure 13.2; Schaafsma 2002).

Further indications of Navajo Apache friendship with the Tewas is in a letter Rogue Madrid wrote to Governor Vargas on November 11, 1696 about Tewas returning to their pueblos: "Sir, I carried out the order your lordship gave me to go to the pueblos of San Ildefonso, Jacona, and Nambe. . . . In San Ildefonso Pueblo, I found seventeen young men who were archers and thirty-six women and children. When I asked them about the rest, they told me that they had gone to the provinces of Zuni and

Moqui and to the Navajo Apaches. Eleven families are there from this pueblo of San Ildefonso" (Kessell et al. 1998:1059). Many of the Pueblos returned to their villages in the Fall of 1696 (Schaafsma 2002).

After 1696 the documents emphasize Apache raids as in the January 10, 1706 certification prepared by Captain Rael de Aguilar (Hackett 1937:366–368) and Governor Cuervo y Valdés's letter of August 18, 1706 (Hackett 1937:381–387), with very little suggestion of conspiracies with the Pueblos.

Conclusions

Overall, this review demonstrates that the Pueblos and Apaches were in various kinds of alliances against the Spaniards through at least 1696. Future research will inform on the changing nature of these conspiracies since the relationships clearly changed over time and were different from one Pueblo or group of Pueblos to the others. It is also apparent that different Apache groups related to the Pueblos in different ways. Some were in more constant partnership with the Pueblos, for example the Apaches de Navajos with the Tewas and Picuris, while others seem to have been more adversarial. The simple picture of the Apaches as always being nothing more than raiders has to be reexamined, and is clearly wrong for the seventeenth century.

Finally, in the documents discussed above, I can find very little that would corroborate the factionalism model proposed by Brugge (1969) and formalized by Ivey (1992). A more in-depth perusal of the primary documents might be able to sustain this interpretation. However, my finding is that the conspiracies were with individual pueblos such as Taos and Picuris or with groups of pueblos such as the Tewas and Tanos.

Acknowledgments

I would like to thank Robert Preucel for inviting me to participate in his 1999 Society for American Archaeology symposium in Chicago. Thomas Chávez kindly gave me permission to photograph the Miera y Pacheco map of 1778.

References Cited

Ayer, Mrs. Edward. E. (translator)
1916   *The Memorial of Fray Alonso de Benavides, 1630.* Privately printed, Chicago, Ill.

Bloom, Lansing B.
1928   A Glimpse of New Mexico in 1620. *New Mexico Historical Review* 3:357–389.

Brugge, David M.
1969   Pueblo Factionalism and External Relations. *Ethnohistory* 16(2):191–200.

Espinosa, J. Manuel
1988   *The Pueblo Indian Revolt of 1696 and the Franciscan Missions in New Mexico: Letters of the Missionaries and Related Documents.* University of Oklahoma Press, Norman.

Forbes, Jack D.
1960   *Apache, Navajo and Spaniard.* University of Oklahoma Press, Norman.

Forrestal, P. P., and C. J. Lynch (editors and translators)
1954   *Benavides' Memorial of 1630.* Documentary Series 2. Academy of American Franciscan History, Washington, D.C.

Foster, M. K.
1996   Language and Culture History of North America. In *Handbook of North American Indians, Vol. 17: Languages,* edited by I. Goddard, pp. 64–110. Smithsonian Institution, Washington, D.C.

Hackett, Charles W. (editor)
1937   *Historical Documents Relating to New Mexico, Nueva Vizcaya and Approaches Thereto, to 1773.* Collected by A. F. A. Bandelier and F. R. Bandelier, Vol. 3. Carnegie Institution of Washington Publication 330(3), Washington, D.C.

Hackett, Charles W., and Charmion C. Shelby (editor and translator)
1942   *Revolt of the Pueblo Indians of New Mexico and Otermin's Attempted Reconquest, 1680–1682.* 2 Vols. Coronado Cuarto Centennial Publications, No. 8. University of New Mexico Press, Albuquerque.

Hammond, George P., and Agapito Rey (editors and translators)
1953   *Don Juan de Oñate, Colonizer of New Mexico, 1595–1628.* Coronado Cuarto Centennial Publications, No. 5 and 6. University of New Mexico Press, Albuquerque.

Hester, James J.
1962   *Early Navajo Migrations and Acculturation in the Southwest.* Museum of New Mexico Papers in Anthropology, No. 6. Museum of New Mexico Press, Santa Fe.

Hodge, Frederick W., George P. Hammond, and Agapito Rey
1945   *Fray Alonso de Benavides' Memorial of 1634.* Coronado Cuarto Centennial Publications, No. 4. University of New Mexico Press. Albuquerque.

Ivey, James E.
1992   Pueblo and Estancia: The Spanish Presence in the Pueblo, A.D. 1620–1680. In *Current Research on the Late Prehistory and Early History of New Mexico,* edited by B. J. Vierra, pp. 221–226. New Mexico Archaeological Council, Special Publication 1. Albuquerque.

Kessell, John L., and Rick Hendricks (editors)

1992   *By Force of Arms: The Journals of don Diego de Vargas, New Mexico, 1691–1693.* University of New Mexico Press, Albuquerque.

Kessell, John L., Rick Hendricks, and Meredith D. Dodge (editors)

1995   *To the Royal Crown Restored: The Journals of don Diego de Vargas, New Mexico, 1692–1694.* University of New Mexico Press, Albuquerque.

1998   *Blood on the Boulders: The Journals of don Diego de Vargas, New Mexico, 1694–97.* 2 Vols. University of New Mexico Press, Albuquerque.

Milich, Alicia R.

1966   *Relaciones: An Account of Things Seen and Learned by Father Jeronimo de Zarate Salmeron from the Year 1538 to the Year 1626.* Horn & Wallace, Albuquerque.

Miller, L. D.

1985   Calendar: Servicios Personales del Maestre de Campo, Juan Domínguez de Mendoza. Ms. on file, Center for Southwest Research, University of New Mexico, Albuquerque.

Reeve, F. D.

1956   Early Navaho Geography. *New Mexico Historical Review* 31:290–309.

1957   Seventeenth Century Navaho-Spanish Relations. *New Mexico Historical Review* 32:36–52.

Reff, D. T.

1994   Contextualizing Missionary Discourse: The Benavides Memorials of 1630 and 1634. *Journal of Anthropological Research* 50:51–67.

Schaafsma, Curt F.

1974   *Final Report on a Survey of Abiquiu Reservoir.* School of American Research, Santa Fe.

1976   *Archaeological Survey of Maximum Pool and Navajo Excavations at Abiquiu Reservoir, Rio Arriba County, New Mexico.* School of American Research, Santa Fe.

1978   Archaeological Studies in the Abiquiu Reservoir District. *Discovery* 2:41–69.

1979   *The Cerrito Site (AR-4): A Piedra Lumbre Phase Settlement at Abiquiu Reservoir.* School of American Research, Santa Fe.

1981   Early Apacheans in the Southwest: A Review. In *The Protohistoric Period in the North American Southwest, a.d. 1450–1700,* edited by D. R. Wilcox and W. B. Masse, pp. 291–320. Anthropological Research Papers No. 24, Arizona State University, Tempe.

1992   A Review of the Documentary Evidence for a Seventeenth-Century Navajo Occupation in the Chama Valley. In *Current Research on the Late Prehistory and Early History of New Mexico,* edited by B. J. Vierra, pp. 313–321. New Mexico Archaeological Council, Special Publication 1. Albuquerque.

1994   Pueblo Ceremonialism from the Perspective of Spanish Documents. In *Kachinas in the Pueblo World,* edited by P. Schaafsma pp. 121–137. University of New Mexico Press, Albuquerque.

1996   Ethnic Identity and Protohistoric Archaeological Sites in Northwestern New Mexico: Implications for Reconstructions of Navajo and Ute History. In *The Archaeology of Navajo Origins,* edited by R. H. Towner, pp. 19–46. University of Utah Press, Salt Lake City.

2002   *Apaches de Navajo: Seventeenth Century Navajos in the Chama Valley of New Mexico.* University of Utah Press, Salt Lake City.

Scholes, France V.

1928   Manuscripts for the History of New Mexico in the National Library in Mexico City. *New Mexico Historical Review* III:301–323.

1936   Church and State in New Mexico, 1610–1650. *New Mexico Historical Review* XI(1–4):9–76, 145–178, 283–294, 297–349.

1937   Church and State in New Mexico, 1610–1650, Chapter VI-VII. *New Mexico Historical Review* XII(1):78–106.

1938   Notes on the Jemez Missions in the Seventeenth Century. *El Palacio* XLIV:61–70, 93–102.

Scholes, France V., and Lansing B. Bloom

1944   Friar Personnel and Mission Chronology, 1598–1629, I. *New Mexico Historical Review* XIX:319–336.

Schroeder, Albert H.

1963   Navajo and Apache Relationships West of the Rio Grande. *El Palacio* 70(3):5–23.

Worcester, D. E.

1941   The Beginnings of the Apache Menace of the Southwest. *New Mexico Historical Review* XVI:1–14.

Young, Robert W.

1983   Apachean Languages. In *Handbook of North American Indians, Vol. 10: Southwest,* edited by A. Ortiz, pp. 393–400. Smithsonian Institution, Washington, D.C.

Chapter 14

The Persistence of
the Corn Mothers

Joseph H. Suina

I walked into the dusty little village of Shongopavi, a Western Pueblo high upon Second Mesa, and approached the plaza with considerable anxiety. Although I had been forewarned that sacred dances and related religious ceremonies were being performed in broad daylight and in full view of non-Indians, I was totally unprepared for what I was about to witness. When I turned the corner and saw what was going on, I was shocked, dismayed, and saddened—all at the same time.

I had heard that Indian women and children along with non-Indians were permitted to stand dangerously and disrespectfully close to the katsinas and that the dancers distributed non-traditional gifts to non-dancing participants instead of the "proper Pueblo blessings." After a lifetime of learning about the sacredness of the religious ceremonies within the Eastern Pueblo communities, I was simply not prepared for what I was witnessing. My worldview was turned completely upside down.

Immediately thoughts rushed through my mind. Did these people really care about their traditional ceremonies? Had they abandoned all respect for their katsinas? Why were tourists, Anglos, and other non-Indians there? Why was this sacred act being presented as some sort of exotic entertainment? What impressions of Pueblo culture would be remembered by these foreign people?

Earlier, at the foot of the mesa I had passed Indian women and children from a traditional Eastern Pueblo that I was familiar with. They were selling home-baked bread and craft items. One lady told me that they were forbidden by their elders to view the ceremony under those conditions and would be selling their products until their men returned at the end of the day. Something was terribly wrong!

Now, after much reflection and careful consideration of my own biases as a member of an Eastern Pueblo, I have come to understand why I reacted so strongly to this event. My reaction was rooted in the different historical experiences that the Eastern and Western Pueblos had with the Spanish colonizers.

The impact of Spanish invaders on the people they called "the Pueblos" was nothing short of catastrophic. In addition to Christianity, foreign social, governmental, economic, and language systems were introduced, often by force, upon us. Many of these new influences were meant as replacements for traditional Pueblo life, a life we Pueblo people already saw as complete. We suffered great loss of life from introduced diseases for which we had no defenses. Dozens of villages simply dried up from death and migrated to surviving Pueblos and other tribes in order to find relief from mental and physical anguish. For over 80 years, we endured until we could endure no longer the threats and acts of religious persecution introduced by the Franciscans and reinforced by the military.

Then the unthinkable occurred. Pueblo communities, otherwise very independent of one another united into a single force to cast out a common foe. An all out battle was launched to reclaim a remembered traditional lifestyle that predated the arrival of the iron clad Spaniards. The struggle was to break the chains of tyranny that engulfed my people since the time of the invasion. Historians tell us that this was the famous Pueblo Revolt of 1680. To my people, it was the declaration of independence! That heavy-handed relationship of the Spaniards towards the Pueblos was never to be again, even after their return in 1692.

In the aftermath of confusion and transformation, the Pueblos retained and maintained the core of their religion, languages, and cultural integrity. Attempts were made to completely rid ourselves of all Spanish introduced items and ideas. Foods, tools, and even Christianity were abandoned in the quest to return to traditional ways. For example, individuals who took spouses in the church were instructed to abandon them and to take the one their hearts truly desired.

The current state of our native Pueblo religion, languages, and culture after 400 years of Spanish influences and two other subsequent governments are the envy of many Indian tribes across the country whose retention of native culture has not fared as well. Perhaps the veneer of Spanish influences wasn't all that thick in the first place! In spite of all that happened, many Spanish influences were not abandoned as was intended. Some of those still prevail in our lives and at some point we "stopped pretending to be Christian" as we did initially. Many of our people are truly committed to the Catholic faith without ever having to let go of our traditional religion. The fiesta and devotion to the saint are genuine demonstrations of the old and the new faiths done separately but together in one spirit on that special day. My guess is that this accommodation came long after the threat of religious persecution was over with and our people could see more clearly the true intent of the religion.

The Pueblo people are neither a tribe, nor a political unit. We are a group of villages each speaking a unique language or a dialect and each governed by our own religious and secular leaders. Our tribal leaders carry canes as symbols of authority introduced by the Spaniards. In addition, we now have canes from Mexico, the United States and the state of New Mexico as recognition of each Pueblo's sovereign nation status by each of the above governments.

We were called "Pueblos" by the Spaniards because our peaceful and communal way-of-life which was in sharp contrast to the nomadic and more aggressive lifestyle of people like the Apaches and the Navaho who were also in the area. Although we all live in villages and share a similar culture, we are each unique. And as noted before, not all of us share the same historical experiences; there can be no disputing the fact that the Eastern Pueblos suffered from the cruelty of the Spanish colonial presence to a far greater degree than the Western Pueblos. My discussion will thus compare the Western Pueblos of Laguna, Acoma, Zuni, and the Hopis of Arizona with the 16 Eastern Pueblos located along the Rio Grande River and its tributaries. These latter Pueblos are Taos, Picuris, San Juan, Santa Clara, San Ildefonso, Tesuque, Pojoaque, Nambe, Santo Domingo, San Felipe, Santa Ana, Zia, Jemez, Sandia, Isleta, and my own village of Cochiti. Many effects of the period of Spanish colonialism profoundly impacted us and, as I will show, some still continue to guide the ways in which we relate to the outside world.

Spanish exploration and eventual colonial concentration in the east was no doubt due to the location of the Rio Grande River. This area sustained Eastern Pueblo farming that, in turn, played a key role in supporting the early colonists. Rich irrigation land came to be highly valued even before it was established that great material wealth of the type the Spaniards were in search of, such as gold and silver, was largely absent. By contrast, to the invaders the Western Pueblos must have seemed like wasteland, located off in the distance. Except for occasional visits out west by early explorers and a handful of missionaries, staying along the Camino Real among the so-called "docile" Pueblos, whose service they came to depend upon, seemed a wise choice for the early colonizers.

There are numerous categories of material and physical

evidence, including religious practices present only in the east that attest to differing colonial impact between the two locations. To begin with, the average size of the Western Pueblos is nearly ten-times that of the east. There are several reasons for this. Not only were missionary and civil encroachments greater in the east, but the demand for land by colonists and settlers in and around these Pueblos was much more pressing. There the ever-shrinking Pueblo population added to the ease with which the intruders came to occupy former Pueblo lands. Today, several Eastern Pueblos have Hispanics residing on Spanish land grants right within the Pueblo population area. Harmony usually characterizes this coexistence. However, many Eastern Pueblos continue to be plagued by encroachment of neighboring Hispanic and Anglos along the borders of Pueblo land.

Several other causes contributed to the population reduction in the east. The most important of these appears to be migration and diseases. Religious oppression and forced labor both took their toll, which resulted in periodic movement of large groups of people to the west long before the Pueblo Revolt. And in 1680, immediately following the successful expulsion of the invaders, the population shifted dramatically with some moving to mountaintop retreats and others departing west to Acoma, Hopi, and Zuni. While many people were fearful of retaliation by the enemy, according to our oral tradition, this departure was also to leave behind all Spanish influences and to return to the traditional way of life.

History informs us that another major cause for the considerably smaller Eastern population figures was the close proximity of the Spaniards and their newly introduced livestock. Both exposed the Pueblos to diseases for which our ancestors had no immunities. In some cases, entire villages were devastated by smallpox.

While land and population both stand out as ways in which we differ, the impact of religious persecution persists. It governs the fundamental approach we employ with outsiders on all matters; even those only remotely connected to the native religion. The Eastern Pueblos' posture on native religion and other areas of the native

culture is still very much guarded, as noted by my experience shared at the beginning of the chapter. To understand the reasons behind this, one must appreciate the severity of the impact of specific historical events on the lives of each and every Eastern Pueblo person. In addition, it is important to understand how protecting this most cherished part of our life played a key role in keeping our communities together during extremely challenging times. This type of guardianship by our people down through the generations no doubt sustained our religion and culture to the degree we still have it today.

Forced Christianity and the ban on certain ceremonies and dances were far too excessive an imposition on our deeply religious people who relied upon the activities of the native faith for daily existence. For us, religion was not then and is not today just a casual one-hour Sunday affair. It is all encompassing and regulates all aspects of our lives. Our dances and ceremonies are never just for show. They are instead for thanksgiving and petitions for further blessings from the spirits.

Unknowingly, the Franciscan Fathers provided us a way out of the horrible dilemma they created. This order of priests actually encouraged Indians of the New World to celebrate Christian events and individual saints through native forms of worship they considered safe. For the Pueblos, this meant an opportunity for at least some of the native dancing, singing, and praying to continue, They only had to stay within the prescribed limits of the church and appear like they were in transition from one religion to another. Pretending to be Christian was a small price to pay to hang onto our cherished religious traditions. Realigning our traditional seasonal calendar with the one the church imposed was a simple matter. Our traditional winter dances were adjusted to coincide with Christmas day and the days following, our spring pre-planting ceremonies were now in line with the Easter season, and the various summer and fall saint's days served us well to continue on through the months. The village patron saint's day became a major annual event among the Eastern Pueblos and two Western Pueblos located closest to them, Acoma and Laguna. This public "fiesta," or more popularly known today as the "feast day," provided an opportunity for trading and the renewal of acquaintances with other Pueblo people and outsiders. But more importantly, it was the opportunity to showcase the Pueblo as a model Christian community "expressing its devotion to the saint" to all outsiders and especially to the oppressors.

Pretending to be Christian in the Spanish mold was just the beginning, however. The Eastern Pueblos also had the risky business of maintaining the remainder of their cherished religious practices. It was the part least understood by the Spaniards and labeled as "paganism." It was what led the Spaniards to commit acts of religious persecutions, such as whippings and even executions of our people who were suspected of participating. The friars with military backing raided kivas and private homes in search of religious leaders and the paraphernalia of the outlawed ceremonies. The latter they would pile high in the plaza and set to flame in a public demonstration of their bitter intolerance for these and any related activities. These search and destroy tactics became a source of major consternation that would eventually lead up to the revolution as the only solution for the Pueblos.

In order to protect and continue these so-called "pagan rituals" the Pueblos had to enlist the help of every man, woman, and child. It became a sworn obligation of everyone to protect religious items, locations, activities, ideas, and leaders. Except for the obvious approved practices, all targeted areas of the traditional religion went underground forever. The meaning of being a member of an Eastern Pueblo rose to a new height. It meant that all were in together on this fight and a deep sense of solidarity was evoked in the people. This was exactly the opposite of what the invaders intended and it may have been the very thing that has kept the corn mothers from ever going away!

Today, those of us of the Eastern Pueblos who carry out the once most targeted religious activities, do so under the greatest precaution for insuring secrecy. Closed villages, late night schedules, and well-guarded conditions are measures commonly employed for security. A secluded location away from the village might serve the same purpose for some events. By contrast, our relatives of the Western Pueblos, specifically the Zunis and the Hopis take little precaution for similar events. For example, the Shalako dance of the Zuni and the bean dances of the Hopi, both forms of katsina dances, include non-Indians among the spectators. Openness of this type is both appalling and even sacrilegious to those of us of the Eastern Pueblos. In recent years both communities have tightened up their policy on open and easy access to these events but for a different reason; that being, that non-Indian guests with their casual and entertainment seeking attitudes have turned these sacred events into circus-like occasions.

Other ways in which we insure protection for our traditional religion involve our youth. Our youngest school children know exactly what not to talk about even to a favorite teacher. Still other more explicit forms of protection that outsiders learn about sooner or later are the following. Prohibition of photography, sketching and tape recording of any type are strictly enforced. In Pueblos where photography is permitted, it is for profit and allowed only in carefully selected areas. Dances and ceremonies are almost always off limits to photography, in-depth discussion and all other curious advances. Even the creation and sale of katsina dolls, a popular economic endeavor among the Zunis and the Hopis are not acceptable practices among the Eastern Pueblos. Teachers are strictly forbidden to probe into matters related to the native religion especially katsinas and other sacred activities. Books and other print materials that include these are not allowed in the school and the home.

Religion is not the only protected area, however. The more traditional Pueblos in the east will not permit their language to be written or allowed in the schools in spite of the push for bilingual education which experts say will enhance their children's learning. In communities where the native language is used in the school, non-natives are not permitted to attend these classes. All of the above and more, some of which I'm not permitted to disclose, are still employed for the sake of keeping our religion, languages, and culture out of harm's way from all outside forces including the U.S. Government. Through the total assimilation policy and removal of children to distant boarding schools, this government also took its shot at Pueblo cultural genocide.

Today, it is in many ways like it was during the Spanish rule, we still must protect and keep secret our most sacred religious activities. And after hundreds of years and generation, after generation of Pueblo people keeping vigil over our religion and traditions, our native faith in the spirits, is far from extinct. Our elders have told us that outside governments will come and go (we have been under three so far), and that if we lose our traditions it will be only because we fell asleep on our watch. That would mean, that not only did we let our guard down but, more tragically, that we became apathetic and failed to honor that for which our forefathers paid a very heavy price and instead gave too much time and attention to the ways of the outside world.

Index

A

Abó, Tompiro pueblo, 9, 21, 138, 143n. 2
Acaxee Rebellion, 172
acculturation, 6, 15, 17, 22, 167, 169
Acho (Rio Colorado) Apaches, 204, 206, 207
Acoma, Keres pueblo, x, xi, 16, 42, 57, 61, 78, 92, 93, 119, 173, 184, 209, 213, 214
Adams, Charles, 81, 129
Agave society, 8
agency, 20, 22, 153–55, 181
Agoyo, Herman, 23n. 1
agriculture, 35, 134, 149, 175
Alamo, Juan del, Isleta interpreter, 156, 157, 158, 159
A'losaka, Hopi deity, 125
Alvarado, Hernando de, 184
American Museum of Natural History, 10, 13, 64, 105
Amoxiumqua, Jemez pueblo, 46, 55
Anderson, Benedict, 21, 149, 170
Antelope Mesa, 114, 115, 128. *See also* Awatovi
Antelope Mesa Rock Art Survey, 121–24
Apaches, 22; alliance of with other Indians, 3, 4, 42, 189, 191, 194, 201–10; at Jemez, 202–3; raiding of, 4, 5, 17, 210; at San Ildefonso, 208; at San Juan, 205–6, 207; at Santa Clara, 207–8; at Taos, 201, 204–5
Apaches de Navajo (Navajo), 3, 4, 191, 198, 202, 205–20
Appadurai, Arjun, 149
Archaeological Institute of America, 10
archaeology: and community, 62, 63; and meaning, 23; Mission, 9–12, 49, 50–51, 64–70; Pueblito, 15–16; Refuge site, 13–15, 33, 52–53, 53–54, 136–38; Spanish site, 16–17
Archer M. Huntington Expedition, 13
architecture, 33–42, 48–54, 138–41
Arenal, Tiwa pueblo, xiii, 173
Argüello Carvajál, Fernando de, governor, 202
arms and armament, 182, 183, 187, 188
Arnold, Dean E., 104
Arvide, Martín de, 46
Asa (or Tansy Mustard) clan, 116
Ashiwi Polychrome, 87–88, *92, 93, 93,* 94, 109, 110
Astialakwa, Jemez refuge pueblo, 14, 19, 21, 48, 51–53, 55–56, 58, 99, 108; attacked by Vargas, 8, 135, 190–92
augite latite, 102
Awatovi *(Awat'ovi),* Hopi pueblo, 11, 21, 79, 114, 115, 116, 117, 120, 121, 122, 123, 124, 125, 127, 128, 147–61; Vargas at, 9
Awatovi Expedition, 11
Ayeta, Fray Francisco de, 204, 205

B

Badger clan, 8, 116, 150, 152–53, 155
Baker, Ele, 49
Bancroft, Hubert H., 4
Bandelier, Adolph F., 10, 13, 39, 54, 56, 99, 168
Bannon, John Francis, 168
Barth, Frederick, 169
Basso, Keith, 148
Batkin, Jonathan, 103
Bautista de Orozco, Juan, 173
Bear clan, 151
Bearstrap clan, 116
Benavides, Fray Alonso de, 21, 46, 54, 83, 116, 198, 199, 202
Benedict, Ruth, 8
Beninato, Stefanie, 5
Berkeley School, 169
Bernalillo, 192
Bhabha, Homi, 21, 168
Bird, Allison, 82
Black Mesa (Hopi), 114
Black Mesa (San Ildefonso Mesa): Tewa refugee pueblo, 14, 21, 47, 106, 175, 181, 208; and Giant's Oven, 186; Mera at, 14; people from San Ildefonso, Santa Clara, San Juan, Tesuque, Cuyamungue, Pojoaque, and Jacona at, 175, 186; people from San Lázaro and San Cristóbal at, 192; Vargas's first attack on, 183, 184–88, 196; Vargas's second attack on, 183, 192–94, 196
Bloom, Lansing B., 49, 50, 51, 54, 55, 199
Bluebird clan, 116
Boletsakwa, Keres refugee pueblo, 19, 48, 51, 53–54, 57, 58, 99, 108; Santo Domingo refugees at, 56, 175
Bolton, Hubert Eugene, 168, 169
Borderlands history, 4, 22, 63, 167, 168, 175
Bourdieu, Pierre, 86
Bow *(Aawatngyam)* clan, 116, 150, 151, 153
Bradfield, Wesley, 49
Brew, John O., 11, 120, 162n. 19
bricolage, 142, 151
Brooklyn Museum, 49
Brugge, David, 199, 210
Bunzel, Ruth, 91, 95
Bureau of American Ethnology, 49

C

Cabeza de Vaca, Álvar Nuñez, 173
Carlson, Roy, 15
Castaño de Sosa, Gaspar, 119, 173

Catholicism: conversion of Indians to, 78, 83; at Dowa Yalanne, 40–41; images in Frijoles Canyon, 136–38, *137;* and modern Pueblos, 213; pro-Catholic factions, 8, 9; religious paraphernalia, 8, 40–41, 93, 135–6; responses to, 132; and Spanish conquest, 171–73, 175–76. *See also* Christianity

Catiti, Alonso, Santo Domingo leader, 7, 79, 133, 135; feasting at Santa Ana Pueblo, 18

Cebolleta, Piro pueblo, 21, 140

ceramics, 80–81, 87–95, 103–10, 119–20

Cerro Colorado (La Alameda), Keres refuge pueblo, 56, 57, 99, 108; Mera at, 14; people from Santa Ana and Zia at, 175, 184

Chakpahu, Hopi pueblo, 114

Chávez, Fray Angélico, 6

Christianity, 4, 5, 9, 81, 114, 117–20, 128–29, 171, 172, 212, 213; Christian Indians, 83, 203; conversion to, 4, 114–29; feigned acceptance of, 20, 47, 213–15; Indian ambivalence toward, 132; symbols of, 20, 80, 81, 132–43

Cibola, 173

Cibola Whiteware, 35

Cicuye. *See* Pecos

Cisneros, Alonso de, 9

Clark, Jeffrey, 38

Clarke, Louis, 87

Clemente, Esteban, Salinas leader, 5

Cochiti (Keres pueblo), 3, 5, 8, 9, 15, 17, 79, 99, 163n. 27, 190, 203, 213; people at Kotyiti Pueblo, 189; Vargas finds vacated, 100, 184

Cochiti Dam Archaeological Project, 17

Cochiti Springs site, Spanish rancho, 17

Cohen, Ronald, 171

collective consciousness, 149, 151

colonialism, 18, 20, 63, 86, 171

colonization, 3, 22, 64, 66, 156, 168, 169, 175

Comanches, 79

Comaroff, Jean, 142, 170

community, 21, 61–63, 100–101, 149

Concepción, Fray Cristóbal de, 115

Copala, Lake of, 18

Corbera, Fray Francisco, 208

Corn clan, 116

Corn Mountain. *See* Dowa Yalanne

Coronado, Francisco Vásquez de, x-xi, 46, 114, 173, 184

Corvera, Fray Francisco, 100, 208

Courlander, Harold, 118, 153

coyote, 176

Cristobal, San Marcos leader, 100, 189

crystalline basalt, 102, 105, 106

Cubero, Pedro Rodríguez, governor, 154, 157

Cuervo y Valdés, Francisco, governor, 17, 61, 64, 192, 210

Cunixu, Luis, Jemez leader, 48

Curtis, Edward S., 151, 152, 153, 154, 161n. 10

Cushing, Frank Hamilton, 13, 33, 39, 183

Cuyamungue, Tewa pueblo, at Black Mesa, 175, 186

D

datura, 156

decolonization, 132

Delgado, Fray Carlos, 23n. 13

Dick, Herbert, 12

Dinetah, 15

discourse: clan, 151; archaeological, 17; documentary, 17; oral history, 17; millenarian, 157; politically situated, 168; power of, 22; revitalization, 20, 103

disease, 21, 22, 64, 79, 167, 168, 175, 212, 214

Dittert, Al, 15

Dodge, Meredith, 55

domination. *See* resistance

Domínguez de Mendoza, Juan, captain, 202, 204

Dougherty, Julia, 52

Dowa Yalanne (Zuni refuge pueblo), 14–15, 33–42, 57, 87, 94, 99; Bandelier at, 13; Cushing at, 13; Mera at, 14; Mindeleff at, 35; question of kivas at, 39–40; Spier at, 13; translations of name, 33; Vargas at, 8, 39–41; view from Zuni, *32*

Dozier, Edward, 5, 78, 167, 175

Durán y Chaves, Fernando, captain, 181

Durkheim, Emile, 38, 149, 161n. 7

E

Eight Northern Pueblos, 23

El Chato, Taos leader, 6, 7

Eliza Seligman Camp, 54

Elliott, Michael L., 50, 53

Ellis, Florence Hawley, 54, 56, 163n. 28

Elmore, Francis, 49

El Saca, Taos leader, 6, 7

El Taque, San Juan leader, 6

El Turco, Plains Indian guide, x

encomienda, 4

El Zepe, Cochiti leader, 100, 189

Enriquez de Alemanza, Martín, Viceroy of New Spain, 172

español, 181

Espejo, Antonio de, 46, 115, 173

Espeleta, Francisco de, 21, 79, 150, 154–55, 159, 160, 161

Espeleta, Fray José de, 116, 154–55, 162n. 20

Espinosa, J. Manuel, xii, 5, 159

Estevanico, x

ethnicity, 18, 169–71, 175–76, 182. *See also* identity

ethnogenesis, 85–86, 95, 170, 175, 176

ethnography, 62, 148, 149, 156, 159, 175
ethnohistory, 78, 102, 114, 117–18, 133, 134–36, 160, 199–201
Eulate, Juan de, governor, 201
event, 155–60

F

factionalism, 77, 86, 100, 110, 153, 199–201
Faraón (Faraones) Apache, 37, 206. *See also* Apache
Farwell, Robin, 54
Ferguson, T. J., 14–15, 23n. 11, 70
Fewkes, Jesse Walter, 148, 153, 160, 161n. 9, 163n. 32
Figueroa, Fray Joseph de, 116
Flute *(Lenngyam)* clan, 150, 151–52, 162
Fontes, Cristóbal, alcalde mayor of Cochiti, 17
Forbes, Jack, 167, 204
Fort Burgwin Research Center, 12
Frijoles Canyon, 10

G

Galaxy society, 92
Galisteo, Tano pueblo, 11, 16, 61, 64, 65, 66, 67
Galisteo Basin, 10–11, 63–64, *64*, 70, 71
Garaicoechea, Fray Juan, 9, 79
García Marín, Fray José, 207
García Olgado, Juan, captain, 203
Garner, Van Hastings, 5
Gauthier, Rory, 50, 53, 54
genízaro, 176, 182
Girl Scout Archaeological Unit, 54
Giusewa (Jemez pueblo), 10, 19, 46, *48*, 48, 49, 54–56. *See also* San José de los Jemez
Glaze E, 103, 108
Glaze F, 54, 80, 91, 103, 136
Gobernador Polychrome, 109, 110
Granillo, Luis de, alcalde mayor of Jemez, Zia and Santa Ana, 47
Great Shell society, 8, 36
Greyrobe, Fray Juan, *(Kwan Tátchui Lók'yana)*, 8, 41
Griego, Juan, San Juan war captain, 112n. 10, 189
Group M (Bandelier National Monument), 136
Guadalupe Mesa, 47, 51, 52, 57, 181, 182, 191, 206; Vargas attack on, 8, 190–92, *191*, 196
Guerra, Fray Salvador de, 162n. 19
Guerta, Fray, 201
Gutiérrez, Fray Andrés, 115

H

Hackett, Charles W., 199
Halona:wa, Zuni pueblo, 16, 41, 87. *See also* Zuni
Hammack, Laurens, 49

Hardin, Margaret, 91
Harlow, Francis H., 103, 112n. 4
Harrington John P., 55
Hawikuh *(Hawikku),* Zuni pueblo, x, 11, 15, 70, 81, 87, 88, 89, 90, 91, 92, 93, 194
Hawikuh Glazeware, 91, 92, 94
Hawikuh Polychrome, 91, *92*, 94, 110
Hawley, Florence, 107. *See also* Florence Hawley Ellis
Hemenway Expedition, 39
Hendricks, Rick, 55, 161n. 2
Herrera, Domingo de, 193
Hester, James J., 198
Hewett, Edgar Lee, 10, 49
Hill, Jonathan, 85
historical imagination, 148
historical memory, 173
Hobsbawm, Eric and Terence Ranger, 18
Hodder, Ian, 77
Hodge, Frederick Webb, 11, 33, 55, 78, 87, 91, 93
Holmes, William H., 55, 56
Homol'ovi, Hopi pueblo, 137
Hopi Tribe Cultural Preservation Office, 121
Hopification, 18
Horn (Cochiti) Mesa, 99, 181; Vargas attack on, 188–90, *189*. *See also* Kotyiti
Hotvilla *(Hotvela),* Hopi pueblo, 150
Hudelson, Sam, 49
Hughte, Phil, Zuni artist, 42

I

icon, 42, 101, 110, 128, 136, 137, 174
identity, 85, 90, 94, 95, 99, 133–34, 142, 149, 161, 168, 181
ideology, 20, 149
index, 14, 101, 102, 103, 110
Indian Arts Fund, 88
Indios, 171, 176
Isleta, Tiwa pueblo, 5, 61, 156, 157, 203, 213
Ivey, James E., 199–200, 210

J

Jacona, Tewa pueblo, 208, 209; at Black Mesa, 175, 186
Jemez *(Walatowa),* Towa pueblo, xii, 16, 19, 47, 50, 51, *51*, 58, 157–58, 213
Jemez Black-on-white, 51, 53, 103
Jemez Revolt of 1623, 5, 46, 174
Jesús, Fray Francisco de, 47–48
Jesús, Fray Juan de, 47, 58
jewelry, 82
Jironza Petrís de Cruzate, Domingo, governor, 3, 47, 56, 157, 184
Johnson, Gary, governor, xiii

Jorge, Antonio, captain, 183, 187, 193
Juárez, Fray Andrés, 202

K

Kapo Black, 136
Kapo Gray, 53
Kawaika'a (Hopi pueblo), 115, 121, 123, 124
Kechiba:wa (Zuni pueblo), 15, 70, 87, 89, 90
Kechipawan Polychrome, *89*
Keen, Benjamin, 168
Kern, Richard, 51
Kessell, John L., 55
Keur, Dorothy, 15
Kiapkwa Polychrome, 93
Kidder, Alfred V., 11, 15, 103, 112n. 15
Kisakovi, Hopi pueblo, 116
kiva wall murals, 81–82
Knaut, Andrew, xii, 5
Kokopnyama (Hopi pueblo), 114
Kolliwa (Zuni pueblo), 13, 23n. 10
Kopytoff, Igor, 142
Kotyiti (Keres refugee pueblo), 15, 21, 99, 175, 194, 195, 196;
    attacked by Vargas, 8, 100, 188–90; excavated by Nelson,
    13; mapped by Bandelier, 13; Mera at, 14; San Felipe and
    San Marcos refugees at, 100, 107, 175; visits by Vargas, 100
Kotyiti Glaze Polychrome, 53, *102*
Kotyiti Research Project, 15
koyaanisqatsi, 9, 160
Kroeber, Alfred, 13
Kubler, George, 49, 54, 55
Kuwanwisiwma, Leigh, 129
Kwaakwant (One Horn) society, 150
Kyaki:ma (Zuni pueblo), 15, 87
Kyaki:ma Refuge site (Zuni pueblo), 11, 12, 14

L

La Alameda (Keres refugee pueblo), 175. *See also* Cerro
    Colorado
La Alameda (Tiwa pueblo), 5, 61, 135, 174, 203
labor, forced, 4, 118, 172, 175–76
La Cienega, 64
La Cieneguilla, Keres pueblo, 65, 207
La Cieneguilla de Cochiti (Keres pueblo). *See* Kotyiti
Ladd, Edmund, 91
Laguna (Keres pueblo), 16, 42, 64, 213, 214
Lambert, Marjorie, 68
language, 83, 175, 213, 215–16
Las Humanas (Gran Quivira, Tompiro pueblo), 90
Las Majadas site, Spanish rancho, 17, *17*
lead, 93

Leonard, Robert D., 63
Letrado, Fray Francisco, 90
Levi-Strauss, Claude, 142, 151
Loew, Oscar, 55
Lomawaima, Hartman, 18, 138, 142
Loololma, Oraibi chief, 155
López de Menizábal, Bernardo, governor, 117, 203
López Sambrano, Diego, captain, 204
Losada, Varela de, alcalde mayor of Cochiti, 17
Los Pedernales, 208, *209*
Lucía, Tewa woman, 207
Lugo, Fray Alonso de, 46, 202
Luján, Francisco, teniente of Cochiti, 17
Lululongturque, Hopi pueblo, 114
Lummis, Charles Fletcher, 168
Lycett, Mark, 12

M

Madrid, Roque de, captain, 15, 182, 186, 189, 190, 208
Manso de Contreras, Juan, governor, 46
Márquez, Lucía, 182
Martínez, Phélix, governor, 157, 158
Marx, Karl, 161n. 7
Matachines Dance, 19
material culture, 19, 22, 80–82, 86, 101–3, 111, 132, 170
Mats'a:kya (Zuni pueblo), 87
Matsaki Buffware, 89, 91, 92, 94
Matsaki Polychrome, *90,* 91, *91*
Maxwell Museum of Anthropology, 49, 80
Mera, H. P., 13–14, 53, 103
mestizo, 176, 181
Mindeleff, Victor, 35, 150
Mishongnovi (*Musangnuvi,* Hopi pueblo), 116, 117, 150, 155
Mixtón War, 172
Mizquía, Lázaro de, captain, 182, 183, 187
Mobley-Tanaka, Jeannette, 141
Mogollón, Juan Ignacio Flores, governor, 16
Moho, Tiwa pueblo, x, 173
Montgomery, Ross, 11
Moreno, Fray Antonio, 208
Morris, Earl, 87
motif, animal, 124–25; bird, 19, 77, 80, 81, *81,* 82, 89, 91, 124;
    checkerboard, 125; clown, 136; cross, 19, 77, 79–82, 83, 92,
    92, 119, 126, *126,* 134; crown/halo, 137; double-headed key,
    20, *108,* 108–09, 111; dragonfly, 19, 77, 82; feather, 20,
    81,*91,* 91–92, 94–95; flower, 82, 119; hooked triangle, *109,*
    109–10; katsina (kachina), 89, 90, 91, 123, 125, 136, 137;
    mask 122, 123, 137; rider on horse, 126–27, *127;* rug/clan,
    122, 123, 125; shield, 91, 124; snake, 136; star, 19, 77, 119;
    stepped mountain, *109,* 110; textile, 20, 92, 94; Virgin
    Mary, 136

movement: cultural revitalization, 18, 99, 153, 155, 160; ethnic, 169; millenarian 5–6, 22, 157, 158–59; pan-ethnic, 21, 171; reformative, 155, 160

Muñoz, Fray Francisco, 47

Muñoz, Fray Juan, 48

Museum of Anthropology at the University of Colorado, Boulder, 88

Museum of Archaeology and Ethnology, Cambridge University, 87

Museum of New Mexico, Museum of Indian Arts and Culture, Laboratory of Anthropology, 49, 50, 80, 103, 105

Museum of New Mexico Foundation, 55

Museum of Northern Arizona, Flagstaff, 119

N

Nagata, Shuichi, 161n. 1

Nakèmuu (Tewa pueblo), 136

Nambé, Tewa pueblo, 16, 182, 208, 209, 213

Namboa, Pedro, Alameda elder, 174

Naranjo, Domingo, Santa Clara leader, 6, 18, 208

Naranjo, Pedro, San Felipe leader, 6, 18, 133

Narvaez Valverde, Fray José, 147

National Museum of the American Indian, 49

nativism, 18

Navajos, 3, 15, 16, 22, 88, 154, 201–2. *See also* Apaches de Navajo

Nelson, Nels, 10–11, 13, 64–66, 67, 68, 99, 103, 105

Nequatewa, Edmund, 7, 118, 128

Nesuftonga (Hopi pueblo), 114

New Mexico State Monuments, 55

Niman (Home Dance), 152, 158

Niza, Fray Marcos de, 173

O

Obeyesekere, Gananath, 148

Ogapoge Polychrome, 110

Ojeda, Bartolomé de, Zia war captain and auxiliary, 182, 189–90, 190, 191, 195, 209

Old San Felipe (Keres pueblo), 108; Bandelier at, 13; Mera at, 14

Old Santa Ana (Keres pueblo), Mera at, 14

Old Shungopavi, Hopi pueblo, 116

Oñate y Salazar, Juan de, governor, xi, 46, 61, 115, 173

Oraibi (Orayvi), Hopi pueblo, 79, 117, 150, 155; warriors plot to destroy Awatovi, 154

oral history, 7–9; Cochiti, 8, 9; Hopi, 7–8, 9, 21, 118–19, 150, 153; Jemez, 7, 8, 135; San Felipe, 9; Zuni, 8, 36

Ordóñez, Fray, 201

Ortega, Francisco de, captain, 203

Ortiz, Alfonso, 5, 6, 153, 167, 168, 175

Otermín Antonio de, governor, 3, 5, 47, 157, 204–5

P

Paaco (Paa-ko), 12, 65, 67–70. *See also* San Pedro

Paaqavi, (Bacavi), Hopi pueblo, 150

Padilla, Fray Juan de, x, xi, 114

Palace of the Governors, 16

Palatkwapi, Hopi pueblo, 160

Parrot clan, 116

Parsons, Elsie Clews, 51

Patokwa, Jemez pueblo, 19, 48, 49–51, 55, 56, 58, 134, 135, 190. *See also* San Diego del Monte

Pautiwa (Ned Zeena), Walpi elder, 153

Pavayoykyasi, wife of *A'losaka,* 125

Payupki (Tiwa pueblo), 99, 116, 157

Peabody Museum of Archaeology and Ethnology, Harvard University, 11, 119

Pecos (Cicuye, Tiwa pueblo), xii, 10, 11, 16, 48, 64, 119, 194

Peirce, Charles Sanders, 101

Peralta, Pedro de, governor, 201

Perea, Fray Estévan de, 117

Pérez, Melchior, 23

peyote, 155–60

Phillips Academy, Andover, 11

Picurí, Luis, Picuris leader. *See* Luis Tupatu

Picuris (Tiwa pueblo), 3, 12, 201, 206–7, 210; Tribal Council, 12

Piedra Lumbre phase, 198

Pindas, San Juan leader, 5

Piros, 155, 204

Pivanhonkyapi (Hopi pueblo), 160

Poheyemu, Tewa mythological hero, 6, 23n. 4

Pojoaque, Tewa pueblo, 61; at Black Mesa, 175, 186

Pojoaque Polychrome, 103

Pooley, Emil, 7

Popé (Pop'ay), xii, 5–6, 78, 79, 99, 133, 134, 173, 174–175, commemoration of, xi-xii; feasting at Santa Ana Pueblo, 18; imprisonment at Santa Fe, 79; role as leader, xi-xii, 5–6, 99; visionary experience of, 159

Porras, Fray Francisco, 115

Posadas, Fray Alonso, 117

Postcolonial studies, 167–8, 176

Potrero Viejo. *See* Horn Mesa

Powamuy (Bean Dance), 150, 152

Prada, Fray Juan de, 202

praxis, 33

pueblito, 15–16

Pueblo auxiliaries, 21, 182; from Jemez, 47, 192; from Pecos, 185, 192; from San Felipe, 100, 189, 190, 191, 192; from Santa Ana, 100, 189, 190, 191, 192; from Zia, 100, 189, 190, 191, 192

Pueblo Blanco (Tano pueblo), 65

Pueblo Colorado (Tano pueblo), 65, 70

Pueblo Largo (Tano pueblo), 65, 67, 70
Pueblo Revolt of 1680, xi–xiv, 3–23, 33, 35–6, 40, 42, 47–54, 58, 78, 79, 85–6, 94, 99, 116–117, 129, 133–44, 174–175, 204–5, 212–13
Pueblo Revolt of 1696, 9, 15, 16, 22, 50, 58, 157, 196, 208–10
Pueblo Shé (Tano pueblo), 65, 70
Pueblo-Spanish war, 61, 181
Puname Polychrome, 103, 108

Q

Quara, Antonio, 156, 157
Quarai (Tiwa pueblo), 9, 12, 21, 138, 143n. 2
Quivira, xii, xiii

R

Rabbit clan, 116
Rael de Aguilar, Alfonso, captain, 210
Ramenofsky, Ann, 12
Ramírez, Fray Juan, 203
reduction, 46
Reed clan, 150, 151, 154
Reff, Daniel, 6–7
refugee effect, 20
refugee hypothesis, 15
Reiter, Paul, 54
Reneros de Posada, Pedro, governor, 3, 47, 184
resistance, architecture of, 19, 138–140; domination and, 18; iconography of, 20, 110, 111; ideology of, 20; modes of, 141–142; passive 18, 78–79, 83, 114, 128–129; Pueblo style of 19, 78–80; ritual imagery and, 77; symbolic inversion as, 138, 140–141; women's, 86,
revivalism, 18
revolt. *See* Pueblo Revolt of 1680, 1696, and individual revolts
Rhodes-Livingston Institute, 169
rock art, at Astialakwa 52, at Awatovi, 120–29, 122–23, *124*, 126–28; at Boletsakwa, 53; at Kawaika'a, 124–24, *124*
Rodríguez de Cubero, Pedro, governor, 147
Romero, Alonso, 187
Ruiz de Cáceres, Juan, sergeant, 182, 186

S

Sahlins, Marshall, 21, 148
Said, Edward, 168
Sakiestewa, Robert, Hopi elder, 7
Salado Polychrome, 89
Salado White-on-red, 89
Saldívar, Vicente de, captain, 173
Saliko, Walpi chieftess, 153
Salmerón Relaciones, 54, 117
San Bartolomé de Xongo Pavi (Hopi pueblo), 116. *See* Shungopavi

San Bernardo de Aguátubi (Hopi pueblo), 115–16. *See* Awatovi
San Bernardo Polychrome, 119–120
San Buenaventura de Cochití (Keres pueblo). *See* Cochiti
San Cristóbal, Tano pueblo, 10, 64, 65–6, 67, 68, 187, 208; at Black Mesa, 192
San Diego Catholic Church, 51
San Diego de la Congregación (Jemez pueblo), 19, 46, 47, 48, 51, 55
San Diego de los Jemez (Jemez pueblo), 19, 46, 48
San Diego del Monte (Jemez pueblo), 19, 47, 48, 58. *See also* Patokwa
San Diego Mesa, 47. *See also* Guadalupe Mesa
San Esteban de Acoma (Keres pueblo). *See* Acoma
San Felipe (Keres pueblo), 6, 17, 203, 213; church in ruin, 132; Cochiti attack on, 9; people at Kotyiti Pueblo, 189, people at Old San Felipe Pueblo, 108; Vargas at, 190
San Gabriel de Yungé, Spanish and Tewa pueblo, xi, 201
San Geronimo de Taos, Tiwa pueblo. *See* Taos
San Ildefonso (Tewa pueblo), 7, 208, 209, 210, 213; Vargas establishes *plaza de armas* at, 186
San Ildefonso Mesa. *See* Black Mesa
San José de los Jemez (Jemez pueblo), 19, 46, 48, 55, 56. *See* Giusewa
San Juan (*Ohkay Owingeh*, Tewa Pueblo), xi–xiv, xiii, 5, 6, 16, 46, 173, 205–6, 213; at Black Mesa, 175, 186
San Juan de los Jemez (Jemez pueblo), 19, 47, 48, 51, 56, 58. *See also* Jemez
San Juan Mesa (Jemez district), 51
San Juan Mesa (Rio Grande district), 207
San Lázaro (Towa pueblo), 10, 64, 65, 66, 187; at Black Mesa, 192
San Marcos (Keres pueblo), 10, 64, 65, 70; people at Kotyiti, 100, 107, 111, 189
San Miguel de Oraibi (Hopi pueblo), 116. *See also* Oraibi
San Pedro, 11, 64, 67. *See also* Paaco
Sand clan, 116
Sandia (Tiwa Pueblo), 61, 132, 140, 141, 203, 213; church in ruin, 132
Sando, Joe, xiv, 7, 50
Sankawi Black-on-cream, 53, 109
Santa Ana (Keres pueblo), 18, 47, 206, 207, 213
Santa Clara (Tewa pueblo), 6, 38, 186, 187, 202, 207–8, 209, *209*, 213; at Black Mesa, 175, 186
Santa Cruz de la Cañada, Spanish settlement, 64, 192
Santa Cruz de Galisteo (Tano Pueblo), 61. *See also* Galisteo
Santa Fe, Spanish villa, 5, 16–17, 42, 61, 64, 154, 156, 185, 188, 190, 192, 194, 197n. 2, 199, 205, 206, 207
Santa María de Gracia (Tano pueblo), 61. *See also* Galisteo
Santa María, Fray Augustin de, 116
Santiago's Day Celebration, 19

Santo Domingo (Keres pueblo), xiii, 7, 58, 70, 203, 206, 213; church in ruin, 132; Vargas finds vacated, 184

Saxete, Miguel, San Juan governor, 209

Schaafsma, Curtis, 112n. 4, 112n. 13

Scholes, France V., 49, 54, 55, 199, 201, 204

School of American Archaeology, 49

School of American Research, 49, 88

Schroeder, Al, 13, 199, 200

Scott, James, 18, 78, 80, 141

Seifert, Donna, 16

semiotics, 20, 101–3, 111

Senecú del Sur (Tiwa pueblo), 147

Setoqua (Jemez pueblo), 51

settlement pattern: during the Pueblo Revolt period, 3, 61, 175; in the Galisteo Basin, 63–64, 70–71; Jemez, 45–46; Zuni, 13, 33

sexual abuse, 9

Shalako (and *Sa'lako*), 92, 152, 153, 215

Shepard, Anna, 103, 104

Shungopavi (Hopi pueblo), 116, 117, 212

sign, 101, 102, 133, 134

Sikyatki (Hopi pueblo), 160

Sikyatki Polychrome, 119, 120

Sikyatki style, 89, 91

Silverberg, Robert, 82

Simmons, Marc, 5

Simpson, Lt. James, 51, 55

slave raids, 172, 176, 203–4

Smithsonian Institution, 49, 88

Snake clan, 150

Snow, Cordelia, 16, 17

Sopete, Plains Indian guide, xii

Southern Methodist University, 12

Southwest Museum, 49

space syntax, 14, 34, 36, *36*

Spicer, Edward, 5

Spielmann, Kate, 12, 80

Spier, Leslie, 13

Spivak, Gayatri, 21, 168, 176

Squash clan, 150, 151; Squash/Sparrowhawk, 150

Stallings, William S. Jr., 54

Stephen, Alexander, 151

Stevenson, James, 88

Stevenson, Matilda Coxe, 78, 88

Stewart, Omer, 155

structure, 148, 149–53

style, 77–80, 88–95, 170, and function, 101, 111

Suina, Joseph Henry, 23

Sun clan, 116

symbol, 18, 77, 79, 83, 101, 102, 128, 132–33, 136, 137, 142, 149, 151

syncretism, 140

T

Taapalo, Awatovi leader, 151, 153, 154, 155, 161n. 10, 162n. 17

Tabira Black-on-white, 82

Tanjete, Francisco (El Ollita, San Ildefonso leader), 7

Tanos, 3, 206

Taos (Tiwa pueblo), x, 6, 7, 78, 156, 204, 206, 210, 213

Taos Revolt of 1639, 5, 174

Tapacito site (Navajo pueblito), 15

Tarahumara Revolt, 172

Teajaya, Cristobal, 156, 157

technological choice, 86, 88–89, 93–95

Telles Jirón, José, encomendero of Cochiti, 17

Tenamaxtli, Mixtón leader, 172

Tepehuan Rebellion, 172

Tesuque (Tewa pueblo), 16, 64, 213; at Black Mesa, 175, 186

Tewa Black-on-white, 103

Tewa Polychrome, 52, 53, 103, 107, 112n. 16, 136

Tewa Village (Hano), 99, 116; people from San Cristobal and San Lazaro at, 175

textiles, 92, 94

Thenorio de Alba, Miguel, secretary, 158

Thomas, David Hurst, 12

Three Corn ruin (Navajo pueblito), 88

Thunder Mountain. *See* Dowa Yalanne

Titiev, Misha, 155

Tobacco clan, 116, 150, 151, 152, 153, 154

Tonque, 65

Torreon site, 17

Toulouse, Joseph H. Jr., 49

Tovar, Pedro de, 114, 115

Towner, Ronald, 88

transcript, hidden, 18, 19, 141; official, 168; public, 18,141; subversive, 80

Trask, Lance, 53

tree ring dates, 54, 58, 59

Treviño, Juan Francisco de, governor, xii

Tricentennial of the Pueblo Revolt of 1680, xii, 23

Trujillo, Fray José de, 116

Tshidi, 142

Tsukuvi (Hopi pueblo), 137

tuff, devitrified, 104, 105; Otowi, 105, 106; rhyolite, 104, 105; Tshirege, 104, 106; Upper Bandelier, 188, 190

Tupatu, Luis (El Picurí, Picuris leader), 99, 205–6, 207

Turner, Frederick Jackson, 169

Tusayan, province of, 114

Tutiqua (Keres pueblo), 56. *See also* Cerro Colorado and La Alameda

Twitchell, Ralph Emerson, 4

Tyuonyi, Keres pueblo, 10

U

Ugarte y la Concha, Hernando de, governor, 5, 202, 203
University of Chicago, 67
University of New Mexico, 49
Ute, 208

V

Vaca, Alonso, captain, 203
Valverde y Cosío, Antonio de, adjutant, 156, 157, 183, 187
Vargas, Diego de, governor, 45, 47, 115, 157; at Astialawka, 8, 47, 135, 190–192; at Black Mesa, 184–88, 192–94; at Boletsakwa, 57; at Dowa Yalanne, 37, 39–40, 40–41; at Kotyiti, 8, 100, 188–90; at Patokwa, 57, 134; recolonizing expedition in 1693, 47; reconquest in 1692, 3, 47, 147, 204, 205; at Santa Fe, 61
Vargas, Eusebio de, 8
Vargas, Fray Francisco de, 47, 48
Vargas Project (University of New Mexico), 19, 45, 55, 58, 197n. 1
Vega, Juan de la, genizaro, 182, 207
Velasco, Fray Francisco de, 201
Vélez de Escalante, Silvestre, 135, 147, 191
Villanueva, Fernando de, governor, 5
Voth, H. R., 7, 152, 158

W

Walatowa (Jemez pueblo), 48, 51, 56, 58. *See* Jemez
Walpi (Hopi pueblo), 116, 117, 150, 152, 154, 162n. 18
warfare, xii-xiii, 119, 172–73, 181–96; Pueblo strategies, 195–96; Spanish soldiery, 181–82; Spanish strategies,194–95. *See also* arms and armament
Warren, Helene, 103, 104, 106
Weber, David, xiv, 4, 7
Weber, Max, 160, 161n. 7
Western Archaeological and Conservation Center, 80
White House, ancestral Keres village, 15
Whiteley, Peter, 79
Wiget, Andrew, 7, 8, 41, 118
Wikvaya, Hopi elder, 7
Wills, Wirt H., 63
Wimaya:wa (Zuni pueblo), 13, 14
Wissler, Clark, 13
witchcraft, 4, 160
Wolf, Eric, 161n. 5, 167, 168
women: and identity, 95, 99; and Kotyiti ceramics, 20, 99–100, 110–11; and resistance, 85-7; and Zuni ceramics, 20, 86, 95
women's societies: *Maraw,* 150, 151, 152, 153; *Owaqöl,* 150, 151, 152, 158
Woodbury, Richard and Nathalie, 88

Wuwtsim (or Manhood) society, 150, 152, 153, 159, 161; *Aa'alt* (Two Horn), 150, 151, 152, 154; *Taatawkyam* (Singers), 150, 151, 152, 154; *Wuwtsimt,* 150, 152, 154

X

Xenome, Diego (Dieguillo), Tewa leader, 208
Ximénez, Fray Lázaro, 201
Xixime Rebellion, 172

Y

Ye, Juan de, Pecos governor, 182, 207
Yoywunu, Walpi elder, 151

Z

Zaldívar, Juan de, maese de campo, xiii
Zaldívar, Vicente de, sargento mayor, xiii
Zárate Salmerón, Fray Gerónimo de, 46, 202
Zia (Keres pueblo), 47, 48, 56, 58, 184, 192, 213
Zue, brother of Cristobal leader of the San Marcos people, 100, 189
Zuni Archaeology Program, 14
Zuni Polychrome, 93
Zuni (*Halona:wa*), Zuni pueblo, 14, 33, 41–2, 78, 87, 213; excavations by, 88; Tribal Council, 14
Zuni Revolt of 1632, 5, 35, 174